P9-CJJ-104

NO LONGER PROPERTY OF
SEATTLE PUBLIC LIBRARY

BLINDFOLD

A MEMOIR OF CAPTURE, TORTURE, AND ENLIGHTENMENT

THEO PADNOS

SCRIBNER

New York   London   Toronto   Sydney   New Delhi

Scribner
An Imprint of Simon & Schuster, Inc.
1230 Avenue of the Americas
New York, NY 10020

Copyright © 2021 by Theo Padnos

All rights reserved, including the right to reproduce this book or portions thereof
in any form whatsoever. For information, address Scribner Subsidiary Rights Department,
1230 Avenue of the Americas, New York, NY 10020.

First Scribner hardcover edition February 2021

SCRIBNER and design are registered trademarks of The Gale Group, Inc.,
used under license by Simon & Schuster, Inc., the publisher of this work.

For information about special discounts for bulk purchases,
please contact Simon & Schuster Special Sales at 1-866-506-1949
or business@simonandschuster.com.

The Simon & Schuster Speakers Bureau can bring authors to your live event.
For more information or to book an event, contact the Simon & Schuster Speakers Bureau
at 1-866-248-3049 or visit our website at www.simonspeakers.com.

Manufactured in the United States of America

1   3   5   7   9   10   8   6   4   2

Library of Congress Cataloging-in-Publication Data has been applied for.

ISBN 978-1-9821-2082-5
ISBN 978-1-9821-2084-9 (ebook)

To Jim Foley, Peter Kassig, Steven Sotloff, and Kayla Mueller.
I wish you were here to tell your stories.

CONTENTS

PROLOGUE

On my first day in my first prison, the Eye Specialist Hospital of Aleppo, Syria, the captors gave me a blindfold—a grime-stained scrap of fabric they called "the cloth." Before every interrogation and during my twice daily excursions through the hospital corridor to the bathroom, they made me tie it over my eyes.

I knew everything about that blindfold. It lay on the floor of the cell I was occupying then, next to a pee bottle, a water bottle, and some bits of bread crust I was saving up. It was an early springtime green. It felt soft in my fingers. It had been decorated with dozens of tiny violets. I became attached to this blindfold, perhaps because, in that world of al Qaeda prisons, it was my only possession.

This cloth stayed with me through many cellmates, sessions of torture, escape attempts, and transfers from one prison to the next. Sandals came and went, as did spoons and pee bottles. I wore the same pair of bloody sea-green hospital pants for half a year. Eventually, they vanished, too. I held on to the blindfold.

At first, I hated this object because it meant total helplessness for me and, for them, a deeper kind of control. But it was such a tattered, threadbare, throwaway scarf that, if I tied it right, it could be used like a veil. I could see, and they didn't know I could see. Later, it occurred to me that it had probably once belonged to a woman (because what would a Jebhat al-Nusra warrior want with purple flowers?), that it might have been used in her kitchen or to keep her hair in place, and so I started to think of it as my connection to the world I had lost: women, civility, cooking. I needed to hold on to it for this reason.

I clove-hitched it around my neck once. It was long enough, when rolled into a rope, to work as a noose. That scarf was my emergency escape route. I wanted it nearby in case it became clear that a quiet slouching into soft fabric, followed by deep sleep, would be preferable to whatever horror they meant to videotape, then send out to the world.

There came a time when this head scarf soaked up my blood. My hair was coming out in handfuls then, like a dying sort of seaweed. When I removed the head scarf, there was more hair to it than there was fabric. I used it as a bandage now and then. It absorbed the sorts of things bandages absorb.

Through the months, the scarf mopped up my sweat and wiped away graffiti I scratched into the walls, then erased in a panic when a guard warned that my defacing their prisons might bring on the car battery. It soaked up soup I had spilled on the floor. Sometimes, when I had spare food, I hid the food within the cloth.

I had no pen during my first eighteen months, and no way to tell myself what was happening to me. The blindfold, I began to think, was a register. Its blood, pus, and hair were the outward, visible marks of an ordeal that was above all else a trial of the spirit. And it had kept me safe. "Where's the cloth?" they used to shout when they opened up the cell door. If I had it in my hand and was busy blindfolding myself, they could see I was complying with the prison rules. They didn't hit me. So I brandished it at them like a talisman, wrapped it around my eyes, and then, in this state of compliance and fleeting safety, I walked out from my cell, into their world.

I could see. I watched them at prayer, at study, in their kitchens and their meeting rooms. I was an unobserved observer in their little Islamic state—so it felt to me—and my safety within it was because of the purple flowers I had tied around my head. Those flowers helped me see. The blindfold was my laissez-passer. It was the little patch of magic carpet on which I traveled.

Now and then, other prisoners needed it. Someone was about to be interrogated. Or led away to god knows where—a torture chamber, the trunk of a car, a grave. "Do you have a cloth?" a guard would ask, banging on my cell door. "I gave mine to Yassin yesterday," I would lie, or I would sigh: "A cloth? No. By god, I have nothing."

Over time, it began to seem to me that the captors meant to tamp down all my senses and that, as a consequence, the senses had woken up. About a year and a half into my ordeal, they decided to allow me a pen and paper. Soon, I found myself writing a story. When I began it, I didn't know much about the plot of this story but I did know that my blindfold would be important in it. For me, that blindfold represented the power of my senses over their ambition to shut them down.

Now I think that in those first months in the eye hospital, they wanted total disorientation for me—and for the other fifty-odd prisoners they kept in windowless cells in that basement. The blindfold was meant to detach me from everything I knew about the world, including my name, which, in those days, became Filth and sometimes Ass and other times Insect. Perhaps I did become a bit unmoored—but as this was happening, my senses were on high alert.

For instance, in a prison, you learn to know what's going on by smelling the air. The prisons in Syria smell of charred wood, burning trash, people throwing up in their cells, and the floor-cleaning fluid with which they mop up the scenes of their crimes. In the evenings, they smell of the feasts the fighters make for themselves: roasted chicken, cardamom in the coffee, piles of steamy, fluffy rice. On Fridays, the day of prayer, they smell of shampoo. When there is torture, they reek of the patchouli oil the men in black put in their beards. Every time you smell the oil, you know those men are on their way into the cell block.

Of course, I also listened. In the blackness of a cell—or when they took charge of tying the blindfold and so cinched it down tight—my ability to make sense of sound was all I had. Over time, I began to think that the auditory faculty runs much deeper than we know, that footsteps and whispers proceed directly to the lizard part of one's brain, and that sounds had helped me see just as my blindfold helped me see.

In some of the prisons you hear the interrogations in high fidelity, as if they're happening in the cell next to yours. Sometimes they do happen there. As they're flogging the guy next door, they will sometimes tell you to thrust your face to the floor or against the wall, and you might well pretend to have heard nothing at all, but you cannot keep yourself from knowing what's going on then. Elsewhere, it's the squawk of the commanders' two-way radios that sinks into your consciousness, and the codes they use among themselves when they are discussing the next checkpoint to be attacked, or the fate of such and such a prisoner. Sometimes it's the sound of a certain commander as he barks at his underlings that awakens your senses, and other times it's the conviction in the fighters' voices as they sing their anthems.

Under such circumstances, what news does your senses bring you? Once, after I had spent an evening with the car battery and a commander in one of their interrogation rooms, the commander came to me in my cell. I was by myself. It was much too dark in there for me to see his face. I could scarcely see my hands. But I recognized the outline of his head against the light from the open door. I listened to him breathing. He shone his flashlight in my face. "Prepare yourself," he said, "little liar. Tomorrow will be worse."

I can handle this, I told myself, but I was drifting away from planet Earth then, and I wanted to drift away. The next round of investigation, as they called their electricity treatments, it turned out, wasn't better or worse, but afterward I lost track of time. During one of the nights that followed, in the darkness in my cell, I saw my mother at her kitchen table. She was alone and hunched over the Boston telephone book, as if she were scouring the pages for my phone number. Didn't I have a phone number? Of course, yes. I've always had phone numbers. But which one? She couldn't find the right one—and so scoured every page. Page after page, she scoured.

During a subsequent night, I found my mother in Vermont. In her driveway, leaning across the hood of her car, her head down. She tried to smile. "Mom," I said, "I'm in Syria now. I'm in the prison here."

We had a dialog then, a little like this:

Me: Things are bad here, Mom.

Her: I know they are. But this is absurd. Can't you talk to them?

Me: No.

Her: Surely . . .

Me: The other thing is . . . The thing is that I'm not coming home.

Her: What? Don't be ridiculous.

Me: I wish I could change it.

Her: What? Where did you say you were?

Now she didn't say a word. Was she confused? She looked into the hood of her car. She spoke to me, but I couldn't hear. I reached across the hood. I was about to touch her. But she was disintegrating. She kept fading away. I needed her to talk to me then. Maybe she would have come back. Probably she wanted to, I thought. But the call to prayer was coming then and I was too awake to see her.

Once during my daydreams, I saw the last town in which I had been alive and free, a minor revolutionary capital called Binnish. The American journalist James Foley, I learned much later, was being kidnapped in an internet café in this village more or less at the hour in which I was seeing it in my imagination. ISIS beheaded him, of course. One night, I had a dialog—inside my cell—with the sweet-voiced shopkeeper I had met here. He had changed some Turkish liras for me. He had given me a paper napkin filled with baklava. Inside my cell, our conversation went like this:

Me: You said that if I needed anything in the world—anything at all—I should come to you.

Shopkeeper: Yes.

Me: I'm coming to you now. I need you.

Shopkeeper: But it's too late. They have you.

Me: But surely you can call for help?

Shopkeeper: You came too far, into a country you never understood, that happens to be under the sway of an unopposable kind of faith.

Me: I see.

A funny thing about the al Qaeda prison system is that this feeling of looking down over your earlier life—over life on planet Earth, among living beings—never quite goes away. It can last for years. Sometimes, in your cell, you feel yourself gazing from an impossible height.

If you keep watching and keep a record of what you've seen, I think it's possible that your sense of hearing, and the sense of sight that comes from being in a blindfold some of the time and in the pitch black much of the rest of the time, might allow you to see the society around you more deeply than those who can look on things openly, without restriction. Now I know that the captors sometimes collaborated in my efforts to see, and wanted me to see. At the time, I hadn't the vaguest notion of what they were trying to do, and their efforts to make me see simply terrified me.

Neither the al Qaeda commanders nor the ISIS commanders with whom I sometimes shared a cell ever forced me to look at anything specific, but I'm sure they did want me, their American invader–enemy, to reckon with the spirit of the times in Syria. They controlled the oil, cities, landscapes, Palmyra. Could I not see how powerful they had become? Did I know this, really, in my soul? They must have felt I did not know.

There were times when they led me from the cell in my blindfold, brought me to the room at the end of the corridor, then had me lie face-first, in my blindfold, on a cement floor. They locked down my hands and legs into a medieval device—an iron cloverleaf sort of thing I felt but never quite saw—behind my back. When they had me lying on the floor with my feet and hands locked in the air in iron loops—I rocked on my stomach like a bloody sort of hobbyhorse—they ripped off my blindfold. They seized my hair by the roots. They thrust their faces into mine. "We want you to see us," an interrogator told me in one such moment. He introduced himself. He introduced his friends. "We are from the al Qaeda organization," he said. At the time, it seemed to me that the interrogator didn't care what I looked at since he knew I would soon be dead. Now, however, I think that he seized my hair by the roots because he thought I was inclined to explain away or deny or, anyway, fail to reckon with the might of their Islamic state. He wasn't going to allow me that luxury. He was going to make me see. Events like this happened more than once. Why would they have gone to such trouble if they weren't trying to make me see?

The interrogators would give me their noms de guerre then— always absurd names, pulled from the pages of Islamic history, or dreamed up in order to suggest that the bearer was a sort of emissary from an Islamic state-of-the-future—the Emirate of Tunis, the Emirate of Canada. Sometimes they would pull down the scarves they had tied around their own faces. "Look us in the eyes!" they would say. "We are from the al Qaeda organization. Do you know who we are now?"

My instinct was to pretend I couldn't understand—or see or know. For two years, whenever I felt I was going to see something I did not want to see I put my head in my hands. I stuffed my thumbs into my ears. But you cannot go on like this forever. Eventually a prisoner will know much more than he's supposed to know.

Over time, I came to feel that seeing an Islamic state from underground—as most of my cells were underground—presents advantages the people walking about in the sunlight, on the surface of the earth, do not have. In an Islamic state, citizens can easily get themselves in trouble for looking too much or remembering too well. A proper citizen in an Islamic state should devote himself to prayer. Making money is okay. Looking after one's family is fine. Keeping a private record of public life—as, for instance, spies do—is not. When people are caught up in the hurly-burly of everyday life, they often forget to look around them. In a war zone, death looms. Here, people are busy acquiring bits of food and fuel for the evening tea. If they have energy left over, they involve themselves in quarrels, love affairs, resentments, schemes, dreamy projects—and of course they stare at screens.

My feeling that I was about to die allowed me to see. In a prison cell, at the very end of your allotment of days, you are in a little eagles' nest, a thousand feet above the surface of the earth. You can see everything. Why do the living struggle and sweat, you wonder, when all they really need to do is to live?

BLINDFOLD

CHAPTER 1

MY PLAN

Antakya, Turkey, October 2012

My plan was to find the cheapest possible dive in Antakya, Turkey. I would sleep there, then make daytime excursions across the border, into Syria. Steering clear of the violence, since I was no combat reporter, I would discover quirky but telling stories about life in the shadow of the Syrian revolution. I would type these up, then dispatch them to editors in New York and London.

For a freelance reporter, the greatest certificate of success was a commission from the *New Yorker* or the *Atlantic*. Those magazines, I understood, paid reporters as much as $10,000 per article. *Rolling Stone* paid similar sums. During the previous years, I had sent out pitch letters to the editors of these magazines. I hadn't gotten a flicker of interest from any of them. Mostly, the editors didn't reply at all. What was up with those people? Maybe they wanted baksheesh. Maybe they awarded contracts only to their college roommates.

I was fine with this. I had options. A year earlier, I had written two essays about the troubles in Syria for the *New Republic*'s website. As I wrote, I was under the impression that a chaotic but beautiful upending of the social order was sweeping through the country. I knew that a few Islamists, probably off in the hinterland, had made their presence known and that the deep cause beneath the violence was the people's wish to be rid of their dangerous-because-very-stupid dictator, Bashar al-Assad. And thus to be free.

In July of 2012, in Vermont, I watched via the internet as crowds ten thousand people strong danced in the central square in Hama, the site of an earlier revolt (1982) against an earlier President Assad (Hafez, the current president's father). The crowds roared with naughty happiness as they sang to their president:

> *Kiss my ass and let all those who bow before you kiss it, too. O, by*
> *god, no one gives a shit about you.*

This looks like good fun, I thought. I knew that financing a reporting trip to Syria wasn't going to be easy. The *New Republic*'s website had paid me $800 per article. I had to ask them to send the money to me in Damascus via Western Union. The Western Union agent in Damascus had taken about $80 off the top each time. An accountant would have added up the cost of the plane to Beirut, the collective taxi to Damascus, the visas, and the expenses on the ground in Syria. To an accountant, it would have seemed that each essay *cost* me about $800. I wasn't interested in accounting.

I had loved writing those essays. I wrote them in the early, heady days of the Syrian revolution, in the summer of 2011. Those essays brought me into the living rooms of religious savants in Damascus. They encouraged me to learn the lyrics of the radio hits there and to interview the Damascene pop stars. The writing had directed me into bits of the Koran I had known nothing about. Composing those website essays had been like a miniature graduate school for me in which the cultural life of the capital was my professor. My fellow citizens were the students. When the articles appeared on the *New Republic* website, I felt I had captured a true, terrifying zeitgeist in the capital about which no one there could speak. When readers commented on my essays, I felt they were attesting to a talent in me—essay writing about Syria—I hadn't dared to believe in myself.

Naturally, a problem cropped up. In the late summer of 2011, as the violence in the Damascus suburbs worsened, the Syrian government, fearing spies, revoked the visas of most of the Westerners living in Damascus. I had to go home to Vermont. And then the owners of the *New Republic* sold their magazine. The new editors did not reply to my emails.

Over the following months, I developed a new plan. I would send out letters to the world's second-tier, lower-pay, low-prestige publications. Didn't such magazines abound in the world? I didn't know. I assumed they must. Meanwhile, there was news to report.

In October of 2012, the nation of Syria appeared to be wandering into a sea of blood. In many of the poorer urban districts, and in all of the rural ones, the government had collapsed. In some places, the government officials had defected to the rebel side. In other places, the police, the state security agents, and the military men had been driven away. Elsewhere, as more than a few YouTube videos attested, the representatives of the ancien régime had been lined up, made to kneel in the dirt, then shot through the back of the head.

"We are your men, O Bashar, and we drink blood!" So went the chants the pro-Assad militias made in the wake of their victories, recorded, then posted to the pro-government YouTube channels.

"To heaven! To heaven! To heaven we will go, martyred by the millions!" So went the chants the anti-Assad crowds made during their demonstrations.

In those days, my general feeling was that the revolutionaries were on the side of the angels. I felt that the Syrian Kurds, whose Iraqi brethren had learned to guide American smart bombs to their targets during the Iraq war, could work with Western air forces and democrats on the ground inside Syria to overthrow President Assad. After the air campaign, I thought, the time would come to storm the barricades. I assumed that the revolutionaries would find me charming. Seeing how admiringly I wrote of them and respecting the freedom of the press, they would, I thought, chauffer me from protest to internet café to village square. Because it would be hot and because the rebel brigades would be in possession of confiscated villas, the rebel commanders, I guessed, would allow me to write out my stories in the shade, by the side of the villa swimming pools.

The genius of my plan was that it required almost no money to launch. No money, in my opinion, would make the reporting better. My affection for Syria, my network of friends there, and my familiarity with the beautiful Arabic language—this, I told myself, was the start-up capital that counted. Penny-pinching would force me to sleep in mosques, to take the city bus, to hitchhike where locals hitchhiked, to eat in the houses of friends, and to learn the secrets of Middle Eastern travel austerity from the resident authorities: pilgrims, itinerant trades-men, and students.

Most people in Syria are poor. Poverty, I told myself in Vermont, ought to be the sine qua non criterion by which editors judged the fit-ness of the reporter who wished to write about the Syrian people.

In the early summer of 2012, I nearly emptied my bank account—and so added to my eligibility as a reporter—by making a trip to Syria. A generous elderly, possibly out-of-the-loop consul in Houston gave me the visa through the mail. No editors in New York and none in London, it turned out, wished to publish the essays I proposed to them. That trip cost me $1,500. Later, in July, in Vermont, on a whim, I bought a Cannondale racing bike. That bill came to $1,800. Running low on cash, I sold a few things. I borrowed from my mother. At the end of the summer, I had enough cash for a new ticket to Turkey. In order to pay for expenses on the ground, I borrowed again from my mother.

I boarded the plane for Istanbul in early October. Assuming that in the fullness of time, when my reporting career was flourishing, I might hop over to the island of Cyprus for a few weeks of cycling, I brought the Cannondale. I spent my first night in Istanbul on the floor, in a room occupied by a friend I had made during my earlier, fruit-less trip to Syria. I told this friend, Freddy, an asylum seeker from the Democratic Republic of the Congo, that I had some reporting work to undertake in Syria. Would he be willing to house my bike during the two weeks or so in which I would be away? Of course, he said.

Freddy, it turned out, objected to all ideas concerning Syria. "What do you want with those people?" he asked. As my host in Turkey, and an able Turkish speaker, he felt himself under an obligation to look out for me. During my twenty-four hours with him, I admitted to him that my American cell phone didn't work in Turkey. It would have cost me

$50 to unblock it. I didn't want to pay. Freddy offered me his. I refused. He insisted. I tried to put him off. In the end, I took it because the mention of the word "Syria" caused him to shiver, because I knew he wanted to look after me, and because my taking it seemed important to him. If I needed to make a call in Syria, I tried to explain to Freddy, I would walk to one of the village shops in which the owner offered pirated international lines at cut rates. I would listen to the other phone conversations underway in the shops, make friends with the patrons, and, in this way, learn about the life of the nation. It wouldn't occur to the proper, professional reporters to go about things this way. So much the better, I told Freddy. Freddy, a refugee in Turkey, couldn't understand why I wished to make life more difficult for myself. "You make me afraid," he told me.

I took the bus from Istanbul to Antakya, the city on the Syrian border in which the international press had established a sort of ersatz headquarters. On the bus, I counted up my cash. I had $200 in my American bank account, available to me through my ATM card. I was managing another $150 in liquid assets, in the form of dollar bills, stray Syrian notes, and Turkish coins. These deposits lived in plastic bags in the interior of my backpack.

So I wasn't rich, at least not in American money, but neither would I be poor. In Antakya, life was considerably cheaper than it was in Istanbul. Accounting for the falloff in prices, technically speaking, I would probably be rich. At least I might feel that way. As for my budget: Many people in these regions, I knew, lived for six months on $350. A single publishing success would bring me, at the very least, $200. This would allow me to live—and write and hike and make new friends—in Antakya for at least six weeks. The first success will bring on the others, I told myself.

Right away, on my first day in Antakya, I began sending out my pitch letters. What about a story focusing on the music of the Syrian revolution? No one was interested. What about the mysterious-because-incommunicative young men from Libya, France, and Holland one stumbled into in front of the military supply shops in Antakya? "Fascinating," said one editor, "but not for us." Austin Tice, a sometime freelancer and full-time law student at Georgetown, had disappeared in Syria in August of that year. A story about Austin Tice? No one was interested. I had an idea about the zany press characters wars attract. What about an update of the 1973 campaign memoir *The Boys on the Bus*, in which the bus would be the Turkish bars where the next generation of war correspondents was coming of age? No one was interested.

I fell into the habit of waking up early, drinking a glass of orange juice in the restaurant next door to the boardinghouse in which I was staying, then scanning my emails.

Two weeks came and went. One Saturday morning, after I had sent out a blizzard of pitches—after they had yielded nothing at all—I sat by myself in the restaurant with my chin in my hands. I gazed through the restaurant's plateglass windows. Every fifteen minutes or so, curious, nosing sheep, in troupes of three or four, ambled by. At a plastic table on the sidewalk, a circle of withered, motionless men sat smoking in the sunlight.

During my first hours of meditation, I allowed my thoughts to drift to the hotel, in the fancy Antakya neighborhood, in which the present generation of war correspondents would have been, just then, sipping the foam from their morning cappuccinos. I half-thought of offering myself to one of these properly employed journalists as a translator or a fixer. Perhaps if I hung out at their cappuccino bar for long enough, a crumb, in the form of an assignment, or an editor's email address, would fall from their table. I would dash off a letter. The editor would bite. Cash would flow. I daydreamed in this way for a little while, then snapped to. Those adventurers were in love with the correspondent flak jacket and the telephoto lens. They knew everything about gadgets and who, in their correspondent bubble, was in love with whom. How could they help me with Syria? It's beneath me to speak to them at all, I told myself. It would make as much sense, I thought, to ask the sheep on the sidewalk for help. The shepherd, wherever he was, would inform me about the politics of the region. If I were to turn to my fellow café patrons—ancient, trembling men—they would share their wisdom about warfare with me.

Toward ten thirty, I decided that the time had come in my life for

Plan B. Maybe I could retire to a youth hostel on the nearby island of Cyprus? If I could get there, I could certainly ride my bike. But then . . . I was pretty sure I didn't have the money to get there. A panic seized me. Did I have enough change to pay the gentle, whispering white-bearded man who pressed his oranges in the back of the café? He had told me that he brought in his oranges from the orchards along the Mediterranean coast, to the south of Antakya, in Hatay Province. Those oranges had tasted like fruit from the heavens to me. I would have died of shame if I had not been able to give the orange juice man his money.

I tried to explain to myself how exactly my cash had dwindled away. During the previous ten years, I had angled and schemed and dreamed of turning myself into a Middle East correspondent. There had been Arabic-language academies in Yemen. There had been a period of study in a Koran school in Yemen and a not particularly successful book about what one learns in such a school. During the three years prior to the war, I had been a full-time resident of Damascus. During this period I had fallen in love, as most foreigners do, with the people, the language, and the culture of this place. My career, however, had foundered.

Naturally, I refused to give up. I dug in my heels. I declared my indifference to money. I don't require rewards from the world of things, I told myself. Now, however, the economics of my career development program were pronouncing a verdict in figures. There wasn't enough money in this business, it was too obvious and much too late for me to note, or if there was, it wasn't for me. I would have to find another way.

For the time being, I required only enough to get myself to Cyprus. In order to come up with that cash, I decided that I would write one last essay. Perhaps the new editors of the *New Republic* would publish it. Perhaps someone else would. That essay would establish, in my own mind, if in no one else's, that my essays were fun to read, revealing, cool, better than the others. There was no cash value in such essays? Fine. Once I had rung the Syria essay bell, I would cut my losses. I would trim my expectations, pack up, move on.

In order to solemnize this decision, I typed out an email to the person whose opinion mattered more to me than anyone else's. She had rescued me from a thousand disappointments, not all of which had involved my being broke. Lately, however, a note of plaintiveness had been creeping into her communications.

"For heaven's sake, sweetheart," she had taken to saying, into the ether, when we talked over Skype. "You need a Plan B."

"I know, Mom," I would reply. "I'm working on it."

"As they say in Georgia," she wrote in an email I received the day before my Antakya restaurant reckoning, "'tell me what you know good.'" This, I knew, was her way of saying, *What in God's name are you doing in Turkey? Please. Stop being an idiot.*

I had been too embarrassed to reply to her question. Now, however, I tapped out a version of the message she wanted to hear:

> I'm still trying with the editors. Nothing definite yet. I mean to get one more piece published. I'll send that around, bargain, negotiate, and maybe this will lead to more steady work somehow. But maybe not. Anyway, I'm planning on writing one more piece. Then, I'm moving on. Okay? Okay?

I had friends in Odessa. There were English-teaching possibilities in Tbilisi, Georgia. Cyprus, however, was nearby. I mentioned these places, wrote a bit about the delicious Turkish oranges, the whispering of the orange juice presser (he spoke a formal old-fashioned variety of Arabic), then pressed "send." Right away, as if from the phone itself, I heard the sound of my mother sighing in cheerful, exhausted relief.

Having thus committed myself, I turned to my current accounts. My room in the boardinghouse—officially, the Hotel Ercan (in Turkish: the Hotel of the Brave)—was costing me $17 a night. I was spending $10 during the days easily—on coffees in the morning, lunch, cell phone cards for Freddy's phone, and cans of Efes beer in the evening. A taxi into Syria was going to cost me $20. I would need at least $40 for expenses inside Syria. My mini-audit told me that about $250 of my freelance journalism start-up capital remained. Under the circumstances, the right thing, I decided, would be to move to a cheaper, more decrepit boardinghouse. But the Ercan, I knew from previous visits, was the cheapest, most decrepit of the Antakya boardinghouses. What to do?

Happily, as if by an act of God, just as I was typing the last of my internal audit figures into my cell phone calculator, Ashraf al-Tunisi (Ashraf the Tunisian), whose musings on the Arab affection for warfare had entertained me during my first mornings in this restaurant, materialized in a patch of sunlight in front of the boardinghouse. I knew him to be the occupant of a room in a cheaper, more slovenly house, in the alleys above the old city of Antakya. I knew him to be in need of money.

I ordered a coffee for him. I stepped outside. Handing him the coffee, I greeted him as my Yemeni teachers used to greet me, high on the top floors of the Sanaa tower houses, when I met them for my first Arabic lessons.

"Morning of the light, Ashraf, my brother," I said.

"Morning of the rose and the jasmine," he replied. Did I happen to have a cigarette for him? He paused. "Never mind! God is generous."

Ashraf had been a student of philology in the Syrian city of Aleppo before money troubles interrupted his studies. When the violence flared in Syria, the regime revoked his visa. He was forced to leave. Now, in Antakya, he disdained the young Syrians who made ends meet by selling vegetables from street corner barrows. They were slaves to the material world. Ashraf preferred to pass the days in contemplation. He read in the mosques. He admired the sunsets. In order to carry on, he sold the TV he had brought with him from Syria. Then he sold an extra pair of shoes, and, finally, his cell phone.

In Ashraf's opinion, the war in Syria was a species of craziness into which Arab countries often tumbled. He thought my ambition to have a closer look at it was a species of American craziness. But if I was determined to go, he told me when I met him, during my first morning in Antakya, I should allow him to vet my traveling companions. Meanwhile, he said, if there was anything I should need in Antakya— a friend, an advisor, connections in Aleppo—I should address myself to him.

In the sunlight, in front of the Ercan, I gave him a minute to sip his coffee. He found a willing cigarette donor at a café table, lit his cigarette, then returned to me. He smiled into the sun.

"I have a question for you, Ashraf my brother," I said. I asked him how much he paid to rent his room.

"Rent?" he said. It was nothing at all—a pittance. Did I not want to hear about the house itself? "Surely you want to improve your Arabic?" If so, his house would be the ideal venue, since it was filled with Syrians from every sect, party, and region. The house sat on the lip of an escarpment, with a view over the twists of the Orontes River, the spiraling Antakya suq, and on the horizon a Turkish alpine panorama. From the curb, he looked up into the warren of gimcrack shacks and mosque minarets that hung like a balcony over the southern half of the city. "By god, from my room, you feel yourself a thousand feet over this filthy city of whores. There are birds, my friend. There are clouds."

"Every night in the Ercan, I spend seventeen dollars," I told him.

"What?" he said, in genuine—or was it simulated?—shock. "Seventeen dollars for a dirty room in this whore of a hotel?" But this rate was exorbitant. It was *haram* to charge even half that amount for such a room. I agreed. His rent, he said, was not unreasonable: 200 Turkish liras a month—about $40. We kept quiet for a moment, and then I mooted my idea. I would bring a blanket and a pillow. I would sleep on the floor of his room. I would pay half the rent.

He thought the matter over for a moment, furrowed his brow, and then a smile of the warmest welcome and shared purpose washed over his face. "Of course," he said. "You are welcome. Welcome, my American friend!"

I checked out of my hotel. We ambled through the suq. From a stall operated by a friend of his, I bought a pink faux-fur blanket (50 Turkish liras) and a pillow (10 Turkish liras). On the far side of the suq, as we climbed through the alleyways, I gave in to the feeling of newfound friendship and serendipity that had hovered over every adventure I'd had in the Arab world to date. I bought each of us a can of beer (10 Turkish liras). He needed a haircut. Okay, I did, too. We went to his friend, a barber whose shop was around the corner from Ashraf's house. "I'll pay for us both," I said (10 Turkish liras).

As we were getting our hair cut, we resolved to strike out, right away, in search of work. Any work at all would do. Did we not both need money? " 'Work is blessed,' said the Prophet, peace and blessing upon him," Ashraf observed.

"Ameen," I agreed.

He felt Antakya was much busier with opportunities for people like us than we knew. Until recently, he had preferred not to search them out. He rather liked to think. "I know what you mean," I said. Lately, however, a feeling had come to him that a little bit of money in his pocket would do him good. And the society of friends at a job site would buck him up. His larger ambition was to save for a ticket home to Tunisia. "May God make you prosperous," I told him.

"May he give us both wealth," he replied.

We spent the rest of the afternoon making inquiries at the construction sites on the outskirts of Antakya. Ashraf felt he would have better luck finding a job if he told the construction managers that he was a Syrian victim of the war, lately evicted from Aleppo, by the helicopter barrel bombs. He felt that I didn't look enough like an Arab for this trick to be useful to me. "Don't say you're an American, whatever you do," he said. He felt that no Turk would believe that an American required work at a construction site. They would assume I had come to spy. They would refuse us both. He thought I could pass for a Russian.

"I'll do my best," I told him.

Shortly before sunset, we happened across a sawmill. The supervisor there wanted to know how strong we were. "We're very strong," Ashraf said.

The supervisor pointed to a pile of stumps that had been dumped in front of a house-sized circular saw blade. "Can you lift a stump?" he asked.

Ashraf seized an enormous block of wood, hoisted it over his head like an Olympic champion, then beamed at the supervisor. The supervisor beamed back. He asked Ashraf where he was from.

"Syrian from Aleppo," said Ashraf.

The supervisor gestured at me. "And him?" he asked Ashraf.

"Russian," Ashraf replied. "But speaks Arabic."

The supervisor cast a dubious look at me. He greeted me in Arabic. I replied in Arabic. His face brightened. He shook my hand. The workday would begin at 7:00 am, he said. "Twelve hours' work. Okay?" We would be paid 50 Turkish liras—about $10—at the end of the day. Were we okay with these terms? "Very okay with them, yes," said Ashraf.

"You'll be here at seven?"

"Of course," Ashraf said.

"Of course," I said.

I'll make use of this bit of luck, I told myself as Ashraf and I wound our way upward, through the alleyways that led to his room, because a compelling, sellable article about the precarious life of the Syrian refugee was to be found at the sawmill. Surely the Turks were subjecting Syrians to something unpleasant at the mill. Dangerous saw blades? Overwork? Perhaps the Syrian refugees employed in this place were organizing a government in exile amid the stumps. Perhaps they were shipping their pitiable salaries back to their friends in the Free Syrian Army? I would find out the details, then write an absorbing, participant-observer essay about the hardscrabble life of the Syrian refugee in Turkey.

I liked the idea when it came, but as we climbed the hillside alleyways, doubts trickled through my head, and by the time we opened the door on Ashraf's windowless, furnitureless room, the story idea, which had shimmered for a moment in the afterglow of a genuine job offer—then caused me to try out opening lines in my head, to daydream about which of the magazines might bite, to see figures and feel cash—was falling in on itself. As we stood in the darkness, it dissolved into a puddle of dreck at my feet.

Had there been a single Syrian among the lumberyard laborers I might have tried to pump some life into it. Yet the material out of which I meant to build my swan-song report to the world consisted, as far as I could tell, of a fake Syrian, a fake Russian, a mighty circular saw blade, and some Turks. I asked myself: Even if, eventually, some Syrian woodmen turned up at the mill, would anyone in New York care if poor Syrians were becoming poorer slowly in Turkey? I wasn't sure I much cared.

At six thirty the following morning, I declined to get out of bed. Ashraf disappeared. At ten thirty a violent banging and shrieking arose from the porch outside Ashraf's room. I lifted the latch on the door. I poked a nose into the fresh air. A white-haired gentleman stood in the sunshine. His eyes were outraged. He held a heavy stick, almost as fat as a log, like a battering ram, in both hands. He advanced across the threshold, strode to the center of the room, then began to shout—partly in Arabic and partly in Turkish, it seemed, or was that Kurdish? As he remonstrated, I stepped backward, then squinted, and then his howling sorted itself into intelligible Arabic sound.

"Working!" he said. "Now. This instant. Go!" A stack of sacks containing cement powder was to be moved from one spot in the courtyard outside Ashraf's room to a spot a few meters away. I was to perform this labor. "You get up. Now!"

I slipped on my sandals. In the courtyard, I picked up one bag, dragged it across the courtyard, then picked up another and another. A few minutes into this task, I noticed that the man was staring at me, mouth agape, as if he couldn't make sense of the alien creature that had touched down in his courtyard.

"You're not an Arab," he observed.

"No," I said.

"Where from?" he asked. "Germany?"

"Yes," I agreed. "Germany."

His face softened. He glanced at the little tower of cement sacks I had made for him. "Thank you," he said in Arabic. "You help me."

"Of course," I said.

When I had moved all the man's cement sacks, he followed me into Ashraf's room.

Ashraf had not paid the last month's rent, he said. Neither had this month's rent been paid. And where was Ashraf? I didn't know where

Ashraf was. The man stared at the blanket on which Ashraf had slept, then turned his eyes to me. "Well, this can't go on," he said. He eyed an open laptop next to the faux fur on which I had slept. Was I living in this room now, too?

"Yes," I admitted. "I am Ashraf's roommate."

The man brandished his stick. "You get out," he said. "This is no hotel."

"Wait," I said. "Please." I reached for my backpack. "I have money." He lowered his stick.

Two months' rent came to 400 Turkish liras—or $80. I counted out the money. I handed it to the visitor. He made a weak smile. He nodded. Holding his eyes on me, he took a step backward. "May God be with you," he said softly. He paused, murmured to himself, reached through his mind for a phrase, and then with a confused but happy expression in his eyes produced it: "Guten Tag!" he said.

"Guten Tag," I replied. He neglected to shut the door. I returned to my blanket on the floor.

During the preceding weeks, an essay about the deep, invisible causes of the war in Syria had been writing itself in my head. I judged its value as a commercial enterprise to be approximately zero dollars, which was why I hadn't bothered to put it down on paper, but as I lay in the semidarkness, it occurred to me that this was the value of all my enterprises, in which case it made sense to write what I wanted to write.

I knew how the writing of this essay would make me feel: missing Damascus, frightened for the country, agog at the paradoxes of the place, and full of admiration for the rebellious crowds. There would be sadness in this essay, since totalitarian societies crushed the life out of a nation's youth. I felt Syria's coming generation was especially hope-filled, curious about the world, happy—though afraid to be so—and pullulating with undiscovered talent. There would be humorous bits to my essay, since Syrians loved to make fun: of the lisping president, the putative stupidity of the citizens of Homs, the Baath Party, the sorry state of the Syrian army's equipment, and the feeblemindedness of the state's bureaucrats. The writing would amble along in this lighthearted mood, since encounters in Syria, even the ominous ones, perhaps especially them, often began in courteous bonhommie.

Yet my essay would come to the point quickly: A sadistic cult of Assad lovers had cast a spell over the nation. Those in the grips of this delirium had so enthralled themselves, with what exactly I would reveal at the end of the essay, that they were willing to shoot their political opponents in the face, openly, on international television, week after week, without a twinge of regret. Perhaps the intoxicating substances at issue here were occult doctrines, arising from Zoroastrianism, fire worshiping, and hatred of Islam, which were now propagated by the president's semisecret religious sect, the Alawites. So the opposition preachers intimated during their Friday-afternoon sermons. Perhaps the current president's father, Hafez, now twelve years dead, had cast his own variety of fairy dust across the nation. So the chanting crowds ("Oh! Oh! May God curse your soul, O Hafez!") seemed to feel. Anyway, that summer, the Assad partisans could be seen on Twitter videos, strolling in plazas littered with corpses. They pumped their Kalashnikovs into the night sky as they chanted: "We are your men, O Bashar, and we drink blood!" During the summer of 2012, the blood had flowed more thickly, in more places, than at any point in the war to date. During my earlier, botched trip to Damascus, in June, I had run across a Damascus journalist friend in a café. "It's just that I don't see any ending to this thing," I told her. She stared at me. "Nor do we," she replied. And then she burst into tears.

My working theory was that emotions driving the violence in Syria didn't have a local habitation exactly, but I felt an attentive traveler could uncover the darkness beneath the placidity of everyday life by visiting the places in which the previous generation of Syrians had murdered one another. Of course, the traveler would have to listen carefully. Of course, he would have to find obliging strangers. Of course, they would dissemble. Of course, the phrases they uttered would mean one thing in a certain cast of light in the morning, then give way to richer, deeper meanings as the day's shadows lengthened. If the traveler was willing to draw no conclusions, to keep his ear to the ground, to make friends, to read, and to watch, the ground, I felt, eventually, would speak.

My plan was to carry out this listening project in a line of villages that runs in the shadow of the Syrian Coastal Mountain Range, north from Homs to the Turkish border. Since this is the frontier along which the mountain people, most of whom are Alawites, give way to the desert tribesmen, all of whom are Sunni, I imagined that some conversation I encountered would be ruled, as it is along the Syrian coast, in the Alawite homeland, by love for President Bashar al-Assad. Other villages I felt would have given themselves to the passionate hatred I was seeing in demonstrations on YouTube. In other villages, I imagined, I would find a muddle.

My idea was to amble along this frontier for a few days and then return with my notebooks to Antakya. There, in the safety of Ashraf's hovel, I would draw up my portrait of the nation. I knew the general feel of the picture: It would show a nation adrift, unsure of its identity, jealous of more eminent, richer rivals, wanting admiration, longing to prove its powers but unable to keep itself from being pulled into the darkness.

Since some secrets are hard to keep, and since I wasn't much in the mood for concealment anyway, I meant to acknowledge that the reporter in the background of this essay had worked his life into a similar fix.

Such were my essay-writing plans. A month or so after they first came to me, I was kneeling on the floor of a cell in the basement of the Aleppo eye hospital. Teenage toughs were making me press my hands and face into the wall above the lice-ridden blanket on which I slept. They laughed as they flogged my back with their galvanized steel cables. I screamed for help. "Oh mi God!" they shouted at me in English. "He is need helb! Helb!"

During those moments, I was aware, on some level, that the idea that had brought me into Syria was a literary travelogue, a bit like Rebecca West in Yugoslavia, a bit like George Orwell in *Down and Out in Paris and London*. This was the butterfly I had chased over the precipice.

In the minutes following these flogging sessions, when my torturers had left my cell, I would stare at the walls. What bubble of self-involvement had I been living in, I wondered, that I should have allowed my life to go floating away—correction, paid my last pennies to cause it to float—into his hell? If only I could wander backward in time to the hovel in which I resolved to pursue the idea, I thought, I would wring the would-be travel writer's neck.

Such is the wisdom of hindsight. That morning in Antakya, as I listened to the landlord clomping about upstairs, I attached myself to my writing idea like someone who falls asleep while driving, nearly comes to grief, then directs a maniacal concentration on the road ahead. I would not be swayed. I refused to permit opposition. I cared about the details of the voyage and nothing else. How much cash should I take? What footwear would be appropriate for October in Aleppo? I resolved to take a pair of plastic sandals. In case I should have the opportunity for a jog, I brought a new pair of running shoes.

Ashraf liked to say that he knew every one of the ten thousand smugglers in Antakya as he knew his own brothers. He had been a café hanger about in the poorer, Arab-speaking quarter of the city for long enough, I judged, for the boast to be more than idle chatter.

Should I trust myself to his friends? I wondered. I didn't much trust him anymore. His lot, I felt, were as likely to finagle my last dollars out of me, then leave me stranded on the windy plains north of Aleppo, by the side of a potato field, as they were to help me. But who in Antakya could I trust? No one, I decided. In which case it made sense to choose at random.

My two weeks of letter writing in Antakya had given me enough time to contemplate a random sampling of travelers. A cigarette dealer Ashraf and I sometimes saw in the evenings, as he rattled through the Antakya alleys on his moped, had a guileless, friendly demeanor. Apparently, he spent his days on jeep trails deep in the Syrian mountains. His customer base, soldiers in the Free Syrian Army, lived under the strafing of the attack helicopters, somewhere in the hills along the Syrian coast. If I traveled with this person, the ride would surely present dramatic scenery. It would cost me pennies, but the risk to life and limb, I felt, was incalculable. And therefore unacceptable. The traveling companion for the voyage I was writing in my head, in any case, was a raconteur, an amateur historian, a singer of songs, and a teller of dirty jokes. I judged the cigarette seller, who was in his twenties, too young and too focused on distributing cigarettes to be useful to me.

A band of young men Ashraf identified as Libyans sometimes lounged at the plastic tables on the sidewalk in front of my ex-boardinghouse. Their story, an obvious fiction to the resident café patrons, was that they had come to the area on a humanitarian mission. They were nurses. Or teachers. Or aid workers or something. One evening, shortly after Ashraf began his lumberyard job, he and I spotted a group of six of them huddling in front of the grocery store across the street from the Ercan. Ashraf rose from the café table, shook their hands, smiled, pointed at me, palavered for a moment, then watched in surprise as their faces darkened. One of them spit on the ground. No, they would not talk to a journalist, they told him, nor would they go anywhere with an American, nor did they have any plans to go anywhere near Syria. "God be with you," they told Ashraf.

A day later, again after his workday was over, he and I wandered into the lobby of a boardinghouse above the Antakya suq in which every one of the twenty or so armchairs lining the perimeter of the room was occupied by a wounded rebel fighter. Some of their faces bore hideous gashes. Others had arms in slings and feet in casts. They grinned as they showed me cell phone photographs of more damaged, bloodier comrades-in-arms. In the photos, men lay on the floor of a sun-dappled forest. Their entrails spilled into the dirt. Some of those soldiers were not quite dead, it seemed, but clasping on to the thread of life, as the Arabic phrase has it. This was why the photographer had taken the picture, a soldier explained to me: to capture the instant in which the martyr's soul entered paradise. Allegedly, the eyes, though lifeless, registered the happiness the soul experienced on seeing the face of God.

In this room, Ashraf declined to identify me as an American. I was a French reporter, he said, who wished to travel into Syria. A half-dozen soldiers interrupted their conversations to offer me a ride into the war. I took down the numbers of two of them, but I knew from the moment I saw the gaping, somehow unbandaged wounds in these men's faces that I would never, under any circumstances, go to the places at which they had been injured. Those people had been in a war. Bullets had flown about. Stuff had blown up. A reporter interested in this sort of thing required a camera. He wore aviator glasses. He would want to write about bravery. Maybe he himself was brave. Maybe he was just reckless. He was not me.

As I said my good-byes to these invalids, I wished for God to send victories to the Free Syrian Army. "Ameen," a dozen mumbling voices replied. I promised to stay in touch, as is proper after an exchange of phone numbers, but I walked down the boardinghouse stairway certain that those men would soon be killed, down to the last man, and supposing that that was what they wanted. What is it about death, I wondered, that young men in this part of the world wish to make friends with it, to carry it around in loving portraits on their mobile phones, and to return to it whenever their wounded bodies allow? I have nothing in common with such people, I told myself, since the only thing I want to return to was a canny, true, colorful essay.

The next morning, a Friday, I made a visit to my old boardinghouse in order to chat with the two young Syrians with whom I had shared a bathroom on the top floor of the Hotel Ercan. Ten days earlier, we had spoken about the possibility of making an excursion together into Syria. They struck me as trustworthy—or anyway as trustworthy as strangers in a frontier town can be. I found Adnan and Gibriel in their room on the hotel's fifth floor. During their three weeks in Antakya, they had roamed up and down the Turkish coast. They had interviewed fishing boat captains, fishmongers, and strollers on the beach. Their understanding had been that, in exchange for a small fee, some such person might drop them on a beach on the island of Cyprus.

Their research had established that the going rate for this crossing was $3,000 per person. They had come to Antakya with hundreds of dollars in their bags—but not thousands. It often happened, they learned, that the boat captains who demanded these absurd sums proved to be bandits who beat their passengers, robbed them, then abandoned them on a desolate stretch of the Turkish coast. So yes, said Adnan, he and his friend Gibriel were indeed planning to return to Damascus. In order to trace their way back to the troubled suburb of Sayyidah Zaynab, where their families lived, they would travel as they had come: by a tortuous concatenation of farm lanes and forest paths on which Syrian government officials never appeared. Some of this smugglers' highway could be traveled by car. Other portions had to be negotiated on foot. The voyage would cost about $75. Because Adnan would be conscripted into the army if the government caught up with him, both friends planned to play it safe: They would never set foot within sight of a government checkpoint.

Their plan was to leave Antakya the following morning at seven thirty. If I wished to come with them, I could meet them in the lobby the next day, Saturday, at that time. Both of these young men made sure that I understood: If I were to travel with them, I would have to assume responsibility for my own well-being. Were I to find myself in trouble, I understood from the stern look in their eyes, I would be on my own.

"Don't you need an ID to get on a bus?" I asked.

Adnan shrugged. "Sometimes yes, sometimes no." I asked about pop-up checkpoints on the highways, the cost of bribing highway officials, whether the officials would be pro-government, pro-rebel, or something else, and what would happen to the traveler if he didn't have the money to pay.

A few minutes later, after we had said our good-byes, when I was outside again in the sunshine, I tried to imagine what was likely to occur during a voyage to Sayyidah Zaynab. It was a regime-controlled, mostly Shia suburb, lately settled by waves of Iraqis in flight from the violence there. Every few weeks, the rebels in this newer Middle Eastern war tried to blow up the Sayyidah Zaynab Mosque, a destination for Shia pilgrims. My traveling companions belonged to the minority Sunni population in this majority Shia suburb, which was itself under assault from the all-Sunni suburbs in whose midst it sat. Could be interesting, I thought. My traveling companions would be on the side of the young men who disguised themselves as women—their childhood friends, so they said—who hid their suicide belts under their black robes, then blew themselves up among the crowds of Iranian pilgrims.

Adnan and Gibriel did not strike me as suicidal. They seemed rather cordial. They were certainly quick to warm to the idea of traveling with me. I was certain they could teach me about the difficulties of escaping to Cyprus. But if I should find myself questioned at an improvised checkpoint along the highway or blocked by an ID-demanding bus driver, I knew—because they had been as explicit as they could be without being impolite—that they would leave me to my own devices. Downstairs, in my favorite restaurant, as I drank a glass of angelic orange juice, I decided that too much of Adnan and Gibriel's itinerary passed through country too thick with Syrian government agents. Those agents were on the hunt for undocumented foreigners in Syria. "American journalist" to government minions in Syria meant "undercover CIA agent." I dreaded the minions. And then how would a voyage to Sayyidah Zaynab help me with my fault line of villages?

Later that day, I walked to the top of the escarpment that overlooks Antakya. I contemplated the views the tourist takes in: The Alexandretta plains about which Gertrude Bell had written in her 1907 chronicle of a voyage through Syria, *The Desert and the Sown*, lay to the left. Beyond those plains, the Mediterranean shimmered. Beneath me, flocks of birds floated over a field of minarets and church towers. I took a picture with my iPhone. I sat on a rock. At my feet, a column of ants was marching away, into a talus field and, from there, upward, into the highest reaches of the escarpment. How duty bound the ants are, I thought, how single-minded, how unquestioning, and how busy. Why was I not capable of living out my life with as much purpose as the typical Turkish ant?

As I walked downward, into the center of town, I turned into the narrow, darkened alleyway by which one entered the Ercan. Almost always, at every hour of the day, Syrians with whom I had a nodding acquaintance could be found milling about in front. On this evening, a café lounger who called himself Abu Firas happened to be smoking a cigarette at a sidewalk table. During our first meeting, I had told him that I was a reporter who wished to travel into Syria. The moment I appeared in the street, when I was still fifty paces from him, he called out my name. I ambled to his table. He invited me to sit. There were no formalities. He proposed a trip into Syria. For $100 in cash, up front, he would take me to any village I wished to visit in Idlib Province. He had grown up in the province. He knew everyone there. Okay? Was I in agreement? Okay?

"Idlib?" I said. "What's in Idlib?"

"Okay," he said. "Fine. Aleppo."

Apparently, during our first café conversations I had related details of my life I don't normally relate to strangers. Or had someone else related these on my behalf? Ashraf? Adnan and Gibriel? Anyway, Abu Firas knew my story: I was the American reporter who wanted to spend no money, was curious about religion in Syria, had once lived in a Damascus neighborhood called Sha'alan, and now lived in a hovel with Ashraf.

"You have memorized well," I said. "You are spying for whom?"

He smiled. "Yes. Spying. Like you."

I smiled back. I asked him how he proposed to take me to Syria.

"A car," he said. "A Mercedes."

"Right," I said. "I should take you there in my private jet." He did not smile. Anyway, I said, if I was going to pay $100, I wanted a proper guide, approved by the Syrian ministry of tourism, with degrees in Roman history, classical architecture, and Syrian politics. "What do you really have, Firas?" I asked. "A bicycle?"

I meant to tease him. Most of the Syrians in the area were more of a mind to blow the ministry of tourism in Syria into little bits than to apply to it for a certification. Firas was meant to chuckle at the mention of their certifications, and to scoff at the idea that anyone should want anything from them.

He stared at me. "You don't like me?" he said.

I told him that I wanted a man of culture as a guide. He spoke a rural, hard-to-understand version of Syrian colloquial Arabic. "What have you studied, my Abu Firas?" I asked. "Anything at all?"

His face darkened. I waited a moment for him to smile. He stared at me, frowned, then turned away. I sighed. Why must I make smart-alecky remarks? I had wanted to be cute. For an instant, I regretted it. I needed to apologize. And then I caught myself. Was not every Syrian café lounger in Antakya on the make?

Perhaps some of the Western reporters in Antakya were easy marks. I wanted it to be known that I was no rube. During our first meetings, Abu Firas had come across as too forward, too aggressively friendly, almost angry. I had felt he was working an angle. I wanted him to take his line of patter elsewhere. So it was okay to have crossed a line with him. I didn't regret putting him off.

Abu Firas, however, was not put off. It took him an instant to swallow his pride. He sucked on his cigarette, then ordered me a tea. We chatted a bit about conditions in Idlib—such government troops as had not yet been killed or kidnapped, he said, were besieged on every side. Sooner or later, they would die. The people would rule. The government would be gone. He sighed. He took another drag on his cigarette. Would I object if he made a phone call?

When his correspondent picked up, Abu Firas stepped away from the table. He began one of those warmhearted conversations, full of Syrian formulae for good wishes, followed by doublings and tripling of the wishes, that affirm membership in a venerable brotherhood. He chatted for a moment under his breath, then returned to the table, the sour mood I had provoked in him earlier vanished. He suppressed a grin.

"I have excellent news for you," he said. The friends he had just now spoken with were journalists themselves. They were Syrians, friendly to the opposition, who would be returning to Syria soon.

"Yes?" I said. "Journalists? Who do they work for?"

Abu Firas wasn't sure. Anyway, his friends were constantly occupied with work. Probably they had many employers. They were in demand because they knew every back road in Idlib Province. They knew the main roads, too. Basically, they were travelers. One day, they were here; the next day, they were elsewhere. As chance would have it, this evening they would be at the hotel above the central taxi stand in Antakya, just around the corner from the Ercan.

"They want money," I told Abu Firas.

Abu Firas shrugged. "Maybe they want free," he said. "Ask them."

"Free, free?" I asked. "Or free now and pay later?"

He shrugged again. He didn't know. "Possibly free, free. Maybe a few liras." I could find out the details myself, since the two people in question would be upstairs, in the first-floor hotel lobby of the Hotel Antakya, that evening at 7:00 pm.

At that hour, a breeze was rolling through a wall of floor-length curtains. Otherwise, the lobby was dead. I examined the reception desk, peered down an empty hallway, then stepped through the curtains. I met my kidnappers out there, on the balcony, in a haze of soft evening light. It cast a coppery glow over their jeans, their baseball caps, and their white basketball sneakers. They had propped their feet on the balustrade. They turned their heads but did not remove their feet. Probably this was a bad sign.

Eventually, Abu Firas stood. He smiled in surprise and awkwardness, then abruptly stopped smiling. He offered me his hand. "This is the American journalist," he said into the slanting rays. I was the one who wanted to visit Syria, the one who spoke Arabic, the one who used to live in Damascus. The kidnappers offered me their hands.

The kidnapper closest to me wore a red baseball cap. His tresses glowed in the evening light. His eyes twinkled. He could have been a model in a magazine advertisement. "Welcome, my brother," he said. "Welcome, my American friend!" He offered me a cigarette. I declined. He put a glass of tea in my hand.

His name, he said, was Mohammed. He was Syrian, lived in Syria now, and planned to return there soon. He grinned his Cheshire cat grin. I like this person, I thought. I liked the way he tipped backward in his chair, his tea perched high above the Antakya din, and his blue-

jeans-and-baseball-cap ensemble. I had to restrain myself from pepper-
ing him with questions.

"Speak English?" he asked me.

"Yes," I told him in English.

"My language speaking very well," he said. "I am study. English, if
you please."

He switched to Arabic. In Arabic he said that he had had to abandon his university course but carried on now as best he could, by studying the grammar on his own, reading stories, and of course watching
American movies.

In the midst of these declarations, Abu Firas announced, out of
nowhere, implausibly, as if he'd been struck by a bolt from the heavens,
that he had left his phone in his hotel room. He apologized. "You'll be
fine by yourselves?" he asked. He is giving us space to discuss money, I
told myself. So Abu Firas, despite my earlier rudeness, was being polite.

"Going?" I said to him. "Stay. Drink tea." This, too, was a politeness.

"I have things to do," he said. He offered me his hand. "Anything I
can do for you?"

"Anything I can do for *you*?" I replied. These were formulaic, situation-
appropriate courtesies, but Abu Firas had gone out of his way to do
me an act of generosity. He couldn't have known what his good turn
meant to me, and I had no way to express my gratitude. Still, I felt it. He
had introduced me to an ideal traveling companion: the Syrian citizen-
journalist. I despised all other kinds of reporters. The citizen-journalist,
however, I liked. I liked the idea of the citizen-journalist and didn't care
about the details. I would learn the details along the way. I wished I
had some truer way to thank Abu Firas. In the event, the only thing
that came to mind was: "God be with you, brother. A thousand thank-
yous!"

Hours later, it occurred to me that Abu Firas probably wouldn't
have sought out my kidnappers for me if, earlier in the evening, I hadn't
made condescending remarks about his accent, his sophistication, and
his car. One oughtn't to tell strangers in Antakya that one is an American. This, too, had been a mistake. Perhaps he genuinely believed me
to be scouting around on the CIA's behalf. I oughtn't to have joked with

him about the possibility. Hours later, when I was trying to retrace my steps, in my mind, to the library of a house in which I was being tortured I kept seeing Abu Firas's half smile in the evening light. I saw his uneasiness, and his urge to slip away. Perhaps the kidnappers had been telling him, before I arrived, of their feelings that Americans deserved to be shot wherever they could be found. I came to know those kidnappers. Declarations of this nature would have been quite in line with their true feelings. Perhaps he had misgivings about sentencing me to a voyage with such friends. Perhaps he half-agreed that Americans should be shot when possible but didn't feel like carrying out the shooting himself, so made an excuse about his cell phone, then slipped through a dusty, diaphanous curtain, and so out of the plot he had set in motion.

In the fall of 2012, he was a common sight at the coffee tables in the Arabic-speaking section of Antakya. His phone number is in my iCloud account. He doesn't answer it now. I never saw him again. Where have you gone, Abu Firas, you travel agent of death?

Though no one offered me Abu Firas's empty chair—though the kidnappers had returned their feet to the hotel balustrade—I sat in Firas's chair. I smiled at my new friends.

I made a remark about the sweeping view the hotel balcony offered. My hotel, I said, was a stack of dark boxes, in a darkened street. Mohammed nodded and grinned. His friend grinned. They gazed outward, into a flock of cotton candy evening clouds just then settling over a ridgeline about ten kilometers to the south. That balcony permitted an expansive view: the busy taxi stand beneath us, the forest of Turkish rooftop bric-a-brac in the middle distance—water tanks, satellite dishes, ventilation pipes—and, beyond this, the falling night.

I was curious about what these young Syrians were up to in Antakya.

"We're tourists," said Mohammed, in an accent that suggested "educated" to me, "middle class," and "Damascus." "Vacation," he said. "Marvelous, Antakya. Yes?" He winked.

I changed the subject. Mohammed had grown up in a rebel-held suburb outside of Damascus called al-Tal, he said, had studied computer science and English at the university in Damascus. Sadly, the violence in Syria had prevented him from continuing his studies.

He wore his baseball cap backward, like an insouciant pop star. I judged this to be a sign of boyishness. His clothing was clean, possibly new. I judged this to mean "comes from a nice family." He was neatly shaven. I judged this to mean "not particularly religious."

As he talked, I scrutinized his eyes for evidence of the qualities I meant to avoid—bossiness, an insistence on having the upper hand, recklessness. Here was someone too into American mall fashion to insist, I thought, on taking me to witness a battle or a bombing. Perhaps he and I would strike up a friendship? That evening, in that light, I judged this possible.

After twenty seconds of conversation with Mohammed, I turned to the other kidnapper—the leader of the plot, as it turned out. "And your name, my friend?" I asked. He thought over my question for a moment. He stared into the distance. "Abu Osama," he replied. Then he turned his face toward the mountains. He grinned over some private happiness.

In prison in Syria, whenever I saw these moments in my imagination, which was often, every detail of the scene made the malevolence of Abu Osama's character flood into my consciousness. I couldn't get these details out of my head. The reason Abu Osama hesitated before giving me his name, I knew after it was much too late, was that he hadn't expected his kidnap victim would turn up of his own accord, smiling and gregarious and ready to be eaten up. I was a fish leaping into his net. The fish spoke cheerfully, in colloquial Syrian Arabic. The singularity of the situation would have thrown him for a loop. So his surprise—and a need to rummage through his imagination for a suitable name—left him at a loss for words. Instead of speaking, he skipped a beat. He stared into the void. And then his stroke of wit in naming himself after the Terrorizer of America, as one of the anthems popular in Idlib at the time referred to Osama bin Laden, made him giggle. He couldn't laugh in my face, and so he smirked at the rising moon, at the Antakya rooftops, and at the painterly clouds on the horizon.

I, however, was too interested in the idea of the citizen-journalist to notice. Probably I wanted to prop up my feet alongside a crew of friendly, principled, moneyless Syrian reporters. Probably I was lonely.

"May the mercy of God and blessing be upon you," I said to Abu Osama. "May he keep you and preserve your parents."

Abu Osama said he was from Idlib. "In truth, Mohammed and I are activists," he said. "Activist-journalists, actually."

Did he write? No, he and Mohammed took photographs. They also made videos.

"I see," I said.

Mohammed turned to me. He spoke in English. "No vacation," he said. "We are work. Journalist sometime. Sometime activist. See?"

"I see," I said. I said I would help him with his English. Of course, it was fine as it was. If he wanted help, I would help him.

"You are welcome," he said.

"So you go out on demonstrations?" I asked. "You also do some reporting. Is that right?"

"I lead the demonstrations," Abu Osama corrected.

His Facebook page, which I didn't bother checking at the time—which I discovered easily enough after I was released—shows that he hardly lied at all during our first meeting. To be sure, he spoke in generalities. I filled in the rest.

As for leading the demonstrations, his Facebook page videos show him to have been a fiery, effective leader of the crowds in his native town, an agricultural outpost on the northern Syrian plains called Marat Misrin. On Facebook, he called himself the singer of Marat Misrin—by which he meant that he led the dads and sons who gathered on the boulevards here in colorful, strident, naughty, outraged song. The crowds—especially the little boys among them—adored him.

His Facebook page shows him to have been a busy Facebooker, with 3,124 friends. He posted new pictures every few days. By 2014, he had married. His real name was Abdou Nijaar. In 2015, he had a son. Naturally, he called the son Osama. Because fathers in Syria often adopt their sons' names, his friends on Facebook began calling him Abu Osama. Probably his wife, who did not post on his Facebook page, called him Abu Osama.

So his fib to me about his name might have been more like a wish—a fiction he would make fact in the fullness of time. The rest of what he told me that night was true. For instance, here he is as a photographer.

A 2012 self-portrait from Abu Osama's Facebook page.

Somehow, in Antakya my feeling was that activist-journalists only advanced the revolution through peaceful means. If they had wanted to be combatants, they might have been, I thought. Instead, principle or temperament or talent led them toward documenting the infinite quantity of facts that would advance the cause of the Syrian people.

I know now that in an Islamic state kidnapping, killing, activism, and journalism are one. The most loved, most widely celebrated citizens do all of these things well. The activist-citizen makes the dream of a caliphate real by rallying the faithful. The journalist builds it by sending out photographs of victories, family happiness in the streets, and the togetherness of the men at prayer. When he puts the video of a killing on Facebook, he shows the world that here, on this stretch of Syrian ground, while the black flag waves, the enemies of God are coming to grief.

When I met Abu Osama, I had no notion of how important the activist-journalist was in the social phenomenon underway, a few kilometers away, on the far side of the international boundary. What does it take to build an Islamic state? A glance at his Facebook page might have brought deeper understanding, though the fake name he gave me would have made it hard to locate. To his 3,124 friends, in any case, and to all others inclined to drop by (his settings were adjusted to "public"), he made his declarations in an international, impossible-to-misinterpret language of symbols.

Here they are, in a self-portrait on his Facebook page. The camera symbolizes journalism. It delivers tidings to the global body of believers, the Ummah, which might not otherwise know of the phenomenon unfolding in the overlooked, untouristed regions of the world. The book gives the law. The Kalashnikov slays the enemy. The face mask—impersonal, unknowable, watching—represents the state. Why can't a believer deploy all of his talents on behalf of the state at once? He can. He should. The brightest believers do.

Sadly, on the night I met these young men I had no notion of civic virtue in an Islamic state. I wanted to know that these young men were journalists, not militants. I dreaded being dragged into the midst of a battle I hadn't the courage or the equipment to document. I hoped that these new friends had found some means of supporting themselves in the profession, unlike me. So I asked Abu Osama where he published his photographs.

"Among the opposition," he said, using the Syrian expression for press outlets operated by government opponents. "TV. Newspapers. Anywhere." It wasn't an implausible story. The opposition television had offices in Beirut and Dubai. I hadn't known they paid photographers in Antakya. But why not?

Abu Osama in 2013, somewhere in Idlib Province,
also from his Facebook page.

I turned to Mohammed. "Peaceful demonstrator," he said. "And photographs, too."

I decided that Mohammed was the warmer, more talkative one of the pair. He said that his purpose was to help the opposition.

"Any particular branch of the opposition?" I asked.

"No," he said. "We help them all."

"And by helping, you mean . . . ?"

Mohammed smiled. He shrugged. He shifted his gaze to the rooftop bric-a-brac. I have badgered him into silence, I told myself. Didn't I have a talent for this? Mohammed's clamming up, I felt, with a twinge of annoyance at myself, was a mark of his intelligence. My questioning proved my naïveté. A canny Syrian, when confronted by a curious stranger, particularly a foreign one in a foreign place, shuts his mouth. I knew this. Yet I had behaved as if I were having a chat on a bench in a London park.

So there were indescribable ways in which these young men helped people of no known affiliation. Fine. Indescribability interested me. I liked secrets. Later, perhaps, after I had earned the trust of these two journalists, they would confide. In the meantime, I meant to control my urge to pry.

Some moments of uneasy silence passed, and then Abu Osama wondered, apropos of nothing, what I wished to see in Syria.

"I don't know," I told him. "I'm open." I wanted to travel and to learn. I meant to write an essay. He nodded. I asked him if his current trip to Antakya involved journalism.

"No," he said. On this trip, he was picking up supplies.

Perhaps they're not journalists after all, I thought. Or if they were journalists, they made their money carrying goods from Turkey into Syria. Did they deal in alcohol? Cigarettes?

"I see," I said. "Supplies?"

"Yes," he said. "Many different sorts of things."

A new silence fell over our discussion. Abu Osama looked at the moon. Mohammed rescued the conversation. He said that he had recently taken an Italian journalist on a tour of the Aleppo front. The journalist's name had been Marco. Marco Something. Actually, he couldn't remember Marco's family name. I asked who Marco worked for. Mohammed searched the air above the balcony. He couldn't remember who Marco worked for.

So there was no Marco, I concluded. Or maybe Mohammed had seen Marco months earlier, on television perhaps, or in passing, in a van filled with combat-vested, pith-helmeted journalists.

"Very famous reporter in Italy," he said. "I can find you his number if you need it."

No, I didn't need it.

Abu Osama interrupted. He had a question for me, if I didn't mind. "Are you Muslim?"

In the Syria I knew, before the war, this had been a rude question. It sometimes meant "in your personal life do you abide by any kind of moral code at all?" Sometimes it meant "I don't trust you." But there were times when it meant, simply, "I have never met anyone like you."

"Does it matter if I'm not?" I said.

"Not at all," he said. He was merely curious.

"Good," I said. "Because I am not a bit Muslim." I told him that I respected Islam, had studied it, but had never thought of converting. Was this a problem?

"Not at all," Abu Osama said.

That evening, the three of us spent about a half hour sniffing at one another. It wasn't unfriendly sniffing. It wasn't hostile. Toward the end of the conversation, Mohammed asked how long I wished to remain in Syria.

"Two days," I said. "Then back here."

Mohammed thought about the program for a moment. He looked at Abu Osama.

"Would that be a problem for you?" I asked.

"Not at all," Mohammed said. Yes, in fact, now that he had given it some thought, that would be easy indeed.

I wanted to know if the voyage they were planning would take them to dangerous places.

"Of course not," Mohammed replied. He went only to the safe places. But what gave him confidence in the safety of those places? "Isn't it our country?" he asked. "We know the roads. We know the people. It's our country." He smiled. "We grew up there, so we know."

"I see," I said. I asked if he could bring me to one of the field hospitals in which European doctors were helping wounded rebels.

"Doctors?" he said. He turned to Abu Osama. Abu Osama nodded.

"Certainly, doctors," Mohammed affirmed.

"What about foreign fighters?"

"The *muhajireen*?" Mohammed asked, using a colloquial term meaning foreign fighters. "Yes, of course." He smiled.

Everything is "yes" to these people, I thought. Of course it will turn out, I told myself, once we start moving on the ground in Syria, that many things are "no" while only some are "yes." So they were over-promising. Was this wrong? Not particularly, I thought.

During the first summer of violence in Syria, before I gave up my apartment in Damascus, I had heard rumors of foreign journalists who, hailing a random cab, failed to suspect that the driver was an incognito regime agent. They asked to be driven to notorious, revolution-fomenting mosques. The drivers agreed, tore through the alleys in the helter-skelter way customary among Damascus taxi drivers, then delivered the journalists to the front steps of the Syrian National Security HQ. The greenhorn reporters were arrested, accused of wishing to kiss up to terrorists or, worse, funding them, jailed, and, after many days of unpleasantness, expelled from the country.

As Mohammed was assuring me of the availability of foreign fighters and foreign doctors, I stole glances at him. I eyed his friend. I took a deep breath. Regime agents? I wondered. It's not their sort of thing, I told myself.

Rather, they were out to make a buck. Was this wrong? It was not. Now that the border crossings outside of Antakya were in the hands of the rebels, some among Syria's vast population of underemployed, undereducated young men wished to establish themselves in the import-export business. And so? Had I been in their place, I thought, I would have done the same.

At the time, in October of 2012, a single Western journalist had disappeared in Syria. That evening, this person, Austin Tice, was on my mind. I wanted my new friends to know what I knew about Austin: An adventurous freelancer and law student from Texas, he had set out for Syria about six weeks earlier, in August of that year. From Antakya, he had traveled to a village in Idlib Province called Khan Sheikhoun. He had been taken in by a family there, according to his Twitter feed, and had then traveled deeper into Syria, toward Damascus. I thought I might be able to learn something of his disappearance from the citizens he had met in Khan Sheikhoun.

I asked Mohammed, "Can you maybe take me to this town?"

He reflected on the question for a moment. "Khan Sheikhoun?" He turned to his friend. "Can we take him to Khan Sheikhoun?" He turned back to me. "Why, yes, I believe we can."

"And how much do you want to take me there?"

Again, Mohammed turned to his friend. The wise thing to do when contemplating an excursion with any Syrian driver, I knew, was to insist on an agreement up front, before any debts were incurred, and to repeat it several times, so that the terms could be affirmed, out loud, by all concerned. Drivers sometimes pretended to be offended by a discussion of money. "Pay what you like," they often said. Later, bitter arguments ensued.

After conferring with Abu Osama, Mohammed turned to me. He held my gaze. He didn't find the question rude in the least. "Your voyage is free," he said. He spoke evenly, in a quiet voice, with a touch of indignation in his tone, as if I had asked to pay for the tea he had offered me. "We're going there anyway," he said. "You are our guest."

I wasn't inclined to believe in "free." I wasn't inclined to believe that these twentysomething hipsters had given me authentic names, or genuine hometowns, either. I was, however, curious about what they got up to in life. What if their work involved something very illicit? In that case, a voyage in their company would give me a marketable story to pitch. So what was their line? Alcohol? Women? Phones? I meant to find out. The finding out, apparently, would be free. So much the better.

Because understandings concerning money in Syria have a way of unraveling if left unattended, I returned to the money matter a few minutes after Mohammed had uttered the word *belash*—literally, without a thing. I put my understanding of our agreement in quasi-legal terms, to make sure that we understood how things were to work between us: "You, Mohammed, and you, Abu Osama, agree to take me into Syria, and to return me here, to Antakya, in two days' time, in exchange for nothing whatsoever?"

"You will pay in a restaurant, for instance, if we stop for breakfast," said Mohammed.

"Of course," I said. "I'll pay for the gas, too." I would be happy to pay more, I explained, but I was a freelancer. I made my money after the reporting, not before. I was sorry about this. I, too, didn't have much. Did they understand this?

They did understand. They nodded. They turned their faces away.

A moment or so of silence passed. I contemplated the view. Who knew how jagged and piney the peaks in Syria could be? They contemplated my stupidity. Who knew Americans could be such fools?

"When do you want to leave?" Abu Osama asked. "Tonight?"

Was he kidding? No, apparently, he was not. He was ready to leave that instant.

I explained that I needed to prepare a traveling bag. I needed to change my Turkish liras into Syrian liras. "Should I take my passport?" I asked.

Mohammed thought about it for a moment, then shrugged. "Sure," he said.

"How much money should I take?"

"How much do you have?" he asked.

"Very little."

"Do you have five hundred dollars?"

"No." I did not. I squinted at him. It was only two days. Five hundred dollars in Syria, I felt, was a fortune.

He shrugged. The checkpoints sometimes required bribes, he said. Gas was becoming expensive. It was best to take extra cash into Syria because there were no ATMs, at least not any connected to the outside world.

"I'll take what I've got," I offered.

We talked about blankets (no need to bring one) and food (falafel and tea, a few pennies per day) and then Mohammed, wondered, out of idle curiosity, nothing else, how many phones I planned to bring.

"I have two," I said.

"One is a satellite phone?" he asked.

"No," I said.

He sighed. He twiddled his fingers through his beard. It was just that he had known other correspondents who traveled with satellite phones.

"Well, I don't," I said.

"That's fine," he agreed.

It took my new friends another minute or so to work through the rest of their desiderata. Did I have a bank card I wished to bring? I did have one, but what good would it do me? Mohammed thought I should bring it on the off chance that we would run across a bank connected to the outside world. What kind of cameras did I have? I had none. I had a laptop. I didn't want to bring it. What if it should be seized at a checkpoint?

"Good point," Mohammed said. "Very clever."

There wasn't anything else of value in my possession. When this realization dawned on my new friends, a silence overtook our dialog. They sighed as if I'd given them news of the death of a distant friend.

They had been hoping, I supposed, that American reporters would behave like Saudi princes, tossing $100 bills in the air, smiling at everyone, and passing out spare video cameras like party favors. After I have disabused them of these notions, I thought, they will see that I have as little as they have. Perhaps then we could get on with our journalism, our travel, and our friendship.

In the meantime, I didn't object to them hoping. Westerners, in general, have. They can always get more. Young men in the Middle East have a bit but not much. They cannot get more.

Rationalizing their acquisitiveness thus, I propped up my feet. I watched the moon rise. My new friends drifted into a whispered conversation. They made warm noises, but not to me. Before I got up to leave I told Mohammed that I could be ready the following day.

"Okay," he agreed. "Nine?"

"No," I said. "Noon, at the earliest."

We agreed to meet at the café next to the Hotel Ercan at 12:00 pm. We shook hands. We wished one another the blessings of God.

I woke the following morning at seven twenty-five. If I hurry, I thought, I can catch Adnan and Gibriel, my friends from the Ercan, before they set out. The three of us would engage the Syrian police in a cat-and-mouse game across the breadth of the nation. Whenever a checkpoint presented itself, we would hike through the forest, chatting, laughing, and never getting caught. In the evenings, we would share our meals. It would feel like *On the Road* meets *Dispatches* with an undercurrent of homelessness.

I threw a notebook, a can of beer, the two cell phones, a passport, $50 in US cash, a paperback copy of the Paul Theroux book *Dark Star Safari*, and my running shoes into a daypack. I put on a white neoprene cycling jacket I had picked up at a used clothing store in Berlin a few years earlier. I was in no mood to try to pass myself off as a local. Locals did not wear white cycling jackets. I didn't mean to present myself as a war correspondent, either. I meant to present myself as me. So I tucked my iPod into the vest pocket of the cycling jacket, then hurried from the hovel. On the way to the Ercan, I practiced the hale-fellow-well-met greetings I would utter to Adnan and Gibriel when I met them in the lobby. "They left this morning at seven thirty," the hotel clerk told me.

At the taxi stand in the center of town, I drank a cup of coffee. I had a stroll. I contemplated the trash in a culvert through which the Orontes River flowed. At noon exactly, Abu Osama was waiting for me at a table in front of the Ercan. A duffel bag sat at the side of his chair. He made an unctuous smile. "Would you like a coffee?" he asked. Syrians never arrive early for anything. When a Syrian agrees to do a favor for free, then waits around in a café, grinning and offering to buy a stranger a coffee, something is up.

"Where is Mohammed?" I asked. Abu Osama, it seemed to me, had a taciturn—even a sour—disposition. I was to travel with him alone? My heart sank.

"Mohammed? Oh, he is waiting at the apartment," he lied. "No coffee?" I declined the coffee.

We caught a minibus for Reyhanli, a Turkish village hard on the Syrian border. In the apartment in Reyhanli, a third kidnapper, also in his early twenties, introduced himself as Abu Osama's brother. He was to be called Abu Said. Abu Said shook my hand. He muttered a welcome, but his blank face and his fleeting eye contact told me that he didn't wish to welcome me at all. He directed me to a couch.

As I sat, the brothers settled into a pair of armchairs on the far side of a carpet. I surveyed their flat: It was no bachelor pad but a cleanly, nicely appointed family home. There were carpets in the living room, a prayer room, a heavy television, a vase of plastic flowers on a coffee table. Someone had vacuumed. Someone had arranged a line of pillows along the back of a sofa. Where were Mom and Dad?

Sinking into their armchairs, Abu Said and Abu Osama retrieved their mobile phones from their pockets. They scrolled. They tapped out messages. I scrutinized their faces. Were they really brothers? Perhaps they are brothers in the "brothers-of-the-faith" sense of brotherhood, I thought. They might have been cousins.

Fifteen minutes passed. Why had we come to this apartment? Who lived here? Why were they sinking away into their phones? I had been under the impression that we were striking out on adventure into Syria. In fact, a pair of postadolescent couch surfers were mesmerizing themselves with their cell phones in their parents' living room.

Another five minutes passed. Abu Said rose. Without saying a word, he disappeared into an interior room. He returned ten minutes later. He sat in his armchair. Then Abu Osama rose. He disappeared behind the same door.

They are having lunch with their mom and their sisters, I told myself. They are embarrassed that they cannot invite me into the women's sphere. They don't know how to make their apologies and are not considerate enough to bring me a plate, and so they say nothing. Perhaps, I thought, I could find a sandwich in Reyhanli.

I yawned. So the smugglers make their contraband run during the daytime, I explained to myself, then come home to Mom and Dad at night. Mom and Dad, I guessed, hardly belonged to the normal run of Syrian refugee families. They had the money to rent a Turkish apartment I couldn't have dreamed of. The wireless internet, the satellite television, the carpets: The occupants of this apartment had been business owners or teachers or civil servants before the violence in Syria drove them into Turkey. They had taken an apartment directly on the Syrian border because they meant to hurry home at the earliest opportunity.

Pillars of the community such as the mom and dad in whose living room I was lounging would not have approved if they had known that their sons were making their money by running goods across the Syrian border. If the sons were to introduce me to their parents, the parents would almost certainly suss out an impending voyage into Syria. The father would be courteous with me, then turn to his sons: "What business have you with this American in Syria?"

An interrogation along these lines could end our trip before it began. Fine, I thought, I shall not pry. If a fatherlike person appears, I thought, I will keep my mouth shut. In the meantime, I wanted to waken my traveling companions from their slumber. I wanted them to understand that our voyage into Syria was no casual, local errand but a project that might easily lead us into mortal danger.

"The two reporters," I said rudely, in the midst of their silence. "The two who were imprisoned near here a few weeks ago. You've heard of them?" My friends had not heard of these reporters.

One was a Dutch photographer and the other a British writer, I explained. I pointed toward a line of Syrian pines on a ridge outside the window. "A band of extremists took them prisoner in a forest. Right here," I said. The incident had played out over several days. The journalists had emerged in good condition, but only after a foiled escape attempt, and only then after the Free Syrian Army fought its way into the extremists' encampment. During the skirmish that preceded the journalists' liberation, several of the extremists, including their leader, I explained, had been killed.

"Really?" said Abu Said, barely lifting an eyebrow. He asked for the names of the journalists. I looked them up online. No, he had not heard of them. And the name of the *katiba* that took the journalists into custody? I searched further, but the militants had had no name, apparently, at least not one I could turn up. The brothers frowned. They returned to their phones. There were angry birds to be dispatched and candies to be crushed. So bands of extremists were trampling around in the forest a few hundred meters from where we sat, the bands had hijacked people quite like me, the hijacking had turned into an international incident, and my traveling companions, on learning this news, could not be bothered to lift their eyes from their phones.

How addicted we've become to our devices, I told myself, and how totally these wicked machines keep us from seeing what's going on under our noses. I decided I had better take a walk.

I announced my intention. The brothers looked at each other. "To where?" Abu Osama wanted to know. "Why?" He volunteered to accompany me. I wanted to be alone. I told him this. He consulted his watch. "We'll be leaving here in fifteen minutes. You can be back then?"

"Of course," I said. At first, stepping out of the apartment, I worried these dour, incommunicative brothers might leave without me, but when I was a hundred meters from them—when their silences and half sentences were no longer annoying me—a dread more powerful than any I had encountered during all previous voyages to Syria washed over me. I ignored it, but the feeling did not go away. The first cold winds of winter were whistling through the trees. No other humans were about.

As soon as I am on the far side of the border, I thought, I will be among people who do not know me or like me, in a war zone, without a working cell phone. I turned my eyes toward the sky over Syria. A bank of heavy clouds hung over low, forested hills. I imagined plumes of mushroom clouds rising from the earth, merging into the cloud bank, then dissolving themselves in the autumnal gray. Perhaps the clouds I was looking at were rather more made up of dissipated explosion smoke than cloud. It was certainly possible. How was one meant to tell the difference between explosion smoke and cloud? I pondered this mystery for a moment. For what reason exactly, I wondered, did I mean to take myself into those killing fields?

I decided that Abu Osama and his brother—or cousin or whatever he was—Abu Said were too silent and too furtive to make the trip enjoyable. The friendlier, baseball-cap-wearing Mohammed had vanished. Good riddance to him, I thought.

In my mind's eye I saw the brothers driving me to a lonely spot on the high plains, north of Aleppo. They would provoke an argument. One of them would insist on my paying hundreds of dollars. Had they not guided me across an international border? Had they not imperiled their lives in doing so? They would demand $300 in cash. I would refuse. And so they would leave me by the side of the road, as bandit taxi drivers in Syria sometimes do.

Or perhaps they would invite me to witness some episode of brutality I did not want to witness. This lot of Syrians would be murdering that lot. I would refuse to witness it, whatever it was. We would argue, they would insist, I would give in, and then, when we had arrived at their "safe" observation post, some bit of twisted metal would fly through the air, lodge in my kneecap, and maim me for life.

I knew what the other reporters would say: "Really had no business being in Syria at all, did he?"

"Probably thought of himself as a bit of a cowboy."

"He's gonna be a one-legged cowboy from now on." And so on. What a useless lot those correspondents were. I longed for providence to arrange for me to meet one or two of them by chance, in a sandwich shop, for instance, or in a collective taxi. I had read the twaddle they published under their editors' gentlemanly headings: "A Letter from Syria" and "A Reporter's Notebook" and "The Aleppo Scene." Most of it was hogwash. I had yet to meet one of these charlatans in person. If chance were to present me with such a meeting, I decided, I wouldn't waste time being polite. I would give the nonentity in front of me a piece of my mind. Why not? Those people deserved much worse.

It occurred to me that I could catch a return bus to Antakya. It would have me back in Ashraf's hovel within the hour. I had my computer there and a pink faux-fur bedspread. Ashraf would appear in the evening. The two of us would drink a beer together, then sleep, and in the morning new safer, wiser career projects would come to me.

At the bus station—a parking lot on a side street strewn with blowing trash—I learned that the bus for Antakya had left minutes earlier. The next one would come in an hour. Or maybe two? The man to whom I put my questions was himself a stranger in Antakya. "Only God knows," he said in Arabic. He cast a mournful glance toward the sky over Antakya, then lowered his head, then shuffled away into the wind.

I will make my apologies to my new friends, I told myself as I ambled back to my kidnappers' parents' apartment. I will bow out and slink away. I walked for a few meters, lost track of where exactly the apartment was, retraced my steps, and as I searched out the lanes that led to their apartment my resolve disintegrated.

It had taken me weeks to settle on suitable traveling companions. The ones I had found were certainly sullen. But their price was right. Anyway, I had cast my lot with them. To change up my plan now would have been to allow my life to be ruled by whimsy and precognition and flights of the spirit.

It was true that these young men had yet to warm up to me. I hadn't warmed to them. And so? In Syria, there would be travel and interviews with actual citizens. In other words, there would be work. Was I afraid of work? I was not. If Abu Osama and Abu Said proved too somnolent or too disagreeable to travel with or wished to bring me into places in which I did not feel safe, I would make my apologies. I would walk away. I had a job to do. Perhaps, when way led on to way, my traveling companions would let me in on their secret. Perhaps then we could be proper friends. Or not. Anyway, I would be back in Antakya on Monday, my notebooks filled with chance remarks, the exact wording of roadside signs, snippets of song, the prices of things, lists of what I had eaten, and transcriptions of what was said in the prayers. In Syria, all such things were as free as the air. In Turkey, in the comfort of the hovel, I would spin them, in my own good time, under the faux fur, if not into gold, exactly, then certainly into $200.

Abu Osama answered the doorbell. "Hurry," he said. The driver had arrived. "Get your things," Abu Osama said. "Now." I was to put them in the trunk of the Oldsmobile that had appeared in front of the apartment. I was to climb into the back seat of the car.

The driver brought us to a dirt road about five minutes outside of the village. To the south, a line of Turkish watchtowers stood over recently plowed fields. We bobbed down the dirt road. Presently we came to a break in the line of watchtowers. We could see the turrets of the nearby towers, but they were tiny eagles' nests atop distant pylons. The driver made a sudden turn into the dirt and then gunned the engine. We roared through the furrows, as in a car chase scene, then jolted to a stop in front of a roll of barbed wire. Abu Osama stuffed a pile of Syrian liras into the driver's face. The driver tossed them to his dashboard. "Hurry," he whispered. "The Turks. Run!"

It occurred to me that Abu Osama was paying for me to be smuggled into Syria. How gallant of him, I thought, as I seized my backpack from the Oldsmobile's trunk. I resolved to return the favor by proving an agreeable, uncomplaining traveling companion. In those moments, I knew, he required me to run. Running I could do. I picked my way through a weakened, trampled-down portion of the barbed-wire roll. I turned to glance backward into Turkey. I paused for an instant, then set out at a healthy pace, as if in an important race at home.

As I ran, I kept my eyes on a line of olive trees on the horizon, a kilometer or so distant. Over there, it seemed to me, the nation whose language I could speak, whose villagers had plied me with tea in the past, beds for the night, and, now and then, beseeched me to marry their daughters, was urging me to run faster. It would take me in, I knew. Every instant of life in that country, I felt, was rich in interpretative possibility. When I was there, I was rich, too.

So I flew through the field. I left my fellow travelers as if they had been standing still. Glancing over my shoulder, I saw that Abu Osama's Santa Claus sack of smuggler's booty was causing him to stagger through the dirt. He stumbled forward, rested his sack in the dirt, hoisted it over his shoulder again, then carried on with his stumbling. What clumsy, slow-witted smugglers I had happened across. They were suited to balcony idling and to languorous tea chat. Such dead weight I had brought with me. Why had I bothered?

On the far side of the field, as the olive grove approached, I slowed to a jog. My mood improved as I approached the safety of the Syrian trees. In the past, I had spent hundreds of dollars and countless hours worrying over my Syria visa applications. Now the ease with which I had waltzed into Syria struck me with the force of a revelation. Why had I troubled myself so? Indeed, why did anybody bother with visas and passports and the like at all? In order to arrive in the desired country, it seemed to me, one slipped into an Oldsmobile. One went scampering away through the dirt. Then came the olive trees. Then came the brand-new life. The reason the common herd insisted on respecting every border regulation in every corner of the world, I decided, was that lines on maps appeared to unthinking people as though they, the lines, had descended from heaven. In fact, bureaucrats in London had plotted them out in bygone centuries. Smugglers, refugees, explorers, and journalists in pursuit of truth, as I was, understood that life does not conform to the notions those long-gone officials entertained about who should go where, for what reasons.

Perhaps I'll apply for a visa when I'm old, I told myself, or out of courtesy for the men and women who work so dutifully at their borders. Henceforth, I decided, whenever visa regulations annoyed me, I would pursue the many alternative routes to which imaginative travelers repaired when officialdom blocked their way.

For a few moments, in the safety of the Syrian olive grove, revivifying thoughts along these lines came to me. I watched Abu Osama and Abu Said stagger under the weight of their backpacks. Whatever they were smuggling into Syria was causing them to weave and stumble like drunkards.

I turned my eyes to a pair of olive pickers. They were propping a ladder against a tree trunk. I approached one, spoke friendly words to him, listened to the pretty Arabic words of welcome he spoke, and felt that I was coming home. A few minutes later, when Abu Said and Abu Osama had joined me, the three of us sat under an ancient, gnarled olive tree, smiling at one another and glancing backward toward the unsafety of the Turkish watchtowers. So far, so good. Presently, a man with a handgun dangling from a shoulder holster appeared, welcomed us with a string of God-saturated phrases, as is common in Syria, then directed us down a dirt path.

The ease by which arrangements of this sort in Syria are made made me feel free. Our success at the border crossing made me feel free. We walked for ten minutes or so. At a roundabout at the edge of this olive grove, Mohammed, the red-capped lounger who had failed to appear at the orange juice restaurant in the morning, was waiting behind the wheel of a yellow-and-white Syrian taxi. Now he wore a crumpled fedora. During his wait, he had lowered the brim of his hat over his eyes, propped his feet on the dash, then fallen, so it seemed, sound asleep. The sound of our voices in the air as we approached the car did not wake him. The sound of my hand on the door handle hardly stirred him. Surely, he was striking a pose? Opening the car door, I understood: He was indeed pretending to be an idle cabbie, waiting for a fare, napping the afternoon away. It just so happened that this cabbie had decided to fall asleep in the middle of nowhere, by the side of an olive grove. It just so happened that we, the weary travelers, laden with bags, needed a ride. What good fortune! What serendipity. It was in this mood of wanting to have understood Mohammed's joke, and wanting to be in on it with him, that I slipped into the passenger seat.

We exchanged greetings. As we salaamed, I noticed that his windshield had been cracked into a panorama of spiderwebs. A screwdriver had been plunged into the car's ignition.

So he took a shambolic approach to car maintenance. Had I been a citizen-journalist in a war zone, I, too, I thought, would have been happy to drive anything that moved. I smiled at him. He smiled back. "Nice ride," I said.

"You like it?" he said.

"Very much," I said. I asked him, as is sometimes polite in Syria, how much his car cost and whether he would be willing to sell it to me.

"For you, of course," he said, smiling, "it will be free."

This made me smile. We shook hands over our fake deal. We waited for the others to stuff their belongings into the trunk, and then to lash the trunk to the body of the car with a strand of twine. The dilapidated state of their car made me smile. Abu Said and Abu Osama greeted Mohammed with great ardor, as if they hadn't seen him for months. This, too, made me smile. We were all old friends, it seemed, about to embark on a road trip in a jalopy, through the freedom of rebel-held Syria. As Mohammed slipped the car into gear, I allowed myself to feel the freedom all travelers feel at the outset of an adventure that is to occur in a beguiling countryside, among friends.

Mohammed, I noticed, was an attentive, rule-respecting driver. He drove as if we were in a driver's ed class. He held his hands on the wheel at eleven and one. He fixed his eyes like lasers on the surface of the road. I guessed that he hadn't had much experience as a driver. "You drive very well, my friend," I told him. He grinned. He did not take his eyes from the road. His seriousness at the wheel—or maybe it was the quiet that descended over the passengers in the back seat once we were in motion—reminded me that we were now in a country at war. Perhaps the Syrian government's helicopters were inclined to target rebel taxis. Such an attack, I knew, couldn't be ruled out. The reason for the somberness that crept over us in those moments, I decided, was that death, in this part of Syria, might come rocketing out of the sky at any moment. My fellow travelers understood this. By their silence, they were giving the situation the respect it was due. Other travelers, elsewhere on Earth, didn't have to think about attack helicopters or IEDs in the roadway. We didn't have this luxury, knew it, and so meant to travel in a silence appropriate to the gravity of the situation. This, I decided, was quite as it should be.

Presently, we rolled through the village of Atme. Atme subsequently became famous for the sprawling refugee camp that established itself on a hillside outside of town. Even then, when the encampment was just a few hundred tents, Atme was overrun. In the village, by the side of the road, refugee families sat on the curbside, waiting like lost luggage. A line of male travelers was filing through the center of the town on foot. Luckier, larger groups had piled themselves onto mattresses, which were strapped to the backs of flatbed trucks. Other families carried their belongings on taxi roofs and, now and then, lashed to the backs of motorcycles. One man had tucked his three infants into a wheelbarrow. He wheeled them along the village high street as if he were carrying a load of potatoes to market.

In the quiet of the olive groves, outside this village, as we crested a hill that permitted a view of the setting sun, it occurred to me that I wasn't sure whose house we would sleep in that night. Would the house be in Aleppo or Idlib? Would we be staying with someone's parents? I understood that prudent journalists did not sleep in schools or mosques, since the regime had been to known to air strike such places. What if their idea of a fitting sleeping arrangement didn't mesh with mine?

Since no one was talking yet we were certainly going somewhere, I concluded that a destination had been decided on, and that neither Mohammed nor anyone else had communicated this fact to me. This, I thought, was discourteous. It occurred to me that if I announced that I wished to sleep, say, in Aleppo rather than in Idlib, my fellow travelers, who evidently had a plan but didn't want to let me in on it, were likely to lie to me about their plan. I could express whatever wish I felt like expressing. They were going to sleep where they wished to sleep. This realization made me feel slightly less than free. It was just a feeling. I let it pass.

I stared at the darkness settling over the olive groves. I have nothing in common with Syrian smuggler-journalists, I decided. In agreeing to travel with sulky small-time criminals I had forfeited the opportunity travel affords to make valuable friendships. I regretted it.

So I have made a mistake, I told myself. Yes, a mistake. And then I thought, So what exactly is wrong with two-bit smugglers? Pretty much the entire point of traveling, I told myself, was to discover. Discoveries of personal character, particularly in Syria, did not always culminate in a glow of virtue. Was this news? Not to me it wasn't. Anyway, voyages in which everyone lived on the same plane of middle-class morality happened to grandparents, were called senior cruises, and finished, every afternoon at the same time, with a glass of warm milk. Was that what I had had in mind?

My theory of travel, which I had developed in libraries in America during graduate school, was that travel allowed you to slip into lives you might have lived but hadn't yet had the time. To give your old life the slip, you had to learn to eat as foreigners ate, to speak the languages they spoke, and to pray as they prayed. The more totally you gave yourself to them, the further you could see into the lives of others. Visions of this kind, I thought, were bound to produce interesting writing.

Asked about his philosophy of travel, a writer I admired, Jonathan Raban, advocated bold self-surrender: "You've got to go naked into the world," he once told an interviewer, "and make yourself vulnerable." In writing his *Old Glory: A Voyage Down the Mississippi*, in which he set out to discover the invisible currents along which the United States floated in the early eighties, his idea had been to deliver himself to the great moving power in the nation, the Mississippi River. He did it as Huckleberry Finn did—that is, by pushing himself into the flow, then watching the stars.

In *Huckleberry Finn*, this is an act of unaccountable disregard for society and personal safety. But in that book, the river is life. The little towns through which the river flows, the book makes clear, have fallen in love with death. They have fake religion. They kill. They scam. They "sivilize"—by which Mark Twain means to say that they turn life into waking death.

For its part, the river cannot be read. It seduces. It carries you away. It teaches courage, especially the moral kind. It represents the imponderable, inhuman powers that work their purpose out beneath the surface of things. Eventually, it brings the travelers in the story into something like harmony with the wild, turbulent, multitudinous nation that was just then coming to life.

My beat-up taxi that wasn't a taxi—this I told myself as we rolled from the village of Atme—will do as a raft. My taciturn smuggler friends, the descending night, whoever else I might meet along the way, their religious feelings, the flows of refugees, their traffic jams, bicycles, donkey-drawn carts—the wide-open wilderness that was northern Syria in the absence of a government—this would do as a river.

I felt—or anyway, I tried to make myself feel—that over time my voyage would bring me an understanding of the invisible currents on which the nation was floating, as Mark Twain's experience of the Mississippi had brought him understanding.

Some dangers on this voyage, I told myself—IEDs, enemy troops, air strikes—would be clear and present. Others would be like the whirlpools and sawyers in Huck's river: to be felt more than seen. If I kept myself in the broad mainstream, where millions of locals were going about their lives, the crowds, I thought, would protect me. It was the cowboy reporters who insisted on tracking down al Qaeda chieftains or photographing the back-and-forth of the battle who got themselves in trouble. I, for one, had better things to do.

So I coached myself that evening. Accordingly, as it was occurring to me that I had surrendered myself—in the matter of sleeping arrangements—to my fellow travelers, I asked Mohammed to tell me where we would sleep exactly once. He pondered the question. "At my house," he replied suddenly, with finality, as if he had made up his mind, then and there, to send out an order. He would command the gates of his compound to be opened. His men would prepare the sleeping quarters. The women would prepare the food. He nodded in silent approval of his decision. So we were retiring to his private domicile. The matter permitted no further discussion.

"You have a house?" I asked. I had been under the impression that he was a refugee from al Tal—an IDP (internally displaced person), in UN-speak—in Idlib Province.

"Of course I have a house," he said. "Everyone here has a house." He turned to his friends.

"I have a house," said Abu Osama. "And my brother, also a house." Abu Said nodded.

"We are with the revolution," Mohammed said. "The Syrian people are with us. If we want a house, we have a house."

This was an obvious lie. They were mocking me with the boldness of their fictions. We would soon be sleeping in someone's parents' living room, I assumed. Mohammed, who wanted to be taken for a grand personage, would tell me that it was his house. Fine, I thought. Eventually, the river of time would sort out who owned what. It would certainly reveal to me where we were going. It would answer all other pressing questions, too. Or perhaps the mysteries I felt settling over our voyage would deepen, in which case I would have involved myself in a proper detective story. What kind of work did my new friends do, really? To whom did they sell their goods? Time would tell.

I decided to leave my fellow travelers to their drama. I turned to gaze at the world. At a junction just south of Bab al-Hawa, along a stretch of highway on which the rebels in Syria had won a series of tide-turning battles that summer, Mohammed angled the taxi right, away from Aleppo. Pity, I thought. Aleppo was the more picturesque, more newsworthy city. In a field off to the left, a Syrian government tank that had evidently been blown from the surface of the highway lay on its side like a giant armadillo. A still more giant predator had pounced on it, then dragged it into the grass. A tangle of blue and red wiring had been pulled from the tank's interior, then left to dangle from a hatch in the turret. What haunting, prehistoric scenery wars created, I thought, and what an unhappy fate would have befallen the soldiers within. The predator, I imagined, would have pulled out their entrails, too.

In a village a few kilometers farther on, we drove through a line of burned-over shops. Swatches of soot covered the white cinder blocks above a row of pull-down steel gates. The walls, however, were intact. It looked to me as though an arsonist had walked down the village high street with a torch, set fire to everything that would burn, then vanished into the night.

So had the destruction been the work of the government? The rebels? Vandals? Was this a necessary, rejuvenating kind of fire? Or was it mere anarchy? I didn't have enough confidence in my fellow travelers to put my questions to them. I am living among unanswered questions, I told myself, as the people in the region who want nothing to do with this war have surely been doing from the start.

Twenty minutes of driving brought us to a village stronghold of the revolutionaries called Binnish. Binnish, my traveling friends had told me, was the only place on our route in which I could exchange the $50 I had in my pocket for Syrian liras. My kidnappers were good sports. Perhaps they didn't want the $50 they were going to acquire once they had carried out their kidnapping scheme exchanged for Syrian liras? If so, they didn't say a word. Mohammed pulled the car to the curb, across from a wall on which someone had scrawled, in spray paint: "To us, the blood of our martyrs is precious. To them, it is to be spilled by the barrel."

In front of the grocery store in which I was to change my money, a gas-powered generator hammered and coughed. It seemed on the verge of blowing itself to bits. One of its lines fed a pastry shop, into which my companions disappeared. Another line fed into the grocery store.

Behind the groceryman's counter, a flat-screen television was showing news scenes of the Syrian war. The groceryman converted my money in silence. I picked out a bottle of juice. I put it on the counter. The man stared at me as if he had seen me somewhere before, as if my appearance in his shop meant danger for him, or possibly for me. He seemed beset by strange apprehensions. I held my money out to him. "You are a journalist," he observed.

"Yes," I said.

He pressed a palmful of sweets into my hand. "Welcome," he said. He declined to allow me to pay for the juice. He stared hard into my eyes. I wondered if he might be on the verge of tears.

"May God preserve you and strengthen you," he said. "If you need anything under the sun, anything at all, you will come to me. Yes?"

"May he strengthen you and preserve your parents, the mother and the father," I replied. I urged him again to take the coins. He refused.

Before the war, during my three years of life as a student and aspiring journalist, I had lived in a series of apartments in downtown Damascus. In those neighborhoods, the citizens to whom I introduced myself as a journalist had recoiled, as if struck by an electric shock. So the revolution has washed this terror away, I told myself. So strangers in this country would speak freely to me. At last! I thought. Personal narratives, jokes, obscenities, memories, dreams, diatribes—my notebooks would overflow. "Bliss was it in that dawn to be alive," I thought. I would have stories for my grandchildren.

As I stepped outside into the generator din, it occurred to me that a few days in the company of my shopkeeper friend would bring me true, wise, revealing stories—without the deadening silences my smuggler friends imposed.

An idea popped into my head: I would make this village store my research headquarters. The storekeeper would introduce me to his customers. When they stopped in for cigarettes and chitchat, I would write down whatever tales they cared to relate. My essay would be called "What I Saw of the Revolution from the Binnish General Store."

In order to put the idea in motion, I required a place to stay the night. I gazed at the graffiti in front of the store for a moment, crossed the street, then turned down a side street in search of a hotel.

I walked for five seconds, then ten. "Whoa! Whoa! Where are you going?" Mohammed called out. His hand was on my shoulder. He put his arm through mine. "Where are you off to, friend? It's not safe here," he said. "Not after dark. Not on your own."

Ten minutes later, when we were again rolling through the olive groves, I happened to notice out of the corner of my eye that the two companions in the back seat were passing some small object back and forth between them. It made clicks and clacks, like a staple gun. It caused giggles to issue from the back seat.

I let it pass for it seemed a private joke. A few kilometers farther on, it occurred to me that a spider or bug of some kind was crawling through the hair on the nape of my neck. I shooed it away with a flick of the hand. A moment later, the insect was back. I clapped my hand over it, then inspected my hand. Nothing. The insect went away for a few moments, and then I felt it cavorting on the side of my head, where my hair overlapped my ear. I shooed it away, then turned to the back seat. My traveling companions gave me dour looks. They said nothing.

A few minutes later, when the twittering in the back seat returned, I turned my head again. My eye happened to fall on a shiny black gun Abu Osama was stuffing into the pocket of his winter jacket. It had a menacing-looking black barrel and a flap, under the handle, that would have been used to snap bullet cartridges into place. The brothers in the back seat made sheepish, guilty grins at me.

Abu Osama produced a bullet from a jacket pocket. He held it by the tips of his fingers, as if he were displaying a tiny, ingenious piece of gadgetry.

"Question, if you don't mind," he said. "What is the price of such a bullet in America?"

"By god, I don't know," I replied. He nodded at a pair of handcuffs, which, to my bewilderment, were sitting in his lap. "And the price of the cuffs?" he asked. I didn't know.

About a day later, as I reviewed these moments in my mind, I knew that when I stared through the cracks in the taxi windshield Abu Osama and his brother were aiming their gun at the base of my skull. I would have turned my head now and then to inspect a bend in the road. Olive trees were casting curiously shaped shadows across the pavement. There were roadside shacks. The moon was rising. Abu Osama would have moved the gun as I moved my head. Naughtiness of that sort was just his thing. He would have nuzzled the gun's sight into my hair. My inability to see or even to feel would have made him giggle. Abu Said would have blanched a bit. Perhaps he giggled. This would have encouraged Abu Osama. He would have clicked the magazine into place loudly, as if he wanted to be discovered at his game. In Arabic, when an assailant uses his weapon to caress a victim he is said to "kiss" him. So Abu Osama was carrying out this form of flirtation. He wanted to kiss me. He wanted me to feel and not to feel it. He wanted his friends to admire—and to keep quiet.

At the time, as I contemplated the presence of a gun, a bullet, and handcuffs in the back seat, I was indignant. I have fallen in with a carload of thugs, I told myself. They were lowlife bullet dealers. Probably they had spent their time in Antakya casing the new rash of military supply shops that had spread through the city. An unscrupulous dealer somewhere in the Antakya hills had sold them the gun. Probably it didn't work. They would show it off to their friends in the Syrian sticks. Maybe they would use it to threaten people. Maybe they meant to rob actual Syrian citizens on the highways of this governmentless backcountry.

"And those handcuffs of yours," I said. "Do you need them?" I addressed my question to the air, in a tone of conspiratorial curiosity, as if I liked the idea of banditry. I wanted to be let in on the secrets of the trade.

"You never know," Mohammed said. He turned to glance at his friend Abu Osama, who shrugged. No one else spoke.

After a minute or so, Mohammed interrupted the quiet. Nowadays, he said, criminals were flooding into Idlib Province. Many of them had been sent by the regime to maraud and to spy. "I could come across a regime lackey of this kind tonight," he said. His word for "lackey," *sha-*

beeh, also meant "spirit" or "ghost." The *shabiha* were regime irregulars in civilian clothing who fanned out across the countryside pillaging and shaking down and abusing all those they thought insufficiently loyal to President Assad. They often appeared in news reports. I wasn't altogether sure they existed.

"The *shabeeh*, he might rob me," said Mohammed. "He might try to kidnap me. We need the gun for protection," he explained. "We need the cuffs to put him in jail."

So in this governmentless part of Syria, there were jails?

"There are many jails," he said. "Do you think we do not have jails? Why would you think that?"

"Of course you do," I said. I didn't mean to underestimate his justice system. I apologized. And then I shut up. I dislike Mohammed, I told myself. I disliked him intensely.

So these young men had appointed themselves sheriffs of the Binnish backcountry. They prowled the roads, profiteered from the war, and pretended they were journalists risking their lives in the fight against tyranny. How cute, I thought. How Lone Ranger–ish of them. When I got back to Turkey, I decided, I would write an article about overgrown adolescents in Syria who imagined themselves vigilantes, gallivanted around in a decrepit taxi, had scarcely learned to drive, and anyway spent most of their time smoking cigarettes on hotel balconies in Turkey. Probably any self-respecting *shabeeh*, I thought to myself, would have overpowered these lightweights in an instant.

I sank my chin into my hands. I stared into my lap. Have they nothing better to do? I thought.

Another ten minutes or so of driving took us to an unmanned barricade—a scattering of stones, a blanket-sized scrap of tin roofing, a mess of tires strewn across the highway, then abandoned, as if by a naughty child. Whispers passed among my companions.

Mohammed turned to me. "In the village ahead," he said. "They're with the regime, Every last one of them."

"Yes?" I said.

"All of them are Shia," he said.

I had been aware of the existence of two tiny Shia atolls in the sea of Sunni Muslims that is the northwest corner of Syria. And then I had forgotten them. Now, somewhere ahead in the darkness, there it was: the divide in the Syrian psyche I meant to put at the center of my essay-to-be. Perhaps I should begin the narrative here, I thought, at this line of rubble in the night.

Mohammed turned the taxi left, then nosed it down a dirt road. "Why not visit the Shia?" I wondered.

"They'll shoot us if we drive through," he replied, as if relaying news too boring to discuss.

A few moments later, at the entrance to a friendlier, unbarricaded village, Mohammed slowed so that I could examine a sign painted across a sheet of plywood that had been propped by the side of the road. A scrawl of white characters, in disorderly, childlike lettering, had been daubed against a black background. The letters read: "There is no god but God." Beneath this legend, inside a white circle, smaller black letters spelled out the rest of the testament of faith: "Mohammed is the messenger of God." The sign I was looking at then eventually became the emblem ISIS used on its flag and official documents. At the time, the feelings that gave rise to ISIS were present enough in this landscape but the group itself did not yet exist. Back then, I didn't suppose that reading the feelings of a place was possible at all. In any case, I was inclined to take things at face value. The testament of faith on a board at the entrance to a town suggested to me that the region was reverting to some older, more reliable, better loved means of governing itself. Why has it taken so long? I felt like asking my traveling companions, but didn't because they were, I was beginning to suspect, inclined to make up random answers—out of boredom, evidently. Mohammed gestured at the sign. "Can you read this?" he asked. I read the testament of faith out loud for him. He nodded. "Good," he said. "Now you know all you need to know."

This village, it turned out, was in the midst of its evening routine. It was carrying on in the electricityless gloom that engulfed all the villages on the northern Syrian plains then. Men in robes were plodding home from the sunset prayer. Revolutionaries piled weapons into pickup beds. Children stared at us with attentive, wondering eyes. A shopkeeper was reopening his vegetable stand.

What stoicism, I thought. The ideals to which these villagers dedicated their lives—piety, freedom—had no need of electricity. They knew this and so carried on with their routines as if electricity had been a fad that flourished for a time among city dwellers, then dwindled away. In this village, I thought to myself, there was moonlight. There were candles. The villagers guided themselves by an inner light.

Such were my reflections at the time. If I had known then what I know now, the darkness of those villages would have worried me. Now I know that the men who have been bringing forth Islamic fiefdoms in Syria feel that the worse things are, the better. Hardship is meant to draw the nation closer to the Koran. It deepens the citizens' reliance on one another. Electricitylessness weans the populace from the government's menu of sexy evening soap operas. The builders of these fiefs feel the soap operas have been conceived to weaken the public love of Islam and to promote pastimes the West loves, like drug taking and wife swapping.

A citizen in an Islamic state should nurture contempt for soap operas in his heart. He should renounce television in general, except the Saudi government television, which shows a live feed of the faithful circumambulating the Kaaba in Mecca. Anyone who's lived in a proper Islamic state for more than a few weeks knows that it's the revolution in consciousness that counts.

When that revolution takes over a landscape, it will leave markers. How can it not? One of them is the destruction of the electric grid. The shops may well burn. Slabs of painted wood will appear at the entrances to the villages. The cars, the water mains, the schools—all such things aren't likely to be maintained in the normal way, at least not for long, because a time of atonement has come, and detachment from the world of things.

That night, some such psychology, it seems to me now, was falling over the landscape. It fell as the moonlight fell, across every house and alley, over the sheep and the abandoned Byzantine villages.

It would have settled over the interior of our car, just as it settled over the hills. I saw it all. I read the signs, letter by letter, but as I had no notion of how to interpret them, they were merely scenic. I felt every sight to be curious and strange, like a field of hieroglyphics. Very intriguing indeed, I thought, as the sights and sounds—and the tingling in my hair at the back of my neck—whispered to me of my fate. I wondered what would come next.

What came next was an hour and a half's worth of driving through the darkness. As he drove, Mohammed fed himself bits of the warm, cheesy pastry—*kanafeh*—he had bought in Binnish. The pistachio bits on the surface of this spongy, sweet cake had sprinkled into his lap. He gestured at the cardboard box the baker in Binnish had prepared for him. "Eat," he told me. "Be my guest."

We chewed in silence. I gazed at the other cars faltering through the darkness. Almost all drove without headlights. Was this in order to avoid attracting the attention of fighter planes? Or because the headlights no longer worked? Many cars bore license plates from Eastern Europe: Romania, Bulgaria, Poland. Others came from Aleppo, Damascus, and Idlib. Some bore no license plates at all. The revolution will have brought new life to the Eastern European stolen car industry, I thought to myself, and perhaps to car thieves everywhere in Syria. I noticed a pair of friends motoring along without a passenger door. Other cars lacked bumpers. Out with the old, in with the older—apparently the revolution had brought some such ethic to aficionados of highway driving in northern Syria. Or perhaps people were driving wrecks out of necessity, because spare parts were too costly. The wrecks rolled along rather well, I thought. Why fix it if it ain't broken?

As we drove, doubts about my conclusions crept into my head. With such an enthusiasm for wreck renovation abroad in the land, it probably wouldn't be long until one of our fellow motorists turned his eyes to our wreck. Surely, useful things could be scavenged from the four of us? I cast worried looks at the cars that overtook us. When I noticed a car limping along behind us (some flashed their brights), I sank into the depths of my seat. I didn't want to show my companions that I was afraid. On the other hand, I didn't want a passing scavenger to empty his magazine into my head.

Happily, the taxi wreck had too little power to delay the wrecks behind us for long. Our followers followed for a minute or so, pulled into the oncoming lane, then roared away.

Late in the evening, the taxi slowed to weave through a pair of hairpin bends, marked out by stacks of boulders in the road. At the end of this obstacle course stood a bullet-ridden oil drum. Behind the drum sat a ring of empty plastic chairs. Two teenagers in civilian clothing emerged from the shadows. In his right hand, the taller boy held a rifle. Its strap trailed through the dirt. He motioned for Mohammed to lower his window.

"Who are you with?" the teenager asked.

"Ahrar al-Sham," replied Mohammed, scarcely glancing at the soldier. Ahrar al-Sham was the largest, most famous militant group in the North.

The soldier nodded. He stepped aside. "Off you go," he said.

Mohammed did not reply.

This dialog occasioned no commentary in our car. So my companions were activist-journalists in Turkey. Inside Syria, they went about as Ahrar militants. Had they lied to me or to the checkpoint soldiers? In any case, they were liars. I let the matter slide.

We drove for a few minutes, and then I brought up the other aspect of the checkpoint dialog that mystified me: What on earth was the point of a middle-of-nowhere inspection in which an anonymous sentry pretended to seek out the identities of travelers who weren't required to use license plates or to present IDs?

Mohammed shrugged. "Security," he said.

But what, I wanted to know, were the security men hoping to intercept? On whose behalf were they providing security? To man a checkpoint in this region of suicide car bombers and attack helicopter air strikes was to invite fatal attacks. Were not the security men compromising their own security?

My mind chased such questions down dead-end alleys. I didn't feel like badgering my companions any longer. I did, however, hope to hear

a word or two about Ahrar al-Sham. How could four slackers in hood-
ies and soccer jerseys in a beat-up taxi be taken for rebel soldiers? Surely,
the sentry might have posed a question or two about a brigade, a superior officer, orders, a base, identity papers? There had been no discussion in our car about anything remotely connected with soldiery. As
Mohammed chewed the last of his *kanafeh*, I asked him if he was really
with Ahrar al-Sham. He kept his eyes on the road. "Yes, I am," he said.

I turned to the passengers in the back seat. "You're also Ahrar
al-Sham?"

"In the beginning of the war, yes," Abu Osama said. "Now, no longer." Abu Said said that he himself had always been a civilian.

"And the teenagers at the checkpoint, also Ahrar al-Sham?" I asked.

Mohammed shrugged. "Probably," he said.

But there had been no uniforms at the checkpoint, no flag, no
badges—no identity markers of any kind. Twenty-four hours earlier, I
had been keen on the idea of slipping away from one's identity. Travel
of this sort revealed the breadth of possibilities before us. It taught
the fullness of the world. It transformed the self. So I liked the idea.
Didn't I? This Syrian version of identitylessness seemed extreme to me,
as if whoever was in charge of the checkpoints meant to invite all travelers to be whoever they felt like being and to flip identities every few
kilometers. Naturally, this checkpoint freedom would spread from a
spot on the highway to a village nearby, and then through a chain of
villages—and so on, across the landscape. Surely, this was the point. So
this bit of Syrian landscape meant to experiment a bit with its identity.
It wanted to invent, to drift away from itself, to try on something new.
How curious, I thought. I hadn't known landscapes might want to do
such things.

Another twenty minutes of twisty single-lane roads—excellent ter-
rain for bicycling, I noted—led us to a village somewhere in a region
Mohammed referred to as the Jebel al-Zawiya, or Corner Mountain. I
knew it by its reputation: wild, unpoliceable hills, a smuggling-based
economy, and an earlier religious rebellion (in 1982) against Bashar al-
Assad's father, Hafez.

Mohammed slowed the car amid a cluster of single-story cinder-block farmhouses. In the darkness, I couldn't make out windows or doors or chimneys. The village looked like a collection of shipping containers that had dug themselves in for the night in the lee of a hill.

Mohammed inched the taxi upward, along a rock-strewn goat path. "So these houses belong to the families of your clan?" I asked him. Technically speaking, he was an adoptee in someone else's clan. I knew this. I meant for him to elaborate on his new living arrangements.

"Yes, my clan," he said. He cut the engine in the front yard of a cinder-block hut. The four of us emerged from the car. The closing of the car doors was like a series of tiny explosions in that silence. The stars lit our way. Sheep bleated. No one spoke.

Mohammed's front door opened on a sitting room. Abu Said and Abu Osama picked through a stack of blankets that had been piled in a corner. "So this is your house?" I asked Mohammed.

He thought about the matter for an instant. "Yes, it is," he said.

Did he own furniture? A kitchen? Live with anyone? He did not speak. He helped me push a foam-rubber mattress into a corner. He lit a pair of candles, then placed them on a chair in the middle of the room. He fetched a blanket for me, which I put around my shoulders. He announced that he meant to sit up during the night with friends. The friends lived in a neighboring house. He opened the front door. "Want anything else?" he asked. He slipped away.

The brothers, Abu Osama and Abu Said, were busy shaking out a blanket. Some of the blankets had lice, Abu Osama warned. Too late now, I thought. The brothers spread a blanket over their laps. They opened a laptop, then lost themselves in a video game.

In Antakya, I hadn't been able to manage much enthusiasm for journaling. Now, however, I was embarked on a proper reporting voyage. It would have felt more professional if I had had a commission or a lead on a commission, but now that I had arrived in an actual war zone, the matter of who might publish what and for how much struck me as too trivial to worry about. The details would sort themselves out with the exchange of a few emails.

I withdrew my reporter's notebook from my backpack. I noted the time and the date. I related my discovery of a new way to cross an international border, the kindness of the shopkeeper in Binnish, and the stringy, gooey *kanafeh* Mohammed had offered me as we drove.

I opened the can of Efes beer. Did beer drinking offend the scruples of my traveling companions? But they had offended me with their silences and their ridiculous ideas about ridding the countryside of *shabiha*. Their absorption in their video game offended me. I drank the beer without guilt.

In my notebook, I noted the weather: bright moonlight, bright clouds, cold gusts. Winter, I told this diary, was on the march. I noted the living room décor: a single carpet, a mess of foam-rubber mattresses, a desk, a chair. There was new vocabulary to add to my war journal: *qammleh*, for which Abu Osama had scoured his blanket before he unfolded it across his lap, meant "louse."

I thought about how the other reporters meant to cover this war. Traveling about in bunches, whispering into satellite phones, dashing off bulletins for the wire, then retiring to the bar to reminisce about the halcyon days in Baghdad and Kabul. They waved at the countries they wrote about, interviewed their drivers, interviewed one another, mistook the lies they encountered for the truth, then went off to the TV studio to discuss how nearly they had escaped death that very morning and how heartbreaking the lives of the local children were. Probably templates in their computers produced these stories for them. They wouldn't dream of altering their templates. Why should they? They were already at the summit of their crummy profession. I hated them. Phonies.

In a distant valley, artillery boomed. I asked Abu Osama about this. A battle was underway for the highway that controlled access to a city about ten kilometers away called Marat al-Nouman. So said Abu Osama. He spoke quietly, scarcely looked at me, then returned to his video game. The computer bathed the brothers' faces in soft blue light. They muttered to each other. Things were being blown up in the virtual world, too. Every few seconds, when something big exploded in their imaginary world, a hint of a smile appeared in their eyes. They did not take their eyes from the screen.

How curious it is, I told my notebook, that my smuggler friends should be so entranced by their laptop game and so indifferent to the slaughter their fellow citizens were carrying out on one another in the valley next door. Was real-life war not worth a moment or two of discussion? No, their virtual world had it all over the real one. So the video game designers have conquered minds even here, where the barrel bombs fall and there's scarcely an hour or two of electricity per day. If only the combatants over in Marat al-Nouman could so enthrall themselves, I told my notebook, they could resolve their differences by banging away on their keyboards.

I did not bother to ask my roommates about their itinerary for the following day.

I resolved to wake up, kibbitz as little as possible, listen and learn. We will take the taxi through the hills, I told myself. The car, I knew, was full of wares. Perhaps my fellow travelers would prove to be the Willy Lomans of the Syrian war, way out there in the blue, riding on smiles and shoeshines.

Probably their customers would be local shopkeepers. Perhaps there would be rebel soldiers standing at an intersection somewhere, waiting for phone chargers or cigarettes or a magazine of bullets. Probably there would be a shady character or two wishing to buy handcuffs. Once my companions have brought me into their trade, I told myself, there won't be a need for secrets anymore. Perhaps then, at last, we could be friends.

It occurred to me that the following day was Sunday. The only thing I would insist on, therefore, was a visit to one of the phone-booth bodegas, which were common enough in Syria at the time, so that I could call my mom. Sunday mornings, her time, were my times to check in in Cambridge, to reassure her, to hear a bit about the weather at home, and, though I didn't like to admit that Mom was wise in ways I was not, to listen.

First, however, I would disclose. I would slip the bit about my being in Syria into the latter half of the conversation—after I had told her that I was making friends, that the weather was lovely, and that the longest extant stretch of Roman road in the Middle East lay just inside Syria, on a pretty hillside, under a line of juniper trees. Actually, I'm not more than a few kilometers from that place right now, I would say. Then I would assure her that I could hear birds chirping everywhere, that I was in a village as serene as the most idyllic Vermont hamlet, that I was keeping as far from the combat zones as was humanly possible, and that the essay I was going to produce about the whole thing—the voyage, the friends, the Syrian war—would probably, almost certainly—well, possibly—be published in the *New Republic*.

I knew I could count on her not to ask about the nature of the commitment I had had from the editors there. She wouldn't want to probe into the details, I knew, because she wouldn't want to force me to admit that the *New Republic* editors had long since stopped replying to my emails. She certainly wouldn't want to lead herself to the conclusion that I had tried to interest all the editors I knew everywhere, had gotten nowhere, had gone off anyway, and was now wandering around the high plains of Syria with no particular aim in view, in the company of people I did not know from Adam.

A conclusion like this might well have provoked a family crisis. She would have been cordial enough on the phone, but after she had hung up she would have steadied herself, then called our wiser, more life-competent cousins. She would have beseeched them to beseech me to knock it off, to come back right away, at least to Turkey, and to breathe not a word of protest. The cousins would have swung into action. I wasn't in a position to say no to a united family front. I would have tucked my tail between my legs, then hurried back to the hovel. From the hovel, I probably would have had to go home.

In short, a single indiscreet question concerning my career might have brought the entire house of cards fluttering to the floor. My mother knew this. Her discretion—and her wish to assure me success—would prevent her from asking.

Instead, she would ask me about the food I had been eating. "Delicious *kanafeh*," I would tell her, and was she aware that I hadn't come to Syria to practice up on restaurant criticism? I wasn't out to tour the local farmers' markets. "Um, Mom? There is like a war going on here. With bombs and stuff like that? Fighter jets?" I would clue her in thus. A moment of silence would open up on the phone line. She would sigh. "Well, for God's sake, be sensible," she would say, at last. I would say that I was pretty good when it came to sensibility if she thought about it at all and that I could probably win about ten blue ribbons in any sensibility contest she cared to mention. She would tell me not to be a smart aleck. There would be more silence. I would know that she was right to be worried and she would understand that I knew. She would sigh again.

"I just don't want you to be a damn fool," she would say.

"Okay, Mom," I would say. "I got it."

"And keep in touch, for heaven's sake."

"Of course, Mom," I would reply.

And that would be that. Such were our Sunday conversations. Probably they did us both a bit of good.

In the morning, shortly after I woke, a fourth kidnapper appeared. Abu Dujanna came dressed as if for an athletic competition, in running shoes and a dark blue tracksuit. He wanted to leave the house right away. I asked for a cup of coffee.

He returned with the coffee in less than a minute. "Can you hurry, please?" he asked.

So rushing was the order of the day. Okay, I would rush. Before we left the house, however, I had a favor to ask of my hosts. I wished to climb up to the house's rooftop. From up there, I hoped to inspect such damage as the regime had inflicted to date. I wanted to guess at the weather to come and to gather in a sense of the topography of the place. I had yet to see the landscape by the light of day. So I asked Abu Dujanna if it would be dangerous for me to stand on the rooftop.

"Of course not!" he exclaimed. He loved the idea. He was a gracious host. He left the room, then returned a moment later with a troupe of villagers, two of whom were carrying Kalashnikovs, and the three kidnappers from the night before. We were a minor expeditionary force. We trooped up a narrow staircase, opened a trapdoor, then stepped into misty morning sunshine. The house in which I had slept, I discovered, was a tiny raft in a sea of rolling, almost entirely uninhabited scrub-covered green hills. A tendril of smoke arose from our raft. Far away, on the horizon to the north, a line of twenty or so smoke tendrils rose into low-hanging clouds.

By what road had we driven in the night before? There were goat paths between the hills but nothing modern or engineered enough to be called a road. Perhaps we had floated in?

Such busyness as there was in Mohammed's neighborhood, I discovered, existed entirely in the animal kingdom. A rooster strode along the crest of a stone wall. Hens pecked at the ground beneath him. A family of sheep browsed at the edge of a stone cistern in Mohammed's yard. Mohammed's village, I decided, lived approximately in the time of the Prophet.

From the rooftop, a Kalashnikov-bearing villager pointed to a pile of boulders in a field about a hundred meters away. "Over there, last week," he said, "the regime sent a jet. Twelve child martyrs. May God not forgive the killer, Bashar al-Assad."

I squinted at his pile. I couldn't make out the damaged building itself, but I could tell from the flatness in his voice and from the stone-like faces of Abu Osama and Mohammed that the mention of Bashar al-Assad's name had ruined the morning. His jets came at random. They killed the children. They zoomed away. In my mind's eye, I saw them roaring low overhead. The sound of their engines would have distributed terror across the landscape. The planes would have streaked through the sky, caused the children to freeze in their tracks and the mothers to weep—and then the jets would have been gone. In their wake would have come bitter curses.

In that morning haze, among those stone-faced villagers, it seemed to me that if the power of hatred could somehow guide the bullets, the villagers' Kalashnikovs would have taken down entire squadrons of the government's fighter jets.

I wished the villagers Godspeed. What business did a MiG fighter jet have with these subsistence herders? Their children would have walked to their schools in bare feet. These people would have lived their lives according to the rhythms of the Koran: prayers; *eids*; Ramadan; sheep slaughtering, then a feast. I had a vague sense that foreign countries might be sending high-tech missile systems to certain rebels in Syria. But the recipients of this kind of aid were professional military men, I felt. They were defectors from the Syrian Arab Army, for the most part, and members of Kurdish militias. They dressed in camo fatigues, gazed at enemy positions from inside sandbag-reinforced bunkers, and carried 3G-enabled encrypted tablets wherever they went, the better to stay in touch with drone pilots on duty in military bases in Florida. In the fields I was looking at, there were no such military men. It seemed to me that if the Syrian government was to bomb here, the most it could hope for would be to bomb the sheep out of existence.

Once, before the war, a snafu at the nearby Bab al Hawa border crossing left me stranded, late at night, on the Syrian side of the border. A passing soldier offered to call me a taxi.

During our drive through the countryside, when we were safely distant from the customs officers, the taxi driver had asked me if I had anything special to do that evening in Aleppo. I had not. Because if not, he said, and if it was all the same to me, I could sleep on his bedroom floor, and in the morning, after a glass of tea, he would drive me to whatever address in Aleppo I had in mind.

He brought a mountain of quilts to his bedroom floor for me. He brought me a nighttime tea. His toddlers came padding in to say good night. Now this man, his toddlers, and their neighbors were the targets of the government MiGs. Why such punishment for such innocent people? I wanted to know. To what conceivable end?

On the rooftop, I whispered to Mohammed: "May God destroy the houses of those who bomb here." I turned to a Kalashnikov-bearing villager. "May he send you victory."

"Ameen," he murmured.

Ten minutes later, inside our taxi, hurrying across the countryside to I knew not where, Mohammed, who was again behind the wheel, told me that Abu Dujanna was the extremist among the four friends. Indeed, as a member of the most extreme among the rebel formations, Jebhat al-Nusra, he had already killed many people.

I happened to be sitting in the back seat this time. Mohammed grinned into the rearview mirror. "He is very extreme," he said of the off-duty soccer player—or track coach or whatever he was—who sat to my right. "From the most extreme of the extremists, *masha'Allah.*" *Such is the will of God.*

I turned to look at Abu Dujanna. He beamed at me. "Go ahead," said Mohammed. "We have brought him just for you. Interview him."

Abu Dujanna cast a radiant glance into my eyes. He looked at me as if he were falling in love, as if I were his bride. "Yes, ask," he said. "I answer. Please! Whatever you like."

"Okay," I said. "Abu Dujanna, my friend." I nudged him in the ribs. "You are a terrorist?"

"Yes," he said. He smiled.

"Good for you," I said.

"Yes," he agreed. "Excellent."

I shrugged. "Jebhat al-Nusra?" Jebhhat al-Nusra had become famous, at least inside of Syria, for the explosive-laden suicide trucks it had been sending into branch after branch of the state security apparatus. Allegedly, Jebhat al-Nusra—the Victory Front, in English—was the Syrian al Qaeda franchise.

"Yes, Jebhat al-Nusra," Abu Dujanna said. He shrugged then turned to inspect the passing scenery.

I shrugged back. "Very good for you."

The actual members of Jebhat al-Nusra, an ultra-secretive, ultra-extreme gang of jihadists, lived, I knew, deep inside the Syrian forest. Or they dwelled in desert tents. They ate bark, did pull-ups on jungle gyms, were bin Laden's disciples, and appeared in public only in videos, and only after having rammed their suicide trucks into the Syrian Defense Ministry in downtown Damascus. Al Qaeda, I thought then, was a Yemeni-Saudi thing, to which a handful of Iraqi fanatics were trying to cling. In Syria, a milder form of Islam prevailed. If there were genuine Syrian al Qaeda members, I assumed at the time, they were dour old graybeards who had radicalized themselves in Afghanistan, at bin Laden's side. The likelihood of my happening across such a personage, or anyone linked to such a personage, was, I assumed, just about zero.

I was, however, willing to play along. Perhaps, I thought, Abu Dujanna dreamed about joining Jebhat al-Nusra. Perhaps he had an uncle who knew a cousin who had a friend who was in the group. I was certainly willing to be intimidated if that's what my friends had in mind. If Abu Dujanna had wanted to threaten and rail, as the al Qaeda exponents did on YouTube, I would have shrunk in my seat. But Abu Dujanna rather seemed to be in a mood to gaze into the middle distance. When he turned to me, his smile was so pregnant and twinkled so merrily that he seemed to want to plant a kiss on my cheek. The smiles in the eyes of the other passengers made me think a terrific joke was being told. They watched me looking at Abu Dujanna, watched him grinning, then turned their eyes back to me. In those moments, there was too much happiness in the taxi for me to carry on with a serious interview. Anyway, I knew they were having a game.

Through the rearview mirror, I made eye contact with Mohammed. "Jebhat al-Nusra?" I said. "Lovely. I'd rather interview you."

Mohammed's expression told me that he didn't think me much of a journalist. Would a true journalist turn down an interview with a true al Qaeda member? Mohammed insisted on the interview. I bridled. He insisted. Eventually, I gave in.

"How many people have you killed to date?" I asked Abu Dujanna.

"Many," he said.

"*Masha'Allah*," I said.

"Yes, *masha'Allah*."

"Why, out of all the possible battalions and *katibas* in the Syrian war," I asked Abu Dujanna, "did you join Jebhat al-Nusra?"

"Who else will defend the Syrian people?" he said. "Who will stand for Islam?"

He said that President Assad's dream was to drive Islam from Syria and that the purpose of the current military campaign was to accomplish by bombs what it had not managed to accomplish with its brainwashing elementary schools, its fake imams, and its program of automatic imprisonment for all those who loved the Prophet more than the regime said he ought to be loved. "Islam in Syria?" he asked, idly, of the air, as if referring to a mythical bird. "It doesn't exist." He had joined Jebhat al-Nusra in order to bring the religion of the people back to the people.

He required several minutes of speechifying to tell me this. When his speech was done, I asked him if his having joined Jebhat al-Nusra meant that he cared for Islam more than the others in the car cared for it. It did not, he said. "Then why hasn't everyone joined Jebhat al-Nusra?" I asked. Abu Dujanna shrugged. The other passengers looked at him but did not reply.

I was interested in this question because terrorists of some variety, I knew not which, had lately struck a prominent building next to the iconic central park in Aleppo. I had seen the carnage on television from the Antakya hotel lounge: Employees from the cell phone company whose offices happened to be across the street from the terrorists' target ambled through the rubble, their shirts spattered in blood. Dozens of civilians had been killed.

A year earlier, the employees in that building had sold me a SIM card, in that downtown office. The women in the office had struck me as faintly flirtatious. They wore lipstick. The men made courteous smiles at me. All the employees wore smart yellow company sport coats. That office had suggested industriousness to me, young people enjoying life in the city center, a high-tech sector for Syria—and so, the future.

"Abu Dujanna, my brother," I said. "You don't support blowing up office buildings. The people who work there are your brothers and sisters."

He thought about my suggestion for a moment. He looked out the window. "It depends," he said. "If you kill two hundred now, those two hundred will not join the army. You may save four hundred later. It might be necessary."

"Killing civilians is necessary?" I asked. I stared at him. His mind, however, was made up. He nodded. I made eye contact with Mohammed in the mirror, then with Abu Osama, who was sitting to my left. Everyone in our car, it seemed, agreed with Abu Dujanna's terrorist math. It was good to blow up small numbers of people now because dozens dead now would prevent thousands dead later.

I thought about this obtuseness for a moment, withdrew from the conversation, sat in a funk for several kilometers, and then understood the game my fellow travelers were playing. They believed I had come to this rebel-controlled part of Syria, as a journalist from the state TV might come, in order to draw up a report that would prove the people's rebellion in the provinces to be a vast conspiracy in which crazed jihadis, paid by "interests" and "lobbies" and "agents," sought to tear Syria apart.

Such was the line the regime-supporting TV channels followed. "They do it because nothing satisfies them, because they love nothing and no one, because they have nothing to cling to, no identity, no home." Thus did the former president Hafez al-Assad explain the rebellions he had put down, in Idlib Province in 1980, and in the mutinous city of Hama in 1982. Now, the Syrian state TV had begun to replay clips of the former president's most stirring denunciations of the "conspirators" and "enemies of the state" that had risen against him in his day. These clips played late at night, over a soundtrack of mournful French horns. There were shots of Syrian wildflowers swaying in the breeze. There were flashes of fratricidal killing in the streets. "We Syrians, however, have a place we call home," Hafez intoned. On came the swelling strings.

Evidently, my traveling companions had decided, on the basis of what evidence I did not know, that I was out to find the homeless marauders the state TV was forever twittering about. They had agreed, among themselves, out of the range of my hearing, to play along with the jihadi-under-every-rock fantasy they thought was dancing in my head.

So they meant to string me along, to allow me to believe that I had stumbled on a veritable nest of little bin Ladens, to watch my unease deepen, to let it drop that Abu Dujanna planned to blow himself up in a crowded Damascus marketplace—and just as my fantasy of journalistic fame and fortune was a true fact before my eyes, all four of them would burst into laughter. "We are not terrorists. We are not homeless. We are the people of this nation," Mohammed would lecture me. If I insisted on finding al Qaeda behind every bush, as the Syrian government journalists did, he would say, I could piss off back to Turkey. If, however, I wished to report the truth—that they were not paid, were not foreigners, and were not terrorists—I was welcome to it. The four of them would help me however they could, and for as long as I liked.

When I withdrew from my Abu Dujanna interview, he had been, I thought, befuddled. *Yes?* his face had said. *Carry on, please. I am ready.*

After several minutes of silence, I decided to begin the conversation anew. "Excuse me, brother Abu Dujanna," I said. "What I think, in case you're curious, is that al Qaeda's presence in Syria, if it is present, is no business of mine. Let them do what they like." It wasn't my affair, and I wasn't interested. I said that in any case, everyone in the world knew everything there was to know about al Qaeda. There were movies and TV shows and professors at all the universities who studied al Qaeda. "I am here to understand the Syrian people's war against the government in Damascus," I said. I looked for Mohammed's eyes in the rear-view mirror.

"You are a Syrian citizen?" I asked. "Yes?" I asked him if his feelings about the government were typical of all citizens' feelings and if he had made his commitment to overthrowing Bashar al-Assad for private gain.

His feelings were indeed typical, he said. No, he was not interested in cash.

"So you are not paid, and you have dedicated your life to the revolution in Syria?"

"Not paid," he said. "Yes, dedicated."

"The reading audience in the West would therefore like to better understand some of the details of your life," I said. I held his gaze in the mirror. "Is that okay with you?"

"Yes, fine," he replied, but quietly, without smirking.

I told him that the reason I wasn't interested in interviewing terrorists was because I didn't feel they represented anything beyond themselves. I wanted to interview him, since I thought he could plausibly speak on behalf of millions just like him. "Do you understand?" I said.

"Yes," he said. He lowered his eyes.

We drove through misty, green hunchbacked hills for a half hour in silence. I didn't have the faintest notion of where we were going. I didn't care.

During my time in Damascus, I, for one, had lacked the courage to look crosswise at the lowest civil servant in an official building.

When I saw government soldiers in the street, I hurried away. I had been much too afraid of them to go anywhere near an antigovernment demonstration. Had I been born a Syrian, would I have been any more courageous? I doubted it. Now, somehow, I had found young men in whom the impulse to give their lives away so that Syrians of the future could live in a more just society was as instinctive as the impulse to dream. Probably they couldn't have squelched it if they had tried. Though I didn't much like my traveling companions in a personal sense, I admired them for a quality neither I nor anyone else I knew in the West had: the instinct for self-sacrifice. The sincerity of their commitment, I decided, was a beautiful, inimitable thing, particular to Syrians, which so outshone their other qualities that it was a mark of my selfishness to have allowed them to put me out.

I wanted Mohammed and his friends to understand the sincerity of my admiration. I respected their cause, their commitment to it, and their willingness to be killed so that Syrians of the future could live in a more just society. I wished them to understand this. Apparently, I was having difficulty persuading my traveling companions of the sincerity of my feelings. As we rolled though the mist, I decided that I wasn't going to allow this failure to ruin my trip.

I told myself that either Mohammed and his friends would quit trying to play me for a fool reporter, open their hearts to me, and speak to me about their lives—frankly, without the lies—or they would not. If they did, the voyage would continue as we had planned it, on the balcony in Antakya.

If they did not, I was not going to tear out my hair. So I wasn't destined to become BFFs with a small-time smugglers' gang on the Antakya-Idlib border. Oh well. In that case, the next time a convenient moment for a leave-taking presented itself—when we arrived in Aleppo, say, or at a busy café, preferably one next to a bus stop—I would shake the hands of all four travelers, look into their eyes, thank them, then be off.

In the meantime, I decided, I required coffee.

The taxi happened to be passing through the revolutionary outpost Binnish as my thoughts brought me to this moment of resolve. On the outskirts of town, an enterprising coffee seller had parked a pickup whose side panels opened up on a mobile coffee bar. I dropped a hint to Mohammed. He slammed on the brakes. The five of us poured into the morning sun. I insisted on buying each of my new friends a coffee. I wanted a picture of the steam rising from the coffee man's espresso bar. The steam floated through a shaft of morning sunshine. How picturesque, I thought. Abu Dujanna saw me taking this picture, then asked to have his picture taken with me. He had Abu Osama stand with my phone—that is, the phone the lot of them were about to steal—in front of the two of us.

In these moments, the clock my kidnappers had set on my dreamworld was ticking away its last minutes. I, however, felt the dream would last forever. In that dream, I had friends, my journalism career was on the cusp of success, and the wave of violence rolling through the Syrian countryside was soon to give way to a time of justice for the victims of the Assad regime. I wanted to document the promise I felt in the air then, so as Abu Osama clicked the button on my camera app—his camera app, that is—I made a jaunty smile. I leaned into Abu Dujanna. I had to keep myself from putting an arm around him, so much did I want to communicate the warmth of our relationship to whatever Facebook friends might someday look at the picture.

Such were my thoughts then. Now I suppose that Abu Dujanna, who asked to be photographed with me, wanted an image documenting the serenity of my dreamworld. He meant to slip into the illusion for a moment, to level an even gaze at the viewer and to say, without breathing a word: *Peekaboo!*

A few days later, by which time I had disappeared into the clutches of the actual al Qaeda organization, my kidnappers appear to have spared me a thought. I suspect they assumed I was about to be killed or had already been killed. Perhaps they only meant to remind a future me of how blind I had been on this morning in Binnish. Anyway, from my iPhone they emailed me a copy of this tourist snapshot, with the subject header "Abu Dujanna." I found it in my inbox, years later.

Sunday morning, October 21, 2012: Abu Osama used my cell phone camera to snap this picture of Abu Dujanna and me as we stopped for coffee in the town of Binnish.

CHAPTER 2

A KIDNAPPING

Binnish-Taftanaz Highway, October 21, 2012

A few miles outside of Binnish, amid spindly olive trees, the kidnappers pulled off the highway. Abu Osama got out of the car. He walked to a cluster of houses at the end of a lane, knocked on the door of a single-story cement farmhouse, spoke briefly with an invisible personage at the door, then motioned for Mohammed to park the car in front of a similar, flat-roofed house about a hundred meters away. Behind this house, a fruit-laden olive orchard rolled away toward the Turkish hills.

This house's front door, we discovered, had been left ajar. In the entryway, children's clothing lay strewn across a tiled hall. A chandelier had been yanked from the ceiling, then tossed to a corner. In the master bedroom, coat hangers, ties, and shoes had been scattered across the bedspread. The closet's double doors stood open, as if the master of the house had woken, thrown his closet doors aside, then vanished. He had left his suspenders on the floor and a box of mismatched shoes.

The glass in a child's bedroom window had been shattered. The shards lay on the floor amid dust, children's slippers, and a naked plastic doll. In the kitchen, an open suitcase, empty except for a pair of child's socks, sat on the floor. Under the kitchen sink, I found a row of five-liter buckets packed with olives.

Mohammed and Abu Osama fetched their backpacks from the car. Without saying a word to me, the four kidnappers set themselves to tidying the place up. They were a crew of conscientious, silent housemaids. The shards from the shattered window required sweeping up.

Mohammed found a broom. In the kitchen, there were cobwebs, deceased bugs, and, over every surface, dust.

Abu Osama folded towels that had been tossed to the floor in the bathroom. Abu Dujanna, I noticed, busied himself making order out of a box of straps and leather belts he had found in the master bedroom. The reverence the young men felt for this absent family's belongings expressed itself in the care they took in folding up the discarded clothing, in their busy sweeping, and in their silence.

Now, at last, I felt, I was observing these young men at work. To those places in which the government had dealt out chaos, they restored order. They brought respect and cleanliness where the government had inflicted panic. They are preparing a field headquarters for the day, I told myself, but their deeper purpose was to do this vanished family a good turn.

During the course of the day, I told myself, they would carry out whatever errands had brought them to this spot in the Binnish countryside. Perhaps they wouldn't want me to accompany them? That would be fine with me. In the child's bedroom, I found a desk but no chair. I'll sit on the desk, I told myself, and commit further reportorial thoughts to my notebook.

The windows in this bedroom gave a pretty view into the olive grove. Above it, on a distant horizon, I could make out the silhouette of a Turkish ridgeline.

From the front hallway, I brought in a scattering of multicolored throw pillows. I arranged these along the back of a foam-rubber mattress, on the floor in the child's bedroom. Now we had a colorful divan. The bed needed to be remade. I made it.

After a half hour of silent labor, Mohammed declared our work to be finished. Abu Dujanna, I noticed through an open window, had drifted outside. I saw him standing on the doorstep, pointing an expensive-looking video camera at the sky. I joined him on the doorstep.

"Do you see it?" he said of a tiny mosquito-like object floating over a village about three kilometers away. I did see it: a helicopter—a barrel bomber, for all I knew—on the way to administer its daily dose of death to the villagers. It seemed to dangle and sway beneath the clouds.

It hovered in this way for a minute or so, declined to fire anything, then withdrew. Abu Dujanna and I watched it making downward-spiraling corkscrew turns for several minutes. Eventually, it touched down in a field. This was the regime's military airport at Taftanaz, Abu Dujanna said.

We were close enough to this helicopter to see the shack next to which the helicopter had landed. We could see the pilot opening the helicopter door, then walking across his landing pad, toward the shack. It would have taken us fifteen minutes, not more, of strolling through open fields to arrive at this shack's front door.

"Why doesn't anyone shoot at the helicopter?" I asked. Abu Dujanna grunted but did not reply. He carried on with his filming. And then I understood. So we are carrying out reconnaissance on a target, I told myself. The target was the military airport. The resistants were my fellow travelers. The saps who were daydreaming the last hours of their lives away were the regime airmen. Perhaps I would write up a report about our spying on the regime operations. The report would discuss how cleverly surreptitious Mohammed and his friends had been in their approach—traveling about in a beat-up taxi—and how their discretion prohibited them from breathing a word about the purpose of their mission before they brought it off.

I half-wondered if the attack was more imminent than I thought. Maybe it was happening, like, now? I scanned the fields for soldiers creeping through the grass. They would disable the helicopter with their shoulder-launched RPG rounds, I thought, then send their homemade rockets at the shack. Mohammed and the others remained indoors. They were cautious, I told myself, perhaps even fearful. I, for my part, did not feel even a twinge of anxiety. Is this my first battle? I wondered. I hadn't wanted to see one. But here I was. If it happened in front of me was I supposed to turn my eyes away? No, I would take hold of my notebook. I would say reportorial things to my journal.

I waited several minutes on the doorstep, hoping. Sadly, nothing happened. Trucks and passenger cars rolled, as they had been doing all morning, along the Binnish-Taftanaz highway. Nothing at all.

As it happened, three months later Jebhat al-Nusra and Ahrar al-Sham used suicide truck bombs to clear the checkpoints the soldiers at this base had erected to keep their enemies at bay. The base really did fall. So my fantasy about the incipient attack was realistic, though I had the timing of it off. Of course, I didn't manage to suss out who would be playing which part, either.

When the filming had finished, Abu Osama came outside. He gave a lecture. With the Syrian Air Force busy, he said, and God only knew what kind of spies passing on the highway, everyone's safety required me to remain indoors. I could watch from a window, he said. He escorted me into the child's bedroom.

Here, I discovered, Abu Osama was in the midst of setting up a minor TV studio on the child's bed. He had planted a tripod on the floor, opened a laptop on the bedspread, and was connecting these to a tangle of USB cables. He motioned for me to sit on the floor, on the foam-rubber mattress—my multicolored divan. Mohammed happened to be lounging here. He was staring out the window, into the olive groves. I plopped myself down next to him.

I peeked at my iPhone. It was almost noon. In another hour or so, my mother would be waking up in Cambridge. "You know what, boys?" I said. I needed to make a phone call. "There is a phone shop near here?"

"It's too dangerous out there," Mohammed said.

"Later," Abu Osama mumbled. "Not now."

Right, I told myself. As soon as my journalist-recon-smuggler friends get on with their morning errands—I imagined them piling into the taxi, without me—I'll take a walk. Probably by the time I ambled away to the nearest village, my mother would be settling down with her morning cup of tea.

Yes, Mohammed and Abu Osama would be annoyed that I had wandered away when they wished me to stay put. I didn't care. My phone conversation with my mother, I told myself, mattered to me, as their airport surveillance mattered to them. I needed to check in with Mom, to tell her that all was well, to hear her voice. Was life carrying on its predictable, peaceful way in Cambridge? I needed to be told that it was.

These thoughts must have distracted me enough for me not to

notice as Abu Dujanna and Abu Said took up seats on the child's bed, next to Abu Osama. Without a word, Abu Osama began fixing the video camera to the tripod. He pointed the camera lens at me. He grinned. He checked the viewfinder, then grinned again.

"You are making a film?" I asked.

"Yes," he said.

"For the opposition TV?" I asked.

"Yes," he said. The report, it so happened, was going to be about me.

"Ah," I said. I frowned. I didn't like the idea.

The arrival of a foreign journalist, particularly an American one, can sometimes be taken as a news event in rural Syria. This report, which I suspected he meant to flog, as I was flogging my imaginary essays—which is to say, without success—was going to narrate the nonevent of an international journalist's two-day tour through northern Syria. Could there be a worse idea?

Lacking anything interesting to do with themselves (where were the buyers of their bullets?), they meant to deploy their journalistic powers on me.

I, for my part, had been meaning to write about them. But this is too silly, I told myself.

So journalists would interview journalists. This is how the professionals back in Antakya liked to pass their time. Their affection for this form of laziness was the forty-eighth item on my list of reasons to despise them.

"Look," I told Abu Osama. "Really?" I was certain I could persuade him that the thoughts of a trucker, a farmer, an olive picker—any flesh-and-blood Syrian at all—deserved more attention than mine.

I made a suggestion along these lines. He thought about it for a moment, then shrugged his shoulders. "You said you wanted to interview Mohammed, yes? So interview Mohammed."

As it happened, Mohammed was leaning his left shoulder against my right. I glanced at him. He grinned. It wasn't as if I had much else going on.

"You want to be interviewed?" I asked him. He nodded. I sighed. No one would ever see this report, I felt, since Abu Osama was probably having the same luck with his editors as I was having with mine. "Fascinating," they were telling him, "but not for us."

"Is the camera rolling?" I asked him. He nodded. I turned to Mohammed. "Your name?"

"Mohammed."

"Your age?"

"My age is twenty-five." He was from al-Tal. He belonged to Ahrar al-Sham. Before the war, he had been a student at the university in Damascus.

I asked him about his favorite day of the revolution to date and his least favorite one. By producing a dull-as-dishwater dialog, I meant to establish, on the record and for the camera, how useless our exercise was.

Though I never saw Abu Osama's film, it didn't take me long to realize that he wasn't the least interested in a straight-up news report, as I had assumed, and that he was working in a newer, far more interesting genre.

At the time, when I was coming to know Abu Osama—when he was dreaming about his upcoming production—a samizdat film, a genre popular among the millions of powerless, video-clip-loving young men in the Arab world, showed an American truck or armored personnel carrier lumbering down a rubble-strewn highway, somewhere in Iraq. Over this footage, an a cappella chorus sang about the self-involvement and purposeless of the earlier days, before the great coming back to God. "I regret, I regret," the voices said. "How I've wasted my days. I'm returning to my prayers. I'm coming back to God." Sometimes the voices (always without instrumental accompaniment) spoke of a coming back to God that had occurred long ago, when the singer and his beloved were one. "Where have our days gone? Vanished in the blink of an eye," those voices sang. In that sort of song, the work of making that beautiful time come again had fallen to the current generation.

Such singing carried on for the first twenty seconds of these films, as the American trucks lumbered and swayed. Then the IED exploded. Sometimes, in some films, bodies could be seen hurtling through space. They were little rag dolls, rolling and tumbling in a shower of debris.

Sometimes the Americans came staggering out of their wrecks. Their clothes were on fire. Or they wandered around in circles until snipers shot them from faraway rooftop parapets. Always the survivors collapsed. Always the music continued.

These films were popular in Syria long before the outbreak of the war. The most spectacular ones, with many episodes of destruction and much music, could be purchased wherever pirated DVDs were sold, which is to say in every suq, in every city.

The jolt these films administered was in the undeniability of the evidence they supplied. Each episode told the same story, and the story illustrated a fact everyone believed but, until the arrival of these films, couldn't prove. The evidence in these films showed that powers far more powerful than the Americans—neither visible to them nor comprehensible to their machinery—lay beneath the surface of things in the Middle East. In those films, the people of Iraq—the ubiquitous "us" and "our" and "we" in the soundtracks—had resolved to change their lives. They regretted that they had estranged themselves, in the bother and hustle of daily life, from the invisible powers. Now they were combing over their accounts. They were putting things right. They were coming back to God—and so bringing themselves into harmony with the powers no one could see and everyone could feel.

Popular as these video clips were, by 2012 the good bits had been seen a thousand times. The soundtracks were old, the plots mechanical. As for the filmmakers, they hadn't much embraced the possibilities of the genre: Here were stories about Americans confronting the eternal powers of the place in which the confrontations were observed from one thousand meters away, through a telephoto lens. There were no voices in the films, no reaction shots, and no notion of character. Nor did any of the believers appear on the scene afterward to read out the lessons the Americans ought to have learned ages ago.

Abu Osama, the journalist-activist, was also an ambitious documentarian, as his Facebook self-portraits show. He meant to improve and update. What does the American's face look like in its time of arrogance? What inanities does he utter? When he is the victim of shock and awe, what does the face look like then? On beholding the true powers in the land, what exactly does he say? Abu Osama's film would give the answers.

In the event, when the actors were in position and the camera rolling, the two protagonists in the drama, I'm not at all sorry to say, gave uninspiring, lifeless performances. My heart wasn't in it. I didn't much like the filmmaker. I disliked his idea of my acting out the part of the inquisitive journalist. Anyway, I was in a hurry for the four of them to wrap things up, to pile into their yellow-and-white wreck, to be out of my hair, and to leave me alone to call my mom. I'm sure my impatience rubbed off on my fellow thespian, Mohammed. He, too, I sensed, wanted to get on with things.

After the first minute or so of filming, I decided I had asked all the questions I was going to ask. I was bored. I looked around the room. I took a deep breath. I tossed out a final volley of questions, out of courtesy: Did Mohammed ever wish he could go home to al-Tal? (No.) Did he regret anything he had done in this war? (No.) Could he imagine reconciling with his enemies? (No.) I doubt he answered a single question sincerely. I listened, watched his face for reactions, felt sleepy, bored, then irritated, and then I turned to the cameraman, Abu Osama. "I'm done," I said. "Let's move on."

Abu Osama stood up. All three men sitting on the child's bed stood up. *"Yalla, ya shabbab?"* said Abu Osama. *Shall we go to it, boys?* He was smiling as he spoke these words. It was a friendly sentence. I heard it as an invitation he meant to extend to me. Because he was rising to his feet as he spoke, and because I was anxious to leave, I leaned forward. I rose to my knees. Mohammed, my fellow actor, would have been prepared for this. He had held himself close during the interview. Now he seized a clump of my hair, then yanked my head to the floor.

Abu Osama kicked me in the face. My head snapped backward. An instrument—I'm not sure what, the handgun?—crashed into the side of my skull. Blood oozed into my hair.

"Oof," I said. Someone else kicked me in the chest. There were blows to my face. Someone was stomping the heel of his boot into my chest. "Oof," I said. There were further, sharper kicks to my forehead.

A KIDNAPPING

A voice called out, "Bring the handcuffs!" In Arabic, the word for "handcuffs" is *kalabshe*. *Kalabshe*? I thought. But we had been discussing *kalabshe* in the car the day before. What is the meaning of this word? I wondered. It was on the tip of my tongue. And then I was lying on my stomach. A boot was pressing into the back of my neck. Someone was locking my hands into a pair of cuffs at the small of my back. Ah, I thought, *al kalabshe*.

For a moment, I was able to bring myself to my knees. Probably my attackers allowed me to do this. I knelt as if in prayer for an instant and then another blunt object, perhaps a boot, swung at the base of my skull. I toppled forward, face-first, into the floor. "Oof," I said.

When at last my vision refocused, I happened to see, out of the corner of my eye, that Abu Dujanna was pointing the handgun I had explained away, in my daydreams, the day before, as a cops-and-robbers toy, at my head. He stood in a sunny corner of the room. He held his eyes on mine—a level, even-tempered gaze.

"Please," I said. "Don't shoot." He did not move. "Please!" I repeated. I pulled on the handcuffs. "What do you want?" Having asked this question of dozens, perhaps hundreds of similarly minded militants in Syria by now, I know how silly a question this is. It almost always elicits a slogan or a string of stock phrases. Then comes an interlude of silent, blank staring. They want the violence. They want to say the slogans. They want to watch as the tables turn. They want to stare.

That afternoon, I saw the staring for the first time. There was love of guns in my kidnappers' eyes, and pride in themselves. There was pleasure in being part of a cool film. I doubt Abu Dujanna wanted anything in particular, however, and so when I spoke he also seemed confused to me, as if I had asked him to solve a math problem too complicated to work out in his head.

I promised that I wouldn't move. "I'll do what you want," I said. "Anything you like." Thirty seconds of calm passed, and then Abu Said lashed a leather strap I had rescued from the master bedroom floor during our straightening-up project around my ankles. Mohammed allowed me to sit myself upright on the mattress. Having managed this, I asked Abu Dujanna to lower his gun. He did not react.

Abu Osama knelt in front of me. He grinned into my face. He touched my hair. The success of his operation—or maybe it was the fear in my eyes—caused him to turn his smile to his friends. He told Abu Dujanna to lower the gun.

"Surprised you, didn't we?" Abu Osama said. I watched as he giggled to himself, then rose, stepped to check on the viewfinder of his camera, patted his friends on their backs, then returned to me. "You are a prisoner now," he said. He asked Abu Said to search the pockets of my jeans. I had to rise to my knees for this procedure. From a back pocket, Abu Said retrieved the $50 I had changed into Syrian liras the night before. In the front pocket, he found my driver's license, a debit card, and a SIM-less iPhone. As Abu Said removed these items from my pockets, he spoke softly to me, as if he meant to forestall my indignation. It wasn't illegal for him to take these objects, he said, but rather proper and customary, since items in my possession were *ghanima*. I had an English-Arabic dictionary on my phone. I asked Abu Said to look up the word. Mohammed interrupted in English: "I think your word is 'booty'? 'Spoils'?" he said.

"In Islam," Abu Osama said gently, as if he were explaining the rules of a game to a child, "we are allowed to take the property of the enemy when he is captured. You are our enemy. You are captured. See?"

I searched the four faces watching me. Was no one winking? Mohammed made eye contact but only for an instant, and his eyes were dead. Abu Dujanna watched me, but without expression, as if he were watching a football game. Abu Osama's eyes were alight with happiness and surprise. Abu Said, for his part, glanced at me, then turned to my phone. He tapped and shook. He made it play music, then held it to his ear.

Abu Osama was kneeling in front of me. He would have been in the camera frame. How was I feeling now? he wanted to know. Did I like the handcuffs? "Do you know who we are?" he asked.

No, I did not know.

"We are from the al Qaeda organization," Abu Osama said, grinning. "You didn't know, did you?"

I glanced at the others. I looked into Abu Osama's eyes. "Al Qaeda?" I said. "I don't believe it." He shrugged.

In his corner, under a beam of sunlight, Abu Said was looking for information about the phone. "iPhone Three is all?" he asked. Newer, more expensive models were available by this time, even in Syria. Did it have a tracking device on it? he wanted to know. Was anyone following me through my phone?

It took several minutes for me to convince him that there was no SIM card in the device, that no one from home knew I was in Syria, not even my mother, and that, as far as I knew, no one could track me through the phone. Everyone in the room doubted these assurances. Abu Osama examined the empty SIM tray, turned the phone off, then turned it on again. Eventually, he shrugged. He returned it to his brother, who slipped the phone into his pocket. Abu Osama stood to adjust his camera, then returned, kneeling, to his spot in the camera frame. He held my hair. He turned my face to the camera.

"Do you think Islam does not permit us to do what we've done?" he asked. I had no intention of engaging this person in a debate. I did not answer. "It is legal for us to kill you, to exchange you for ransom, or to let you go. Do you think we are making this up?"

I turned to Mohammed. He stared at me but did not smile. I glanced at Abu Dujanna and Abu Said. They met my eyes but did not speak.

Abu Osama recited a line of scripture. I barely caught its meaning. He glared at me, then uttered further, louder words from the sacred texts. His eyes flashed around the room.

"You killed our sheikh, Osama bin Laden," he said.

I stared at him.

"Why did you invade Iraq?" Outrage filled his eyes. "Do you think this is normal? This is not criminal behavior? Where are your morals? Where?"

My silence must have encouraged him. The Vietnam War, the Hiroshima bombing, the killing of the Plains Indians—episodes and places in American history came at me in volleys. Each item on his list made his lip curl in disgust. "You are animals," he said of Americans in general, of all eras. The killing of Saddam Hussein, drones in Yemen, Blackwater contractors, Abu Ghraib, Guantánamo—every word astonished him, and the astonishment made him turn to me for answers.

"How can it be?" he asked several times, of . . . what, I did not know. The astonishment issued from him like bile that had been caught in his throat. It had caused him great suffering, over many years, even, and now, finally, after choking on it for much of his adult life, chance had allowed him to spit it away. So he spat. He did it in a kind of a trance, his eyes alight, his mind churning. "Do you think you are the policemen of the world?" he asked. "Do you think we want your freedom?"

It was our arrogance, he said, that he would never understand. Also, our preoccupation with sex. Also, our submission to "the Jews." "You are their slaves!" he exclaimed. Periodically, during the course of his denunciations, he paused to goggle at me, as if he couldn't get his head around the scope of our wickedness. Still, he was in no mood to reconcile himself to anything. The situation, he seemed to feel, called out for further, louder lecturing.

The Americans, he said, had entered into a secret alliance with the Shia in Iraq in order to kill "our brothers" there. "You don't know? How can you not know this? Liar." He felt Obama had organized a pact with the Shia-esque government in Damascus to the same end. He felt Americans believed themselves to be immune to all forms of retribution. "But this is your stupidity," he said. "You're all stupid like this, and every one of you will learn from us."

There was more. The racism in America, the adultery, the alcoholism—did I know there wasn't any such thing as an American? "The real Americans are the Indians," Abu Osama said, lecturing now more to his friends than to me. "The land on which they built their country belongs to the Indians," he said. He used an old-fashioned Arabic word for "Indian," which translates as "Red Hindus." He turned to me. "You killed the Red Hindus. Yes! In order to take their land. So you are thieves, on top of everything else."

"The Red Hindus?" I asked.

"Shut up, Animal," he replied. "If the Americans come looking for you, we'll kill you. Do you understand?"

"Yes," I said.

"If the Americans set foot in Syria—one toe inside our country—we will kill them. Then we'll kill you."

"Yes," I said.

"We will put Obama's head in the trash."

"Yes," I agreed.

Before he switched off his video camera, he announced to me what I would have to do to save my life. Islam, he said, entitled him to sell me back to my family for the value of a quarter kilo of gold. The cash equivalent, he said (incorrectly, as it turned out), was $400,000. "You can get four hundred thousand dollars?" he said.

I pretended to consider the matter. "If my life is in danger, yes."

In that case, he said, I was to have one week of life. If I could bring him the cash within a week, I would live. If not, I would be killed.

I nodded. A wound on the back of my head was causing blood to trickle down the back of my shirt. I asked if I could have a towel. Abu Osama sighed. He asked his brother, Abu Said, to turn off the camera. Abu Said rose, clicked a button on the camera, brought me a towel, then dabbed it—gently, as if he felt himself under a moral obligation—at my face.

He threw the towel to the floor, but the blood returned right away. It had drenched my T-shirt. It was smearing itself across the plaster above the divan. I told Abu Osama that if my hands were handcuffed in front of me I could clean myself up on my own. In addition, I could preserve the cleanliness of the house. My suggestion caused Mohammed and Abu Osama to exchange glances and then whispers. A key appeared. My hands were unlocked, then locked again in front of my body. I retrieved the towel. I asked to be allowed to undo the leather strap that bound my ankles. "If you run, we shoot," Abu Osama said. I nodded. Abu Osama allowed me to untie my legs from the leather strap. When I was done cleaning the back of my head, I asked to be allowed to pee. Mohammed escorted me to the bathroom. He waited for me outside the door, then escorted me back to my spot on the divan.

When I had resumed my place, Abu Osama smiled at me. He yawned. "Are you hungry?" he asked.

This lunch, I sensed from the twinkling in my kidnappers' eyes, was to be a festive occasion. Sunlight filled the room. It filtered through the iron filigrees that had been welded, I noticed just then, over the outside of the window frames. It splashed across my multicolored divan.

For the kidnappers, there were ablutions, then prayers, and then Mohammed was sent off in the taxi wreck to comb the countryside for suitable fare. Twenty minutes later, when he pushed open the bedroom door, he was carrying four white plastic bags, all of them stuffed, and pulling themselves toward the floor. Rich, steamy lunch smells wafted through the air.

The kidnappers arranged themselves in a circle on the bedroom floor. Mohammed passed around sheets of newsprint to be used as place mats. There were deep-fried potato wafers, plastic tubs of mayonnaise-garlic sauce, two two-liter bottles of orange soda, an uncountable quantity of smaller water bottles, and at the center of the circle, on its own bed of newsprint, a steaming roast chicken. My cash had paid for the feast, apparently. Mohammed held up a chicken leg. "Thank you, Obama! To your health." Everyone laughed. The kidnappers wished for Obama to send them more agents. They wanted him to come to Syria himself, and to bring his wives and daughters. "Please, Abu Hussein," said Mohammed, using a nickname for Obama common in the Arab world. "Be welcome! Welcome!" He gestured at a space by his side. "Eat," he told me. "You are our guest. Welcome, please."

I was too shocked to eat. I was too afraid and too sickened by their happiness.

They stuffed swabs of bread into the corners of their mouths, then chased the bread down with drafts of orange soda. They wrapped bits of bread around the skin of the chicken carcass, tore at the flesh, then sank their fingers into their mouths.

Halfway through lunch, Abu Osama paused with a tub of mayonnaise in his hand. He held it out to me. "Eat?" he said. He stared for a few moments, then shrugged. A question occurred to him. Why, during the "arrest operation," as he put it, had I allowed myself to be taken into custody without a struggle? Why?

"Four against one," I said. "What would you do?"

He thought about my remark for a moment. "Good point," he said.

"If it were me, I wouldn't spy for the CIA. If I were a spy, I wouldn't come to Syria."

This made his friends laugh. They poured orange soda into their mouths.

Later in their feast, Abu Osama recalled that the Prophet had advised Muslims to beware of dining with non-Muslims. "Actually, it is forbidden to eat with you," he said. Because of the non-Muslim's contamination by alcohol, pork, and, possibly, drugs, a Muslim risked infecting himself when he shared his food with a non-Muslim. The solution was for me to sit at a distance from the kidnappers, in a corner, by myself. Abu Osama nodded at a pile of dusty children's clothing we had swept into a corner. The suggestion hung in the air for a moment. I declined to move. Then Mohammed reached for the sheet of news-print on which a pile of potato slices had been laid out for me. He rolled it into a package, then carried my lunch to the corner. "Sorry," he said as he walked, in a tone of voice that I thought might have conveyed something like regret.

From my corner of indecency, I watched the diners gnawing on their chicken bones. As they smacked their lips, I tried to reckon with the psychology that had brought the five of us to this fix. It seemed to me that some sinister accumulation of photos from Abu Ghraib, rumors from Guantánamo, and YouTube diatribes from bin Laden had worked themselves into a froth inside my kidnappers' brains. Abu Osama was the most affected, but the feeling was present enough in everyone's blood to have pushed them all out into the blue, beyond reason, unreachable in any language, citizens of some parallel reality. I wondered how the transformation had occurred and when. Abu Osama, I told myself, dressed as an everyday Syrian twentysomething but concealed beneath his hoodie the kid killer, the recluse, the sort of failed joiner who hopes to be liked in school, is shunned, takes to watching videos of people being killed, and finally contrives to produce such a video himself. Abu Osama, I guessed, was the Syrian cousin of the American schoolboy killer. During his school years, he would have collected guns, obsessed over slights, and dreamed of himself as an avenging angel.

I felt the others in the room were passive enough and stupid enough to help Abu Osama live out his fantasy. Now, in this land without a government, there was no one around to tell the lot of them not to kill me.

As their eating slowed, my heart raced. They have nothing to do with al Qaeda, I told myself—correctly, as it turned out. But I thought they might shoot me on behalf of the vanished tribes in the American West or because they felt the time had come to avenge bin Laden's death or because they wished to put themselves through the experience of a killing—in other words, for fun. The video camera would egg the lot of them on. I gulped at the water bottle Mohammed had put in front of me.

In subsequent months, when I was learning to adjust to life as a prisoner, I found that even brief, not-especially-injurious beatings left me desperate for water. My mouth felt like cotton against my tongue. My throat ached. Why such thirst? Maybe it was the effort of pleading with my assailants as they hit me. Maybe it was the strength I wasted in straining against my handcuffs. Probably terror makes you thirsty. Probably it was a bit of everything. I never lost much fluid during these beatings and hadn't been especially thirsty beforehand, so the craving for water that overcame me seemed irrational to me, as if something unknown and belonging to them had taken control of my body. This frightened me, and the fear, in the darkness in my cell, turned into panic.

I learned to prepare for beatings by hiding extra water bottles in the wool blanket on which I slept. I learned not to swallow all the water in my cell in the minutes after a beating because sometimes the men in black left the cell, entered the neighboring cell, beat that prisoner for a few minutes, then came back to me. My only relief when they left was my hidden water.

On this occasion, in the child's bedroom of a sunny farmhouse, the thirst came to me like an attack. It seized control of my instincts. It made me pour liters of water down my throat. Naturally, right away, I needed to pee. During my first trip to the bathroom, Mohammed brought me to the toilet. He waited, then brought me back to the child's bedroom.

The second time I asked permission to use the toilet, about fifteen minutes later, Mohammed gave me a skeptical look. "Is it fear?" he asked.

"Yes, fear," I agreed.

He shrugged. He looked at Abu Dujanna. Abu Dujanna looked at the handgun. Eyebrows were raised, but no one moved. I was allowed to walk to the bathroom on my own. Inside the bathroom, I ran my eyes around the window's frame. I might have been able to yank it, then crawl through, I thought, but it seemed to open only onto an air shaft. In the corridor outside the bathroom, however, I was alone. The front door, I could see, had been left ajar. Beyond the front door, a public highway beckoned to me, and beyond that was an olive grove. The bathroom, I told myself, is my friend.

During the postprandial drowsiness that settled over the kidnappers, Abu Osama busied himself with his laptop. Abu Dujanna retreated to a corner. He fingered the handgun but did not point it. Mohammed announced that he needed to sleep for a few hours as he had stayed up late with his friends the previous night. It was decided that there were too many helicopters about at the moment for the five of us to go off in search of a phone or an internet-connected computer on which I could initiate whatever procedures were required to bring Mohammed and his friends their $400,000 of *ghanima* within seven days. We would set off in the evening, Mohammed said. In the meantime, he needed a nap.

Abu Said decided to fill the time by emptying the contents of the backpack I had brought from Antakya onto the floor in front of the divan. He pushed a paperback edition of the Paul Theroux book *Dark Star Safari* around on the floor with his toe. He bent over the white cycling jacket. He held it in the air. "What is the cost of this?" he asked. I told him. He ran his fingers over a pair of New Balance running shoes. "And these?" he asked. I named a price. He shrugged.

He collected my passport, my driver's license, and my phone, then retreated to a corner, next to the door. There followed the gentlest of all interrogations that have ever occurred in Syria. Surely, he had never been on either side of one before. He sat. I sat. There were no weapons. My hands were cuffed in front of my body. A conversation ensued.

Why were there Yemeni stamps in my passport? Because I had been a journalist there.

"You worked there for the CIA there?"

"No. For the *Yemen Observer*."

There were entry stamps from the Damascus airport in my passport.

"The CIA sent you to Damascus?"

"No. I sent myself."

He examined the passport's remaining pages, asked me to confirm the dates on which I had entered and left Syria, then put the passport aside.

We moved on to the driver's license. He passed it to Abu Osama, then on to Abu Dujanna, and then Abu Said brought it to where I sat, on my divan. He held it under my nose. "We know who you work for," he said.

"That's my driver's license," I said.

He shook it at me. A flash of anger passed through his eyes. "Don't tell me this is a driver's license," he said. I insisted. He shook it again. "We know exactly who you work for," he said.

"I don't work for anyone," I said. Each state gave out driver's licenses, I said. The state that had given me mine was called Vermont. The letters on my document spelled out this word. "The CIA is in Virginia," I told him. Virginia was not Vermont.

A moment of wonder followed, then silence. Slowly, Abu Said returned the license to his pocket. He retreated to his corner by the door.

This interrogator was my angel, it turned out. He pursued his CIA theory for an instant, lost interest, then abandoned the interrogation altogether. Later that evening, he disappeared with the phone, the passport, and the driver's license. In the absence of my documents, I could be whoever I wanted to be. "I am an English teacher," I told subsequent interrogators. I gave them my mother's name, Curtis. "I am half-French," I said. The al Qaeda interrogators didn't much care about my name, but they did want to know about my work. "I teach poetry," I told them. "For years I have been living in Damascus." I mentioned the names of the regime-loving neighborhoods in which I had lived. "Every day, I ate under their noses. I know the worshipers of Bashar better than you do. I taught them Shakespeare." Perhaps this line of talk helped a bit. It couldn't have hurt me. I hoped that the secret that could have hurt me—that I had published a book, under the name Padnos, about my life in the religious academies of Yemen called *Undercover Muslim*—had disappeared with my IDs. The title of that book would have made them think I had spied on the religion itself. I despaired when I thought of the title. They could not have overlooked a crime like that, I thought—even if they managed to persuade themselves that the American government would give them millions in exchange for my life.

After Abu Said lost interest in the passport, he turned to my bank card. I gave him the PIN. I told him that there was less than $200 in the account and that he was welcome to it. He shrugged. He returned to the phone. He pulled up an email I had sent to an editor. Letter by letter, he sounded out a sentence in which I had mentioned a region in northern Syria called the Kurdish Mountains, then under the control of rebel forces. "You have contacts there," he said. "Who are they? Regime spies?" I was in touch with regime spies, he concluded, currently undercover among the rebel brothers in the Kurdish Mountains. What was the CIA planning to do to the brothers in the Kurdish Mountains?

"It's a letter to an editor," I explained. I had hoped to go to that region in order to write about the war. The editor had not replied. "I am here, in this region, on this trip, with you," I explained, "because nobody wanted me to go to the Kurdish Mountains." They had not paid me a red cent to go anywhere. They hadn't even replied to my emails. "You see?" I said.

Abu Said did not look at me as I spoke. He found further suspicious emails. He wondered what eBay was and what Audible might be. He wanted to know if the phone's GPS function could be turned off and on. I wasn't sure. He examined the photo archive. The greenery in Vermont impressed him, but not for long. He tapped for a few minutes more, then sighed, then returned the phone to his pocket.

All in all, it took about ten minutes for Abu Said's curiosity about me to exhaust itself. After the last of his questions had been answered, he retrieved the running shoes from the pile of backpack contents. He put these by his side. He tilted his head against the wall. He began to doze.

I looked out the windows of the child's bedroom. Olive branches fluttered in a gentle breeze. It seemed to me then that I had been out for a lark in the Syrian countryside, had driven much too fast, overshot a corner on a mountain road, crashed through a barrier, nearly died in a fiery wreck, but somehow, by the grace of God, I had managed to stagger away with only a cut on the back of my head. I've been an idiot, I told myself. I was by no means out of the woods. I remained in a dangerous fix. Yet it wasn't so dangerous, I felt, that it couldn't be remedied by some smooth talking and maybe, if it came to that, decisive action in a moment of need.

I must tiptoe away from this trap, I told myself. Whenever I managed to tiptoe to within reach of a thoroughfare, I thought, decent citizens—rather than the loons I had stuck myself with—would see my distress, wrap their arms around me, then whisk me away to safety.

In fact, as these thoughts were passing through my head, a stream of traffic, about a hundred meters from where I sat, was flowing along the Binnish-Taftanaz highway. I could hear the whoosh of the trucks. Now and then, the wind carried the voices of distant children at play.

That highway is safety, I told myself. A motorist, a shopkeeper, a housewife, a strolling family—all such people were safety, I thought. I needed to bring myself into contact with any such citizen of Syria, I imagined. If only I could make contact with a human being, I thought, I would make my truth known in an instant in plain declarative Arabic sentences—or in sign language, if need be. The goodness of the Syrian people would take care of the rest.

There came a moment after Abu Said began to doze when Abu Osama announced to me, in his own version of bold Arabic sentences, what exactly was going on out there, beyond the windows to which I kept turning my eyes.

"We will put the black flag on the White House," he announced.

"Okay," I said.

"For every one of your George Bushes, we have an Abu Musab."

This, I knew, even then, was the al Qaeda in Iraq leader, Abu Musab al Zarqawi, killed in action in 2006.

"Okay," I said.

"We are a nation," he said. "The leader of our army is God. The constitution is the Koran."

"Yes," I agreed.

"Bashar al-Assad is nothing," he said. "He is filth. When our armies finish with him, we will attack the real enemy. First Damascus," he said, "then Jerusalem."

"Good for you," I said.

"You don't think we can do it?"

"No, I don't think you can."

He shrugged.

A week later, when I had had further glimpses into their Islamic state, the memory of my incredulousness made me want to pull out my hair by the roots. I held my face in my hands.

I assumed Abu Osama to be bragging about a fairy realm in which sane people did not believe. I suspected that he himself didn't much believe in it. He meant to intimidate and to impress, nothing more.

"The mosques here are full as never before," Abu Osama told me that afternoon. There were morning study sessions for women, afternoon study sessions for children, and everyone, everywhere, loved the heroes, the sons of the land—the mujahideen. "Every man in every family," he said, "is a *mujahid* on the path of God."

I scoffed. A week later, the shimmering olive leaves beyond the window of the child's bedroom kept coming back to me. I saw them in my sleep. I could not get them out of my mind. If I had been capable of taking this person's ranting seriously, I would have known that safety for me lay out there, in the thistle and prairie grass, between the lines of trees. Instead, I dreamed about a random encounter with Good Samaritan housewives. In an Islamic state, Good Samaritan housewives exist, I know now, but they do not leave their houses. They will make food for a prisoner if they are so ordered. But they cannot speak to him. They certainly cannot help him. As for being rescued on the public way: I know now that a foreigner in an Islamic state who comes running along with a bee in his bonnet about being a journalist ("Help me! Help me!") must be presented to the authorities. The foreigner could be a spy. He could be a Jew. He could be spying on behalf of that Elders-of-Zion-esque fraternity that, it is thought, works out its purpose through its figurehead, Bashar al-Assad. In an Islamic state the learned men know exactly how to find out who the stranger is. The man with the bee in his bonnet must be brought to them. If the Good Samaritan fails to do this, it is probably for a reason. What is this reason? The men of learning will want to find out for themselves.

As it happened, Abu Osama's threats meant nothing much to me. Such nonsense he talks, I told myself. Eventually, he himself lost interest in issuing his threats. He had begun a computer project. Cables had to be removed from backpacks. None of the cables wanted to connect his camera to his laptop. The tripod had to be folded, then returned to its case. There were fresh batteries to remove from backpacks and notes to be typed into his laptop.

That afternoon, Mohammed must have slept for hours. No one wished to disturb him. Anyway, no business pressed. I understood that we were to set out in the evening in search of the $400,000 in cash. For the time being, an afternoon of sunlight pouring through the trees, then splashing on the carpet, stretched out before us.

During the early part of the afternoon, Abu Dujanna and Abu Osama were vigilant kidnappers. Abu Dujanna, the sentry, held the gun. Abu Osama played with his computer cords. Every twitch of my knee or sigh caused Abu Dujanna to turn his eyes on me. As they were preparing for the Asr prayer, which comes at about three o'clock, it was decided that two of the kidnappers would make their prostrations while a third, Abu Dujanna, would watch me. Only after his friends had made the last of their prostrations did Abu Dujanna rise, hand the gun to Abu Osama, and begin his prayers.

Later in the afternoon, however, a different prisoner-guarding strategy emerged. The lot of them appeared to drowse. One by one, without a word, they slipped from the room.

Alone in the child's bedroom, I pulled on the bars of the windows. I stared at a farmhouse across the lane. I padded around the perimeter of the room. I am a panther in a cage, I told myself. The bedroom door was closed but not locked. I sat for twenty minutes, rose to try the door, then stopped myself. I could see the kidnappers in my mind's eye. They sat in the shadows, at the end of the corridor. They wanted me to try the door. They were begging me to do it. They would have had the gun trained on the bedroom door. Probably, I thought, they would have allowed me to run, at least a few feet. I had no intention of falling into their trap a second time.

So I sat under a window in the bedroom. I gazed into my lap. I pondered the pattern on the absent child's bedspread, then stared for a while at my shoes. I sat in this attitude of bewilderment for an hour. Later, I rose to watch the sun sinking, then stared at the shadows on the carpet, then sat. I plunged my face into my hands.

By the time Mohammed woke from his nap, shortly before sunset, I was afraid. I was lonely. It was late on Sunday morning in Cambridge. I felt that if only I had been allowed to speak to my mother, she would have warned me. I would have heeded her admonitions. All would have been well. Why hadn't I tried harder to make the call? My regret and my inability to help myself brought me to the verge of tears. Perhaps they themselves will not kill me, I thought, but I didn't doubt that other, more malevolent people nearby would be happy to do the job. I wanted to stay with these kidnappers, particularly with the baseball cap–wearing Mohammed. During my afternoon reveries, I managed to convince myself that he and I could talk, that he didn't have any reason to want to kill me, and that the passage of a few days in his company would cause him to see reason and so to abandon his absurd your-money-or-your-life highway robbery project.

So I was pleased when he padded into the bedroom in his socks. He was wearing my white cycling jacket. He removed the iPod mini I had hidden away in a breast pocket. An expression of warm appreciation fell over his face, as if I had brought him a gift. "An MP3 player?" he wondered.

I lifted my face from my hands. "Yes, it is," I said.

He tilted his head. He pretended to be flattered. "Thank you," he said.

"No problem at all," I said. For a moment, he seemed genuinely moved. I was his friend. I had brought him an expensive toy from America. "A thousand thank-yous," he said, winking.

"Where have you been?" I wondered.

He smiled. "You're angry. Don't be angry."

I denied being angry. Or rather, I was angry, yes, but only at myself.

"Because you trusted me?"

"Yes, yes, trusted you," I said.

He sighed. He sat down on the mattress next to me.

When the regime had arrested him earlier that year, he said, on charges of using Facebook to organize demonstrations, he had also been angry. Like me, he had had difficulty eating at first. "That will pass," he said. He felt I could take comfort in being the prisoner of a just cause. The regime officers in his prison had been beasts. Their highest ideal had been Bashar al-Assad, an animal. Whereas his cause was Islam. As a prisoner, I would be treated according to the rules laid down in the Koran. "We are Muslims," he said. "Everything we do, we do under the eyes of God."

After a few moments, he rose from the mattress, wrapped his fingers around the iron filigree I had been holding a moment earlier, then stared out into the dying light. Distant trucks rolled along the Binnish-Taftanaz highway. "Is four hundred thousand dollars a large amount for an American family?" he asked in a voice that resonated, he seemed to want me to feel, with academic rather than personal interest. "It isn't really, is it?" We discussed the budgetary realities of typical American families for a few minutes. He felt $400,000 would be easy to raise. I wasn't so sure. I wondered what he meant to do with his $400,000. "Buy me a Doshka," he said—a high-caliber Russian machine gun.

"Good for you," I said. He wanted to mount his Doshka onto the back of a pickup truck, then drive it hither and yon across the countryside. When an airplane appeared in the sky, he would shoot it down. "Good for you," I repeated.

I was curious about how he had gotten on during his three months in his Damascus prison. He had been terrified, especially at first, he said. His family had no idea what had become of him. Inside the prison, he had to contend with savage overcrowding, hunger, and lice. But there had been moments of fellow feeling and collective passion for God. He had wept in the arms of his parents when he was released. The following day, he said, he set out for Idlib Province.

I was curious about the fate of his fellow inmates. Some had been tortured so badly they could no longer see, he said. Some had been released. Others had disappeared. "The regime is stupid," he said. It had created the rebellion on its own, inside the prisons. The prisons had taught the soldiers in the opposition how to hate and had given the revolution's leaders time to study the Koran, to fall in love with it as if for the first time, and, by the way, to split up the country into areas of revolutionary command. As for his own experience inside the prison, it had been painful but good, since he had learned to give himself to God entirely. Now, as a free man, this was how he meant to live out the remainder of his life: by walking, in every moment of every day, on the straight path of God.

"*Masha'Allah*," I said.

"*Masha'Allah*," he agreed.

The other kidnappers drifted back into the child's bedroom shortly before sunset. They, too, appeared to have been drowsing and chatting the afternoon away. They listened as Mohammed finished his tale of having been imprisoned for a handful of Facebook postings. They shook their heads in sadness.

At last the time for the sunset prayer came. There were ablutions, then prostrations, then handshakes among the believers on the child's carpet.

When the five of us climbed into the taxi, at about seven in the evening, we had resolved, I felt, to find a telephone on which I could call one or both of my parents. I would inform Mom or Dad or whoever I could raise on the line that I would soon be killed. I would utter whatever words had to be uttered in order to accomplish the mission at hand: $400,000 in cash had to be delivered to a point somewhere near us, at any rate inside Syria, within seven days.

I had made it clear—by listening, I felt, and by making sympathetic noises—that I sympathized with the kidnappers' cause. Obviously, I could not approve of the means by which they meant to advance their cause. But we didn't discuss means. We had discussed the near-term goal: their suitcase of cash.

I was on board with their plan. They understood this and so did not hector or threaten.

Thus the mood that evening as we set out for where I did not know was one of businesslike collective purpose. We would cooperate. They would get what they wanted. I would get what I wanted. In the meantime, I would have to wear the handcuffs. I would be a prisoner—but not, as in the regime jails, an object of contempt or abuse. We were business partners, in a manner of speaking, and now we were embarking on our first business trip. Though an exact hour for the expiration of the deadline had yet to be set, I assumed that it would come soon enough. Thus, in addition to our purposefulness, I felt that we were in a bit of a hurry.

"It's the exchange of prisoner for dollars that makes things complicated." Mohammed sighed as he inched the taxi out onto the Binnish-Taftanaz highway. "Very, very complicated."

I agreed that the swapping of a prisoner for a small mountain of cash wouldn't be a routine transaction, exactly, but neither would it be unheard-of. Somewhere, in today's world, I said, an oil company executive or politician was kidnapped practically every day of the week. Always the kidnappers demanded a ransom. Always an insurance company paid. In Yemen, every time a tribe in a distant province needed a new road or wished for a visit from the president, the tribe kidnapped a handful of tourists. "He who is kidnapped in Yemen is the luckiest victim in the world, since his hosts always feed him qat, treat him to delicious food, and in the end the government always builds the new road," I said.

As I talked, I didn't feel a surge of kidnapper confidence in my confidence, but neither did anyone scowl or contradict me or order me to shut the hell up. I supposed that the kidnappers' ransom scheme might have daunted them a bit. Perhaps their response to looming difficulties was to ignore them. Anyway, my kidnappers declined my invitation to chat about how the ease with which kidnappers in this day and age secured their ransoms. Their minds seemed rather focused on the camera Abu Osama cradled in his lap, the gun Abu Dujanna was babying in his, and on recent additions to their wardrobe.

Mohammed caressed the sleeves of a white cycling jacket. It looks quite like something I own, I thought to myself. Abu Said, I noticed, wore a pair of new New Balance trainers. Smiling to himself, he propped his foot on his knee. Someone had doused himself in cologne.

At a rise in the road that offered a view north into Turkey, Mohammed wondered, apropos of nothing, if I felt the ransom might come more quickly if we announced to the world that I had been kidnapped.

I thought about his idea for a moment. "We could call Al Jazeera," I suggested. I had no experience with TV journalism. I knew no editors. Or reporters or interns. I wasn't at all sure that it would be possible to persuade someone at Al Jazeera that this was no crank call. I did, however, want to get on the phone to someone. The idea of my being on TV made smiles appear on the faces of my kidnappers. "However you'd like to proceed is okay with me," I said. I said that I knew many people at Al Jazeera, and could call the studio whenever they liked.

"We'll see," said Mohammed.

We drove without headlights. The moon lit our way. After about fifteen minutes of driving, a road sign indicated our arrival in the village of Marat Misrin. As the car drifted past apartment blocks on the outskirts of this agricultural settlement, it occurred to me that as long as someone was going to be robbed of $400,000, it might as well be the US government. It occurred to me that as long as the kidnappers were asking for $400,000, they might as well ask for millions. "Let's ask Obama for ten million dollars," I said into the moonlight. "You all can have nine million. I'll take one. Everyone's happy. Okay?"

The kidnappers grinned but did not bite. The road led us through fields in which squat olive trees stood in orderly rows. In the midst of one such field, at a bend in the road, Mohammed stopped the car. That evening, ours was the only one we had seen. He didn't bother pulling to the side of the road.

Abu Osama stepped out, then ambled down a dirt track. At the end of this track stood a single-story house, almost entirely obscured by overhanging foliage. He knocked, waited a moment, then disappeared within.

I needed to pee. My captors allowed me to step out of the car in my handcuffs. I stood in the center of the road, gazed at the moon, then walked a few steps into the olive grove. As I stood in the dirt and looked forward through shadowy lanes, it seemed to me that a vast darkness stood before me, that a helter-skelter sprinting through the tree trunks could well bring me to a provisional kind of safety and that a Marine, a Navy SEAL, or anyone true physical courage would have made a run for it. I didn't dare. I cursed myself for lacking the courage to seize the freedom that was everywhere around me. But then wasn't it wiser, I wondered, to play to my strengths? I wasn't the type to go Jason Bourne–ing it through the wilderness. It occurred to me that I wouldn't have been able to sprint in handcuffs, would have tripped in the olive grove furrows, panicked, and eventually collapsed, on my own, in a heap. When he caught up with me, Abu Dujanna would have put a bullet through my thigh. If, that is, he was feeling friendly. Neither in this moment nor at any other did I believe a ransom in dollar bills might somehow reach Syria within seven days. I'll get myself out of this on my own, I told myself, by playing the strongest, safest hand I have to play. I would charm, chatter, and cajole. Eventually, I hoped, the kidnappers would see the folly of their scheme. They would come to reason, lose heart, then let me go.

So when I returned to the car, I told Mohammed that "Doshka," in Russian, meant "little soul." I said that we would get Obama on the phone, insist on $10 million, right away, to be delivered via helicopter, and that with this money Mohammed could purchase a little army of little souls. And brand-new pickup trucks with which to carry each Doshka around. I said that peeing in handcuffs wasn't at all as easy as it looked. "I want my million at the end of this," I said.

I think everyone in the car knew I was kidding. But we were faced with a knotty problem. It had to be solved somehow. I was coming up with ideas. Was this wrong? I think the captors rather felt it was right. Why shouldn't the US government supply Syrian rebels with Doshkas?

Why wouldn't a well-meaning American wish to help in the supply-the-rebels program? In any case, all the kidnappers understood, I think, that my heart was in the right place, that I wished to make myself useful, and that if we played our hand wisely, the lot of us might well bring our current dilemma to a positive conclusion.

Thus, after ten minutes of waiting for Abu Osama, when he and a companion emerged from the house at the end of the lane, the mood in our car was cheerful. It was one of bemusement, with a tinge of comedy.

The companion ruined everything. He was Abu Osama's cousin Behajat Nijaar—also a photographer, as it turned out. Here is his Facebook self-portrait:

An undated self-portrait from Behajat Nijaar's Facebook page.

The themes in Behajat's Facebook photo archive are as follows: the joy that waving the black flag brings to demonstrators in Marat Misrin, the savagery the Syrian Air Force inflicts on the citizens of northern Syria, the heroism of the defenders of the faith, the impossibility of driving them from the land and the bravery of the local photographers.

The war he depicts on his Facebook page has two sides to it: the believers and the enemies of Islam. In his photos—and in the friends' many comments, too—the believers are winning, though the outside world, knowing nothing of the happiness belief brings and never guessing at the invulnerability it supplies, doesn't understand this. How to communicate these facts to the world? The solution Behajat the photographer has devised is for him to post photos of Behajat, the defender of the faith, to his Facebook account. These photos dare the enemies. They summon the believers to take up the fight. Here is Behajat with his surface-to-air missile:

Another undated self-portrait from Behajat's Facebook page.

Behajat was carrying a Kalashnikov when he emerged from his house. He and Abu Osama climbed into a separate car. Abu Osama motioned for the taxi wreck to follow theirs. We were in motion. I breathed a private sigh of relief. I hadn't wanted to enter that house, in the dark, in handcuffs. As we drove, I tried to think positive thoughts. I told myself that the companion was bringing the Kalashnikov to enhance the safety of our little business enterprise. Were there not bandits about? Was there not a significant sum at stake? We require more gun and more guards, I told myself. In the taxi, as we followed the sedan, there was further chatter about Al Jazeera. It seemed to me that the momentum of things was turning in my favor. There would be a village soon, I thought—Binnish, perhaps—then lights, dinner, maybe a phone.

The sedan led us to a block of shuttered, electricityless flats on the edge of the village of Marat Misrin. We parked in a gravel-strewn patch of dirt. As we were climbing out of the cars, something enormous—a van? a boulder?—hurtled through the air above us. It crashed into the upper floors of a nearby building. I dropped to my knees. Bursts of tracer fire arced through a deep purple sky. "Careful of the shelling," said Behajat. I could see now that he was older and stockier than the others. He directed us to a flight of stairs that led to a landing at the base of one of the apartment buildings. A key materialized. A door opened, and then we were climbing an interior stairwell. We walked up a single flight of stairs, then entered a spacious, carpeted apartment. Cell phones lit our way, and after a few seconds inside the apartment candles appeared. I stood in my bare feet in a clean sitting room. A heavy sofa upholstered in olive-green faux wool sat to my left. There was a velvet painting of a verse from the Koran over the sofa in this room, shuttered windows, and a dining table. In the kitchen, there was a stove and a sink. In the bedroom sat a single well-made bed and a TV set.

The six of us filed into the bedroom. Behajat sat on the side of the bed. He laid his Kalashnikov on the bedspread. He motioned for me to sit at his feet. He twinkled his eyes at me. He shook his head in slow wonderment but did not speak.

He wore a navy-blue wool sweater and tiny reading glasses with a dark octagonal frame. The glasses made him look a bit like Benjamin Franklin. I can deal with this person, I thought.

"It's nice to meet you," I said. I'm sure my voice trembled. I'm sure he noticed this. I asked him his name.

He grinned. "Why do you want to know?" he asked. He gave me a nom de guerre. Was it Abu Baraa, *Father of the Innocent*? Abu Masaakin,

Father of the Poor? It was something obviously fake, along these lines. I don't remember.

We stared at each other for several long seconds. Eventually, Abu Osama interrupted our silence. He sat on the bed next to Behajat. He opened his laptop, tapped at some keys, then invited the others to gather round.

The five of them peered into the laptop screen. Their faces glowed. When the video began, it stopped all movement in their faces. They watched in a trance for thirty seconds or so, and then smiles appeared at the edges of their mouths, and then I heard my own voice from the laptop:

"What is your name?" I said.

"Mohammed," Mohammed replied.

"How old are you?" I asked. He replied.

"I have no more questions," I said. "I'm done."

An interval of silence followed. Abu Osama's voice emerged from the laptop speakers: "Shall we go to it, boys?"

There was a crash, a pause, scuffling, and then my voice came again. "Oof," I said.

The faces in front of me erupted in violent laughter. There was snorting, hand slapping, and more laughter. It seemed to me that the film had done for the new kidnapper what the real-life attack had done for the four people who had enacted it: It brought him into something illicit and delightful. It surprised, though he knew just where the plot was going, and comforted, since the resolution (me bleeding in handcuffs, Abu Osama lecturing) proved that all was right with the world.

The audience wanted a second showing. The second time around cast the same spell of motionlessness over the audience in the beginning and brought out, at the end, the same thigh-slapping mirth and oneness.

Hearing my own voice made me curious about the film. I asked to have a look. Behajat reached for his rifle. He held the sole of his foot in my face. "You sit, Animal," he said.

There was no time for a third viewing. Behajat was in a hurry. He had committee meetings to attend, he said. He had books to read and articles to write.

"Really," I said. "What kind of books?"

He glared at me. He did not speak.

Before he left the apartment, Behajat took a minute to go over the security procedures that were to be observed during the night. He brought me to the sitting room. He unlocked my left hand from the cuffs, then had me sit on the sofa. He smiled, pulled at the empty cuff, then locked it to the sofa's wooden armrest.

"You sleep here," he said.

If my hand was to be locked to the sofa's armrest, I was going to have to sleep sitting up and to hold my arm in the air. I pointed this out.

He shrugged. "Aren't you an agent?" he said. "Haven't you been trained for this? Do your best."

I told him that I would need to pee during the night. He thought for a moment, then stepped into the kitchen. He returned with a plastic bucket. He planted it under the armrest. His quick thinking—or maybe it was the prospect of my being made to pee in a living room, then sleep next to my urine—made his face light up in happiness. "Anything else you need?" he asked. "Any service for you?"

He cocked his Kalashnikov, then handed it to Abu Osama. He made loud whispers into Abu Osama's ear. I didn't catch what was said, but it occurred to me that the Kalashnikov had been brought for me and that I—rather than enemy soldiers or bandits in the night—was the enemy the gun was meant to keep at bay.

Before he left, Behajat took a moment to wish me good night. He stood over the armrest to which my right hand was locked. "Sweet dreams, hero," he said. "Do you need a pillow?" I did not answer him. "Tomorrow will be fun for you. You will meet many friends. Do you like parties?"

Moments later, he and Abu Said slipped out of the apartment. I never saw Abu Said again.

At first, in the silence after their departure, I sat by myself in the darkness. The three kidnappers who remained in the apartment chatted among themselves in the bedroom. I inspected the armrest to which I was locked. My hand had been fastened to a sturdy, milled dowel. It was much too robust a piece of wood to dislodge without an axe or sledgehammer.

The new addition to the kidnappers' gang, I felt, had materialized like a sinister guest. He had refused to tell me his name, had made mocking, honey-voiced threats about a party, had not uttered a word about a phone call or a ransom, and had brought a new, steely sense of purpose to the group, though what this purpose was I could not discern. I hoped he would not return. Mohammed, at least, had told me his name. Perhaps it was false. Fine. He, at least, had a past, was willing to chat with me about it, and did not snicker when I spoke to him.

I hoped he didn't mean for me to spend the rest of the evening by myself, locked in a darkened room. I called out for him. He came right away.

Within seconds of his sitting down next to me, I knew—from his quiet voice and from the personal nature of the conversation he initiated—that he sympathized with my plights.

He said that many, many innocent people had been imprisoned in this war. In his opinion, if I was truly innocent—if I could prove that I had nothing whatsoever to do with the CIA—I would be let go. In the meantime, there were things I ought to know about life in detention. It was natural that I should be afraid now and natural that I should have no appetite. He said that the fear would give way to boredom, and the boredom to loneliness. He told me about the room in which he had had his first interrogation: a cavernous empty hall in a branch of the Syrian state security apparatus, outside of Damascus. The emptiness of the room had terrified him. The officer had screamed at him. At one point during the interrogation, the police had brought in one of his Facebook friends. The friend, he learned then, had all along been working with the secret police. Every incriminating thing he had said to his friend— and there were many—had been printed out on reams of computer paper. He had been certain that they meant to kill him that evening.

Mohammed was speaking to me then in quiet, courteous tones. *We are not such people*, his stories told me. He and I agreed that the regime was afraid of its own shadow and that if it would only agree that its people were good and so leave them in peace all would be well. The state, however, insisted on poking its nose into the minutest details of private life. It was afraid of Islam because it knew nothing of Islam. It hated Muslims. It meant to crush the life of anyone who dared to believe. We shook our heads in sadness. He said that he meant to die before he allowed himself to be imprisoned again.

After a few moments of silence, he rose without a word of prompting from me, whispered with Abu Osama in the neighboring room, and then both of them returned to me.

A handcuff key appeared. I was released from the sofa. I was allowed to pee in the bathroom, to drink without handcuffs, and to eat a bowl of lentils that materialized from the kitchen.

Mohammed turned to Abu Osama. "Where should he sleep?" he asked.

Abu Osama reflected. He gazed at me, grinned, then made a proposal: "Sleep with me. I'll handcuff your hand to mine."

I stared at him. "Really?"

"Like my wife," he said. He smiled.

I protested. There was giggling.

I pointed out that they already had two guns. Handcuffing me to a sleeping body was overkill. "I'll sleep next to you, but no handcuffs. Yes?"

There was more giggling. "You can have the sofa with the cuffs," he said. "Or the bed. With the cuffs. Up to you."

I chose the bed. It was decided then that Abu Osama and I would sleep on the bedroom floor, on a foam-rubber mattress. Mohammed would sleep in that room, on the bed with the bedspread and the pillows. Abu Dujanna and the Kalashnikov would sleep in the sitting room, on the sofa.

Moments after he pulled the cover over our bodies, Abu Osama began to snore. Mohammed's snores were louder and came on just as suddenly. I lay at Abu Osama's side. I felt the warmth of his body through his clothes. My mind reeled. I wanted to twist and gyrate and thrash on the foam-rubber mattress like a cat. But I had to be a considerate bedmate. Abu Osama had taken pity on me. I did my best.

During the first hour of their slumber, I pretended to myself that I was dead. I tried to recite the alphabet backward and to count sheep. After an hour of suppressing my urge to jangle the cuffs, it occurred to me that I could no more fall asleep than I could drift away to the last safe place in which I had slept—Ashraf's hovel. I needed to pee. I wanted to scream.

Around two in the morning, the electricity in the neighborhood decided to turn itself on. The bedroom television flickered to life. A cartoon was playing. "I can't sleep," I announced. Mohammed rose from the bed, turned off an overhead light, turned down the TV sound, then twisted the TV stand so that I could watch from my mattress. "Watch this," he said. I watched *Tom and Jerry* for an hour. I listened to my kidnappers snore. Once, in the small hours of the morning, I reached across my body with my free hand, found the handcuff with my fingers, held it, then wriggled the locked hand. Abu Osama had locked the cuff loosely, out of the goodness of his heart, apparently, but it wasn't so loose that I could ease my hand out. I let the handcuff go. I watched another hour of television. When I could stand it no more, I jangled the cuffs. Abu Osama woke. "May I pee?" I said. A fit of graciousness must have overtaken him. With his free hand, he searched the pockets of a pair of pants he had discarded by the side of the mattress. He found the key, fiddled under the covers, then clicked the cuffs open. This bathroom was inside the bedroom. It had no window. I looked for an air shaft or a loose panel in the ceiling. Nothing.

When I was again lying next to Abu Osama, I held out my wrist to his. He felt for my hand, held the handcuff over my wrist, then closed the ratchet down. "Ouch," I said. "Not too tight."

He loosened the cuff by a single ratchet. *Click* went the cuff. "Better?" he whispered.

"Yes, better," I whispered. The snoring returned. I wriggled my hand halfway through the cuff. I held it there—halfway in, halfway out. I didn't dare move. In those moments, I remained a cooperating, amicable prisoner. This entente was going to save my life. I was much too frightened to hurt it. I wriggled my hand back to where it was meant to be. My heart thumped.

When the dawn prayer came, it was announced via cell phone alarms. The shutters on every window in that apartment had been locked down tight. Against flying shrapnel? To protect the occupants from sniper fire? To pretend that no one was home? That apartment, in any case, was like a cave at the center of the earth. There might have been a muezzin on the apartment's front steps. We wouldn't have heard him. We certainly would not have seen the dawning light. The cell phones, however, brought everyone to life. The kidnappers awoke shortly before four.

Again, Abu Osama brought the handcuff key under the covers. He unlocked the cuffs from both of our wrists. He made his ablutions, waited as the others made theirs, then invited me to use the bathroom. As they prayed, I waited on the mattress for Abu Osama. When he was again by my side and the lights were off, I again held out my hand to his. "Not too tight, okay?" I whispered to him as he closed the handcuff over my wrist.

"Shut up," he said.

It took a few minutes for the kidnappers to put themselves to sleep. When their snores were again filling the room, I wriggled my hand until it was half inside the cuff and half free. If Abu Osama had woken then, I could have told him that I was trying to make myself comfortable, that I had been asleep, that I hadn't realized where my hand had gotten to.

A moment later, I slipped my hand out of the cuff altogether. I let it rest by Abu Osama's side. If my bedmate had woken then, it would have been harder to persuade him that I was a cooperative, good-natured kidnap victim. Still, I might somehow have managed to make him believe that I had wriggled free in my sleep. Even when I stood up and looked down on his slumbering body, I imagined that I wasn't exactly putting myself in danger since I might have been able to insist that I only meant to pee. I had done it a dozen times already. I knew the rules. What was the big deal?

Imagining myself reciting some such lie, I stepped over Abu Osama's sleeping body. I eyed the handgun next to Mohammed's pillow. I paused by the bathroom. Then I floated across a tiled entry hall.

I caressed the latch on the front door. I whispered to the doorknob. I floated down the stairwell.

At the bottom of these stairs, sunlight streamed from beneath a heavy steel door. I was certain it would be locked. In a panic, I thrashed at the bolt. I kicked at the base of the door. An ungodly din rose through the stairwell. I kicked again. The door popped open of its own accord, as heavy steel doors that are not locked sometimes do. I stepped into the dawn.

I was no longer my kidnappers' friend then—no longer a cooperative, curious, wry prisoner who wanted to call up Al Jazeera because why not? I was, however, free. I began to sprint.

When I encountered a traffic divider about twenty meters from the apartment steps, the curb sent me sailing through the air. I experienced that crash in surreal slow motion, as people who fall from high places sometimes do. It was a sensation of soaring through golden sunbeams. I felt the pavement coming but also felt I could put off the impact, turn down alleys as I flew, and keep on flying, perhaps for several minutes.

The crash, as it happened, caused a pleasurable jolt to run through my body. I skidded on my palms for a moment, popped to my feet, then ran much faster than I had run before. Even if Abu Osama and his friends had been reaching their fingers around my shirt collar, which I thought faintly possible, I was certain my body had more agility to it and more power than theirs would ever have, so I ran like a real-life Jason Bourne, as if their catching me meant their killing me, as it might well have done. So I tore through the morning light. I raced down the central boulevard in Marat Misrin. I flew over the traffic dividers, dodged the parked cars, and rocketed through the center of the village's clock-tower square. I did not stop until about four kilometers of village scenery had gone by—ample time and space, I hoped, to have lost my kidnappers for good.

CHAPTER 3

THE FALCONS OF THE LAND OF SHAM

Marat Misrin, October 2012

Later that day, the officers of the Free Syrian Army post to which I fled decided that a proper Guantánamo-like interrogation was in order. They hung me by my wrists from a sort of a scaffolding that had been erected over a cement irrigation pool. They poured water into my face as they beat my head and hands with steel cables. They wanted to know where I had been trained and which branch of the American government had done it. "How many people have you killed?" they yelled. Somehow, the sight of an American struggling to breathe under an ad hoc water torture struck these officers as comical. My interrogation, for these officers, was more of a comedy than it was an interrogation.

At first, however, they were the picture of chivalry. In the morning, when I presented myself at their door—it would have been just past six—they greeted me like law-and-order men anywhere in the world greet a victim who comes to them for aid and protection. They were well aware that a tide of lawlessness was sweeping through the district. But when they heard what my kidnappers had done to me, and when I told them that the kidnappers had announced themselves to me as members of al Qaeda, they were indignant. As I talked, they shook their heads in silence. They promised that they would make things right.

I had introduced myself to them in a panic.

At first, imagining that Abu Dujanna and Abu Osama were breathing down my neck, I threw myself at the steel door of their HQ. A brigade of the Free Syrian Army had established itself in the police station in Marat Misrin. I shook the door and screamed. Abu Osama and his friends, I assumed, were hot on my heels. "Journalist!" I yelled. "American journalist!"

I'm sure I woke the neighborhood. Eventually, after a minute or so, a boy—about ten?—let me in.

I flew past him, tore down a hallway, then burst through an open door. I paused on the threshold of a spacious office, the perimeter of which had been lined with cots. A half-dozen soldiers were waking from sleep. They propped themselves on their elbows in their beds. They squinted at me.

I was incandescent with fear. I didn't care who knew it. I assumed that the child who had opened the door had not had the wit to lock it again. If Abu Osama and Abu Dujanna were pursuing me, as I assumed they were, they would burst through the doors, level their guns, then open fire. I didn't want to die in a hail of bullets.

So I searched the room for the safest, most bullet-resistant spot within it. In addition to the beds, the room contained a heavy desk, office chairs, a blackboard, and a conference table on which the soldiers had laid out their Kalashnikovs and their cigarettes.

Eyeing a dark corner, under a cot, I pushed my way past the conference table. I shoved a pair of boots and a stray Kalashnikov a soldier had stored under his cot out of my way. I tucked myself in under this soldier's bed. Even if my captors had strafed the entire office with gunfire, they wouldn't have been able to aim at my head, I felt, since it was well concealed behind the flap of an army blanket. I pressed my cheek into the floor. I didn't move a muscle. I meant to wait for things to calm down out there, in the world beyond my hiding place.

It took at least a minute for the soldiers to reckon with my arrival. "What's wrong with him?" one of them wondered, eventually, in a voice heavy with sleep. A hand lifted up the flap of the army blanket. A smiling face hovered over the floor. "Come out from there," the soldier said. "You're in safety. What's wrong with you?"

The boy spoke for me. "He says he's a journalist."

"You're in safety," the soldier said. And then a chorus of men's

116

voices repeated versions of this assurance: "No one can hurt you here." "You are with the Free Army." "You're safe."

I decided that the voices were probably right. By cowering under a bed, I was making myself ridiculous. If I undo my mistake, I told myself, I might recover a measure of dignity before too many of the soldiers figure out what's going on.

So I pushed the army blanket out of my way. I smiled at the soldier nearest me, crawled from under his bed, then sat on its foot. "Those people!" I stammered. "Kidnapped! They have guns! They were going to kill me."

A half-dozen men, each face groggy but surprised and half-smiling, gaped at me. "Calm down," the voices said. Was I okay? Had I been injured? Who were those people?

A half hour later, after the door boy had been sent out for breakfast— when he had returned with plates of falafel, hummus, plastic sacks of bread, and pickled vegetables, as I was drinking my fifth glass of tea—it seemed to me as though I had stumbled on a passageway that led back through time, into the Syria I had known before the war. All six soldiers in the room had a glass of tea and a mobile phone on the conference table in front of them. Each had a cigarette in his hand, and each seemed to feel that the time had come to draw deeply on a cigarette, to smile at the absurdity of life, and to wait for other, still more absurd things to happen. Nobody was in a hurry to do a thing. The men drew on their cigarettes and smiled as I told my story.

Even when I uttered neutral, unfunny phrases—"A half hour ago, I felt myself two feet from the grave," "I ran like a lunatic," "I can't believe I am here with you," and so on—the soldiers burst into appreciative laughter. They smiled at every sentence I uttered. An odd but delightful form of entertainment had come to them. It produced one hilarious phrase after the next. They smoked and giggled. Nobody in the room, it seemed, wanted the fun to stop.

Somehow, the flow of conversation took us to a *fatteh* and shawarma restaurant in my old Damascus neighborhood called The Goat's Beard. I repeated a judgment I had heard once on the lips of a university student in Damascus: Given that their chicken sandwiches were made out of goat meat, lunch there ought to be cheaper than it was. I spoke of the Damascus pop band I used to listen to and of the mosque on the hillside above the city in which I used to study the Koran.

In the midst of my ramblings, a soldier whose bull-like neck and shoulders suggested a past as a professional weight lifter excused himself to place several nearly wordless calls. Yes, he said after he hung up. The higher-ups in this *katiba*, or battalion, were on their way to the police station now. In the meantime, did I need more tea? Did I know which branch of the Free Syrian Army I was dealing with? He pointed to an insignia that had been drawn over the office chalkboard. The group called itself "al Katiba Suqor as Sham Idlib" or the Falcons of the Levant, Idlib Battalion.

The weight lifter retrieved his mobile phone from the table, set it to play a Fairuz ballad I happened to know, then returned it to the breakfast table. "Remember the last time I saw you?" she crooned. "For so long I haven't seen you and now I do. So how're things?"

Since I was the first foreign journalist to turn up among the Falcons, the weight lifter told me, the leaders of the group would want to make sure I was okay. They would want to hear my story for themselves. I waited for him to say, "After which they will bring you to wherever you would like to go." He did not say this.

Yet these soldiers certainly believed my story. I had related it in plain language, without contradicting myself. I gave the soldiers the names the kidnappers had given me, and offered a physical description of each one. I described the car, the apartment from which I had escaped, and the house in the olive grove from which Abu Osama's cousin had emerged. "We'll find them, don't worry," the weight lifter assured me.

As he was filling my tea glass, the *katiba*'s ten-year-old motioned for me to turn my ear to his lips. "They'll be executed," he said of my kidnappers. He grinned, then pushed a plate of roasted eggplant toward me. "One bullet," he said. "That's it."

Around nine thirty in the morning, the weight lifter asked me in a friendly tone of voice to explain what exactly I had come to Syria to do. Was it normal, he wondered, that a journalist should come to Syria from America with nothing more than a cell phone camera and a notebook? "No press ID and by himself and fifty dollars in Turkish liras in his pocket?" he asked. "What newspaper do you work for?"

"I work for many newspapers," I said, lying. I tried to explain about the difficulties of the freelancer's life. "Most of the editors are pretty ignorant, if you ask me," I said. "They don't want anything to do with Syria because they can't understand." Their indifference was the reason I had to go it alone, and on a shoestring.

He sighed. He dropped the topic.

Another university-age soldier whose friendly, inquisitive eyes and flowing tresses reminded me of friends I had known during my earlier life in Syria wanted me to discuss the relationships I had had when I lived in Damascus. Had there been any girls? No, I lied. But I had had male friends with whom I studied and others with whom I had played sports.

He wanted to know where these people lived. I named a pair of rebel-friendly neighborhoods.

Before the war, I said, I had been under the impression that Damascus was like a mosaic in which all the pieces came down from their places during the daytime, swirled around together, then went home again in the evenings. For me, living in that turbulence of religions and customs had been like living in a movie in which, every few minutes, the characters taught me new things about life.

I knew Syrians could get along, I said. I had seen it myself and had felt it. I wished that the warring parties could figure out a way to talk through their issues. The soldiers in the room stared at me.

"To be honest," I said, "I had many friends. Some with the president. Some against him."

The weight lifter gave me a skeptical look. "Two and a half years in Damascus," he agreed after a moment, nodding. "And many friends. Good for you." He checked his phone. He looked around the room. He wondered if I thought I would be able to find the apartment in which I had been held the previous night.

"Probably," I said.

"In which case, we'll fetch your friends right now," he said.

"They have guns," I told him.

He smiled. "Our guns are bigger."

I looked around the room. Did everyone think this was a good idea? "I'm happy to be alive," I said. It had been my mistake to surrender myself to bandits. "I didn't lose anything of value," I said. "I don't care about the passport."

"You will get your shoes back," he said.

"Okay," I said.

"And your money, passport, and phone. You don't want these things?"

I did want these things.

"These criminals might well kidnap us, too," he explained. "We need to find them for our own sake." In any case, he said, before I went anywhere the leaders of the *katiba* would have to take my statement. Maybe they would want me to identify suspects. Nothing could happen without their signing off on things.

So I was caught within the workings of a Syrian bureaucracy. It was hardly the first time. In Damascus, I had come to know the central offices of the bureaucracy and the branch ones. I had come to know what they smelled like: military men, smoke, tea, sweat. I had come to feel that while no human could know the details of its inner workings, eventually, in the fullness of time, it would deliver the things I wished it to deliver.

Around eleven, when combat vests had been donned, handguns tucked into shoulder holsters, and packages of cigarettes stuffed into breast pockets, it was decided that the time had come to set off in search of the criminals. I murmured words of protest. They were ignored.

A jeep whose markings indicated that it had been appropriated from the former government sat in front of the police station. I climbed into the front seat. The weight-lifting soldier dropped his Kalashnikov on the bench seat next to me. He swung himself into the driver's seat. Two Kalashnikov-bearing soldiers hopped into the rear seat. A second jeep followed us. Our posse rolled forward, along the avenue I had sprinted down at dawn that morning. The purpose of this mission was to apprehend bandits and to recover my stolen property. Since I was telling the soldiers where to go, I was in charge. As we drove, I tried to think thoughts along these lines, but ten minutes into our search, when the jeep stopped in front of a dirt pit by the side of an apartment building and the soldiers dismounted, then pointed with their Kalashnikovs down a flight of stairs that had been chopped into the clay, I declined to go where they asked me to go. They uttered courteous phrases: "Be our guest." "Don't be afraid." "You're with us." I couldn't do it. Eventually, one of the soldiers walked down the stairs himself, smiled, shone his cell phone about, and then reached for my hand.

Inside the pit, following a warren of passageways that led toward the nearby apartment building, we found a second set of stairs that led upward, into a neat, silent, unoccupied apartment. It could have been a hotel room for business travelers. Its windows had been shuttered. The bed was made. The kitchen was spotless. We sat for several minutes on a couch. When the soldiers from the other jeep turned up, one of them handed me a plastic bag. It contained new shoes, underwear, pants, a shirt, and a razor. I was shown to the shower.

My old clothes went into the trash. A soldier pointed me to a bottle of cologne in a medicine chest in the bathroom.

Thus spritzed up, I returned with the soldiers to their jeep. We came across Abu Osama right away, within a hundred meters of the apartment. He and a friend I did not recognize were emerging from a fruit and vegetable seller's shop. Abu Osama held a bunch of bananas in his hand. A soldier descended from our jeep, accosted him and the friend, and then I watched from the safety of the jeep as an argument erupted in front of Abu Osama's taxi. Passersby gathered. Other soldiers descended from the army jeeps. Abu Osama stood stricken in front of a crate of apples. He stared at the crowd for a moment, began to shout, and then one of the soldiers delivered a sharp smack to the side of Abu Osama's head.

This ended whatever argument had begun. Abu Osama surrendered his keys. He allowed the soldiers to search his car. On the floor of the back seat, a soldier found the red backpack that came with me from Turkey. The weight lifter had it brought to me.

The soldiers conferred for a moment. It was decided that one soldier should sit in the taxi back seat with Abu Osama and his friend, while another drove the taxi wreck back to the police station.

When we arrived, the weight lifter escorted me to the chalkboard office in which, by this point, a gathering of some twenty-five men, most of whom wore long beards and combat vests, had assembled. A voluble discussion was underway in which each of the twenty-five, it seemed, wished to hold the floor.

The discussion abated for a second as I took my seat at the conference table. Eyes fell on me, but no one spoke to me. Abu Osama and his friend, I understood, were being taken to a cell. As my eyes adjusted to the interior light, I could not help noticing that the new men at the station, even the two watery-eyed, gray-bearded sheikhs who watched me with gaping, quivering mouths, were covered in weaponry. The younger men, most of whom were standing, had turned up at this meeting with knives and handguns tucked into their belts. The elder men wore their handguns under their shoulders in police-style holsters.

After he had made his greetings, the weight lifter asked me to pour the contents of my backpack onto the conference table. The items Abu Osama and his friend had left me were the Paul Theroux book, a pair of orange plastic sandals, and a loaf of Turkish bread I had brought for snacking. The contents were returned to the pack and the pack returned to me.

One of the new men in the office was the chief to whom I was meant to relate my saga. But which one? I scanned their faces. None of them seemed eager to discuss matters with me, but when the soldier who had driven Abu Osama and his taxi to the station appeared in the office doorway all the eyes in the room turned to him. He turned his eyes to me. "You are from the CIA?" he said. He smiled. I smiled back. The absurdity of the remark spoke for itself, I thought. "Anyway," he said. "They arrested you for spying."

I protested. The phone call to Mom and Dad, the quarter kilo of gold, the al Qaeda claim—I blurted out the details of the story I had related earlier in the morning. As I spoke, my eyes darted around the room. The assemblage listened to the first words I spoke, but a wave of deep-throated argumentation overwhelmed the second sentence and the third. I persisted. I sought out the weight lifter's eyes. He ignored me. The argument increased in volume.

I tried to chip in. After five minutes or so, a lull in the argument gave me my chance.

"The CIA is against Bashar al-Assad," I said to no one in particular. "They're on your side."

The weight lifter turned to me. "Bashar protects America's baby girl, Israel," he said under his breath. "No matter what they say, under the table, the Americans will always be on Bashar's side."

"I am not from the CIA," I said. I held my cheap backpack and my plastic orange sandals in the air. "This isn't CIA stuff," I said. The weight lifter glanced at my exhibits for a moment, smiled, but perhaps only to himself, then returned to the argument his colleagues were having. I tried to follow it. It concerned previous military engagements, places I did not know, and people I had never heard of. I waited for someone to bring order to the gathering.

After ten minutes or so, a gunshot went off in an adjoining room. The argument stopped dead. Now they have killed Abu Osama, I thought. I made eye contact with the weight lifter. He listened for a moment, then made a sheepish grin, then shrugged. The tea boy appeared in the doorway. His face radiated impish happiness. He held a Kalashnikov in one hand. One of the soldiers—an elder brother?— barked at him. The boy had had permission to fire the gun into the air, he said, but not from the courtyard next door to the conference room. "What is wrong with you?" said the elder soldier. The boy lowered his head. He walked the Kalashnikov back to its owner, surrendered the gun, took a playful slap on the cheek, then walked out of the room, his eyes dancing with happiness.

A few minutes later, when Abu Osama was brought before this assemblage, the backpack he had brought from Turkey into Syria was emptied out onto the conference table, as mine had been. He had staggered under the weight of that backpack two days earlier, during our crossing over. Now I watched as a little treasure trove of handcuffs, balaclavas, black woolen gloves, a bundle of plastic zip ties, a pair of

Leatherman-like foldable vise grips, a scattering of empty cell phone cases, camera bags, cables, and flashlight lasers spread itself across the table. The weight lifter swirled his hand through the loot. He picked up, then dropped a heavy wad of American bills. There would have been several thousand dollars in that bundle. The weight lifter shone a laser flashlight around the room, then returned it to Abu Osama's little lake of goods.

Abu Osama launched into a defense. His panic made him blurt out his sentences in a pitter-patter of disconnected phrases. He knew for sure that I was a spy because I spoke Farsi (I do not) and Hebrew (I do not), had been exchanging messages in Russian on my mobile phone (true), had CIA contacts in the Kurdish Mountains (a lie), had spied for years in Yemen (more lies), then come to Syria in order to track down Muslims the CIA might wish to assassinate. "They've been training him for years." He explained that during the arrest, I had fought like a lion, was far stronger than I looked, and had mastered a series of mental tricks. "He knows how to break out of handcuffs. He doesn't sleep! He doesn't eat!" The weight lifter did not bother to dignify these accusations with a reply. He smiled indulgently at Abu Osama. He did not look at me.

Eventually, one of the Falcons spoke up. If Abu Osama had begun to doubt that I was actually a journalist, the Falcon asked, he might have brought me directly to the police station. What business did he have in detaining me overnight? He was not the law enforcement authority in Marat Misrin. "You have no job," said this soldier. "Where do you get your money from?"

The room erupted in new volleys of shouting. So no one is in control now, I told myself, the argument is the point, they adore shouting at one another, and when the excitement of it all passes, a ranking officer will allow me to say my piece.

So when this stormy weather passes, I told myself, I will recount the facts. The officers will listen. Eventually, I knew, someone would bring me my passport and my cell phone. Someone else would bring me back to Turkey. The community would deal with Abu Osama, in the fullness of time, however it saw fit.

As I was thinking these thoughts, Behajat burst into the office. "Salaam *alaykum* to everyone!" he called out. He greeted the officers by name, then reached across the conference table to shake these colleagues' hands. I stood up to offer him mine. He declined to shake it.

Behajat launched himself into a speech. His cousin, as everyone knew, had a strong faith in God. Behajat urged anyone doubting the sincerity of Abu Osama's commitment to Islam to consult with the religious authorities of Marat Misrin. In addition, Abu Osama had been present at the most important battles in the war to date, which he had filmed, then uploaded to the internet. There could be no doubting his valor. As for the American spy, Behajat said, he didn't know if I had come to spy for Russia, America, the Jews, or all of them, but having spoken to me the previous evening and having examined my passport and my mobile phone, he was certain of one thing, which was that my story about being a journalist was a lie. "If he is a journalist, let him show you a press pass. A business card? Who does he work for? No cameras. No colleagues. Why has he come? What business does he have here? Ask him. He will lie to you in five different languages."

Toward the end of his speech, Behajat asked that I be removed from the room. A younger soldier, carrying a Kalashnikov, showed me to a chair in the center of an adjoining empty room. From this office chair, I listened as Behajat fulminated for several minutes. At last, the soldiers from my earlier morning posse came to fetch me. They took me by the elbows, escorted me outside, down the police station's front steps, and then into a crowd of about twenty young men who had gathered in the street. "Welcome!" voices in the crowd called out in English, and, "Hello, my friend!" And also: "Fuckyoo!" and "Donkey!"

The soldiers asked the crowd to make way. I was allowed to climb into the back seat of a Land Cruiser. One of the soldiers sat to my left, another to my right. Other soldiers climbed into other jeeps and Land Cruisers, and soon a minor expeditionary force composed of pickups, Land Cruisers, and one beat-up taxi was rolling out of Marat Misrin, into the fields beyond.

It took us about twenty minutes to reach the border-crossing station at Bab al-Hawa. As we were pulling into the parking lot in front of an administrative building here, the driver of our Land Cruiser rolled down his window. A sentry approached. "It's Monday," said the sentry. "The court doesn't meet on Mondays."

"Bring the judge," our driver said.

"You bring him," said the sentry.

This exchange prompted the soldiers in our Land Cruiser to get out, to consult with the other drivers in our column of SUVs and pickup trucks, and then everyone was tapping numbers into mobile phones.

"Where is the judge?" the soldiers near me said into their phones. "Can he come now? Why not? When can he come?"

"I'll bring him myself," our driver barked into his phone. "Where is he?"

Eventually, the judge's transportation to the court was sorted out. It was agreed that the Falcons and I would wait for his arrival in his office.

Thus about twenty soldiers, Behajat, Abu Osama, and I were escorted upstairs, into one of those spacious wood-paneled offices in which, not so many months earlier, a portrait of the president would have beamed down from above the enormous desk at the front of the room.

There were no portraits in this office. A man with a mustache and neatly trimmed hair, wearing a button-down camouflage shirt, sat at the desk. A pair of elderly gentlemen, their hands resting on their canes, napped on a sofa to his left. The Falcons settled themselves into armchairs and a dilapidated sofa. The younger man sat on the floor. Now we were all at the mercy of someone else's bureaucracy. The Falcons knew just what to do. They pulled out their mobile phones and their cigarettes. Abu Osama and Behajat sat together in a corner. They whispered between themselves.

I introduced myself to the man at the desk. I told him that I was a journalist, that I had written about the character of the regime, and that I hoped to understand the deeper causes of the war. I repeated some phrases I had heard on the lips of a rebel in a YouTube clip. The war had started out as a popular uprising, involving all classes of people in Syria, I said, but the government had taken to mobilizing its own religious sect against the demonstrators. The result was that its sect, the

Alawites, who practiced a religion that had almost nothing to do with Islam, was now making war, for God only knew what reason, against the Syrian people. "So, yes," I said to the official at the desk, "it has become a sectarian war. A minority is trying to rid itself of the majority. This is what I write about. This is what I want the officials in Washington to understand."

The official at the desk reached out his hand to me. We exchanged grave looks. "You are always welcome in Syria," he said. He told me his name, volunteered to speak to the judge on my behalf, told me I was an honorable journalist, then offered me a glass of tea, which I accepted.

As he and I drank our teas, he examined his mobile phone. I turned to Behajat and Abu Osama. Catching Behajat's eyes, I told him that I wasn't angry, that I didn't think he had done anything wrong and didn't want anything from him. I raised my voice so that the entire room could hear. "There is nothing between us," I said. "You owe me nothing. I owe you nothing. Okay?"

I was within a thousand feet of the Turkish border then. If my kidnappers had agreed not to press the issue, I could have walked myself to safety.

"Okay?" I asked again. I might as well have been speaking to the wind. My kidnappers did not reply to me. The soldiers watched me pleading but said nothing.

Eventually, the judge breezed into the office. He was in his mid-twenties. He wore a ponytail, a silky white shirt, and flowing Pakistani pants. He stood in the center of the room in order to better address everyone at once.

"What's happened here?" he asked. "There is a problem?"

A white-bearded Falcon who later became known as Abu Jaber, the front man for a coalition of rebels calling themselves the Front for the Conquest of the Levant, spoke on behalf of the Falcons. Nodding at me, he said, "The young man said he is an American. He came to us this morning. He said he'd been kidnapped. The others say he's a spy. That's all."

The judge turned to me. "American?"

"Yes," I said.

He turned back to Abu Jaber. "You'll have to bring us a translator."

I didn't realize then that something like a trial was about to happen, that I was a defendant, accused of spying for the US government, that the presence of two witnesses against me constituted something like an indictment, and that these witnesses would be my kidnappers. I had the feeling I was meant to explain myself to a judge. He would find the articles about Syria I had written on the *New Republic* website. Maybe he would look at my Facebook page. Satisfying himself that I was indeed a journalist, he would let me go.

"Never mind about the translator," I told him. "I'll speak to you myself. I have nothing to hide."

The judge smiled at me. "Excellent," he said. "Shall we begin?"

He invited Behajat and Abu Osama into his chambers. I remained in the office with the soldiers. I drank more tea, stared out the window, and searched the room for a sympathetic pair of eyes. sky. After an hour of this, the judge returned Abu Osama and Behajat to the room in which I was sitting. He had a soldier escort me to an inner office. The judge sat behind a heavy wooden desk. He adjusted the video camera he had mounted on a tripod on his desk. "Sit," he said. "Tea?"

I declined.

"You are not a Muslim?" he asked.

"No."

"Do you speak Farsi?"

"No."

"Russian?"

"Yes, a little."

"How many times have you visited Tel Abib?"

"Never."

"And Moscow?"

"Never."

He paused. He gave me a sympathetic smile. "Are you afraid?"

"Yes," I said.

"But why?" he wondered, in a baffled voice, as if I hadn't a reason in the world to be afraid. "What is the reason for your fear?"

I said that I didn't know why I was afraid. "I need help. I am not a spy," I told him. If he could give me access to the internet, I said, I could prove to him in an instant that I was a journalist.

"I'm sure you have written many articles," he said. "You'll agree that that doesn't mean you are not, also, a spy?"

He wondered what I had been doing during the two weeks I had spent in Antakya. I told him about Ashraf's hovel, my dwindling supply of cash, and my plan to write a sweeping essay about Syria.

"So money was the reason for you coming to Syria? You admit this?" I didn't want to admit anything. He pressed me. In fact, I had come to Syria to make money.

"I never do anything for money," I said. "If I had wanted money, I would have stayed home."

He gave me a dubious look. "But you did not stay home. You must have come for money. Why not admit this?"

"Yes, okay," I said. "I needed money."

"Good," he said. "Very good." He asked if, in my opinion, anyone at all could come out for the jihad.

"Of course not," I said. "A *mujahid*"—one who fights in the jihad— "must have learning from the Koran. He must understand why he does what he does."

The judge nodded. He looked into the viewfinder in his video camera. "True," he said. He rubbed his chin. "You're not a journalist, are you? Not really, right?"

I insisted that I was a journalist. We argued. I had no press card. I had no fixed employer. I knew no other journalists who were currently working in Syria. "Yet you are a journalist, you say. Very well," he said. "Is there anything else?"

"Will you allow me to show you my articles on the internet?" I asked.

"Of course," he said. "Is there anything else?"

There was not. He called out to a sentry posted outside his office. "Prepare a room for him downstairs," he said. The soldier escorted me out of the office, down two flights of stairs, then into a basement cell block. He opened a black steel door. He pushed me through, into a dank closet, about the size of a phone booth, then locked the door.

This cell's previous occupant had left crusts of bread on the floor. A tin dish sat in a corner. The cell reeked of sewage. I stood on a squishy, discolored patch of carpet, the center of which sagged over a hole in the floor.

The soldier told me to lift the carpet when I needed the toilet. He would be in the next room. If I tried to escape, he would shoot me. "Need anything else?" he asked, then walked away.

I stood to the side of the hole. I examined the steel door and the cell's window, which was about ten feet off the floor. A hatch in the base of the door, like a flap for a cat, seemed big enough to accommodate my head. I knelt on the carpet, then tucked my head under the flap. From the hallway outside my cell, the soldier spoke: "We'll shoot you," he said. "You want a bullet?" I withdrew my head. Several minutes later, a tapping from the cell next door to mine drew my attention: "Put out your head, brother," said a voice.

I poked my head through the flap. The occupant of the cell next door, a middle-aged man whose hair had been neatly trimmed into a white crew cut, poked his head through his flap. He made a gentlemanly smile. "Welcome," he said. "Where are you from?" His head withdrew and then a boy, about twelve, poked his head through the same flap. As our eyes met, the boy's face lit up with happiness. "How are you doing?" he whispered. "What is your name? What is the news from your side?"

I asked him what he had been accused of. He made a sheepish grin, then nodded toward the room from which the soldier had threatened me. "We're Shia," he whispered. He made a mocking face at the room next door, as if we were naughty students. The guards were rule-bound schoolmasters. The boy was ready for recess. "What did you do?" he asked.

"Nothing," I said. "I was kidnapped."

"Kidnapped?" he said. He gave a surprised laugh. "Us too!"

To my left, the occupants of a larger cell, about the size of a small elevator, which contained about six prisoners, were listening to this dialog. I was just beginning to introduce myself to these people when a guard came to unlock my cell door. He seized my wrist, then escorted

me into a hallway in which the mustachioed chief from the upstairs
office stood staring, as if stunned. The dark shadow that had fallen over
his face told me he had bad, maybe devastating news to convey. In fact,
he said nothing. He stepped aside. From the shadows behind him, Abu
Osama, Behajat, Mohammed, and a cluster of new comrades—perhaps
six people in all—grinned at me. Abu Osama reached out for my hand,
as if greeting a long-lost friend. Behajat seized me by the elbow. Abu
Osama took the other elbow. We marched up a flight of stairs, through
a series of rooms in which soldiers lounged, then outside, into a parking lot. On the courthouse steps, more young men, some in jeans and
T-shirts, some dressed for the jihad, with scraps of white cloth bearing
the testament of faith around their foreheads, turned to stare at us.

At the rear door of the taxi wreck, Abu Osama put me in the handcuffs I had wriggled out of earlier that morning. People I did not know
climbed into the seat next to me. Abu Osama, beside himself with happiness, sat in the front seat. His eyes gleamed.

He would have been through my mobile phone by this point. He
would have found the Facebook messages I had written to an acquaintance in Russian. As the car pulled away from the station, he turned to
me and patted my knee. *"Kak dyela?"* he chortled. *"Ochen khorosho?"* In
Arabic, he asked me, "So you work for Russia, too? Iran? Israel? All of
them?"

Behajat undid the scarf he wore around his head. He thrust the
scarf into the hands of a comrade in the back seat. "Blindfold his eyes,"
he said. The comrade seized my head. He wrapped the scarf around
my head in a fury, like someone fighting to tie down a spitting cat, then
thrust my head toward the floor. Hands punched at my shoulders and
at the side of my head. A boot sole pressed itself into the back of my
neck.

The car drove slowly. "Nobody talk," Behajat ordered. The car
purred, then picked up speed, and then we were soaring down a
highway.

We drove at high speeds for about ten minutes, then came to a stop
over crunching gravel. Hands reached into my hair, then dragged me
from the car. I remember staggering down a lane, the shouting of my

captors—to hurry, to shut up, to run—and then the door to a house was opening. Fists were ripping at my clothing and my hair. I was in bare feet being hurried across a carpet, possibly in a living room. My blindfold slipped enough to allow me a glimpse of a man on a mattress on the floor. He was waking from sleep. He propped himself on his elbow. Above his mattress an enormous black flag, big enough to cover the breadth of a living room wall, bore the testament of faith in an ornate cursive. I held the man's eyes for an instant, and then I was being pushed through further rooms. A door opened. I was outside and running again, this time with many hands pulling my head by fistfuls of hair.

My feet sank into the dirt. I fell, was dragged to my feet, then ran on. About a hundred meters from the house, in the midst of what I imagined to be a recently plowed field, my captors paused. I felt my legs climbing down into the earth. At the bottom of a tiny flight of steps I was made to kneel. The butt of a gun hit me across my back. I tumbled, headfirst, into soft earth. Above me, there was light. I knew that my captors were up there, on the surface of the earth, crouching at the rim of this pit, but how many of them there were I did not know. Ten? Twenty? I heard the sound of cocking Kalashnikovs. They kicked clumps of earth into the pit. I clenched my eyes shut. So I was to die in a pit in a field? How suddenly one's fate presents itself, I thought. I hope it's over quickly, I told myself. But how will my parents ever find out what has become of me? I raised my elbows over my head. Probably, I thought, the bullets will not hurt. Because no bullets came, I listened to the men above me jeering. "Bring the camera," a voice called out from somewhere above me. A second, faraway voice, possibly answering from the house through which I had just been trundled, replied, "Where is the camera? Which one?"

As the camera issue was being sorted, the men lobbed insults at me. I was an enemy of God, a devil, filth. Their boots kicked splashes of earth over my body. "Hey, you. Animal!" a voice shouted, in a tone used to frighten dogs in the street. "You comfortable?" Another person climbed into the pit with me. He slammed the butt of his rifle into my chest. He kicked at my legs and thighs, then climbed out. From the lip of the pit, he launched himself through the air. He landed with both feet on my chest, balanced for a moment, then stomped his feet down on my elbows and shoulders, as if he meant to pound my body deeper into the earth. This soldier wanted me to call him "sir." He wanted me to tell him that I had come to Syria to spy, that my name was Spy (and Jew-American and Animal and Filth), and that I would soon be in hell.

"Yes, my name is Spy," I told him.

He slammed a rifle butt into my chest. "Your name is Spy, what?" he asked.

More blows from the rifle butt came. Eventually, I caught on. "Spy, sir!" I called out.

"Good!" he said.

"And a Jew-American?"

"Yes, Jew-American, sir!" I called out.

This person, whose voice, I was sure, had been with me over breakfast, as we listened to a pop song about love, asked me if I liked the taste of dirt. He—or someone—must have had a shovel. Heavy showers of dirt poured over my stomach. They splashed over my legs and covered my feet. "Eat," voices told me. "Very good Syrian earth. You like?"

As the ordeal dragged on, a fake argument broke out among my tormentors over whether or not my life was worth the cost of a bullet. "But the bullet is twenty-five Syrian liras," said one voice. "Please. Give him the knife." A voice screamed: "Animal! Hey, devil! The knife in the neck you want?"

Another voice countered: "But he is a polite little boy, isn't he? Yes. So give him a bullet."

Moments later one of the tormentors again climbed into the pit. He bent down, then whispered into my ear, "Shh. Don't say a word. I am from the Air Force Intelligence." He said that he knew of a way to deliver me into the care of his friends in the Syrian government. It would cost me. Did I want his help?

"Yes," I murmured.

"It'll cost a thousand Syrian liras," he whispered—about $16.

"Gimme quick, okay?" I did not reply. "Wait," he said. "What? You're all out?" He climbed out of the pit. He addressed his friends: "Says he's got nothing. Not a penny. Busted flat. What a time to go broke!" The group burst into laughter.

There came a period during my ordeal in this pit when Abu Osama and Behajat put religious questions to me. Behajat announced to the six or seven people crouching at the lip of this hole that I had memorized bits of the Koran. "Recite!" he ordered. I recited a pair of lines. "You see?" he said to the others, as if my having memorized the Koran were the crime for which I was being punished. He wanted to know if I believed in the angels of God. "I don't know," I screamed. Did I believe in the reality of paradise? I didn't know.

"Do you believe in the Prophet of God?" he asked.

"I don't know," I screamed.

So I had lived in Yemen and Syria for years, he observed, had memorized bits of the Koran, and never, not once, had I wished to enter the religion of Islam?

"No," I said.

"Why not?"

"I don't know," I said.

"Devil," a voice replied. More dirt dribbled into the pit.

"Who is the Prophet of God?" a voice asked.

"Mohammed?" I answered.

"Not Jesus?" said the voice.

"I don't know," I said. A heavy shovelful of earth spilled over my forehead. Much later, I discovered that a few weeks after he inflicted this torture on me, Abu Osama posted a video to his Facebook page, which recapitulated this scene down to the smallest scraps of dialog. The video, an animation with cartoonlike characters and an orchestral soundtrack, was produced by a website called IslamExplained. com. What shall become of the unbeliever in the moments after his death? According to a legend known as the Trial of the Grave, a pair of angels bearing mighty hammers will come to the unbeliever just as he is settling himself into his crypt. An interrogation will begin. After the unbeliever has admitted the faithlessness with which he has gone about his life, the angels will smite him, over and over, until his body sinks away into the abyss beneath the grave. I suspect now that Abu Osama and his friends' real purpose on that afternoon wasn't so much to punish me for spying or for my lifelong refusal to become a Muslim but to make the old myths come true. I doubt Abu Osama knew much about the old myths. Yet echoes of them would have come down to him through the animated videos in his social network. Now and then, the religious authorities in his life would have reminded him of the imminence of a reckoning with these angels. Rewarding the virtuous and punishing the wicked, this pair of angels assures that a principle of justice, however invisible, undergirds the universe. The hour of reckoning, this legend promises, cannot be escaped.

In the Syria in which Abu Osama grew up, it would have been difficult to discern the operation of a principle of justice. I suspect now that Abu Osama and his friends were out to change all of that. They meant to make the cheats and the swindlers pay. They wanted punishment for the lawless, and they didn't want to wait until the afterlife to see justice upheld. Thus their little pit, and the drama they staged within. I suspect I wasn't the first sinner to whom these wannabe angels appeared, nor was I the last.

Later, a voice I didn't recognize made a halfhearted effort to inquire into the course of my career as a CIA officer. Where had I been trained, the person screamed at me, how many people had I killed, and how much had the CIA paid me? "I don't know! I don't know! I don't know!" I replied to every question. This voice tried to persuade me that he had found concrete proof of my connection to the CIA in my wallet. "Your card," the person said. "We tried it out on the internet. It opens up straight to the Pentagon."

"The green card?" I murmured. It was my debit card. I tried to explain to the voice what a debit card is.

"You lie," the voice replied. "Shut up, Animal!" Clumps of earth fell across the blindfold.

It was the cocking and recocking of the Kalashnikovs that made me feel the end was seconds away. It was also the rage in the men's voices. Of course it was the little avalanches of dirt, and the fact of being bound up, inside a pit. Somehow, the rage in their voices fright-ened me more than the rest of it. They screamed as if they themselves were being killed. I tried to imagine that I was about to embark on a voyage. I hoped it would take time to reach my destination, that as I traveled I would watch the fields and the rivers floating by, and that when I materialized wherever I was going I would be surrounded by friends.

During my first moments in their hole, I had kept my elbows raised over my face. Now I told myself that elbows do not block bullets. I rested my hands and their cuffs on my chest. I had tried to respond to questions, as if a right answer might help me. Now I stopped talking. I wanted them to get on with it.

In the late afternoon, they brought me out of their pit. A menu of tortures floated in their imaginations, apparently. The next item on their list involved locking my neck and knees inside a used tire, then beating the soles of my feet. After the tire came a CIA-agent-appropriate water torture. There were handcuffs, a scaffolding that had been erected over an irrigation pool, and ridiculous questions ("Why did you join the CIA?" "Where did your training take place?" "For how many years did it last?") that were to be answered as they poured water over my face.

Later, when the sun had gone down and I was shivering in a heap beside their irrigation pool, they handcuffed my hands around a post. They cinched my blindfold down so tightly that I had no vision whatso-ever. I sat cross-legged at their pole and listened as voices and footsteps clustered around me. Someone brought me a bowl of *labneh*. A hand pushed a glass of tea into my hands. But I was trembling too much, was too cold, and was too tightly locked to the pole to do anything but pour the tea down the front of my shirt. I tried to eat their *labneh*. I had no appetite and couldn't see the spoon or the dish. When I gave up, the captors understood my unwillingness to eat to be a CIA resis-tance technique. They forced the spoon into my mouth. I spit it out. There was much screaming into my ear. Someone reached into my hair, seized it by the roots, then throttled my head back and forth as if the person felt he were holding a coconut, filled with milk, that wanted to be shaken about before it could be cracked open. The shaking made me dizzy. The dizziness made me nauseous. But they were screaming at me. I had to eat.

Toward midnight, it became apparent to me that a crowd was gathering. The many singsongy ring tones of the cell phones, the overlapping conversations, and the footsteps near the pole to which I was attached filled my head with images of tormentors streaming through the house, then collecting on the patio by the pool. The crowd seemed to have materialized out of the night. Somebody would have sent out an internet bulletin. Perhaps the news of my arrest had gone out over the radio waves. Ostensibly, a CIA officer had been caught. The men came to poke the barrels of their rifles into my chest and to ask me the sorts of questions revolutionary interrogators might ask captured agents: "Who do you know in Damascus?" "What are their names?" "Who sent you?" Nobody, it seemed to me, took more than a moment's worth of interest in my ostensible crime—spying for the CIA. I was guilty of something deeper, I felt. It seemed to me that the men had gathered for a ritual of some kind, that it was to involve my humiliation, possibly my killing and that as I was being killed, the onlookers meant to celebrate. I felt as though I had stumbled into the clutches of a tribe of hunters. I was a buffalo that had fallen into their trap. So God had sent them a gift. Now they meant to tear the gift to pieces, and to sing and dance and smile as my blood drained into the earth.

So it seemed to me at the time. Probably the crowd was considerably smaller in fact than it was in my imagination, but I was drifting away from reality at this point. I imagined that the puddle of liquid in which I was sitting was my own blood. I felt that whatever had been done to my feet had left them too shredded and too pulpy to touch. Later, however, the handcuff chain happened to catch in my toes. They were in fine shape, I discovered, as I rubbed them with my fingers—normal toes. My underwear was soaked. I was certain it was soaked with blood. But I poked my fingers down beneath my waist enough for them to get wet. I smelled them, then put my fingers to my mouth: water.

At one point that evening, the crowd got hold of an air rifle. Its members played at pressing the barrel of the gun against my heart, then pulling the trigger. *Puff!* said the gun. I startled. The crowd laughed.

There really was some dried blood in my hair and on my face. This attracted the flies. I shook my head to shoo them away. This caused my forehead to smack into the post. More laughter. "Wait!" said a voice. "Flies bothering you?" A person approached with the air rifle. He shot it at my temple, at my throat, and thrust it under my ribs, then pulled the trigger. *Puff! Puff! Puff!* went the rifle. Each member of the crowd wanted to have a turn hunting the flies. Some of the hunters spoke warm, mocking words into my ears as they pretended to pick off the flies. Some whispered insults. It seemed to me that the flies belonged to my tormentors and that the flies, the screaming voices, the laughter, and the darkness were all part of a single, encroaching malevolence.

At first, during my first moments attached to this pole, I had it in mind that I might speak to this malevolence. Now I knew this to be impossible. I felt that only one person I had seen that day—the judge— was capable of holding a rational conversation. My mind fastened itself to the judge. I was certain that I had said all the wrong things to this reasonable figure and that if only they would let me speak to him again I could persuade him that I really was a journalist.

"Please," I told them. "I need to see the judge." Now, as the flies and the laughter swirled around my head, I decided that this judge, who had had a serene, even a kind demeanor, had been my last hope. He had had an office. He lived in an official world. He had been willing to hear me out. But he had washed his hands of me. Now I had been dispatched out onto the plains, into the darkness, where the forces of nature held sway. Out there, a black, inscrutable savagery—something that set upon me as the flies had done and meant to savor my death— was going to kill me. It spoke no language. It took pleasure in killing. My tormentors belonged to this power but didn't control it any more than I did.

Sooner or later, I felt, the government would come with its attack helicopters. It would raze these men's houses. It would burn the fields and shoot the men full of holes. But it wouldn't lay a finger on the power, since the power dwelled in the fields and in the orchards. It fell from the nighttime fog. In trying to explain myself to this force—in speaking about my life as a journalist, then begging to be allowed to revisit the judge—I imagined I was talking to human beings. Really, I had been talking to the night.

A wise person, confronted by a wickedness such as this, I told myself, would understand that it meant to kill him. The wise person would know that resisting could only make his suffering worse. He would submit. I understood this instinctively, at first, in my first moments inside the pit, and then knew it consciously, in a way I might have articulated in speech, as I sat by the side of their pool, waiting for one of them to slit my throat. The men seemed to be drawing the thing out for their own pleasure. This, I felt, was a hideous, indecent way to die. I wanted decency. I wished that they would get on with it.

Later, perhaps around three in the morning, footsteps climbed a set of stairs. They approached the pole to which I was handcuffed, then stopped. A voice ordered me to stand. I stood up. The voice ordered the guards to see that I remained on my feet until the morning. The footsteps walked away.

During the following hours, the guards made sure that I did not sit, but after the prayers, as the first light appeared in the sky, the man in charge of this vigil relented. I was allowed to remove the blindfold for a moment, to clasp a glass of tea, and to guide it to my lips. I needed to pee. One of the men unlocked my cuffs, escorted me to the bathroom without violence or curses, and when I was again locked to the pole, the person told me to sit. Someone tossed me a blanket. "Sleep," said a voice. I must have slept for several hours. When I woke, under strong sunlight, I had no idea where I was. I remembered that something disastrous had happened to my life, but what the disaster consisted of, I couldn't recall. With a start, I thought: Yesterday, I committed suicide. I tried to bring the reasons for my suicide to mind. The silence with which editors in New York and London had met my efforts to kick-start my career must have affected me more than I wanted to let on. So had my downward social trajectory in Antakya. Yes, I had been depressed there, and hadn't realized. I had been in a dangerous state, I concluded, and hadn't known a thing about it. In fact, the condition had been dangerous enough to cause me to want to end my life. Without being aware of it, I surmised, I had resolved to commit suicide, had wandered off to Syria to get the job done, had botched it somehow, and now here I was, in the midst of my suicide attempt but somehow not dead. How has this happened? I wondered.

CHAPTER 4

INTO THE DARKNESS

Aleppo, Winter 2012–2013

The actual al Qaeda men came for me about ten o'clock in the morning. By this point, Abu Osama's amateur al Qaeda gang had cinched my blindfold down tight. They had chained my ankles together and cuffed my hands behind my back. Someone in this group must have wanted to exhibit his zeal to the coming al Qaeda squadron. This amateur lashed a rope to the chain that bound my ankles. He threw one end of the rope over a branch above me, then hoisted my feet into the air until I hung, half-suspended by the rope, half-slumping on my right shoulder. I couldn't keep myself from flopping and twitching. I felt like a prize marlin or a tuna—pulled from the ocean, suspended from a hook, then left to gasp and bleat under the gaze of hostile onlookers. I wasn't allowed to say a word. I grunted. It began to rain.

The commander of the actual al Qaeda men discovered me in this attitude of helplessness. He ordered that I be let down from the rope.

This new group of captors had no use for the head scarf the Falcons of Marat Misrin had been using as a blindfold. They tossed it to the ground. They replaced it with an extraordinary-rendition-appropriate black hood. They replaced the Falcons' handcuffs with two pairs of their own, then locked my hands behind my back. A commander seized my arm from behind, locked my neck into a half nelson, then pushed my head to the floor. He asked for my complete name, and for any aliases I had used. "If you lie to us, we will kill you," he murmured. He wanted to know where exactly in the US I was from and whether or not I held citizenship from a country besides the US. I did not. As he trundled me down the stairs beside the irrigation pool, he lifted up my hands and pushed my face downward, so that I stumbled forward, half–doubled over, like a felon paraded before a line of cameras. "This is how the Americans themselves did it," he whispered in Arabic, to whom I do not know.

Somewhere near the bottom of these steps a covered pickup or van was waiting. The members of this squad lifted me into the back of their truck without a word. It seemed to me as though a tactical assault squad, from some rarefied, high-performance branch of the Syrian rebellion, had come to push the plebeian Falcons and their friends aside. A half dozen of these professionals climbed in behind me. I lay at their feet on a metal floor. One of them allowed me to rest my head on his boot. For a few moments their truck rolled at walking pace, making many turns. Nobody spoke.

When we had driven for a few kilometers, the truck slowed to a stop. I happened to overhear a checkpoint dialog. The checkpoint man, I guessed, would have seen that our truck carried overwhelming fire-power. His voice faltered. The checkpoint checking that occurred then sounded like this:

Guard: Where are you from?

Driver: From here.

Guard: Who are you with?

Driver: With the Front.

Guard: [*Pause. Silence.*] Off you go, boys!

On the far side of the checkpoint, when we had picked up speed— when it was clear that we were sailing through the open countryside, with the engine at full throttle and the wind kicking the dust in our faces—the soldiers, as if obeying an unheard, invisible cue, began to sing. It wasn't normal singing. It was joy. It was love of God.

When they came to the end of one song, a moment of whispering took place and then they launched themselves into a new song. Everyone knew the words to every song. "Our leader, bin Laden," they sang. "The Terrorizer of America. All the soldiers have sold their hearts to the Mullah. Their souls are with God."

These were showmen. This was a performance. I was the audience. Looking back, it's easy enough to see that these men were performing their solidarity for me—and for themselves. At the time, I hadn't slept much during the previous forty-eight hours. I had been arrested, had escaped, been buried, then unburied, then tortured. Now I was flying away to the country in which bin Laden's men lived. I was too shocked and too terrified to feel sorry for myself. What a newsy magazine article a narrative of this voyage would make, I thought to myself, since it is a voyage into death. It felt to me as though the music were carrying me away, that we might well be flying in a literal sense, and that when we touched down, the country in which we alighted would ring with al Qaeda singing. No one was performing a thing, I thought. This was how things happened in al Qaeda land—their state of nature. In a way, I thought, I am making a discovery, since no outsiders know what this nature is like. Whenever we actually touched down at our destination, I would be, I assumed, torn limb from limb. So I was grateful for the flying sensation. I didn't want our excursion to end.

As it turned out, a kind of harmony really did reign in the house to which these men brought me. At first, I saw nothing of it. They carried me up a flight of stairs, then had me kneel on a carpet. I was aware of a sharp blow to the back of my head. "Oof," I said. I tumbled forward. When I woke, I was seated in a chair. I couldn't see. A man had wrapped his fingers around my throat. He was throttling me. I was trying to answer his questions. Others had sunk their hands into my hair. Someone was clubbing the side of my head, possibly with an open palm, according to the rhythm of my interrogator's shouted questions.

"I sent myself," I was saying. "No one knows I've come. Not even my mother." There came a crashing blow to my head, then another shouted question, then another crash.

It seemed to me that somewhere on the surface of the earth, a person vaguely connected to me—a childhood friend, perhaps—was sitting in a chair, in a bloodstained white T-shirt. His head lolled back and forth. The old friend in the T-shirt was being strangled to death. I myself—Theo—wasn't much concerned. I was moving on. It disturbed me that I wasn't moving on fast enough.

After the interrogation, if that's what this was, I was made to lie in my cuffs and a blindfold, in a corner of the room. "Press your face to the wall," voices told me. "Do not move." It pained me to lie on my side. Perhaps a rib had been broken. "May I lie on my back?" I asked. A rain of kicks to the head descended over me. "Shut up your mouth!" voices screamed in English. "Not a word, not a single movement, not so much as a breath!" they shouted in Arabic. So I pressed my face to the wall. I slept.

When I woke, early the following morning, a Koran lesson was underway in the room at my back. Somewhere in my vicinity, a teacher with a fluid, melodious command of the verses recited a passage. Then came a less fluid, less confident voice on the far side of the room. The French-accented students bumbled through their lines. There were other beginners among the students, and some experts who recited beautifully, as if they'd been practicing just these verses all their lives. The teacher was the best by far. He was mournful when the text required this quality in his voice and foreboding when he was meant to warn and threaten. He made his voice hover over the long vowels, drew his breath, then paused for an age at the ends of the lines. When a new line came to him, he struck out along a new melody, in a new tone of voice. At the end of his recitation, the room fell into the sort of silence no one wished to break.

After the lesson, there was tea. The students chatted, as in any normal classroom. I kept waiting for the students or the teacher to acknowledge the blindfolded, handcuffed body lying in a corner of the schoolroom. I didn't exist. Soon a general running away into the outdoors occurred, as in any normal school.

When the students had gone, I nudged the blindfold upward—just enough to open up a thumbnail-sized field of vision. I turned my face from the wall. The young men had scattered their Kalashnikovs across a sun-dappled carpet. A floor-to-ceiling bookshelf, stuffed with gold-embossed biographies of the Prophet, commentaries on the Koran, and legal rulings towered over the guns. The bookshelf was the room's only furniture.

Somewhere in this house, a cook or a group of cooks were at work.

I could hear the clinking of pots. A stove emitted the smell of roasting onions. Outside, sheep bleated. Traffic droned on a distant highway. In a field or driveway not far from my room's window, young men began to kick a soccer ball. Now and then, helicopters buzzed through the air above us. Presumably, they were looking for us.

My interrogator in this house wanted me to know that only he, among all the mujahideen in Iraq and Syria, was entitled to speak on behalf of al Qaeda. In describing his position, he used a word, "spokesman"—*mutakallem*—that made me think of government officials delivering pronouncements on Al Jazeera. This person screamed more than he spoke. During the interrogations, it was all he could do to keep from throttling me to death. Somewhere on the high plains north of Aleppo, a David Koresh–like lunatic had risen up, I guessed, declared himself the local Syrian al Qaeda oracle, recruited a dozen village youths to help him, and now a band of homeless young men, one or two of whom might have come from Europe, had taken shelter here. Perhaps, I thought, terrorism experts would have heard of him. Perhaps not. For my part, when I heard his voice outside the room in which I was being held I knew that someone would be wrapping his fingers around my throat soon. The interrogator seemed to me like the type who was inclined to murder his victims as he questioned them. During one of his interrogations, he pressed a knife into the soft flesh under my chin. "Do you know what this is?" he cooed as he breathed into my ear. He made me say the word *sakeen* (knife) out loud. "What will I do with this knife?" he asked.

"You will kill me. You will kill me!" I was meant to scream. I did scream this.

From the handful of interrogations he conducted with me, I understood that the spokesman felt that wherever on Earth Islam was growing strong, there the US government sent out its agents to kill.

The spokesman believed that the CIA had lately become aware of a growing power in northern Syria and so dispatched a team of undercover agents that consisted of English teachers, doctors, and journalists. He felt the agents would be equipped with high-tech hidden listening devices. He had his assistants lower my trousers, then search inside my underwear. They searched through my hair and in the back of my mouth. The spokesman wanted to know if I had had any surgeries lately. When he had satisfied himself that I carried no CIA spying devices on my person, he set about identifying the Syrians I meant to bribe or otherwise induce into my spying scheme. "I don't know anyone here," I told him. He wanted to know what I knew of the people who had brought me into Syria. "They gave me fake names," I said. "Maybe they were smugglers?"

When this line of inquiry ran dry, the spokesman turned to the network of agents he believed to have been dispatched into Syria. He asked me to write out a list of all the American journalists currently working in Syria. I wracked my brain for the name of the *New York Times* correspondent. I couldn't bring it to mind. What other American journalists did I know in Syria? Austin Tice had disappeared in the Damascus suburbs weeks earlier. I put his name on my list. I filled out the rest of my list with American journalists whose names I could recall. TV personalities came to mind. Wasn't Peter Jennings a Canadian? I put down Dan Rather instead. I invented some names. "I'm not sure all of these people are in Syria now," I said to the spokesman as I handed him my list. He shrugged.

The next time the spokesman came to me—a day later, possibly two days—his questions were about Islam. I was not a Muslim, yet I had been studying Islam for years. Why?

"In order to understand?" I replied. He wanted to know where I had studied, under whom, and which books I had read. I could answer these questions, unlike the ones about my CIA network of agents. The answers led into something that felt like a conversation. I wanted my captors to see my respect for their religion and to understand the lengths to which I had gone in order to understand. So I babbled. I rambled about medieval philosophy, the origins of Salafism, the Muslim Brotherhood, my struggles with Arabic grammar, and my interest in learning to recite the Koran.

In the midst of my speech, it occurred to me that I was establishing myself as a CIA specialist in extremist thought. I had studied founders of the philosophy in order to track down the contemporary exponents.

By the time I realized my mistake, I had recited a half-dozen lines from the Surah Ar-Rahman and boasted of having studied "Milestones," a poetical work by the al Qaeda patron saint, Sayyid Qutb. "It was long ago. I don't remember," I told the spokesman, after it was too late, when he asked why I had studied Sayyid Qutb. "I read the book because I was curious?" I told him.

"Yes, and because you're a spy," he replied.

One morning, after I had been lying in his living room library for about a week, the spokesman threw open the door, marched across the room, then wrapped a rope around my ankles. He took off the handcuffs I had been wearing, had me put my hands behind my back, then cuffed my hands together. He cinched down my blindfold. A half-dozen assistants carried me into the sunlight. The assistants dropped me into the back of a waiting car. On the passenger bench in front of me, men were cocking their Kalashnikovs. No one spoke. Probably the library is too clean a place for an execution, I thought.

I knew that messing with my blindfold would bring trouble. On the other hand, I felt I couldn't allow myself to leave the world without a glimpse of clouds, trees, civilians—planet Earth. So in the back of the spokesman's SUV, as he roared through the countryside, I propped myself up on one elbow, rubbed the side of my head against the upholstery like a cat, writhed, nudged, and shoved, and at last managed to remove an edge of blindfold from the corner of an eye. Through a side rear window, I watched the world go by. There were highway road signs, pretty tree branches, and alternating patterns of sun and shade on the upholstery. When we arrived inside Aleppo I could see the topmost stories of destroyed apartment blocks.

In the midst of one especially violent stretch of city driving, when it seemed to me as though explosions were causing the neighborhood buildings to collapse as we drove in front of them, the spokesman slammed on his brakes. Without a word to his assistants, he opened the driver's door, strode to the rear door, opened it, climbed inside, then began to kick at my back and at my head. He kicked as if he had discovered a rabid dog in the back of his truck, as if he meant to stove in its head, then drop its body into the street. I might have lost consciousness during these moments. I remember that several minutes later, when we were again flying through the midst of a combat zone, one of his assistants murmured a question into the air: "What did the prisoner do?" There was silence, then more skidding through the corners, and eventually the spokesman spoke up from the front seat. "He uncovered his eyes," he said.

By this point, the spokesman had wrapped the entirety of my face in a head scarf. He tied it down tightly enough to keep me from moving my eyelids. I was having trouble breathing.

As it happened, my first underground cell was in the basement of the Aleppo eye hospital. On the afternoon the spokesman dropped me off here, a cluster of foot soldiers met the spokesman's SUV at a turnaround at the bottom of the hospital's front stairway.

One of the spokesman's assistants trundled me out of the luggage compartment. Other assistants removed the rope with which the spokesman had tied up my ankles, freed my hands from the handcuffs, loosened up my blindfold enough to allow me to grasp a water bottle, to drink, and to walk.

We hurried through a rock-strewn courtyard. They held my elbows. Somewhere in the air above us, rooms and walls and slabs of cement were exploding, then tumbling to the street. Streams of broken glass tinkled through the elevator shafts. A minute of brisk walking through this combat zone brought me to the edge of a gaping hole in the earth. Evidently, my captors understood the reluctance with which prisoners approached this void. "Slowly, slowly," they murmured to me in English as they pushed me forward. "Take care. No quick. See?"

I stepped forward but did not see. Beneath my feet, I discovered, there were steps. I could feel that they were steep, that they led into an enveloping darkness, and that as we descended, a welcoming committee, led by a man with a flashlight, was climbing up out of the depths. There were greetings and salaams. My handcuffs were removed and then I was being ushered downward, through an M. C. Escher–like endlessness of stairs. Eventually we came to a landing. The landing led to a corridor, and the corridor to a closed wooden door. Standing in front of this door, I had time to make out the letters WC, in English characters, which had been scrawled across a panel at eye height. Presently, a hand was pushing a key into the door handle's lock. The door swung open. "Get in," said a voice. I stepped forward. The door slammed behind me. Expecting a blow, I froze for a moment, listened for the presence of other bodies, then removed my blindfold. I was by myself. I stood on the threshold of a large, barren room whose only window, a shoebox-sized rectangle high on the wall opposite the door, admitted a dull glow. Someone, I was surprised to see, had painted the walls a soothing pastel pink. It occurred to me that this shade of pink, the hanging fluorescent light trays, and the high ceilings were often found in state institutions in Syria. So was I in a classroom? An asylum? A military barracks? I couldn't decide. My eyes fell on a small pile of dung that had been deposited some days earlier, apparently, on the floor in the center of the room. Wherever I was, the men who controlled the facility, I concluded, despised it.

During my first moments in this cell, I wandered along the walls in a haze of exhaustion. I was still frightened but I felt more relief then than fear. During that week, my tormentors had hovered about me. They had screamed at me for the pleasure of seeing me startle. They had insisted that I keep the blindfold on at all hours of the day and night. Now, I was free to look about. I had no handcuffs. My tormentors from the library, I hoped, had gone away in the car in which they delivered me. Now I am in an institution, I told myself. Here, some saner, or anyway, more official, more comprehensible dispensation holds sway.

In the late afternoon, three men opened the door of my cell. They pushed a hospital cart across the threshold. Without saying a word, one of them withdrew a round of bread from a plastic bag, then tossed this onto a blanket that had been lying on the floor. A colleague had me pick up the bread, kneel by the side of the cart, then hold the bread in the air, at his waist. He scooped two spoonfuls of *halawa* from a cardboard box on the cart's bottom shelf. He deposited these spoonfuls in the center of the round of bread. He asked me to stand, to carry my dinner to the blanket, and to sit. "Eat," he said, when I had done this, "then sleep."

Later in the evening, these men returned with a pair of white pleather dress shoes for me, a clean T-shirt, a pair of hospital pants, and an empty soda pop bottle. I was to surrender the clothes I was wearing and to put on the hospital clothing. I was to keep the shoes and the bottle in a corner of the cell, next to the door. In the morning and in the evening, said a man in a tracksuit, I would be brought to a bathroom, outside my cell. I was to put on my shoes before leaving the cell. I was to fill the water bottle from a faucet in the bathroom. "Do you have a cloth?" he asked.

"A cloth," he repeated. "For your eyes." He turned on his heels, disappeared into the corridor, shouted inaudible words to people I could not see, fell silent, and when he returned, several minutes later, he held a pale green rag, about the size of a bandanna, in one hand. He tossed his rag to the floor. "When you leave the cell, you will put the shoes on your feet and the cloth on your eyes," he said. "Understand?"

Over the following days, the pitch of the battle outside this hospital complex was so intense, the guards so often thrust their guns against my skull, and so cheerfully discussed my upcoming execution that I stopped hoping I might somehow survive. I must face facts, I told myself. Soon I would be killed. I assumed I would be shot in a court-yard somewhere or hanged from a pipe in an underground torture room. But when? At first, thinking about my execution paralyzed me. I felt myself too weak and too frightened to do anything but stare at the walls but as the hours passed, I decided that it was an abomination to sit around like a frog on a lily pad as my captors prepared to do me in. I must plead with them, I told myself. Why wasn't I trying to seize one of their guns? I needed to discover who exactly was in charge of my execution. I didn't imagine that begging for mercy with the orderlies who delivered food to my cell could accomplish much. These people seemed to be teenagers. Some of them were preteens. No, I needed to figure out who among my captors was the chief. I needed to throw myself at his feet.

When I asked the orderlies if I could speak to their leader, they screamed at me. "Shut up, Animal!" they yelled. "Put your face to the wall." When I pressed my face to the wall, they thwacked my back and shoulders with electrical cables.

If I am to save my life, I told myself after about twenty-four hours of such treatment, I must acquire true information about how the execution is to occur. Who exactly will carry out the deed? When exactly?

The only way for me to acquire this information, I judged, was by means of sustained, careful, hypervigilant eavesdropping. Thus, during my first days in this prison, whenever voices could be heard in the vicinity of my cell, I tiptoed to the door. I crouched on the floor. I held my ear to the crack beneath the bottommost panel. Snippets of conversation came to me then, and much pattering of feet. There was screaming now and then, some singing, some solitary reciting of the Koran and much cocking and recocking of the Kalashnikovs. Not once did I pick so much as a shred of information concerning what was to become of me.

I need to see my captors in order to understand their plans, I told myself. At first, whenever a person who seemed as though he might be important came to my cell, I peered into his eyes. I weighed the tone of his voice. I read into his remarks as a literary critic would, attentive to double and triple meanings. This got me nowhere.

For a little while, it seemed to me that I had discerned a pattern in the noises the war, which was occurring outside my shoebox-sized window, produced. Every night a few hours past midnight, it seemed to me, the firefights and the exchanges of artillery fire culminated in a grand, Fourth of July–like symphony of explosions. I imagined that the large explosions were caused by a wave of advancing regime tanks. When these explosions seemed to occur within a kilometer or so of my prison, as they did during my week there, I imagined that this advancing violence meant defeat for my captors and an imminent rescue for me. But if my captors were to abandon their stronghold, wouldn't they shoot their captives first? And what if Bashar al-Assad's military apparatus, the Syrian Arab Army, were somehow to overtake this al Qaeda redoubt? I wasn't at all confident that they would be any sweeter to me than the al Qaeda men had been. Though I found the battle sounds entrancing, and did my best to weigh the meaning of every whistle and boom, it didn't take me long to give up imagining that the racket outside my window might somehow bode well for me.

During this first week of my new life as a prisoner, I felt the lack of anything to read like a physical pain. I tried to read the scratches earlier prisoners had made on the walls. I tried to picture books I had read in the past, to open their covers with my mind's eye, and to see what was written on page one. This exercise deepened my frustration. One afternoon, I begged a guard for a book. "Any book at all," I said. He burst into laughter.

"You wish to read what, Filth?" he said, chortling. He named the two most famous compilers of the hadith, or statements of the prophet. I had in mind to read the compilations of the hadith?

"Ok," I said. "Sure."

He scoffed. No, he concluded for me, I was no scholar. "You are rather a spy," he said. "Shut up. Put your face to the wall." He slammed the door.

Eventually, of course, I despaired of being given a book. I abandoned my mission to sort out who would kill me and when. They'll never tell me a thing, I concluded, and could knowing the hour of my death really save me? I doubted it could.

By far the softest, most comforting object in my world at the time was my blindfold. Because I could see through it, I Imagined that it was my ally. Because, for the most part, they didn't hit me when I was wearing it, I thought of it as a magical fabric that warded away their blows. Because it was old and had been worn down to its threads by what processes exactly I could not tell, I imagined that it was rich in meanings.

During my first days in its company, I imagined that it had been salvaged from the corpse of a recently executed prisoner. But there was no blood on it. The fabric had been dyed to a pretty pea green and printed with tiny violets. It looked like no blindfold I had ever seen. Probably, I decided, I am the first to use this object as a blindfold. It had been worn thin at its center. It would have taken years for such fabric to wear away into the tissue of threads it had become at its center. Jebhat al-Nusra was much too young and way too brutal to have subjected my piece of fabric to such a gentle kind of wearing down. I told myself that the cloth had probably been retrieved from this building's kitchen, which, I was beginning to see, had once belonged to a hospital. It would have been left there by a woman. She had been a cook or a cleaner, had sweated into her head scarf for years, I decided. In her affection for the patients in this place, and because she believed in her work, she brought them delicious, restorative coffees and baklava. When she appeared before these patients, I imagined, she always wore this headscarf.

It took me a week or so to warm to my blindfold. At first, I couldn't bear it. It was another instrument in their arsenal of torture instruments. After a few days, however, I started to see the good in my blindfold. It was soft and translucent. If ever I could bring myself to cry, I thought, which I wanted to do but couldn't, it would wipe away the tears. I liked to hold it to my face and to breathe in its scents. It didn't smell like anything but must, but when I held it to my nose, I imagined that I was in the presence of the former owner. I felt like she was talking to me, and that the era of kindness in which she had lived when she worked in this hospital was still with us. For this reason, I pressed it to my face a lot. I took to hiding it beneath the blanket on which I slept, lest some crazed Jebhat al-Nusra guard should try to steal it away. There was no way that I could escape, but I knew there was nothing to prevent an innocuous object like the cloth to go sailing out into the world. After just a day of use, that blindfold was saturated with my sweat. It held tangles of my hair. If a well-disposed visitor were to carry it away or if, for instance, a gust of wind were to pluck it from the windowsill, it could find its way to a DNA expert. I wasn't much up on the science of DNA identification, but I assumed the expert would draw the obvious conclusion: The residues in the fabric gave incontrovertible proof of my being alive. So I wanted to keep hold of the blindfold for this reason. I felt it was my last reasonable means of sending out an SOS.

About a week after my arrival in this cell, the prison manager came to me with a pen and sheet of paper. "Write out your name, your birthdate, and your mother's and father's names," he said. He slammed the door. He returned after an hour to fetch his sheet of paper but forgot to retrieve the pen. A few days later, I offered to write out some English lessons for a teenage guard who felt the other guards were better at English than he was. When he came to pick up his lesson, he left me with two sheets of blank paper.

At the time, thoughts about the writer Paul Theroux were rumbling around in my head, probably because his *Dark Star Safari* was the last book I had had my hands on. In his books, I told myself, he often found himself stranded in rooms every bit as dingy and disconnected from the world as the one in which I was imprisoned. Theroux positively sought out dinginess and disconnection. Confronted with such qualities in a place, he didn't agonize as I was agonizing. He invented characters, confected a plot, and plucked interesting dialogs from the air. Pretty soon—within minutes, I imagined—he had lost himself in the twists of a novel. It would bring out deep, hidden truths. Probably, it brought him loads of money, too. I wasn't much interested in publishing success at this point, but I did envy real writers their ability to sweep themselves away into imaginary worlds. How hard can it be? I asked myself. Was this ability to invent not a human quality present in us all?

The idea that came to me that afternoon was a Paul Bowles–like tale in which a too-confident, oblivious American finds himself in a village, somewhere in the Central American highlands, surrounded by hostile natives. He has come to photograph them. In the tale I began to scribble in my cell, the villagers accosted the photographer. They draped his cameras around their necks, threw his notebooks into the air, and dashed his telephoto lenses on the rocks. Soon they had him blindfolded and trussed up on a stretcher like a mental patient. Drinking heavily and singing, they hoisted the stretcher into the air, then paraded it into a disused church. My plan for my story was to have these tribesmen sacrifice my tourist protagonist to their gods. First, however, they would torture him.

I wrote out the first few paragraphs of my story quickly, with great confidence, as if I were Paul Bowles himself. I was telling a tale of American hubris getting its comeuppance. I meant for the writing to pause over the details of the torture in a mood of methodical, first-this-then-that attention to detail. Since every night, bloodcurdling screams issued from a room somewhere outside my cell, I felt myself well enough acquainted with torture to give this important topic author-itative treatment. My torture descriptions, I imagined, would cause shivers of unease to run down my reader's spine. He would feel him-self in the presence of something unnameable but essential in human nature. Perhaps the *New Yorker* would be interested in my tale? Anyway, I wasn't worried about where exactly it would appear. The important thing, I thought, was to give my readers a round of instruction in the darker, more invisible regions of the human spirit.

At first, I found the atmosphere and the plot of my story intriguing but when I came to the point in the story in which the villagers were to begin their torture, I stopped writing. I reflected. Late at night in this prison, a kind of screaming arose from behind the steel doors at the end of the corridor, which made me think that my captors were mur-dering their prisoners, one by one, possibly with axes.

Had I meant to entertain an audience by tossing some true-sounding, fictional torture details at them? But I was the audience. I had not found real torture sounds entertaining. The idea of making up a torture in order to divert myself repelled me.

I did, however, believe that fiction can reveal the mysteries of human behavior as, for instance, news reporting never can. Didn't I believe this? In the kind of story I was hoping to write, a putatively smart but actually dim person—a scientist or a journalist, for instance—finds himself wandering through a beguiling landscape. There are whisper-ings, signs, and uninterpretable languages. Soon, he falls into a trap. He sputters and gesticulates. As darkness gathers round, the story's writer escorts the reader into a reckoning with all that the protagonist, who is revealed as a callow, feckless tourist, has failed to grasp about life.

As I tried to work my way through the writing of this tale, it occurred to me that somewhere in the background of such tales, there must be a knowing writer. The problem with my attempt, I felt, was that there was no such person on the scene. What understanding did I wish to bring to readers? I understood that a band of fanatics had risen up, taken over a state institution (possibly a hospital?), converted it into a prison, arrested their neighbors, and now the fanatics were torturing the neighbors. Why? What did my captors intend to do to me? What did they intend to do to the world? I suspected that the torturers themselves could not have shed much light on matters. I suspected that the world's war correspondents had yet to guess at the most basic facts of the world into which I had stumbled. The world's far-seeing novelists would have known still less than the reporters knew.

I am on my own, I told myself. I crumpled my sheet of paper into a ball. I stuffed the ball into the pocket of my pants. A few days passed and then one afternoon, after a visit to the prison bathroom, a guard happened to pat down my pockets as he pushed me into my cell. He pulled a wad of grimy paper from my pants. "What's this?" he said. He locked me into my cell, then returned a minute later with the prison manager and two guards. Under a foam rubber mattress, the guards found my pen and the rest of the paper. The manager thrust them into my face. "What are you writing?" he screamed. "Who gave you the pen?"

I explained: He himself had given me the pen. I meant to write a fiction. My story took place far away, in *Amrika al Latiniya*, I said. I had written it in order to divert myself. The manager stalked around the room for a moment. He stared into my eyes and clenched his fists. "Why do you lie?" he screamed. He kicked over a water bottle, then kicked a soccer ball I had made for myself out of the stuffing in a quilt the captors had given me. The assistants shook out the quilt, then patted down my clothing. They tossed the foam rubber mattress across the room. When the manager had satisfied himself that he had found the pen and every bit of purloined paper, he gathered his assistants, then strode into the hallway. An assistant slammed the door.

During the following days, I clung to the feeling that the fragments of Kafka's stories I had learned when I studied German could help me understand the world in which I was trapped. "'How did I get here?' I exclaimed. It was a moderately large hall, lit by soft electric light . . ." These first lines of a Kafka parable called "The Cell" seemed to offer a promising beginning. But I couldn't recall the rest. Why had Kafka written parables at all, I wondered, and what had he been on about in "The Cell?" I had no idea. One evening during this period of desperation, I managed to persuade myself that the complete text of *The Trial* could sort things out for me. Of all the stories in my memory, this one, about a man arrested one morning in his bed ("without him having done anything wrong") seemed to most truly describe the events that had overtaken my life. So I grasped after suggestive scenes in that book, half-recalled them, fell asleep, then woke in a mood of frustration and fear. Kafka had described the world of a Jew in Prague at the start of the twentieth century. I needed to know about Arabs in al Qaeda in Aleppo a hundred years on: al Qaeda reality. I wracked my brain for the bits of "In the Penal Colony" I could remember. There had been torture in that story. Had the victims survived? If so, how? Recalling nothing useful, and feeling that no amount of seeing into made-up stories could help me, I tore at my hair.

Nowadays, I suspect that the world I was living in at the time had much more in common with dreams and hallucinations—and novels and plays, for that matter—than I knew. Now I think that the people in charge of that prison were consumed by their own kind of creative mania. Their passion was to conjure an age-old Islamic dream from the Aleppo rubble. That dream was of Muslims living in serene harmony with the land and with themselves, invincibility before the enemies of Islam, and oneness with the Koran.

In the days after the prison manager confiscated my writing materials, I spent most of my time lying prone on the foam rubber mattress. I might have had a bit of a concussion. When the fluorescent light bulbs in my cell turned themselves on, as they did now and then, the light seemed to pound and flash in my head. Rising from the floor brought on dizzy spells. Sitting down made the dizzy spells come back. I tried to move as little as possible. In order to pee in this prison, I had to walk down the corridor in the blindfold, with a pair of guards at my sides. Right away, they guessed that if they let go of my elbows I would stagger into the walls. During the first steps of this excursion, I would step forward, holding my hands in front of me like a zombie. I would float for a moment, feel the vertigo, bump into something, then crumple to the floor. The spectacle invited onlookers. The onlookers helped me to my feet, ushered me forward ("Quickly, you! Quickly!"), then kicked obstacles into my path. Or they held out their feet, or they pushed me into someone else's extended foot.

When I tripped over the obstacles, a general hilarity spread through the corridor. Despite the dizziness in which I lived in those days, or perhaps because of it, I felt I was beginning to understand what the young men in the corridor were talking about as I stumbled around at their feet. I felt I knew what they were dreaming about.

By my calendar, my first weeks in the Aleppo eye hospital occurred in the last days of October 2012. By their calendar, a time of reckoning—of reaping what had been sown and each being rewarded according to his merit—was dawning over Aleppo. The physical center of the reckoning was the hospital basement. Early on, during my first days in this hospital, a visitor to my cell who was neither armed nor wearing military clothing at all—who seemed, I thought, only interested in helping me understand the facts—told me that this underground corridor was the place in Aleppo to which the defenders of the faith brought its enemies. Competent judges were determining the facts. The innocent were being let go. Those with "things upon them," as the Arabic phrase has it, were being made to pay.

Right away, I could guess something of how the system worked because I could hear the commanders in the hallway as they opened the doors of prisoners in the neighboring cells. "Time to take what you have earned," the commanders would say. What had this person earned? By doing what? I would listen to the handcuffs coming out, and then would come the order: "Stand!" A few minutes of silence would intervene. Then from a room at the end of the corridor, the screaming came. It would last for twenty minutes or so, and when it died away the crack of electric shocks would break the silence. There was more screaming then, and after another twenty minutes or so the voice faltered, then died away. There was more electricity then. Then, nothing. Every few days, new prisoners were brought to the cells next to mine.

In those early days of the Syrian war, ISIS had yet to break away from the Syrian al Qaeda affiliate, Jebhat al-Nusra. Except for the owner of the library, the al Qaeda spokesman, the fighters who frequented this basement didn't seem to think of themselves as members of any sect or branch of the rebellion. They were Muslims. They had come out to defend Islam. Most of the young men who distributed food in the hospital spoke in Syrian-accented Arabic.

My first conversations with the people who brought food and water to my cell in the hospital were about paradise. Did I feel I would ever be in paradise? they wanted to know. "I don't know," I said. They knew just how they would live out the rest of their lives and how they would die. Every moment that remained to them on Earth would occur in battle, against the enemies of God. In the instants of their deaths, they would be transported to the side of God. He dwelled on the highest of the ninety-nine levels of paradise. Here fellow martyrs were watching them and waiting for a beautiful reunion. Everyone would live in happiness together. "Allah has purchased the lives and the wealth of the believers," reads a line in the Koran that came up often in casual conversation in that basement.

For that, they shall have paradise. So they fight in the cause of God,
and kill and are killed. It is a true promise God has made. . . .

Perhaps others elsewhere have different ways of glossing this passage. In this basement, it meant that long ago, at the dawn of time, God had offered a solemn contract to these young men. They had contemplated the offer, then accepted it. Accordingly, they would kill and be killed. Afterward, the ascension. Then, the togetherness. For now, all was well. They would fight and die. Then God would honor his side of the agreement.

"You also might be killed this evening," the fighters in this hospital would tell me—not so much to threaten me, I thought, but because they knew life here, on our planet, to be unpredictable. They wondered if I was prepared for my death as they were prepared for theirs. "You've done nothing to prepare?" they asked. They smiled. It seemed to me that these young men had at last understood that the were the holders of a binding contract with God himself. Now they meant to live and die by the terms of their contract. In this respect their oneness with the sacred book wasn't entirely a dream.

Down there, the caliphate was real, too. As any resident of one of the Islamic statelets in Syria and Iraq will tell you, a caliphate does not come because a swell in a robe and a Rolex declares that now is the time for a caliphate. The believers in a caliphate think it comes because fifty thousand years ago, at the dawn of time, the angels wrote that the current generation would throw up such a quantity of heroes so filled with divine purpose that they could not keep themselves from making the dream come true. Yet even the believers will admit that a caliphate is also a psychological phenomenon that settles over crowds, then works its way through neighborhoods, cities, landscapes.

In October of 2012, the soldiers of our Islamic state weren't asking the citizens to pledge their allegiance to anyone in particular, nor did they want to give their caliphate a name. The armed men called themselves Muslims or Believers or sometimes, simply, "us." Their ambition wasn't to bring an al Qaeda government to Syria but rather, they said, to bring Islam.

There were no uniforms. At the end of the corridor outside my cell, there hung a black-and-white flag emblazoned with the seal of the prophet. The trucks in which the armed men drove their prisoners around often flew this flag or the al Qaeda flag from their antennae.

This state's bureaucracy, I gathered, was a work in progress. In our Aleppo neighborhood, there was an emir (he never appeared, though allegedly you could write him letters). Above at higher levels of this new government, were other emirs, elsewhere. Some, I understood, were judges. Others were historians. Others were military experts and still others were state planners. Collectively, the emirs were referred to al ulema, or "the men of science." In this state, there was an internal police force with an investigative branch and punishments for criminals that suited their crimes. You could be hung by your wrists from pipes beneath the ceiling for having insulted God. You could be shocked with car battery cables for having tried to chat up a girl in the street. Their caliphate was real, even then, more than a year before it announced its presence to the world, in that Alawites were being arrested in the street, charged with apostasy, then dragged into underground cells. This apostasy had occurred, so it was alleged, in the eleventh century, when the first Alawites appeared in the mountains along the Syrian coast. Only now were the Muslims of Syria, as my captors liked to refer to themselves, getting around to holding these apostates to account. Many of the apostates had been soldiers in the Syrian Arab Army. Now they faced execution—not for anything they had done in the army of Bashar al-Assad, but because the punishment for apostasy in Islam, so the feeling in that basement had it, is death.

Happily, the law of God allowed for prisoner exchanges.

Sadly, the Assad regime refused to negotiate with terrorists.

The Alawite prisoners were being kept alive, for now, I understood, in the unlikely event that the regime should change its mind.

As for the soldiers of this caliphate: Many had already killed and died in order to take over the border-crossing stations on the Turkish border. On the day they overran the crossing at Bab al-Hawa, on the Antakya-Idlib border, in July of 2012, one of the commanders yelled into the camera as the banner that later became the ISIS flag waved over his head, "As you can see, we control the entirety of this place. And we announce from this day forward the existence of an Islamic state under the laws of the noble Koran. We are now forming suicide cells to make jihad in the name of God!"

Before I set out for Syria, as it happened, I watched this video. I'm sure all the reporters who were writing about Syria then saw it, too. Its existence was reported in the *New York Times*. We wanted to keep up to date. So we read the *Times*. But then . . . I didn't believe a word of it. There had never been an al Qaeda presence in Syria. Where would they find their suicide bombers? The extremists in the video lived in a tiny bubble, I told myself. Soon they would blow themselves to bits.

Down in the hospital basement, it would have been impossible not to believe in what was going on. Every few days, Soldiers of the Land of Sham, as they called themselves using a word for the Levant in sacred histories of the region, brought in new prisoners of war. They came in handcuffs and blindfolds. Every few days, new young men in combat gear, some of whom stumbled through the simplest phrases in Arabic, trooped through the basement corridor.

In a caliphate, I discovered, people are no longer afraid to disclose the contents of their hearts to strangers, and all the believers, even the most innocent-seeming children—perhaps especially them—reveal themselves to you at the drop of a hat.

Ask an eight-year-old child of a commander inside a caliphate what he wants to be when he grows up. *"Ingimassi,"* he will say, lisping through his gap-toothed smile. An *ingimassi* (from the Arabic verb for "to plunge," as in "plunge into death") carries a Kalashnikov in order to kill as he himself is being killed. Sometimes, in some cases, he carries out his suicide mission, survives by a miracle, then returns in the evening to hang out with his friends. He has submerged himself in death yet somehow lives. In that hospital, I think we all came to know what life feels like when you have left the earthly plane yet carry on, alert, wiggling your toes and fingers, waiting for what comes next.

About the things society once hid from view: In certain private conversations in Syria, even before the war, it wasn't uncommon to hear Sunni Muslims discussing the Alawites' secret-but-all-the-more-real-for-that talent for making themselves invisible. Having no special feeling for Islam themselves, Alawites, it was thought, were okay with dressing up as Muslims, inserting themselves into the prayer rows, then eyeing their neighbors as the neighbors spoke to God. If the faithful prayed too well, studied too much, or came to understand the power of the religion too well, these enemies of Islam, the Alawite agents, pounced.

Now that the caliphate had come, the agents were visible to everyone. Many had already been seized. Inside the hospital, it was easy enough to identify these formerly invisible spies. The men in the military uniforms being made to clean the toilets were Alawites. The men on their hand and knees who swabbed the corridor tiles were Alawites. The foreigners and children who stopped to peer at these house cleaners didn't always understand what was going on. *"Nusayris,"* the men with the guns would murmur, using a derogatory term for Alawites.

One afternoon, not long after my arrival in this prison, a guard left the door to my cell open as he ladled soup into a bowl for me. Behind him, a line of six men in blindfolds shuffled in slow motion, like sleepwalkers, through the corridor. Some of the men wore military pants. Some wore green hospital scrubs. Each man clasped the shoulders of the man in front of him. A guard had hung a tether around the first prisoner's neck. The guard walked with a handgun in one hand and his end of the leash in the other. Some of the prisoners craned their necks at the ceiling, as people in blindfolds sometimes do. Others walked stooping over, as if they were scouring the ground for lost coins.

"*Nusayris?*" I asked the guard who had brought me the soup.

"Yes," he said. "And Pigs." I wanted him to tell me that these men were not going to be killed. "Are they not killing us?" he shrugged in response to my question. The laws of Islam, he said, required murderers to be put to death. The laws also required cleanliness in the streets. Now that the people of Aleppo were living under Islam, he himself could not have intervened to help the condemned men even if they had been his best friends. To interfere in the disposition of their cases would have been to supplant the law of God with whim. When the male Alawite population of Syria had been killed, the Alawite women and children, he thought, might be spared. Perhaps Israel would be willing to take them. Perhaps they could travel from nation to nation, he suggested, like Gypsies.

By October of 2012, the American spies in their caliphate had run out of time. We were being unmasked. It wasn't just my journalist cover they meant to shear away but my hair, the orderly civilian clothing in which I had come to Syria, and the veneer of decency beneath which my truer nature lurked. To remind me of my true nature, they gave me new names. Often I was Pig. Sometimes my name was Donkey or Insect or Filth.

One afternoon, a few days after my head had been shaved, a man in a mask who spoke English with a Canadian accent and his boss, a Syrian commander, put me in an orange jumpsuit, then set me before a tripod-mounted camera. At the time, their caliphate was such that, in this facility, at any rate, they had only a single orange jumpsuit. After I had made my film, about which there will be more later, they made me undress, then turn the jumpsuit over to the prisoner in line behind me.

As I was pulling on my everyday jail clothing again, I showed the commander the tennis jacket I had been living in during the previous weeks. It disgusted even the other prisoners. Lice were living in its seams. I had been dragged up and down the hospital corridor by its collar. It was covered in floor grime. "Sheikh, the jacket . . . it's disgusting," I said. I had played my part in his film. Could he give me a new jacket?

The filmmaker fixed his eyes on mine. "It's not the jacket but the wearer who is disgusting," he replied. He declined to give me new clothing.

In fact, all of the prisoners in that basement were disgusting in the same way. We had all been pounced upon, and so all of our clothing was smeared with blood. We all wore similar lice-filled, grime-stained rags. There were times when we vomited on the floors of our cells. We had nothing to clean up with. The filth the men on the path of God imputed to us was real. Their disgust was real. They lived in a world of patchouli oil for their beards and Head & Shoulders for their cascading curls. Their cleanliness was in the way they smelled, in their pink and white prep-school shirts (Ralph Lauren was popular in Aleppo then), in the zeal with which they performed their ablutions, in their immaculate robes, and in their speech. Normally, in Syria, when young men wish to express contempt they bring up your sister's vagina. Or they tell you that you are the son of a whore. In this hospital, even when the fighters had discovered the inmates defacing their cells, as they sometimes did, and so screamed at the top of their lungs, they did not bring up vaginas or whores.

In their caliphate, the truth about hidden financial dealings was coming out. Anyway, so it was felt. One afternoon during my first week in prison, a pair of heavily bearded, heavily armed visitors to my cell had a discussion about ransoms. It began like this:

First visitor: The Americans don't pay. Too bad for him.

Second visitor: By god, the Americans pay twice what the other countries pay. They lie about it in public more. In private, they pay more.

Whenever men came to my cell to speak about ransoms, I was happy. Their tone made me think that they were willing to horse-trade and knew how to carry out swaps. But when I questioned them, I could see right away that they didn't know who in America they might call to advance their ransom project and didn't want to find out. All of them were too locked inside the Arabic language and too preoccupied with killing regime soldiers to have a go at charming the CIA into a cash drop. How would they begin such a dialog? What demands would they make exactly? They didn't have a clue. I knew, in any case, that if an operator at the US embassy in Amman or Ankara or Cyprus, or anywhere, for that matter, managed to figure out what the person who claimed to be an al Qaeda commander in Aleppo was on about (unlikely but conceivable) the operator would reply, "Freelance journalists are known for getting themselves in trouble. This one went to Aleppo? How unfortunate. It's been nice talking to you. Good-bye."

If the US government wouldn't pay, perhaps someone else would? I clung to vague hopes like these during my first weeks in prison, but the more I discussed matters with my captors, the more obvious it was to me that the sums they required were too vast and the crimes America had committed against Muslims too unforgivable for them to accept a simple cash payment in exchange for my life.

One visitor to my cell wanted me to know that an army under his command had positioned itself across the neighborhoods outside the prison. The army was planning to attack a regime-controlled village in the evening. "Do you think anything you can pay us will last my men beyond breakfast time?" he asked. Other visitors chuckled happily to themselves, then asked, in pretend politeness, about the amount of money I thought I might be able to raise on my own. Maybe I could hawk peanuts in the street? What was my plan, really? Did I wish to sell my kidney? A lung? A liver?

In any case, money, I soon understood, couldn't possibly get me out of my fix. All the fighters were certain that the American army had killed one million Muslims in Iraq. "You think we will be satisfied with money for this?" The fighters would ask me this question, hold my eyes, stare into them in quiet curiosity, and then, as the enormity of the American misadventure in Iraq dawned over us, they would shake their heads.

Almost every day, the younger guards in this prison found a way to mention my upcoming execution. Did I have any last wishes? they would ask. Did I prefer to die by hanging, by the knife, or by a bullet? I assumed at first that the delay in killing me had to do with the emir's desire to set the scene. He would have wanted a good camera, flags everywhere, a happy crowd. Yet after a month of life as a prisoner, it became clear to me that they had all of these things on hand.

During my first weeks in prison, I attributed the delay to a need I imagined in them for a moment of maximum religious solidarity in which to carry out the crime. Such moments normally occur on the holidays, in the early afternoon, after the prayer. Those hours came and went. Nothing happened. I began to think the emir in charge of such matters was away. Whenever he returned—that's when it would happen. I waited for an emir-like figure to materialize on the threshold of my cell. Many men in robes appeared. Some of them had powerful beards. Some didn't. Nothing happened.

Meanwhile, the corridor outside my cell was evolving into a bustling underground boulevard in their caliphate-to-be. In the bathroom, I heard Russian, French, Turkish, and Kurdish voices. In the mornings, when teenage guards escorted me in a blindfold through the corridor, I listened as the men of the caliphate recited the Koran. Some lifted weights then. Others feasted. A kitchen opposite my cell had equipment with which to make stews and soups for dozens, maybe hundreds, of visitors. Along our basement corridor, there were dormitories for travelers, a sitting parlor for distinguished visitors, a mosque, and at the end of the corridor, in the windowless cavern that housed the hospital furnace, a torture room.

I learned to ignore the children. When I happened across them in the bathroom, the ten-year-old boys would ask me, "Do you know what I will be when I grow up?" I knew that they had been brainwashed into telling strangers that they dreamed of becoming suicide bombers. I tried not to engage. "Do you know what they are planning to do to you?" the kids would ask. I ignored them. The older, more distinguished-looking visitors to my cell talked much less. Unlike the children and the teenage soldiers, they never sang. The older men held their tongues and I assumed them to be in possession of secrets—or anyway, of information relevant to my fate. When these make spoke, however, the things they said were every bit as outlandish as the things the children said.

One afternoon, four elderly men in gold-fringed black robes, the picture of sobriety, it seemed to me, slipped into my cell. They collected in a semicircle over the mattress on which I was sitting, then stared at me. Their formal regalia, long beards, and grave faces made me think they had come to make a declaration or to issue a formal judgment. Eventually, one of the men pulled back his robe to reveal a knife and a handgun fixed to his waist. Like a movie villain, he removed his knife from its sheath, then ran his fingers across its blade.

A minute or so of collective knife admiration went by and then one of the visitors wondered, apropos of nothing, how much I thought my life might be worth, in dollars. The men ran their eyes over the objects in my cell: a pee bottle, a water bottle, a tin dish. They massaged their beards. "You could sell your blood," one of them suggested. "Do you have AIDS? Your liver is worth something?" The other men turned their faces to me, as if genuinely interested in my thoughts. "You want to try?" said one. I watched their eyes to see if they were joking. I couldn't tell.

After they had left the cell, I scoffed. A band of dodderers had wanted to frighten me. I had seen through their game. Men of this age, in this clothing, in Aleppo, I knew, spent their days reciting the Koran to themselves on sun-filled patches of mosque carpet. They gossiped. They might have fantasized about selling the blood of their enemies. In real life, they were harmless.

I clung to my theory for the rest of the day, but in the evening, as the light drained out of my cell, my theory began to disintegrate. If my captors were operating on prisoners, the operations might well occur in the basement of a hospital. If they were killing their prisoners, why wouldn't they take an organ or two first? Perhaps their own soldiers required transplants. Anyway, night after night, in this hospital, an inhuman screaming, as if from beasts in a slaughterhouse echoed through the cells. Could this be the sound a human makes when his insides were being ripped apart? Maybe it is, I thought. Anyway, the sounds I heard in this prison indicated that ghastly things were being done to prisoners. Sooner or later, ghastly things, I concluded, would be done to me.

In the darkness inside my cell, I clung to one theory, then clung to its opposite. My captors were on the side of the Syrian people, against the dictator, I told myself. Basically, they were good. I answered myself: Do good people torture their neighbors? Would a good person do to anyone what they were doing to me?

One afternoon, a commander opened the door of my cell, poked his head in, then told me that I should prepare myself, for I was to be executed in five minutes. "In the Islamic manner." He slammed the door. He returned five minutes later to lecture me, apparently, but not to execute me. In the midst of his lecture, the call to prayer came. He turned on his heels. "We're busy," he said. Again, he slammed the door.

After this incident, I began to think that they were keeping me alive because the sight of a blindfolded, terrified American shuffling through their corridors gave them visual proof of a truth the citizens of their state believed in but could not see. Americans cower, they wanted to believe, by nature. We covered up the fact with ridiculous technologies. Now, in their basement, I covered myself with a pair of hospital pants, a bloody T-shirt, and a tennis jacket. In other words, they had taken my cover. "Your rights are with us now," a commander told me.

This meant, I assumed, that I no longer had any of my own. Their right, for their part, was to behold the true nature of the enemy, to look on him as he really was, without his technologies, without any adornment at all.

As it happened, the true nature of this enemy was to tremble. In the darkness, in the presence of flashlights, he held his hands in front of his face. When he was in cuffs, he held these in front of his face. He hardly spoke. When the eight-year-old children told me to drop to my knees, I dropped. Thus the longer my life went on, the more Muslims from every corner of the Earth could see the inner qualities of this enemy:

He was not above pleading with the cubs of the jihad, as the preteens called themselves, for food. He flinched when the cubs slapped him. "Why are you afraid?" the boys would ask, laughing. "Are all the Americans as fearful as you?"

But if I was a walking exhibit, my value, I judged, wasn't much. "Your life is cheap to us," the teenagers used to say as they escorted me to the bathroom. "It will cost us only a single bullet." Maybe they were kidding. Maybe they were half-kidding. Yet the handguns they poked into the base of my skull when they guided me to the bathroom were certainly real. The screams from the torture room were real. Were they killing people down there? I was much too frightened of the answer to this question to ask it of anyone. But when they were torturing someone, I sometimes put it to myself. The answer came back in my head: This is the sound of someone being murdered.

The fighters in this hospital were often bored. To relieve their boredom, they abused me. When I passed them in the hallway, on my way to the bathroom, they slapped the back of my head. They locked their elbows around the back of my neck, wrestled me to the ground, then sprang to their feet in mock triumph and real, unfeigned happiness.

When I had lived through a week or so of such assaults, I decided that my safety required me to avoid the bathroom as much as possible.

I converted my water bottle into a pee bottle. I kept away from the corridor during the times—the dawn prayer, for instance—when I knew the most violent, abuse-prone commanders would be present.

One afternoon, when I judged that no commanders at all were about, I banged on the cell door. A teenager led me to the bathroom in perfect tranquility. He escorted me back to my cell in the same silence. I began waiting for these silences.

Most of all, I feared the prison manager. I imagined that he was in touch with faraway al Qaeda bosses. He could plead my case to them. Or condemn me in front of them. His hatred for me seemed a personal thing, so I feared his voice above all others, but there were stretches of days during which it seemed to vanish from the hospital corridor. He often went about in a suicide belt. Maybe he had blown himself up? Maybe the regime had caught up with him? There were times when, listening for this commander's voice, it occurred to me that the other elder, important-seeming al Qaeda figures had vanished, too. Were they hiding out in the hills? Away on vacation? There were intervals of four or five days in which only the teenagers, it seemed to me, had been left to run the headquarters.

During these periods, it often happened that schoolchildren (the commander's sons?) and a few of their teenage friends would bring a soccer ball into the corridor. They would have penalty shoot-outs. Or they would gather round, as I was being brought to the toilet, to ask questions about the details of my life in America. We all knew they weren't meant to be interested in the dreck and trivia of everyday life in the United States, and yet . . . One of these basement teenagers had somehow convinced himself that over there, in the vast *Playboy* mansion that was an unmarried man's life in America, I had had nine girl-friends.

When he was in the mood for it and when the commanders were away, this young man, Yassin, and I would have cheerful discussions about nine beautiful, willing American women, all in love with me. Didn't I feel it was immoral to "sit with" (his phrase for "have sex with") so many women? How did I find the time and the money? There weren't that many, I replied, I didn't just sit with them, they weren't all American, I didn't pay them, and I was glad for those relationships because they had helped me learn about life. Almost all those young men understood at least something of how complicated romance in America can be because of the "It's complicated" button on Facebook and because in Syria, everyone under forty has seen at least a few episodes of *Friends*. All young people everywhere, of every faith in Syria, can sing in English at least a line or two from the Celine Dion ballad "My Heart Will Go On."

In that basement, when the commanders were absent and when the subject of American love was in the air, the caliphate took a nap. It was still there, but for a few seconds no one cared. In those moments, it was clear to everyone that a girlfriend was good, not bad. My logic was impervious to argument, not theirs. A girlfriend would open the world to you. Her presence in your life would fill you up with pride, not shame. Why had I ever left America? the teenagers wanted to know. What on earth had brought me to Syria?

Once, in those early weeks, when no one special appeared to be lurking in the basement, I told a teenager who seemed, on some days, to be interested in English lessons that I liked his hotel just fine but had some business to look into and needed to check out. "Now," I said. I smiled. He smiled back. He was standing on the threshold of my cell. He flung the door open. "Out you go, then," he said. He stepped aside. "Be my guest." For an instant, the hospital was just a hospital. This young man was just a kid from the neighborhood. He played soccer. Before the war, my rapport with the soccer-playing teenager was the single thing in this nation of invisible realms and mercurial people that I could rely on. Soccer had been like a universal code for friendship. The feelings a game brought waited in every alley, in every village. They were as natural and as good as the sunlight. For an instant in the hospital basement, this teenager was one such friend. I was his American guest.

And then, an hour later, the young man with the bee in his bonnet about my nine girlfriends, Yassin, would be standing on the threshold of my cell with a length of three-quarter-inch galvanized steel cable in his hand. Something, what I did not know, had woken the ancient, collective dream. "The floor of your cell is filthy!" he would shout. There was a pee bottle on the floor of that cell, a lice-filled, woolen army blanket, and nothing else. How was I to clean the floor? "You clean it with your tongue!" he would say, shouting. If the floor didn't sparkle when he returned in ten minutes, he threatened, "the *shabab*"—the other young men in the corridor—would make me regret my filth. I would search Yassin's face for a hint of a smile. He would stare for a moment more, then have me lower my head to his waist, then push my face to the floor.

The caliphate had come back.

Toward the beginning of December in 2012, a band of teenage Turkish fighters took up residence in a room next door to my cell. In the mornings, they lounged on an armchair in an alcove outside my cell. In the evenings, after the prayer, they lifted weights and staged wrestling tournaments in which they threw themselves from the chair's armrests. It didn't take them long to discover that the prisoner in the cell across the way was an American and afraid.

Somehow, the Turks acquired a cattle prod. Somehow, they acquired the key to my cell. Perhaps the Syrian guards had gotten bored of escorting me back and forth to the bathroom. Perhaps the Syrians wanted to allow their Turkish friends some fun.

For several weeks that December, whenever the door to my cell opened, a band of bored Turks would appear on the threshold. I would tie up my blindfold, then allow myself to be led into their recreation zone. They would leap on my shoulders and laugh and ask me to carry them along as if I were a camel. Eventually, they evolved a game in which several of them leapt on my shoulders at once and tried to make me run. I would stagger to the floor. They would kick me in the ribs. They would apply the cattle prod to my backside and to my head. I would scuttle down the hospital corridor in my blindfold.

I resolved to collect spare bottles I found in the toilet stall, to hide them behind the door in my cell, and to pee into them. A guard found me out. He removed the bottles from my cell. A puddle of radiator water stood in the back of this cell. I peed into this. The odor outraged the guards, who informed the prison manager, who appeared, out of nowhere, on the threshold of my cell, surrounded by four Syrian assistants. They sprinkled disinfectant over my head, then dragged me from my cell, then beat me with their shoes in front of the Turks. "Your name is Shoe!" they called out. "What is your name?"

So I was a shoe. I still had my pee problem. The situation, I felt, was degenerating. I knew that I was becoming disgusting to my captors. If only the Turks would leave me alone, I thought, I could bring the prison manager, with whom I shared a language, at least, to an accommodation. If only I could pee in peace, I thought, I could turn my thoughts toward a long-term survival strategy. As things stood, however, whenever the Turks felt like it they subjected me to their blindfolded piggyback game. I was too afraid to use the bathroom. I wasn't sure I could survive the Turks, never mind the punishments the Syrian authorities had in mind.

One afternoon, after a trip to the bathroom, the Turks followed me into my cell, then shut the door. I crouched on my haunches in a corner. One of the young men carried a weapon. A knife? A piece of shrapnel? He concealed it in his hand, but after he had slapped the crown of my head a few times, blood began to trickle down my forehead. It leaked in strings, onto the floor. I screamed at this person. He screamed back at me. The prison manager must have heard that a hullabaloo was underway inside my cell. He strolled through the door, folded his arms, then took up a position a few feet from where I lay. I crawled to his feet. "Please," I said. "Please!" The manager ordered everyone out of my cell. An hour or so later, he returned by himself. He crouched by my side, withdrew a child-sized toy like a handgun from the rear pocket of his jeans, then tapped its butt on my head.

"Anyway, you needn't worry about the Turks," he said softly, like a snake. "If anyone here is going to kill you, it will be me."

In the hours after this episode, I began to think that my captors wished me to see deeply, into the truth of things, just as they did. They felt, correctly, that I didn't want to see. So they had decided to play a game, the purpose of which was to present my fate to me in the form of torture sounds, the songs I heard in the corridor, and the tapping of the pistol butt on my forehead. The fun of it was to lead me into the most intimate, undeniable contact with the truth, to watch as I refused to look at it, to laugh at my blindness, and then one day to present the truth to me in the form of a row of masked men, a camera, and a man with a knife. I had lived through their drama's initial acts. I understood where the crime would happen (their torture room) and who would commit it (the prison manager). I knew about when it would happen (late at night) and who would witness it (the Turks, the teenagers).

One evening during this phase of my ordeal, the prison manager entered my cell with two companions. The electricity had gone out in the hospital. The visitors carried flashlights. The manager stepped forward, seized my head by the hair, and then aimed his flashlight into my eyes.

"Why do you fear?" said one of the men. He promised not to hit me. "Only looking," he said. "Okay?"

The prison manager explained that the men had lately arrived from Iraq. He shook his fistful of hair. My head bobbed on my shoulders. "This," he said, "has lately arrived from Washington."

One of the visitors bent over, shone his flashlight into my eyes like a doctor, pondered me for a moment, then stood up. "He is certainly one of them," he agreed. He felt that I had their eyes and was just as frightened as—by which he meant the American soldiers he had encountered in Iraq, I presumed—they had been.

After a moment, the visitor addressed the prison manager: "I just want to step on his head. May I?"

"Of course," the manager replied.

The manager had me lower my head to the floor. The visitor put the sole of his boot on the back of my head. He scuffed off the grit and mud into my hair. "We're going to step on all the Americans," he said. "Do you know we killed thousands of them in Iraq?"

"A bit too late for regrets, isn't it?" said another voice. "You came for information? I hope you found what you were looking for."

In the darkness, after these men had left my cell, it seemed to me that my tormentors had exposed a new angle of attack. I felt I could defend the US government's involvement in Syria. The American government, I thought, might well have been provisioning at last some of the rebel groups in Syria with training and guns. Apart from this, however, America really had nothing to do with Syria at all. The American government's involvement with Iraq, however, was a different matter.

Now it seemed to me that in the wake of the US military's evacuation of Iraq, the insurgency there had not melted away, as I had assumed, but had gone underground, dug tunnels, crawled away into Syria, then popped up in the Aleppo eye hospital. The American media hadn't reported on the seeping into Syria because the members of this media corps were back in Antakya, lounging by their swimming pools.

Reflecting on my encounter with the Iraqis, it seemed to me that they had been on their best behavior. They meant only to act out a simulation of revenge. Whenever the less-well-behaved Iraqis caught up with me, I supposed, there would be less acting. There would be more revenge. How far behind could they be?

In the minutes before each of the five daily prayers in this hospital, the heavyset, grenade-laden father figures would trample through the corridors. It sometimes happened that I would find myself in the communal bathroom as these men prepared themselves for their prostrations. They leaned their Kalashnikovs against the wall, removed their boots, then showered their feet with cold water. They splashed their faces, caused streams of water to trickle through their beards, then ambled dripping into the hallway. As they walked, they called out to their children, "Prayer, boys. It's time for the prayer!" The hospital corridor filled with footsteps and the sound of cheerful, burbling voices.

As December turned into January, it began to seem to me as though my captors were praying to be allowed to kill me. Their prayers were their time to make evil deeds holy. In their prayers, the sadists transformed themselves into avenging angels of God. The sex obsessives became saintly soldiers. They gazed at the purity within. They would live forever, they told themselves. I would die as God wished for me to die, in the dirt, on my knees, probably soon.

I started to despise the hospital muezzin, a Turk who had fallen in love with the power in his voice. His call was their summons to a collective psychosis, it seemed to me. Their psychosis couldn't be reasoned with, couldn't be seen, and couldn't be escaped. Since I had no books and no way to write, I couldn't crawl away to a sanctuary in my head.

After about six weeks in prison, I found myself turning my attention more and more to my cell's window. It gave out on ground level, flush with the pavement. I had ignored it at first, because the soldiers kept a stack of sandbags piled in front of this window. They draped a blue plastic tarp over the sandbags, then tossed bits of broken office furniture and old ventilation fans over the tarp. It permitted a view, I thought at first, of precisely nothing. Yet there were times when the wind kicked the tarp away. Sometimes soldiers busy with construction projects borrowed a sandbag or two. When fate arranged the pile of debris just so, I found that I could peer out through a tiny channel in the stack of sandbags to a spot high on the facade of a building across the way. In the early evening, just before the Maghreb prayer, pretty, coppery light glinted off a broken window on that building's topmost floor. I had no idea where in Aleppo this hospital was, but one night around Christmastime, gazing into what remained of the window-pane, I decided that that hue of sunset light meant that the window commanded a view over the western horizon.

No traffic noises drifted into my cell. It occurred to me that the incoming shells whistled in the air for an age before they crashed into the floors above me. These clues, I told myself, meant that our hospital had been built far from the center of things, on an eastern ridgeline perhaps, or a plateau, high above the city, as sanitaria sometimes are.

If only they would let me climb up to the shattered window across the way, I thought, I would stand behind it, shield my eyes, then peer out into the setting sun. The vastness of the Aleppo slums would roll away at my feet. I would watch the birds arcing over the rooftops. The Aleppo citadel would hover over the city. I would hold my gaze on the dark silhouette of the Syrian coastal mountains in the distance, look above it into the sky and below it into the middle ground where traffic rolled along a distant highway.

They wouldn't allow me such an excursion? Fine. If somehow I could climb to my own window, I would clasp its bars, hold my eye at my channel in the sandbags, then take in whatever view presented itself. Perhaps the parking lot sloped away into banks of clouds. Perhaps, beyond the parking lot, grasses waved in the winter rain. It was possible. Why not?

The windowsill in my cell was about ten feet off the floor. If I had had a desk or a radiator to stand on, I might have been able to reach the sill, hold myself steady for an instant, then lunge at the bars. As it was, in the mornings, when I had energy, I leapt at the wall. I tried to run my feet up it, then tried to stand on a water bottle, if there was one in my cell or a blanket. When I leapt, the bars I wanted to clasp were only about twenty inches beyond my fingers—close, but far. My view might as well have been on the moon.

There was a radiator in the bathroom. There were sometimes buckets and plastic sacks full of trash in this bathroom. If only the guards would leave me alone in the bathroom, I thought, I could clamber over the trash bags. I could leap at the bathroom window. But the guards never left me alone in this room, nor, for that matter, did the window, when I examined it up close, appear to give out on anything but a wall.

One morning that December, I woke, walked to the spot in my cell from which I could look at the building across the way, and happened to notice a shower of ashes—no, snowflakes—drifting into the war zone.

A few hours later, a guard came with breakfast. "Take me into the snow," I told him.

He put a bowl of olives and a round of bread on the floor for me. He smiled. "Sorry," he said.

"Bring me a snowball," I said.

"Sorry," he said. He shook the snow off the collar of his jacket. It fluttered to the floor. "That will do?" he asked. No, it did not do.

Later that night, this guard, some of his friends, and the prison manager at last took me into their torture room. I was in my blindfold. Though I had walked by this room dozens of times and knew well enough what went on inside, I was too disoriented and too terrified to realize that I was being tortured. It didn't occur to me that I was meant to pour out a confession.

They had locked my body into a truck tire. They did this rather gently, without shouting. Then they cuffed my hands behind my back. They flipped me over so that the weight of my body rested on my knees and my forehead. My hands and feet writhed in the air. I flopped around on the floor, like a trout that's been pulled from a brook. When the pain began, I guessed that they were hacking at my hands and feet with hot knives. My clothes filled with warm liquid. They had begun their hacking at the feet. They were going to work their way upward. Soon they would be slashing their knives into my skull.

In fact, the liquid was water. The knives were only steel cables. They hit only my feet and my hands. Their kind of cables didn't break the skin. Because I couldn't see with my eyes and because I seemed to be squirming in a pool of blood, I guessed that I was being murdered.

I screamed. After a few seconds, the hacking subsided. In the silence after the pain, the manager put a question to me. I answered it. The hacking began again. Our dialog proceeded like this:

Manager: What are you?

Me: Please! What?

The knives cut into my feet. I screamed. The knives stopped cutting.

Manager: You are not a journalist.

Me: No?

The hacking started again. At last it stopped.

Manager: Not a journalist, no. What are you?

Me: An American? An unbeliever?

Manager: You are a liar.

Me: Yes, yes! A liar!

Manager: Do you want to live?

Me: Yes!

Manager: If you want to live, you will speak with sincerity. Why did you come to Syria?

Me: Writing! I am a journalist. Please!

There followed more hacking and more screaming. At last I cottoned on. By the end of this torture session, I had confessed to helping the CIA kill Anwar al-Awlaki in Yemen, to being gay, to wishing to rape Syrian women, and to having coordinated my attack-Islam campaign with the Syrian government's plan to do the same. I had volunteered myself to the CIA because my journalism career had foundered. The CIA had paid me $1,000 in order to get the goods on al Qaeda in Aleppo. "You came to uncover us. We uncovered you. Is that it?" the prison manager explained.

"Yes!" I screamed.

When I had said all—or most of—the things the manager wished me to say, he ordered me released from the tire. I lay on the floor. He seized a fistful of my hair, then brought his face down to the level of the floor. He looked into my eyes: "If so much as a single letter in this confession is untrue, we will kill you. Under torture, we will do it. Did you lie to us tonight?"

"No, I swear to you by God," I said.

The following morning, the assistants brought bread and *labneh* to my cell. Why are they wasting their food on me, I wondered, when I will be dead in the evening? The manager didn't bring me into his torture room that night, but he did the next, and on the following afternoon he did it again.

As he was leading me to the torture room for the third time, he paused at the bottom of the staircase down which I had been escorted about eight weeks earlier. Now, when the manager lifted up my blindfold, sunlight from a door or window at the top of the stairs streamed into my eyes.

"Do you know what this is?" the manager asked about the sun. "This is the last time you will see it. Do you understand?" He brought me into the bathroom. He made me stand in front of the mirror. Again he lifted up my blindfold. "This is the last time you will see your face," he said.

Inside the torture room, the blindfold held itself in place for several minutes. Eventually, a combination of their kicking and my writhing knocked it loose. I'm sure my eyes were rolling in my head as they hit me. But when they stopped hitting, when I was meant to carry on my dialog with the manager, I could see well enough that a crowd had assembled, that Yassin was holding a cable over his head like an axe, that the teenagers who fed me and escorted me to the bathroom twice a day and sometimes spoke kind words to me were now torturing me, also with cables, and that the elderly, long-bearded visitors with whom I had discussed organ harvesting had collected in a corner. They watched like figures in a tableau—silent, rapt, motionless. For their part, the Turks had kitted themselves out in their finest war regalia. They wore combat vests and military-style cargo pants. At least two of them had gone to the effort of tying bandannas over their faces. I knew who they were because I recognized their silhouettes and their expensive-looking basketball shoes.

There were no windows in this room. Someone had strewn a line of candles across the floor. Emergency LED lamps hung from pipes beneath the ceiling. The manager had laid out his instruments across a corner of the floor in rows, like items in a museum display: three pairs of handcuffs, screwdrivers, a pair of work gloves, a neatly coiled chain, jumper cables, and a car battery.

During an interval of calm toward the end of this session, it occurred to me that someone was brushing the fronds of a broom over the soles of my feet. I managed to twist my upper body enough to see a pair of eight-year-old children standing as if in a trance. They held out their cables over the soles of my feet like fishing rods. They were doe-eyed children waiting for something interesting to bite.

"Don't you want to hit him?" a man's voice wondered. The boys stared but did not hit.

In this session, the manager began with questions about paradise. Did I understand I would never be taken into *jenna*? Did I understand I would soon be in hell? Next, he moved on to sex. He wanted to know that I had been a libertine in America and that wherever on Earth I went, I went for sex with the women in my address book. By nature, however, I was gay. Also, sick with sexually transmitted diseases. In Washington, the CIA had planned for me to infect the Muslim—not the Christian or the Alawite—women I came across in Syria. My diseases would sterilize these women, thus advancing the CIA's program of attacking Islam through population suppression.

Halfway through the interrogation, the manager picked up a line of inquiry related to my CIA controllers in Washington. They knew perfectly well where I was, he seemed to think. Yet they had made no effort to come get me. Why not? I didn't know anything about CIA controllers. It turned out that he knew: The CIA had abandoned me to this hospital basement because it had so many cleverer uncaught agents crawling through the city, because it knew that in the past the information I brought them had been a confection of lies, and because the CIA was in the habit of using its agents for a while, then kicking them to the side of the road. So people behaved when their only law was money.

Toward the end of this interrogation, the manager wanted to speak about the vanished American journalist Austin Tice. He couldn't recall Tice's name. I reminded him. "Yes," he said, "and he, too, was a CIA agent. They sent you to bring him back, yes?"

"He's dead," I said.

"No, no," the manager said. "He isn't dead. He's with us."

About a week later, when I was recovering from this torture session and bracing myself for the next—when I was hiding under the quilt on the floor of my cell—a scene came to me out of which I probably could have made the beginning of a short story, not that I was thinking about writing then. It seemed full of news about myself. It seemed to tell the truth about the past and to disclose the future. I didn't want to look at it because it frightened me but did want to look because it explained.

The scene took place on a winter afternoon, at dusk, in Vermont. A young woman in a summery dress stood on the heights of a ruined dam. Heavy snow showers tumbled down from the mountains above her. Snowflakes settled in her hair.

Climbing upward, over rotting planks, her sneakers slipped on the rime frost. She paused, tossed them into the river, then kept on. A few seconds of clambering brought her to a single plank, fixed over the void like a diving board. She listened to the roar of the river for a moment, looked downstream, over village rooftops, then leapt.

Inside the water, she drifted for a moment, then began to panic. Because the current was carrying her toward a shelf of overhanging ice, she reached both hands into the air. She snatched at the ice. But a cascade of black water was dragging objects much bigger than her— tractor tires, tree trunks, refrigerators—into the darkness beneath the ice shelf. The current pulled her under.

I woke from this vision with a start. I reflected on it, pushed it away, forgot about it, then examined it again.

It seemed to me that the broken-down dam was my life before Syria. It was my dying car at home, my abandoned writing projects, and my career in journalism. As an edifice, it was in an unsteady state, yes. But it existed. It had held me up.

The summery dress was my defense against the elements in Syria. A proper reporter comes into a war zone with a combat vest, fixers, editors in New York, something. I had wandered into Syria in flip-flops.

The outstretched hands in my Vermont scene described my helplessness before my captors. In their torture room, my hands had been cuffed behind my back. As they flogged my feet, I waved my hands at their cables. The first time this happened, their cables crushed my fingernails into bloody fragments. The third time it happened, my fingernails were gone. Still, I wriggled my fingers at their cables.

As for the flood, this was the current of electrocutions, songs, screams, and chanting soldiers that washed through the corridor in the evenings outside my cell. It was the old insurgency in Iraq joining forces with the new one in Syria. It was longing for revenge, plus garden-variety adolescent discontent in Europe, plus the terror that comes to a population under siege, at the mercy of the barrel bombs.

Sometime in January, the al Qaeda spokesman dropped by my cell for a visit. I understood then why this person's underlings so rarely spoke in his presence. He lived in a private fortress of incandescent rage. When he spoke to me, he screamed. "Alive! Alive!" he called out that morning. "We've caught an American alive!"

I know now that at the time the spokesman was a rising star in the international jihad. According to his Wikipedia biography, this ISIS commander-to-be, Mohammed al-Adnani, began his career as an apprentice to Abu Musab al-Zarqawi during the war against the Americans in Iraq. During al-Adnani's time in an American prison there, he seems to have bonded with the future ISIS leader Abu Bakr al-Baghdadi.

Later on, after al-Adnani had broken with Jebhat al-Nusra, it was he who led the European fighters in their jihad against the West. "If you are not able to find a bomb or a bullet, then smash his [the unbeliever's] head with a rock," he urged the readers of the ISIS fanzine *Dabiq* in 2014, "or slaughter him with a knife, or run him over with your car, or throw him down from a high place, or choke him, or poison him."

In Syria, I knew him by the nickname his underlings had for him, Abu Taha. That January, when Abu Taha was done exalting over having caught an American alive, he strode to the blanket on which I was sitting, tore the balaclava from his face, beamed a radiant smile at me, and then asked, in an innocent tone of voice, if I remembered him. In fact, I had caught glimpses of his face. I had seen it well enough when, three months earlier, he alighted from his SUV in the midst of the war zone to punish me for having pushed his blindfold away from my eyes.

Mostly, though, I remembered him by his voice. During his interrogations, he had burbled into my ear. His speeches had gone on for hours. I listened to him ordering people about, tiptoeing to the chair on which I sat during his interrogations, withdrawing his knife, then pressing its blade against my throat. As he pressed, he whispered into my ear. I wasn't inclined to forget this voice.

On the morning he came to visit me in the eye hospital, he wanted the underlings there to know that he had done some Google research on me. "If you put his name in the internet," he called out to the half-dozen attendants accompanying him that morning, "you'll see he has been in Yemen. He has published a book about it called . . . called what?" He turned to me. "What was the name of your stupid book?"

My stupid book had been called *Undercover Muslim*. In it, I wrote, truthfully, I thought at the time, about what one learns as a student in the Salafi academies in Yemen. I hadn't loved the title. I had, however, loved the idea of selling books.

I didn't bother trying to explain myself to Abu Taha. I said that I had written a book called *By the Light of the Crescent Moon*. To Abu Taha, himself the author of several books, my title didn't ring a bell. He turned to his underlings. Could any of them recall the title of my book? They could not. An underling in his thirties who was taller and more confident than the others picked up Abu Taha's line of questioning: "So you have been spying on our brothers in Yemen?"

I denied it. Abu Taha shrugged. He launched into a new diatribe. I had been a spy in Yemen, he said, had come to Syria in search of al Qaeda, and now I meant to spread further lies about al Qaeda in America. I would see soon enough, he promised, just what the mujahideen had in store for the spies of America. For several minutes, he ranted for several minutes in this manner.

When he ran out of things to say to me, he turned to his attendants. They had collected in a corner, to the right of the door of my cell. "So we have an American alive," he said again. "He's alive, praise God!"

Was he pleased because he imagined he could swap a single living American for a thousand terrorists, as Hamas managed to do when they released Gilad Shalit? Or because my being alive meant Abu Taha could enjoy the pleasure of killing me? In the hours after he left my cell, I debated the matter with myself. I couldn't decide. Because the hospital was a large structure in the midst of a war zone, while the library in which he first imprisoned me was in a farmhouse somewhere, far from the war, I assumed him to be a field commander. I assumed that the real bosses were upstairs somewhere, in a suite of doctors' offices on the hospital's upper floors, planning out their war. I told myself that my fate was in their hands, that Abu Taha was merely a blusterer who, thankfully, kept himself to the provinces. He will continue to forget the title of my *Undercover Muslim* book, I told myself, and none of his underlings will Google my name. If somehow this could be true, I hoped, and if Abu Taha's discovery of my having written a book about Yemen never worked its way up the chain of command, the book would be forgotten. All would be well.

Later that January, the hospital commanders brought a photojournalist from Long Island named Matt Schrier to my cell. During the preceding weeks, Matt had embedded himself in a Free Syrian Army unit in Aleppo. He had been arrested on New Year's Day during the course of a taxi ride that he hoped would take him from the battle zone, in Aleppo, to the Turkish border. The men who arrested him brought him to the eye hospital's basement. Here, they confiscated his cameras, brought in native English speakers to interrogate him, accused him of nothing in particular, then remanded him to a solitary confinement cell. After twenty days alone, feeling himself going crazy, he resolved to draw the attention of the authorities. He spoke no Arabic. His English-speaking interrogators had disappeared. His strategy was to bang his head against the door of his cell, to scream, and to inquire what was wrong, to beg to be shot. The guards brought him to an office. They seated him in a chair, gave him a glass of tea, and spoke calmly to him. He was under investigation, he was told. If it should turn out that he had violated no laws, he would be free to go.

Shortly after this conversation, the hospital administration decided to move him into my cell. On the night they brought him to me, there was a power cut in the hospital. My cell was as dark as a cave at the center of the Earth. When the door opened, a little crowd of voices seemed to spill into the cell. Some of the voices spoke in broken English, some in Arabic, and one of them sounded like it had come from Long Island.

During those moments, I squinted into the Jebhat al-Nusra flashlights. Matt had wrapped one of the hospital blankets around his waist. He seemed to be wearing it as a skirt. Was this a *futah*—a sarong-like wrap—as men in Yemen often wear? He shouted, almost if he were shouting at friends in a locker room, toward figures whose faces were shrouded in darkness. He seemed to know their first names. Would Mohammed fetch his other blankets, he wanted to know? What about his woolen cap. "Can you get my water bottle, too?" he asked. Because of the sarong, the darkness, and the manic kind of rapport Matt seemed to have established with this entourage of Jebhat al-Nusra guards, I assumed at first, that he was one of them.

As soon as the two of us were alone, however, he began a monologue. No, our captors did not belong to al Qaeda, he explained. "We're in an Islamic court," he said. The prisoners in the cells along the corridor were rapists and drug dealers. So one of the men who had escorted him to my cell, a civilian, apparently, with whom Matt had friendly relations, had told him. Most of the other prisoners, said Matt, were Syrian Arab Army POWs.

Since cameras and business cards on which the word "photographer" was printed had been found in his possession during his arrest, our captors, he said, knew him to be a journalist. They weren't angry with him, hadn't hit him or tortured him, and were currently busy confirming the facts he had given during his interrogation. He had persuaded himself that the interrogators would soon bring the results of their investigation before a judge. Since he had done nothing wrong, and since he was sure the interrogators would communicate this fact to a judge, he would, he felt, be on his way to Turkey soon. From Turkey, he would fly back to California, where he had lately rented an apartment. He meant to abandon photojournalism as a career idea. It had brought him considerable bad luck and no money. As soon as he got back to LA, he would focus on his screenplays. His true talent, he felt, lay in screenwriting.

At a pause in his monologue, I told Matt that I was pretty sure we were being held by Jebhat al-Nusra, an al Qaeda affiliate in Syria. I said that I had lately been tortured. I admitted that during the torture, I had confessed to spying for the CIA. A moment of silence opened up between us. I could feel him staring into the darkness. At length, he asked me if I thought I was going to be killed. I stammered. I considered the matter as if for the first time. I stared at the darkness for a few moments myself, and then I sighed. "I dunno," I said.

"But you confessed?" he asked. "Why?"

I began a discussion about my state of mind during the torture but couldn't find the right words, lost my way, and then lost interest in explaining myself. If this person cannot understand why a prisoner might confess under torture, I thought, I'm not going to go into it.

Matt began a new monologue. Our captors could not be al Qaeda, as I seemed to think they were, he announced, because the real al Qaeda would have killed us already. No, our captors were simply Muslims—obviously very devout ones—who wished to bring Islamic law to the rebel-held areas of Aleppo. He knew all about the real al Qaeda, he said. Bin Laden, 9/11, Zarqawi, the beheading of contractors in Iraq and Daniel Pearl in . . . where was it? He couldn't remember. Anyway, we were dealing with a different kind of animal.

"Yes," I said. "The Syrian branch of al Qaeda."

"Would you stop saying that?" he said. He felt I had no idea what I was talking about. The proof of my idiocy was that I had confessed to being a CIA agent. I had all but dug my own grave. He, on the other hand, enjoyed the confidence of our captors. They positively liked him. As soon as the investigators briefed the judge, he would be set free.

During the first hour of this lecture, I kept silent. Perhaps, he's right, I thought to myself. But the more he talked, the more obvious it was to me that, having no prior experience of Syria, Islam, or the Arabic language, Matt could not see the most basic facts about our world. In his blindness, he spun out fantasies for himself. Was he doing this because he was afraid? Too stubborn to see? I couldn't decide if it would be wiser to clue him in or wiser to leave him to his fantasies. What would be best for him? For us? I wasn't sure.

My circumspection did not last. Within hours my tactless side had won the day. "You've got the facts all wrong," I told him. No, he countered, his facts were right. Mine were wrong. Okay, I decided, after we had been through several rounds of this argument, if he refuses to listen, what is the purpose of talking?

It took us about twenty hours of on-again, off-again arguing to properly despise one another. By the morning of our second day together, he had taken to acting out the screenplays he had written—and memorized—about juvenile delinquency on Long Island. To him, the screenplays, of which there were twenty, were his proudest achievement. But they were full of people being beaten and shot. I couldn't bear to listen. As he recited, I stuffed my fingers in my ears. I looked away. He took my dislike of the screenplays as a rejection of all he had achieved in life, of his very identity. In the evenings, when the guards brought us our nightly ration of bread and olives, he would turn his eyes to them as if they could appreciate how excruciating it was for him to be locked into a cell with a priggish, unsmiling person like me. He would search the guards' faces. "How ya doing?" he would say. They would not reply. "As you can probably tell," he would say, gesturing at me and grimacing, "me and Shithead over there don't really get along."

The guards, most of whom were teenagers, would stare. Sometimes, they would whisper to one another in Arabic: "Which one is the spy?" one of them would say or "What is that one saying?" or "Are they really Americans?"

Toward the middle of February, the hospital authorities brought a Moroccan jihadi, Abu Sofiane, to our cell. For a few days, the arrival of a third person relieved the tension Matt and I could only make worse. Abu Sofiane had been arrested on a quiet afternoon, about a month earlier, in the Aleppo suburb of Anadan. He had gone to a Jebhat al-Nusra office there to volunteer himself as a medic and a fighter. After a meeting with a commander, he emerged into the street. A pair of Jebhat al-Nusra fighters followed him to the car in which he and a friend had driven to the office. As he was getting into this car, the Jebhat al-Nusra fighters accosted him, told him that he was under arrest, and when he resisted, one of them shot him through the thigh. He was packed into the trunk of a second car. An hour or so later, his limbs were being lashed to a metal bed frame in the basement of the eye hospital. During the following four weeks, the Jebhat al-Nusra authorities did not allow him to move from this bed frame. A "doctor"—or, anyway, a Jebhat al-Nusra partisan of some kind—had wrapped Abu Sofiane's thigh in an Ace bandage. His wound received no other treatment. He peed through a catheter. When the guards brought him to our cell, he staggered forward, hopped about a bit, then collapsed in a heap. A few minutes later, I was unwrapping the bandage that covered his wound. His thigh had swollen up to the size of a watermelon. The skin around that wound was a thin membrane of flesh beneath which a soup of black-and-yellow liquid rippled. As I unwound the bandage, a gush of pus poured onto the blanket.

Somehow, Abu Sofiane had convinced himself, as Matt had convinced himself, that the Jebhat al-Nusra high command liked him. In his view, a misunderstanding had cropped up lately between him and some of the middle managers at the hospital. He believed—or pretended to believe—that the matter would be cleared up when the more senior authorities came to the hospital to redeem him. In the meantime, as he waited for his deliverance, he was anxious to forget about the pain in his thigh. Having lived for much of the previous decade in suburban Virginia, he spoke English well. "Do you like movies?" Matt asked him during our first evening together. In fact, Abu Sofiane did like movies.

"Great," said Matt. He had written twenty screenplays. He had memorized them all. Did Abu Sofiane want to hear one?

Indeed he did. In this way, in the evenings, our cell became a little theater. Matt acted out all the parts. Abu Sofiane listened like a child at bedtime He laughed at the right moments. He wondered what had become of Matt's characters and why they acted as they did. For my part, I tried to tune the two of them out. For a few weeks that spring, this movie-inspired entente brought a kind of peace to our cell.

• • •

One afternoon in mid-March, a guard brought an electric razor to our cell. He shaved Matt's head and mine. Abu Sofiane, who had short hair as it was, didn't require a shave. A day or so later, the same guard brought an orange jumpsuit to the cell. "You will make a video," the guard explained.

When it was my turn to stand in front of the camera, a Canadian-accented jihadi asked me questions, in English, about my career as CIA agent. The prison manager who, by this point, I had come to know as Sheikh Kawa, stood in the background. Prompting the Canadian now and then, Kawa held his chin in hand. He nodded. He listened carefully. At the time, Kawa's control over me was such that he didn't need to threaten me to get me to reply as he wished me to reply. He had tortured me. I knew well enough what he wanted me to say.

As the camera rolled, I confessed to being a veteran CIA agent, to having suborned more Muslims into spying for the CIA than I could recall, and to having done it all out of hatred for Islam.

When I was done, I took off the orange jumpsuit Kawa had brought for the occasion. The cameraman escorted me back to the cell in silence.

CHAPTER 5

THEIR NEWS

That spring, I found I couldn't get the suicidal girl who had come to me once or twice in January darkness out of my head. In the evenings, as the light drifted into the cell, and whenever I was trying to make myself sleep, I saw her poised on her plank, high above a river in Vermont. She gazed into a curtain of falling snow. She swept the flakes from her hair, contemplated the roar at her feet, and did not jump. At first, it was the might of the flood and the impossibility of surviving it, even for a minute or two, that held her attention, but the more she stared the more she marveled at the entirety of the scene. The bobbling of the debris in the river held her attention, and then she wondered at the tendrils of woodsmoke rising from the village houses and how busily the inhabitants of this bedraggled ex–mill town went about their lives. They scurried back and forth along the highway that functioned as a village main street. They piled into their cars, drove up the lane a bit, then piled back out. Upstream somewhere, other villagers appeared to have tossed their backyard furniture—and possibly some of the contents of their living rooms—into the flood.

There were picnic tables, propane tanks, sofa cushions, and stray car doors. The more she stared, the more the sight of the debris moved her. She had presumed these effects to belong to the underlying structure of the place. Now they were bobbing away in the troughs of the waves. How fragile life is, she thought, and how prone things are to being swept away.

Looking back now, it seems that this teenager appeared in my imagination because I required a means of seeing how suddenly disasters can descend on a life. I had not known. I hadn't had occasion to reckon with my own impermanence.

Of course, I badly wanted to understand what was happening in the war outside my window, too. I suspect this is why my thoughts kept returning to a person balancing in the air, high above a landscape. I required a seer, a reader of the shifting currents, and a neutral observer. I couldn't see the facts for myself so I invented a watcher, imagined her to be wise, and tried to see through this person's eyes.

Nowadays, I know that during this period in the war, an important kind of news really was developing on the other side of my cell door. That March, the Iraqis and the European fighters in Jebhat al-Nusra were making plans to form a new group, to be called the Islamic State of Iraq and the Levant, which wouldn't fight only in Syria but across the globe. Outside my cell door, this splinter faction within Jebhat al-Nusra was developing its secession plans.

For their part, the loyalist Jebhat al-Nusra commanders were focused on the battle against the Syrian Arab Army. They were keen to show the citizens of Aleppo that as the Syrian Air Force carpet-bombed eastern Aleppo, they alone defended Islam. Accordingly, Jebhat al-Nusra, once a secret organization, launched itself into a high-visibility hearts-and-minds campaign. The sub-commanders affixed the black al Qaeda flag to the antennae of their pickups, and sometimes attached loudspeakers, from which they broadcast Jebhat al-Nusra anthems, to the roofs of these trucks. When their soldiers had nothing special to do, which was often, they piled themselves into the pickup beds, then drove the trucks in columns, at walking pace, through the streets of eastern Aleppo.

From time to time, these pickup caravans parked themselves in front of my window. Looking up from the floor of my cell, I could see the boots of the passing fighters. I caught glimpses of the black flags they flew from their trucks' antennae and heard the anthems playing over the loudspeakers. Many of these parading soldiers were not Syrians. Through the window that had bars but no glass in it, I could hear their broken Arabic. I could see the foreignness in their faces.

By this point, I had long since stopped daydreaming about writing the news article that would rescue my career. Still that spring, as the dream of a caliphate came to life outside my cell, I often wondered what my erstwhile reporter colleagues were making of the recent turn of events in Aleppo. A local hospital had been converted into an al Qaeda command and control center. Martyrs-to-be from across the world were filtering into our basement corridor. The torture of American reporters, their orange jumpsuit videos, the al Qaeda flag–bedecked pickup trucks—surely, I thought, an enterprising reporter would find rich material in such a setting.

Now I know that during the hours in which thoughts along these lines were running through my head, the Beirut bureau chief for the *Washington Post*, Liz Sly, was upstairs in the reception room researching a story about our hospital.

The report that eventually appeared in the *Washington Post*, "Islamic Law Comes to the Rebel Held Areas of Syria," published March 19, 2013, noted that Jebhat al-Nusra, though ostensibly a terrorist organization, had turned itself to civic administration. It had adopted the eye hospital as a kind of "wartime city hall." Here, it concerned itself, as Sly wrote, with "administering day-to-day matters such as divorce, marriage, and vehicle licensing." Toward the end of the article, the report quoted a demonstrator who had been locked up in the city hall basement as punishment for having pushed the al Qaeda flag aside during the course of a march. In the basement, the detainee had been beaten. "It didn't hurt," Sly quoted this person as saying because the pipe with which he had been beaten was thin, "like the ones used in a toilet. It was just a reprimand, a way of saying, 'Don't do it again.'"

Looking back at this article now, I marvel that the hospital authorities allowed her to poke around their premises at all. Perhaps they assumed that she would miss all the important news, as she seems to have done. Certainly, their notion of "the news," in any case, would have born no relation to hers. For these authorities, the important news was that a divine form of government was descending over the Land of Sham. A great, global coalition of enemies, they believed, would soon be attacking this government. They trusted that a critical mass of Muslims, composed of citizens from every nation on earth, was on its way to Aleppo in order to fight and die in its defense. The hospital authorities would have been keen to meet a trustworthy Muslim, capable of transmitting this variety of news to the world's Muslim population. They would have regarded a *Washington Post* reporter as an enemy from the capital of a land of enemies. It's a wonder they didn't arrest her.

Thinking back on that time and place now, it also seems wondrous to me that a reporter could come away from this hospital with the impression that it meant to administer city affairs. In fact, the authorities here meant to put heretics to the rack. They dreamed of an imminent combat between good and evil, millions dead, and a gorgeous utopia, only for Muslims, rising up from the Aleppo ruins. In March of 2013, they were busy making their dreams come true. Did a tour around the hospital's first floor reveal nothing at all of this coming to life? Perhaps this reporter was especially blind? In the years since my release, I've often pondered such questions. I'm inclined to think that this reporter was no more blind than any other. The coming of a caliphate, I know now, is above all a spiritual phenomenon. It occurs within the collective psyche. It's not the sort of thing one could take a picture of. Still less could one interview it. It might be that the best way to report on such an event is to lock oneself into an underground room, to listen to the prayers, and to feel the terror in the air. In this way, over time, the thing that's happening to the city's psyche is bound to happen to yours.

Over time, Jebhat al-Nusra developed a news apparatus of its own. Because its reporters were Muslims, the news they produced was thought to be immune to the Jewish hoodwinking.

Their productions addressed the general news consumer, as the news-like videos the ISIS hostage John Cantlie made for ISIS did. At it happened, these videos covered more or less the ground the *Washington Post* correspondent covered during her Aleppo trip. The news in these reports was that in the ruins of the old institutions citizens, assisted by the principles of their faith, were cobbling together a new civic order. When prisons were referred to, they were said to be for leading wayward citizens back to God. There was no torture. In the civilian population, there was despair and deepening piety. Among the rebel leaders, there was serene conviction. Such is the al Qaeda news. It never changes.

CHAPTER 6

THE VILLA BASEMENT

One morning in April, the prison manager, Yassin, and two prison guards I did not know opened the door to my cell. Yassin held a handful of plastic zip ties in one hand and strips of light blue fabric, to be used as blindfolds, apparently, in the other. I said that I had my own blindfold. "Fine," Yassin said. "Blindfold yourself, then give me your hands." When I had completed this operation, he had me step into the corridor. Out there, I could hear that other prisoners up and down the corridor were also being blindfolded, handcuffed, then made to step into the corridor. The guards were in the mood for jokes, it seemed. One of them leaned a hand on my shoulder, then spoke as if he were a tourist guide, in bright, foreigner-appropriate Arabic. "Have a pleasant journey," he said. "We thank you for your visit!"

That morning, the Jebhat al-Nusra administration escorted twenty-eight prisoners out of their cells in the eye hospital basement, walked us up a flight of stairs, then herded us into the backs of waiting trucks. Outside, in the hospital parking lot, I was made to lie in the bed of a pickup with two other prisoners. A Jebhat al-Nusra fighter who might have been in the bed with us but also might have been sitting in the pickup cab murmured threats at us. We were not to say a word. We were not to move. If we moved or spoke we would be shot.

I waited for the truck driver to turn on its engine, then nestled myself against a wheel well. A few minutes later, we were rolling. It was easy enough to nudge my blindfold upward a bit. I could see that we were rolling down a broad city boulevard. A little knot of commuters waited at a bus stop. By the side of the road, children sold vegetables from the backs of upturned plastic crates. There was a traffic roundabout and, beyond this, a district of junkyards and cement shacks, which dwindled away, after about fifteen minutes, into dandelion fields.

Nestled against the wheel well, I watched the road signs rolling by: Kafr Hamra, Babis, Anadan. We were in the northwestern Aleppo countryside, apparently, heading north. An hour and a half of driving along meandering country roads brought us to the service entrance of a stately villa. There was a line of cedars, an entry gate, a guardhouse, and a flight of stairs under an eave, which led downward, into a basement. Under the blows of the Jebhat al-Nusra guards, the twenty-eight prisoners were hurried down this stairway, through a corridor, then into a basement cell. We were told to sit in rows, to face the back of the room, to keep our mouths shut, and not to move.

I didn't know this then but found out later that about half the prisoners made this voyage in the body of a fuel transport truck. Their clothing stank of diesel fuel. By this point in our travels, most of our blindfolds had fallen away. Some of the prisoners had wriggled their wrists out of their plastic zip tie handcuffs. As we sat with our backs to the door of the cell, we snuck glances at one another but did not speak. In this cell, a bank of boarded-up windows on one of the walls admitted a gray, milky light. We could make out faces by this light but wouldn't have been able to read. In the silence our captors had ordained, we peeked at the windows, smelled the diesel fuel in the air, and did not glance over our shoulders.

From somewhere behind us—the doorway, no doubt—came the sound of men fussing with their Kalashnikovs. They clicked their magazines into place and hoisted their shoulder straps over their shoulders. They murmured among themselves but did not speak to us.

In those moments, I'm sure all the prisoners felt that Jebhat al-Nusra had brought us here to shoot us or to light us on fire. What could we do? I, for one, was too afraid to speak.

After several tense minutes, the captors slammed the cell door shut.

I happened to be sitting next to a prisoner whose ability to read the religious codes in Syria was sharper than mine. He eavesdropped for a moment on our fellow prisoners, then turned to me with a look of terror in his eyes. "They're all Alawites," he whispered.

I glanced at my fellow inmates. Many were wearing combat fatigues. By this point, the Jebhat al-Nusra psychology had worked its way into my own. In a flash, I saw what had happened at the eye hospital. I had been picked out as a political enemy. The other prisoners had been deemed religious enemies. Now we had been brought into the quiet of the countryside. Soon we would be shot as the Nazis shot Jews in Poland in the early part of their war: in the darkness, in the basements of abandoned buildings in the countryside. Afterward, our bodies would be incinerated.

In fact, a group of three captors returned to our cell within minutes to snip away the zip ties. The prisoners who were still wearing their blindfolds were allowed to untie them. Without speaking, the captors handed us bottles of fresh water. They went away without a word but returned an hour later carrying piles of woolen army blankets.

After they had locked the door again, we laid the blankets out over the floor in order to make a sort of patchwork carpet. Our cell was a narrow, rectangular room. There was just enough space in it for each of the prisoners to claim a spot at the base of a wall, to tuck his left shoulder into the flank of the neighbor on his left, to do the same with the neighbor on his right, and to stretch out his legs. Sitting in this way, our toes overlapped with the toes of the prisoners who sat on the opposite wall. We were packed in tightly, in other words, but the conditions were not unbearable. From the eye hospital many of us had brought plastic shopping bags in which we carried extra T-shirts and underpants. Some of the prisoners managed to bring their winter coats. One of them carried a bundle of cloth that, when unwrapped, turned out to contain three door-stopper-sized editions of the Koran.

The military men in this group had been held, it turned out, in the cell next to mine in the eye hospital basement. They knew one another well enough. Now they turned their eyes on the eleven civilians they did not know. Gradually, the air filled with questions: "Where from?" "Who caught you?" "Where?" "How long have you been in prison?"

I'm sure the day's events had shaken us all. I found out later that one of the half-dozen soldiers who made the voyage in the bowels of the fuel truck had lost consciousness in the darkness, as the fuel sloshed over his clothing. He had felt himself suffocating to death.

At one point during the morning voyage, our convoy had bumbled into a confrontation at a highway checkpoint. During this contretemps, the prisoners in the pickup beds watched from under their blindfolds as the Jebhat al-Nusra warriors alighted from the trucks, then ran screaming toward a foe at the head of the convoy, beyond our field of vision. Many large, exotic, expensive-seeming rifles were brandished. There was much shouting. Bursts of gunfire erupted. At the height of this drama, the driver of the fuel truck emerged from his cab, shouted something unintelligible, then reached his hands into the suicide belt at his waist. Withdrawing a pair of wires, he clutched one in each hand, then walked forward through the stalled traffic, waving his wires in the air, screaming.

It took ten minutes for this checkpoint confrontation to resolve itself into a squabble and another ten minutes for the squabble to de-escalate into a discussion. Something must have gone right during the discussion. Soon we were again rolling through the dandelion fields.

Because a Jebhat al-Nusra warrior cannot lay eyes on a prisoner without screaming curses at him and because no prisoner likes to sit on a floor in a pair of cuffs and a blindfold as Jebhat al-Nusra men point their rifles at his back, our first minutes in this basement occurred in an atmosphere of blank terror. The terror dissipated, of course, as it had always done in the past, and within an hour a warm conversational hum, as in a movie theater before a show, hovered over our cell.

Seventeen of the prisoners, I discovered, were indeed Alawite officers in the Syrian Arab Army. They had been wounded on the battlefield, or ambushed or put to siege, then dragged away behind enemy lines. There was an Alawite member of Parliament among us, and seven Palestinian Syrians who stood accused of working as irregulars in pro-regime militias. There were three foreign prisoners: the jihadi

from Casablanca, Abu Sofiane; Matt Schrier, the photojournalist, origi-
nally from Long Island; and me.

Even in the best of times, army officers in Syria can be counted
on to regard people who sneak into Syria without visas, as the three
foreigners had done, as plotters, sent by the CIA, to slit the throats of
the Assad loyalists. In fact, Abu Sofiane really had come to Syria with
some such purpose in view. It would not have taken long for the officers to deduce that a wounded Moroccan in Aleppo who made noises
about having come on a humanitarian mission, as Abu Sofiane did that
night, was a genuine terrorist. If they had met him under other circumstances, these officers would have put some perfunctory questions
to Abu Sofiane, or not, then shot him on the spot. Though they were
too polite to say so, the officers suspected that Matt Schrier and I had
snuck into Syria to provide money and knives to the Abu Sofianes of
the world.

That night, inside our cell, our instinct was to make peace, not war.
We were aware that the occasion required cover stories. We indulged
one another. I introduced myself as an English teacher specializing
in poetry. I had studied Arabic in Damascus before the war and had
returned in the hopes of helping teacherless children in the war-torn
areas. Abu Sofiane declared himself to be a doctor who, after training
in America, had come out to Syria to aid the victims of the war. Matt
Schrier was a photographer from Los Angeles. Our stories were lies or
partial lies. "Welcome to Syria," the officers said to us, smiling as we
relayed our cover stories. They did not probe. Doubtless, they too had
secrets they wished to preserve. Nobody wanted to pry.

By this point Matt Schrier, following Abu Sofiane's instruction, had
decided to convert to Islam. Matt had taken a Muslim name: Nasser.
He introduced himself as Matt. Abu Sofiane corrected him. Matt gave
out the religiously correct name, Nasser. "Welcome, Nasser," the officers said. They wanted a Syria-appropriate nickname for me. In order
to dilute my Americanness, I had introduced myself as half-French.
On the universally-known-in-Syria sitcom *Bab al-Hara*, which is set in
Damascus in the 1920s, in the time of the French mandate, the neigh-

borhood spy-collaborator is called Abu Steyf. He is a comical figure, liked but not trusted. One of the officers proposed the name for me. Twenty-odd faces turned to me, smiling and winking. "Welcome, Abu Steyf," they whispered.

At one point that evening, a Jebhat al-Nusra commander came to our cell to denounce the seven Palestinian Syrians among us. He made them raise their hands, state their names and the names of the places they were from. By agreeing to serve in pro-regime militias, according to this commander, the Palestinians, who were Sunni Muslims, had turned against their families, their villages, and God himself. If matters had been left up to this commander, all those who had betrayed Islam in this manner, he said, would be taken into the yard this evening, then shot.

In the silence after this visitor left the room, one of the Alawite officers leaned forward, then stage-whispered in the direction of the Palestinians, "May God release you from this captivity."

The Palestinian prisoners replied as a group: "May he release us all," they said. "May he return us to our families, each of us, healthy and sound."

This exchange of civilities, it turned out, ushered in a veritable competition of gallantry. Abu Sofiane wanted the officers to know that he loved Syria and that he considered all Muslims to be brothers. In Abu Sofiane's view, the problems in Syria were the fault of the American government, which, out of hatred for Islam, was encouraging Muslims to destroy one another. He elaborated on this theme in a loud whisper for several minutes. Meanwhile, many of the rebels, in Abu Sofiane's view, wanted to spread destruction because they were bored and because destroying things was fun. The right thing to do, he said, was for the Muslims to leave off bickering among themselves and to take the fight to Israel and America—inside Israel and America. Alas, he said, Arabs loved pursuing their family squabbles more than they loved fighting their true enemies.

In this cell, these were anodyne sentiments. They were the equivalent of declaring April weather pleasant. Abu Sofiane spoke for several minutes in these tones. His words brought saddened, knowing smiles to the prisoners' faces. Everyone agreed that the Arabs must unite and that at the root of everything lay the machinations of the Jews.

As the comfort these clichés brought spread through the room, a cadet whose military academy had been overcome by a coalition of rebels nudged me in the ribs. He wanted me to know, he said, that he regretted the manner in which I had been treated during my time in Syria. He cast a bewildered look at the steel door of our cell and at the line of prisoners huddling on the floor beside it. "We are meant to show you the beautiful things," he said. "Here you are seeing the worst."

If I were to visit him in his city, Safita, in the mountains to the west of Homs, he said, I could live for weeks without seeing a hint of war. Also, Damascus—well, most of Damascus—was peaceful. All along the Syrian coast there was peace. "Why didn't you go there?" he wondered. I shrugged my shoulders. Next time, if there was a next time, I said, I certainly would.

That night, we were so eager to talk and talked so volubly that the ranking officer from among the military men, a colonel, had to raise his voice to us more than once. Whispering, we skirted all the sensitive issues, as conversation in downtown Damascus often does. We relied on the formulae for expressing good wishes in which the Arabic language abounds, and when we had exhausted these we asked about the names of one another's children and for descriptions of the things our new friends missed most from home. It was obvious to us all, I think, that while we might still be killed, we didn't exactly belong to the war anymore. We had become spectators. Having withdrawn to the sidelines, it was obvious to us that a madness was consuming Syria. It had possessed us all, and now, inside this villa basement, it did not possess us. We were coming back to our senses. Nobody wanted to kill anybody else. We rather wanted to live and let live.

Toward midnight on our first night in this cell, the Jebhat al-Nusra guards brought us five pots of rice and twenty-eight rounds of bread. In order to spare us the indignity of having to scrounge around in the darkness for the food, they brought us flashlights. There wasn't enough rice to feed half of us, but we were so determined to exhibit our best selves that each person scooped a handful of rice for himself, nibbled at it thoughtfully, as if his mind were on higher things, devoured the bread, then pronounced himself full.

During the course of our dinner conversation, it emerged that Jebhat al-Nusra was working out a swap with the Syrian regime in which inmates from the Aleppo Central Prison would go free in exchange for the seventeen army officers. The Palestinian prisoners would likewise be freed in exchange for Jebhat al-Nusra–friendly Palestinains in regime custody.

The following morning, when the guards came to the cell with breakfast I made my way to the door. I tapped a middle-aged Jebhat al-Nusra factotum on the arm. This person was dressed in an Oxford shirt and pleated trousers. Perhaps he had been a businessman in an earlier life? Perhaps he still was a businessman. "You are negotiating with the Syrian government to free the others," I said. "Are you negotiating with the American government, too?"

He gave me a blank look. "Yes, of course," he said. He flashed his cell phone at me. The number on the screen, he said, belonged to the American ambassador. He didn't say which ambassador or where this ambassador lived or what business he, the man who distributed packages of bread to prisoners, had with the American government. I didn't care. I was anxious for good news, even if there was more fiction to it than fact. Perhaps the bread man really was working a sideline in international hostage negotiating. It could be. Why not?

Over the ensuing days, I pestered the other business-casual Jebhat al-Nusra visitors to our cell. Perhaps they were also moonlight negotiators. For good measure, I importuned the bright-eyed twentysomethings who appeared before us, as if from central terrorist casting, with the testament of faith emblazoned on their headbands. I questioned the stone-faced middle-aged men in robes and one gang of teenagers who wanted me to know that they had recently arrived in Aleppo from a city on the Iraqi border called Al-Bukamal.

All these visitors told me what the bread man told me. Yes, of course negotiations were underway. No, they knew nothing of the details.

During my first days as a Jebhat al-Nusra prisoner, I had scoffed at the idea of the US government horse-trading with the Syrian branch of al Qaeda. If al Qaeda was calling, I didn't think the US government would pick up the phone. I didn't think Jebhat al-Nusra was capable of finding the right phone number. But time had passed. Now, after six months in their custody, I understood that Jebhat al-Nusra was competent enough to keep the Syrian army at bay in Aleppo, to control roads and villas outside the city, and to besiege the Aleppo Central Prison. Evidently, it was working out the details of a twenty-five-person prisoner swap. The reason there had been no progress in my case, I deduced, was because Jebhat al-Nusra didn't have the competence to carry on negotiations with a faraway government.

I felt I could supply the missing know-how, so one morning, after about a week in this cell, I tugged on the sleeve of the bread-delivering businessman just as he was closing the cell door. One of the magazines I had worked for in the United States, I whispered, exaggerating boldly, if not quite lying, had lately been bought by the Facebook founder.

He gave me a quizzical look. "Wait, I remember his name," he said. He scoured his memory. No, he couldn't recall.

"Zuckerberg," I whispered. Actually, I explained, the new magazine owner was Zuckerberg's best friend. Anyway, both of them behaved like Saudi princes with their money. I was their star reporter. Naturally, they would pay for me. Zuckerberg and his friends were capable of spending a million dollars on breakfast or a birthday party or a remodeling of their swimming pool. "Whatever you want," I said, "it will come quicker and there will be more of it if you put me on the phone."

The bread man made a chivalrous smile. He handed me a plastic bag containing a single round of bread. He didn't want money, he said. He certainly didn't want Zuckerberg's money, which was for Zuckerberg. "What do you want, then?" I asked.

Again came the chivalrous smile. "We want what we have always wanted. The victory for Islam," he said. "And we want death."

Whatever grandee owned the villa in whose basement we were imprisoned had planted ornamental trees in his garden and had laid down crushed gravel paths, which were now frequented by Jebhat al-Nusra's sheep. Inside our cell, we could hear the tinkling of the sheep's bells.

We could hear the sheep browsing on the shrubbery. In the evening, when the fighters went out for a stroll, we could hear the garden's gravel pathways crunching under their boots.

Though the guards had boarded up three of the four cell windows with plywood, the fourth one, against which a pile of dead tree branches and broken crates leaned, permitted a view of a miniature weeping willow. During the long afternoons, while many of the prisoners slept, some prayed, and others huddled with the Koran, scatterings of prisoners used to collect in front of this window to peer out at the willow and to catch a glimpse of the browsing sheep. This was our entertainment in those days. We didn't know if we would ever return to the world of willows and sheep, so we watched them carefully, as if by studying their movements we might somehow recover what we had lost.

In earlier times, our basement cell would have been the grandee's hot-weather sitting room. There were crown moldings at the tops of the walls, a frieze in the ceiling for a chandelier, and a row of windows set inside round-headed arches, as in a monastery or a country library. Lately, a cinder-block wall had been run through the middle of this divan. A steel door had been substituted for whatever had gone before. On the other side of the wall, Jebhat al-Nusra was constructing a row of single-occupancy isolation cells.

I never saw more than a glimpse of the outside of this villa. During our first week in its basement, however, we learned that somewhere above us a swimming pool needed to be emptied of the leaves that had drifted in over the winter, then scrubbed. Also, Jebhat al-Nusra's fleet of trucks and SUVs required washing.

To perform these tasks, a Jebhat al-Nusra commander chose a fisherman from among the officers and a barber. One afternoon not long after we had settled in, a commander who appeared before us surrounded by a retinue of well-armed teenagers happened to remark, out of sheer happiness, apparently, that the villa had also come with a tennis court. Yes, and the most unfortunate thing about it, he said, was not one of "the boys"—he nodded at the teenagers behind him—knew a thing about tennis. The commander seemed to have been genuinely saddened by this circumstance. He stood on the threshold of the cell, cast his eyes over the twenty-eight prisoners at his feet, then gave his beard a contemplative pull, as if he was trying to puzzle out a solution for his men.

"I'll teach you," I offered.

He turned to me. He smiled. For an instant, I thought he liked the idea. He unslung his Kalashnikov from his shoulder, knit his brows, then waved the gun in an arc over his belly. "Like this you do it?" he wondered. It turned out that he didn't want tennis lessons after all. His men were busy with the jihad, he said. There would be time enough for play when they reached paradise. But could they not practice up a bit now, I asked, for the great tennis games to come?

The commander did not reply. Perhaps he hadn't heard me. The half-dozen teenagers and twentysomethings in his entourage did, however, hear. They smiled at me with their eyes, as if they would have been happy to have a game or two of tennis were it not for their crummy boss. I smiled back. I would have liked to make it clear to them that tennis is preferable to slaughter and that they could have a game right now, without bothering to ascend to paradise at all, if only they could manage to give their boss the slip. Of course, prisoners are not meant to invite guards into sedition. These guards weren't meant to speak to the prisoners at all. So I grinned at them for a few moments, they grinned back at me, and then the commander herded his charges out of the room.

Over the following days, I learned that these younger Jebhat al-Nusra fighters had adequate means of supplying their own form of amuse-ment. Many of these younger men would have served for a time in the national army. Their idea of fun was to run the prisoners' twice-daily bathroom excursions as a kind of satire on the parade ground drills the officers would have imposed once, in an earlier time, on those under their command.

The mechanics of it worked like this: At about midday and just before dark, a teenager ordered the twenty-eight prisoners to form a line at the cell door. When a Jebhat al-Nusra sentry in the doorway gave the word, the prisoner in the front of the line was to break into a run, hurl himself through a corridor, then into a bathroom, relieve himself, wash, then sprint back to the cell. "Twenty seconds!" the cubs, as the Jebhat al-Nusra preteens referred to themselves, called after us. They crackled their cattle prods in the air: "Nineteen. Eighteen . . ."

Over time, this exercise developed mockeries appropriate for CIA officers (stress positions at the base of a wall) and the member of Parliament (he was made to crab walk to the toilet and to sing an anthem in praise of Bashar al-Assad as he scuttled along).

Some of the prisoners had once belonged to the ruling class in Syria. In addition to the MP, there was a general, two captains, and a handful of lieutenants. All of these men had studied at universities. They owned cars and houses. Their children would have frolicked by the sea during family vacations. In the government offices, the families would have been greeted by courteous clerks. Those clerks would have served the officers with a smile as if they had never dreamed of demanding *baksheesh* from anyone.

Our bathroom exercises told us that the time in which this class of citizen ruled over Syria had come to an end. Now it was their time to hurry through a darkened corridor in a panic, as guards brandished their broomsticks at us. In fact, whenever a normal citizen in Syria wants anything from the government he must screw up his courage, step into a darkened corridor, then fling himself into an obstacle course of absurd regulations. The reward at the end of it all is never much more than a pile of dung. Perhaps these younger Jebhat al-Nusra fighters knew this and so meant to satirize citizen-government interaction in general.

Certainly, the guards knew that the time had come to smirk at the people who used to do the smirking.

When then guards called out, "Hurry!" we sprinted. If we ran too fast, the blown-out flip-flops we used for bathroom sandals flew off our feet. Or we tripped over the bags of cement the guards left strewn across the basement corridor. If we ran too slowly, school-age children ran after us, brandishing their Taser-like electric shockers. The shock these devices delivered wasn't much more painful than a bee sting, but they emitted a hideous crackling and zapping, like tiny electric chairs.

When the children ran after us, they zapped their Tasers at us, watched us leap in terror, then burst into peals of laughter.

Of course, the toilet overflowed. Of course, we had to wash ourselves with fetid water Jebhat al-Nusra had brought in in a bucket. Two pairs of bathroom sandals were meant to suffice for all twenty-eight of us. Of course, we tried to wash our sandals, which were half-destroyed and rotting to begin with. Of course, they got filthier as the exercise progressed.

Some of the guards, I felt, regretted this humiliation. They didn't know us well enough to despise us. Many were too young to have developed a hatred for the ruling class. They wore preppy cotton sweaters, had bright, intelligent eyes, and though they brandished their cables and broomsticks at us, it was obvious, at least to me, that they were playing a part. The scornful, outraged look in their eyes was a pretense. Many allowed us extra time in the bathroom. The more thoughtful ones kept the cattle prod–bearing children from zapping our backsides.

One afternoon during our twice-daily bathroom humiliations, a Jebhat al-Nusra teenager I recognized from the eye hospital tapped me on the shoulder as I scurried past his spot in the corridor.

"Hey," he whispered. "Remember me?"

"Of course," I said. In the eye hospital, he had ladled lentils into my bowl. He had told me of a dream he once had to study economics in Germany. "You are the Sheikh of Economic Science," I said, using the nickname I had given him a few weeks earlier. "How are things?"

He leaned toward me. He winked, then whispered, "What will you give if I let you go?" He cocked his head to the side, then allowed a smile to spread through his eyes, as if he meant to invite me into a private joke.

I promised him my car.

"Oh, yes?" he said. "What kind?"

It was a Subaru Outback. It had four-wheel drive. "Goes great in the snow," I said.

He smiled again. "I wish I could," he said.

"You want my bike?" I asked. He did not want a bicycle. He did not want a million dollars. "Ten million?" I asked.

He smiled again. "Sorry," he said. He was, however, curious about the snow. Back in the hospital, romanticizing with abandon, I had told him that at home it sometimes snowed for a week at a time. Now and then, drunkards were lost in the snowdrifts. They were old men without families. Their bodies turned up in the spring. Evidently, this public drunkenness problem of ours was still on his mind. He pointed out that Islam prohibited drinking. In Syria, he said, such disorders did not afflict the society and people in general were more respectful toward old people than they were in America. When he came to the end of this mini-lecture, a shadow fell over his face. He seemed to lose himself in thought for an instant. Had I ever come across a corpse in the spring snow? he wanted to know.

I was meant to be hurrying back to the cell. He was meant to be counting down my twenty seconds. Instead, he waited for me to deliver my thoughts about snow and bums in America, then made an embarrassed smile. He gestured with his eyes at a cluster of fellow teenagers who had gathered in front of the bathroom. They were thwacking the bathroom door with their broomsticks. "Hurry, you animal!" they were shouting at the door. When the prisoner in the bathroom did not emerge, they hit the door harder. "You are sick?" they shouted, and then, laughing, "Five seconds! Four . . . Three . . ." The sheikh of economic science shrugged his shoulders. He grinned and shook his head slowly, as if marveling at his friends' zaniness. "Sorry about this," he murmured.

In those moments, I half-wanted to reassure this young man. Jebhat al-Nusra was fun and games, I might have said. It was stolen pickup trucks, conquered villas, and willing brides for all. To confide one's future to Jebhat al-Nusra hadn't been a mistake at all, I could have said. Anyway, it was God's will.

I doubt this young man would have believed me much if I had had a go at speaking like this. I suspect both of us were coming to understand that the will that guided our lives sat in a carpeted sitting room in an upper floor in this villa in front of a flat-screen television. Somewhere up there, a pasha was lounging with a remote-control clicker, an iPad, and high-speed internet. Such men spent their days spitting sunflower seeds across the floor. They clicked between Al Jazeera and Al Arabiya, barked out orders over their two-way radios, and did not rise from their couches.

For a few seconds in the hallway, I managed to interest the teenager in a conversation about the car I had in mind for him. Was it more like a tractor with big wheels that crushed the snow, he wanted to know, or like a boat that sailed on its surface? A bit of both, I told him. He wanted to know if I could supply a girlfriend with the car. She had to be a Muslim and had to be the sort of girl who would cherish him, not me. "Would you mind bringing me across to that sort of place?" he asked me. "Go ahead. I'm waiting."

At least that's what I thought he said. Perhaps I was only listening to my thoughts.

Allegedly, we were sinners. Allegedly, Jebhat al-Nusra had arrested us because, in their Islamic state, sin was to be punished. Jebhat al-Nusra didn't issue indictments. The specifics of our crimes varied according to the mood of the person making the accusation, but nobody in Jebhat al-Nusra doubted that we were in prison because we had strayed from the straight path of God. Similarly, nobody doubted that we could regain the path. Sinners could repent. God could forgive. Even if a sinner were to repent at death's door, after a lifetime of continuous, egregious sin, everyone in Jebhat al-Nusra, including the preteen children, understood that God would wash the sins from his soul. Transformed by the magic of grace, the sinner would be taken into heaven as if he had lived out his days like a saint.

Now and then, when spells of optimism overcame me, I sometimes imagined that behind the scenes somewhere, Jebhat al-Nusra was busy negotiating for my release with authorities in the US. Thinking of the US, however, made me despair. I saw a cubicle deep in the bowels of the State Department basement. It was occupied by a bureaucrat. The bureaucrat's job was to keep an eye on and make occasional notes in a file marked "Theo Padnos, disappeared in Syria." I supposed that this official resented me for having overlooked the State Department's many warnings against travel to Syria. Perhaps, now and then, a note from my captors, I imagined, did make its way across the oceans, then through the State Department input charts, to this bureaucrat's desk. He or she would have sighed, examined the communication, then filed it away in the depths of the department's disappeared person file. I wasn't altogether wrong about this, I discovered later. The US government, I found out when I got home, scrutinizes communications from terrorists more carefully than I had imagined and does its best to comfort the kidnap victims' families. Yet its policy of no concessions of any kind to terrorists allows the bureaucrats only to pretend to negotiate. Actual negotiations are forbidden. Thus, communications from terrorist gangs do indeed make it to bureaucrats' desks. There they languish. And then they are filed away.

In the villa basement, the details of US hostage policy weren't much on my mind. I felt I had to negotiate for myself, as indeed I did. So I beseeched the teenagers. This gave them an opportunity for a mini-lecture. I had made the error of placing my trust in fallible, mercurial humans, they said. In this instance, I seemed to believe in negotiators. It would be far more efficacious for me, they thought, if I were to put my faith in God. "When he decides that you shall be free, that's when you will be free," they told me.

"And there's nothing I can do?" I would ask.

I could enter the religion of Islam, they replied. I could pray.

Several teenagers used to urge me to fast. Jebhat al-Nusra sustained its prisoners on two rounds of bread, one in the morning, one in the evening; handfuls of olives; and, occasionally, in place of the olives, a single falafel ball. The prisoners were hungry all the time, especially after having eaten. Nevertheless, the younger, more ingenuous Jebhat al-Nusra fighters felt the wisest thing we could do was to abjure the bread and the olives we got in the morning. They felt that all the prisoners ought to busy themselves with penance, which is to say, with fasting, prayer, and the recitation of the Koran. By these means, and by no other, they seemed to believe, could we bring ourselves into harmony with God. As soon as we brought ourselves into harmony with God, God, they assured us, would take note, then deliver us to our families.

The fact that God had yet to deliver us was, for these young men, proof of the insincerity of our penance. They felt the sincerity would come through a more total commitment to prayer and recitation. "We are reciting. Of course, we pray," the officers would protest, under their breaths, whenever a teenager tossed a round of religious counsel into the cell.

"Yes?" the teenagers would reply, innocently enough. The officers who were holding our cell copies of the Koran in their hands would raise their books into the air—proof positive, it seemed to me, of active reading.

The teenagers would shrug. Perhaps they had been told that Alawites are incapable of prayer—a libel common enough among hard-line Sunnis in Syria. When Alawites pray, it is sometimes alleged, they are only shamming. Some of the teenagers appeared to think that while God could, in theory, pardon anyone, he would never pardon us. Our sins were too grave. "It's no use praying now," the most well-programmed young men would whisper to us, "since God has already decided that you are going to hell."

Such was the logic around which discussions with our guards often turned. To me it seemed that somewhere beneath their carapace there lived wondering, curious, amicable young men. We had no way to crack the shell. Probably the teenagers themselves couldn't crack it. Whenever this exoskeleton of religious wisdom spoke to us, we murmured before its superior understanding. "Very well," we told it. "In that case, we will pray."

My case was slightly more complicated than the other prisoners' cases, since I was the only non-Muslim in the cell (the Jebhat al-Nusra authorities did not question the sincerity of Matt's conversion). It was presumed that, knowing God only through the Christian Bible, I couldn't be expected to know how or whom to worship. Yet Islam, as every Sunni in Syria knows, is no secret. Nor does it consist of recondite dogmas. It requires only the will to believe. Any human who wishes to learn to make a proper Islamic prayer may learn in a quarter of an hour. Neither do fasting nor memorizing a sampling of the most well-known Koranic verses present unusual difficulties. "God made Islam simple for you," the fighters used to tell me when milder, friendlier moods overcame them. Islam would not complicate my life but simplify it.

To the more credulous fighters in Jebhat al-Nusra, our path out of jail was an open road. We could walk the road any day we liked. We had to resolve to hew to that which God had ordained for Muslims, to eschew that which he has prohibited, as tens of thousands of normal citizens in Aleppo did every day, to pray and to repent. If we were to live in this manner, even for a single day, the fighters used to tell us, we would bring ourselves closer to God. If we were genuinely penitent and if God accepted our penance, no judge on Earth, they believed—or prison or coil of chains—could keep God from sending us home to our families.

It wasn't as if we had difficulty being penitent. We had all made catastrophic errors. Our errors had brought us, if not to the brink of death, then certainly to a place from which we could discern a gaping darkness in the territory ahead. Meanwhile, apart from reading the Koran, we had nothing to do with our time but reflect on how we had worked our lives into this fix.

Abu Sofiane was thirty-two. In his twenties, he had had a go at immigration to America. Settling in Falls Church, Virginia, he turned to drug dealing, then insurance fraud. He married and had kids, but the marriage fell apart.

Eventually, the US authorities deported him back to Casablanca. At home in Morocco, he fought with his father. "A loser is what you are," his father had told him. How could he prove to his father that he was no loser? He rather saw himself as a hero—or felt, at least, that heroic qualities he'd never been allowed to express lived inside him. Yet his father, the American immigration authorities, his wife in America, who was herself an immigrant, the officials in the mosques in America and Morocco—all such people had stifled him.

After his deportation, he took a series of menial jobs in Casablanca. He felt that his supervisors paid him little and mistreated him. The pointlessness of the tasks they made him do, and their habit of firing him every few weeks, made him lose interest in work.

In the wake of an argument with his father he resolved to give his life to the jihad. He flew to Istanbul, then took a bus to the border. He crossed into Syria as I did, with about $50 in his pocket. His idea had been to make friends with a shadowy rebel group he had heard about in the news, Jebhat al-Nusra. When he presented himself at a Jebhat al-Nusra headquarters, outside of Aleppo, the men there had appeared to welcome him, but things had quickly gone wrong. Later, after the shooting, there had been a month of unspeakable agony. There had been no treatment for his wound. There had rather been insults and little food. Nor had anyone in Jebhat al-Nusra bothered to explain to him why the organization had shot him, packed him into the trunk of a car, then chained him to a bed frame.

This shooting had occurred in January. By April, he could hobble. He had stopped obsessing over the proximate causes of his misfortune. When he was feeling close to God, he understood that the primary cause was God. God was testing his faith. He felt he had passed through the worst of it and that when he returned to the field of battle he would be fighting out of love of God rather than out of a wish to make himself great—or heroic or worthy—which had been his original motive. During the long, sleepy afternoons, he often managed to persuade himself that the Jebhat al-Nusra commanders had arranged this ordeal for him after all. They meant to try his spirit. They meant to try his body. In those moments, as he daydreamed, Abu Sofiane's face filled with pride. He felt he was passing the tests with flying colors. He felt he was astonishing everyone, including himself.

Abu Sofiane had a flare for the dramatic. He was capable of bowing his head over the holy book, reading out a line in an even, conversational tone of voice, pausing to master his emotions, giving in to a tear, then carrying on half-sobbing, half-shouting, as if, in those moments, his encounter with the Koran was wracking his soul. It was obvious to everyone within hearing range that he was putting on a display. But a display isn't necessarily a lie. Anyway, his emotions when reading the Koran were a matter between him and God. By Jebhat al-Nusra's lights, which were the lights that guided all the thinking pertaining to Islam in our cell, no human being could doubt him.

As for the brutes who had shot him in the leg, on reflection he had decided that they had nothing to do with Jebhat al-Nusra. Perhaps they had been regime spies posing as Jebhat al-Nusra men. Perhaps they had been rogue Jebhat al-Nusra fighters—criminals, rather than men of the jihad who fought on the path of God.

Anyway, if, on his release, it turned out that they were authentic Jebhat al-Nusra men, he would forgive them. His ordeal in prison had taught him that he ought to forget petty disputes. Now he understood that the highest, most beautiful thing he could do with his life was to run forward, in joy and self-awareness, toward martyrdom.

So he said. He spoke this way in his penitent moods, when he was in direct conversation with the Jebhat al-Nusra men, or when they might have been able to overhear him, and when he was speaking in Arabic.

When he spoke to Matt Schrier, he spoke in English. His conversations then were about movies and drugs and sex. When he wanted to speak without being understood by the Arabs in our cell or by Schrier, he and I spoke in French. He spoke a ghetto French. In his ghetto French, he sometimes daydreamed about working in a hotel on the Moroccan beaches, making mountains of money in tips, drinking during the daytime, and buying himself expensive clothes. In French, he confessed to having had gay experiences in America. Maybe he wondered this was the true and hidden reason for his imprisonment? God was punishing him for past episodes of gay sex.

During the long afternoon hours, as we waited for the Jebhat al-Nusra men to bring us our bits of bread and our handfuls of olives, Abu Sofiane and I would have quiet conversations about such matters. We whispered, usually in English. We spoke about the past, speculated about what life would bring us when we were released, and promised to help each other find work—some day. If my journalism career were to prosper, which probably it would do, I said, I could employ him as a helper and a guide or pay him to introduce me to friends of his high in the Jebhat al-Nusra command structure. If he were to find work in a hotel on the beach in Morocco, he said, he could find work for me in the same place.

We would chatter in this way for hours and then, as the sunset prayer approached, a key would rattle in the cell door, the lock would turn, and a phalanx of commanders would be standing before us in black robes, covered in guns. These men liked to hold their Kalashnikovs in one hand, with their fists wrapped around the barrels, as if they were shoppers in a marketplace clutching baguettes. They showed off their handguns by tucking them into their belts or by allowing them to swing from their shoulder harnesses. It wasn't at all uncommon for the younger fighters to appear before us with three guns somehow attached to their persons, a line of grenades stuffed into vest pockets, knives in their belts, and bandoliers slung over their shoulders. They were like children on Christmas morning who, astounded by the abundance before them, make up their minds to wear all their presents at once.

Inevitably, the sight of these men would send waves of happiness washing over Abu Sofiane. When the Jebhat al-Nusra men finally turned their eyes to him, he would beam: "Peace upon you, brothers," he would say. "I am from Jebhat al-Nusra!"

Because he hoped to be taken for an important person, and possibly also because he believed it, at least a little bit, he would announce that he had studied medicine in America. "Yes, for eleven years," he would say. "A Sunni since the day I was born. My medical specialty is the heart. My profession is the jihad." He had to ask me for the name of the bone—the femur—through which he had been shot. He wouldn't have been able to pass a class in remedial English in a US college. But the other prisoners didn't know any better, the men of the jihad certainly didn't, and so in those moments Abu Sofiane was our cell's broken-legged terrorist-cardiologist-hero. The men of the jihad were his kin. Had they come to carry him away to a comfortable hospital bed and a future of hot, hearty meals? He hoped so. "I am from you, like me like you, may God send you many victories, brothers!" he would call out.

As the commanders stood in the doorway, they would smell the air. They would survey our rags and our disorderly beards. The officers would stare into the floor. Abu Sofiane would point to his leg. He would explain that he had been wounded in battle. He was mending up here. He would be out soon. Often, he would mention the Aleppo suburb Anadan, in which he had been shot. Here, he felt, he was widely known. All the important citizens, and especially those who occupied high positions in the jihad, loved him well. "Will you be going to Anadan soon?" he would ask. "You will ask about me there?"

One afternoon, one of the visitors, humoring him, apparently, said he would be happy to take Abu Sofiane to Anadan. Alas, the visitor only had a motorcycle. Abu Sofiane, being wounded, would require a car.

"No, I don't! No, I don't!" he shouted, hobbling to his feet. He leapt forward on one leg, held out both arms to the visitor, then staggered toward him like a mummy in a horror movie. The visitors gaped for a moment, then staggered backward, into the corridor. For a moment, they seemed to worry for their safety. When they had directed Abu Sofiane to take his seat again, they mumbled among themselves for a moment, then withdrew.

During our first weeks in this prison, Abu Sofiane must have bragged of his medical expertise and his willingness to give everything he had for Jebhat al-Nusra to a dozen visitors' delegations. Not one of them offered him so much as a smile. Nevertheless, every time a new line of commanders appeared at the door he grinned at these dour men like a winning child in school, then explained about his eleven years of medical study in America. "Take me with you," he would tell them. Apparently, at the time, these men didn't require volunteers. They had too many as it was. "Maybe tomorrow," they would tell him.

"Okay, my brothers, tomorrow?" he would reply. "Wonderful! I'll be here. I'm waiting for you. Take care!"

Though I wasn't much aware of it then, it seems to me now that Abu Sofiane's desperation wasn't so different from the desperation we all felt. We lived through this period in our imprisonment in a state of low-level panic, as if we knew the execution party was lumbering its way toward our cell, as if we believed that despite everything, we could persuade our captors to change their minds about us. As we waited for the killers to open the door, we whispered to one another about the lives we had led before jail. Often, those lives seemed like strangers' lives. We had run about this way and that, filling up our days with trivia and never turning our minds to the important things in life. Why not?

One of the officers, a draftee-cadet at the military academy in

Aleppo called Ali, had had a chance to slip away to Beirut at the beginning of the war. Out of laziness, he had instead moped around his family's house in Safita, at the base of the Krak des Chevaliers, as the date on which he was meant to ship himself off to the academy approached. When it finally came, he got on the bus hoping, vaguely, that a spell in the military would improve his physical fitness. Almost as soon as he arrived in Aleppo, the rebels put his academy to siege. The higher-ranking officers hoarded the food. The plebs starved. Many were killed. When the rebels took the survivors into custody, the Sunni cadets were dispatched into the care of the Free Syrian Army because their crimes, whatever they were, could be adjudicated by the revolution's secular authorities. The Alawites were sent off to Jebhat al-Nusra, since it was presumed that they had committed crimes against God. It was thought that only in Jebhat al-Nusra were there judges who understood the will of God well enough to punish them as God wished for Alawites to be punished.

Ali had hoped to marry. He had begun a course in French at a private institute in Homs. He hoped to try German, too. His dream was to become a computer scientist. Now the Jebhat al-Nusra commanders were threatening to hang him because the Alawites were fire worshipers, who had come down from Iran nine hundred years ago in order to make war on Islam.

In conversation with me, he wondered why had he known nothing of the fanaticism in his own country. He had read about it, of course, and seen it on television, but he never imagined that actual al Qaeda terrorists would surround a Syrian government armory, starve the cadets within, kill some, and take everyone else hostage. All of a sudden, the fiery-eyed zealots on television were at his throat.

Ali was twenty-eight years old. He felt his time had gone by in the blink of an eye. Unlike many of the officers, he didn't believe much in paradise. He was ashamed that Jebhat al-Nusra—or their friends, or a coalition of al-Nusra and friends—had triumphed over the academy, half of Aleppo, and now appeared to control all of the countryside beyond. "We're very sorry for this," he used to say smiling in embarrassment. He shook his head in disappointment, as if we were all tourists on an excursion into the countryside that had gone awry. As a Syrian citizen, he had believed in the essential decency of the nation, at least a little bit. And now this. Now the people he had once admired— colonels and generals—were covered in lice. They had only rags for clothes. All of us were desperate for the tiniest scraps of food.

"Tell me about America," he used to say when we had eaten the bits of bread Jebhat al-Nusra had given us for dinner. He wanted to know how much a typical family in America could expect to make in a week, how the siblings got along, what kind of a car a normal, every-day American family might drive, and if, were he to travel to America, he would more easily find a job in Chicago or in California. Was France maybe a better bet for him in the future or would Germany, which had a better economy, hold more promise?

Of all the prisoners in our cell, Matt Schrier was the least inclined to regrets. He didn't feel he had made any mistakes at all. He blamed the taxi driver in whose car he was riding when Jebhat al-Nusra arrested him. He felt he had endeared himself to the Jebhat al-Nusra command by converting to Islam, that they appreciated his zany sense of humor, and that while the rest of us had made grave miscalculations, he, being well liked, would soon be let go. But he had been arrested in January. By April, it was becoming clear that he had misread the situation. He didn't know who to blame. His regrets came to him almost against his will, like epileptic seizures. They took hold of him totally, lasted for a few hours, then disappeared without a trace.

When he reflected on the course of his life, he regretted that in his thirty-six years he hadn't accomplished anything in which he could take pride. He was proud of a website he had built to house his photos. But at the moment, it was merely a shell. The reason he had come to Syria was to fill the site with photographs. He meant for the website to be his showcase. It would show the world all he could do with a camera. But Jebhat al-Nusra had stolen the three cameras he had brought with him. All of the pictures he had accumulated in the weeks before his arrest were now in Jebhat al-Nusra's hands. The thought of their thievery enraged him. The way they had derailed his career just as it was taking off enraged him. Their refusal to tell him anything about why they had locked him up, what had become of his cameras, and what they meant to do with him brought the blood into his eyes.

For Matt, Jebhat al-Nusra's irrationality recalled the irrationality of the institutions that had hemmed him in as a child. Understanding nothing and unable to make himself understood, he felt himself locked up in an evil, Koran-heavy version of reform school.

The Jebhat al-Nusra prison system was hardly the first institution with which he had clashed. In high school on Long Island, there had been fights with the teachers, a series of expulsions, and, finally, jail. His father, a basketball coach, had dismissed his abilities as a basketball player. In order to make money, and because he was bored, he and a band of friends used to drive to the suburb next to the one in which he'd grown up, break into prosperous-looking houses, case the bedrooms for jewelry and guns, then sell the loot to high school friends. Eventually, one of the members of his burglary ring was caught. The friend confessed. When the police confronted Matt, he also confessed. In the end, he took a plea. The plea required him to spend several months in jail.

Photojournalism was supposed to have allowed him the freedom he had sought as a younger man. He would document other people's problems. He would step out of his own. Before his trip to Syria, he had taken photos of the Occupy Wall Street demonstrations, had sent these to editors, but no one had been willing to hire him. He wasn't bothered because in Syria, he felt, his physical courage would win the day. He was willing to put himself into situations no sane photographer would approach. He would succeed, he hoped, because he had nerves of steel. As the buildings nearby went up in clouds of smoke, he would point the lens, then shoot. Career success would ensue.

He had also meant to do good. His plan had been to direct some of his attention to the plight of Syrian refugees. In fact, he did manage to tour one of the refugee camps before his arrest. When Jebhat al-Nusra brought him to their interrogation room in the eye hospital basement, their investigators examined these photographs. To his surprise, the photographs produced rounds of laughter. The interrogators laughed at the refugees for their bedraggled clothing and at the photographer for having gone to the trouble of photographing such decrepit people.

In those moments, as they were snickering, Matt decided that the Syrian people ought to draw the world's attention to their plight on their own. His subsequent weeks with Jebhat al-Nusra convinced him that the Syrian people had problems no amount of attention-drawing newspaper photography could solve.

He first encountered Abu Sofiane in February in the eye hospital basement. Right away, during the first hours of their meeting, Abu Sofiane persuaded Matt to convert to Islam. A conversion to Islam turned out to entail, as an opening bid, a new name, complicated ablutions before the prayers, five prayers per day, and regular tutorials in how to recite the seven-line opening chapter of the Koran. Meanwhile, it didn't affect Jebhat al-Nusra's attitude toward him in the least.

He felt he had been conned into the conversion. Since the punishment for apostasy in Islam is death and since Abu Sofiane had trumpeted news of Matt's awakening to God to every commander in the eye hospital (they had wanted to watch with their own eyes as Matt recited the testament of faith), Matt couldn't very well renounce Islam. So he had fallen into a trap, and now the trap enraged him. He felt that as he was falling for this con I sat by, smirking. The smirking enraged him.

In his opinion, Jebhat al-Nusra would believe in the sincerity of his conversion, but only if I converted, too. I'm not sure why he thought this. Perhaps he didn't believe much in his own conversion. A second, reinforcing conversion might have made his own seem more plausible, at least to him. Perhaps he felt that my refusal to convert gave the lie to his too-willing acceptance of Islam. In any case, my refusal, for him, amounted to my collaborating with his killers. As the killers sharpened up their knives for both of us, he believed, I refused to lift a finger. So I was going to get us both killed out of loyalty to some insane scruple. Whenever the subject of my refusal to convert came up, he would clutch both hands to his head. Under his breath, he would seethe. His lips filled with spittle. "You're driving me crazy!" he would whisper as the saliva dribbled from his mouth. "What's a matter with you? Prick. You fuck. Do it!"

There were times when Matt knew that this much rage, in such a tiny cell, when all of our lives were hanging in the balance, was a moral failure. He didn't want to be remembered for bitterness. He liked to think of himself as a Randle Patrick McMurphy type who battled the Nurse Ratcheds of the world. He felt his truest talent was in screenwriting. In screenwriting, he brought his insouciance to life, his understanding of teenage drug consumption on Long Island, and his affection for Quentin Tarantino.

During his seizures of regret, he saw the child he had been. He understood how implacable the schools and prisons he had confronted as a kid were, and regretted that this child had butted his head against such unappeasable foes. He ought to have given in and gotten along, he said. He regretted the fights he had had with his teachers. He especially regretted fighting with his father. "He's a dick," Matt said of his father, "but I knew that. It wasn't worth fighting with him over everything." When the despair took over Matt totally, he sank his face into his palms. Uncontrollable tears seized him. "I should have been a better son," he would say, clutching his head. "I should have been more respectful. I shouldn't have argued so much." He apologized for the fits of rage that overtook him in the cell.

When he finally got home, he used to say, he would rent a new apartment, this one close to his mother, on Long Island. He would dredge up his old screenplays. He would buy a small bag of pot, smoke a bit, not too much, then plunge himself into weeks of productive writing.

The God the officers addressed in their prayers was a warmer figure than the one I had heard evoked in earlier visits to mosques in Syria. He took a personal interest in the community's welfare. He took no notice of Matt's errant youth, accepted his conversion without question, and wasn't at all resentful over my refusal to convert to Islam. He could be spoken to in a calm, reasonable tone of voice as if he were a wealthy old uncle who had betrayed his family, moved away, stopped returning phone calls, but hadn't meant to do anything evil and anyway could be brought around to reason in the fullness of time.

A radar technician called Abu Ayoub who had memorized more of the Koran than anyone else in the cell and so was often chosen to lead the noontime Friday prayer used to address this God. He would speak to him quietly, as if God were ambling around in the garden outside our cell. As the prayer leader, it was his job to divine the community's most heartfelt wishes and to communicate these to God.

Abu Ayoub was a considerate prayer leader. He made an effort to express polite wishes to which no one could object. In Abu Ayoub's understanding of things, our community wished first of all that all martyrs be accepted into heaven. He didn't say which side's martyrs he had in mind. Next, it wished for protection for the families of the martyrs, and then for protection for all innocents, everywhere in Syria. Eventually, Abu Ayoub would ask God to consider our plight. "May this be our last week, O Lord, our last week, our last week," Abu Ayoub would say, in an even tone, at conversational volume, as if the uncle were listening through a clear, well-working cell phone connection. Abu Ayoub wanted God to forgive us our sins and for him to keep our moms and dads safe.

A fraction of a second after Abu Ayoub spoke, the Muslims in the room who could speak Arabic would whisper these wishes into their cupped palms. The Muslim who could not speak Arabic, Matt, would mumble. "May he send all of us back to our families, every one of us, each of us safe, each of us sound," Abu Ayoub would say. "Oh, please, my lord. Lord, my lord. Oh, please." The Arabic speakers would repeat these words.

I enjoyed listening to these prayers at first, but over time, they came to exasperate me. Any reasonable uncle, it seemed to me, even a reprobate one who had moved away and turned off his cell phone, would have done something for us by now. If the uncle were listening, I would think, he wasn't reasonable. Probably he wasn't listening.

As far as I could tell, God's silence brought frustration only to the Westerners in the room. The Syrians with whom I discussed the matter seemed to feel that for the time being, God was asking us to be patient.

Perhaps he was busy with other things. Certainly Abu Ayoub felt that the best thing for it was to make further pleas in the same tone of voice at the following Friday prayers.

Nowadays, I regret my exasperation. Nowadays, I recall how Abu Ayoub used to make a point of including Matt and me in his remarks to God. He wished for God to keep us safe, and to lead us home. He wished this for the unjustly imprisoned everywhere. As he spoke, the prisoners at his back would furrow their brows. They would wait a fraction of a second, then whisper exactly the words he had spoken, in unison, as if more perfect synchrony in their whispering would at last move God to set us free.

Toward the end of April, a youthful cleric in bare feet and long, stringy hair came to us to announce that we were all going to hell. God, he said, had reserved a special stratum in his hell for the exclusive use of Alawites. Here, the intensity of the heat, he said, would reduce the bodies of the Alawites into a kind of ashy powder. No amount of penance, in this person's opinion, could save the Alawites from the torments that awaited them. The rest of us, by this cleric's way of figuring, had aided the Alawites in their war against Islam. We were therefore as wicked as they and condemned to the same tortures in the afterlife.

My discussions with the younger fighters in the eye hospital in Aleppo had given me the impression that in their view, my refusal to convert to Islam was a matter between me and God. God would punish me, they seemed to feel, when he saw fit—possibly right away but possibly also at the end of time. According to this stringy-haired sheikh, matters had changed. Now God had decided to eliminate all unbelievers from the face of the Earth and to dispatch them all to hell. "Whether you live now or die now, it's not up to me," he said. It was up to God. But God, in his view, had already determined that we had not kept the faith. Some of us, he said, had mocked it openly. He didn't tell us when we would die exactly or how we would be killed, but that it was Jebhat al-Nusra's job to do all of us in he did not doubt. He pretended to have been saddened by the situation. Perhaps when we met God in the sky, he said, God would forgive us. He himself had come out (his expression) to bring the law. Having come out, he was merely a slave of God. He was certainly in no position to hand out personal exemptions.

One afternoon at about this time, a pair of commanders appeared before us with cell phones in their hands. They had come to announce a new Jebhat al-Nusra initiative: The officers and the member of Parliament were to be given three minutes each of unsupervised cell phone conversation with their families. If it should happen that, as a result of these conversations, the prisoners' families pressured the Syrian government into accepting Jebhat al-Nusra's terms, the officers and the member of Parliament could go home within the week. If, however, the families could not persuade the government to act, the prisoners' fates would be in the hands of God. The commanders made a point of stressing how serenely indifferent they were to the result of these phone calls. The Syrian government could save the lives of its officers if it liked, a leader among them said. Or not. Anyway, the matter was no longer in his hands.

The phone calls were to begin the following day. After the commanders left the room, a minor windstorm of whispering swept over the cell. Lieutenants huddled with lieutenants. A colonel, a captain, and a general huddled in a different corner. The member of Parliament sequestered himself in his spot at the base of a wall with a Koran, as he had taken to doing in recent days.

As the other prisoners whose fates were hanging in the balance whispered among themselves, he read to himself. He kept at it for hours. Now and then, he set his Koran on a ledge beneath a window (to keep it from touching our lice-ridden blankets), rose without a word, made two private bows to God, as the Sunnah—literally, the Traditions—say Mohammed himself often did, then returned to his reading.

In the evening, the collective prayers were carried out in the normal mood of solemnity, but afterward, during the interlude of handshaking and well-wishing that occurred as the officers were rising from their knees, hands seemed to linger in hands much longer than they normally did. There was much kissing on the cheek and many teary-eyed smiles. The moments after the prayers felt vaguely like a departure ceremony, as if news of an agreement in principle had come during the prayers.

On the following afternoon, some of the officers were indeed able to raise their moms and dads on the phone. During the course of their conversations, they discovered that the government didn't intend to concede so much as twenty-five Syrian pounds—less than a dollar—to Jebhat al-Nusra. Nor had Jebhat al-Nusra presented anything like a set of demands to the government. Various Jebhat al-Nusra commanders had made various demands of some of the families. One of the callers insisted on the regime's total and unconditional surrender. Another wanted the equivalent of $100,000 for one of the officers—the fisherman, as it happened.

But when the families tried to pursue the negotiations, the parties at the phone numbers they had been given did not pick up. Or the person who answered the phone call issued general threats of the "we'll be coming for you all" variety, then hung up.

According to the officers with whom I spoke, their families were at their wits' end. There were no demands to force onto the Syrian government. There were no Jebhat al-Nusra negotiators. There were rather random Skype names and cell phone numbers of people who called once but did not call again. Meanwhile, the bureaucrats in Damascus didn't want to get involved. Apparently, they were moving on.

One of the officers with whom I spoke said that he had taken advantage of the time he had on phone to speak to his twin daughters, who were ten. He didn't know what to say to them. He had tried to give them some words of advice about life in general. Perhaps he had wanted to say good-bye. But the mother had not yet explained to the kids what had happened to their father. The twins appeared to think that all was well. Another officer had spoken to a sister. Over the Jebhat al-Nusra phone line, she had been too terrified to say more than a handful of words. "Are you well?" the brother asked. There was silence. Then there were tears.

In the evening, several hours after the last of these phone calls, one of the commanders returned to us to announce that Jebhat al-Nusra had now officially done all it could do on the officers' behalf. "If they were Muslims," he said of the government, "they would try to save you. But there isn't a Muslim among them." Henceforth, he said, the matter, as far as he was concerned, lay in the hands of God. With that, he turned on his heels. He stepped out of the cell, then slammed the door.

In the moments after this commander left the room, the conclusion hanging in the air was too obvious to speak of: Our lives had been delivered into the hands of a disorderly, shambolic, slacker God. He made absurd demands. Then he shrugged, wiped his nose on his sleeve, and walked away. Evidently, Jebhat al-Nusra hadn't reckoned with the recalcitrance of the other side's negotiators. Nor had it imagined much about the fuss and bother of feeding us, hiding us away from the world, attending to our problems with lice, making up stories for us about a possible breakthrough in the negotiations, all while escorting us out, every few hours, to the bathroom. What a lot of bother we were.

At the beginning of May, an older, more august, more menacing species of cleric began to appear on the threshold of our cell. These clerics brought little crowds of bodyguards with them, many of whom wore something like a uniform, with similar-looking tactical vests, combat boots, and Kalashnikov magazines bulging from every pocket. Sometimes stone-faced teenagers milled around behind these visitors in little clusters and lesser beards. They wore sneakers instead of combat boots, and knives in their belts rather than handguns.

Sometimes the door would open on a tableau of hulking, big-bearded men in suicide belts. The lesser warriors—the ones without the suicide belts, evidently—would be arrayed in a circle behind the big men. These elders would glower at us, murmur at one another, rub their teeth a bit with the minty sticks—*siwak*—with which the Prophet is thought to have rubbed his teeth, then leave without a word. What was the purpose of such exhibitions? It felt as though the exhibitors imagined us to be an audience at a fashion show, that they were runway models, and that their suicide belts were this season's most audacious item. Soon they would be parading their suicide belts through the marketplace and selling them in the market stalls. They were fashion-forward terrorists who knew how to pout, to invite stares, and to exhibit their indifference to being stared at.

Since we knew these men were trying to terrorize us, we shrugged our shoulders at them—after they had left the cell, of course. But toward the beginning of May, these clerics began inviting unlucky prisoners to step outside of the cell with them. These were purposeful, well-executed, often silent exercises in terrorism whose purpose, if they had a purpose, we could not fathom.

They happened like this: In the late afternoon, as the light was draining out of our cell, the twenty-eight of us would be sitting on the floor, murmuring among ourselves and hoping to be fed. Footsteps would sound in the corridor. The prisoners sitting closest to the door would stage-whisper a warning to the rest of us: "They're coming!" Or: "It's them!" A hush would fall over the room. As keys jangled in the lock, we would avert our eyes from the door, then press our foreheads into the walls against which we had been sitting. Such was the attitude in which we were supposed to greet the opening of the cell door. The visitors would keep us in this position for thirty seconds or so as they stepped into the cell. We would feel their eyes on us, listen for a clearing of a throat or a cocking of a gun, and eventually, in the silence of their staring, in slow motion we would turn our faces toward the door. The visitors would stare for a moment more, and then their leader would whisper the name of a village or neighborhood in which one of the prisoner's families lived: "Krim" or "Safita" or "Baniyas." Sometimes we knew that a regime-orchestrated atrocity had occurred in one of these places. Other times, we had no idea why they were angry at this place. Perhaps they meant to avenge some crime that had been committed by a previous generation of Alawites against the fathers of the current generation of fighters. Perhaps they were angry at a custom or the rumor of a custom. Among the Jebhat al-Nusra fighters, it was widely believed that Alawites do not marry but rather pass their wives around among themselves, as one farmer will pass a fertile cow or a sheep to another farmer, since Alawites, the Jebhat al-Nusra fighters believed, did not hold women to be fully human. Many of the fighters believed that in the Alawite prayer the man prostrates himself to the woman's vagina. When the commanders screamed at us, they made allusions to such occult Alawite practices. Did Jebhat al-Nusra mean to punish the officers for their heresies? We never knew. But what if the heretical practices existed only in the commanders' minds? They never made explicit accusations. We could only defend ourselves against the general one: unbelief.

Yes, we do believe, we said.

No, you don't, Jebhat al-Nusra replied.

When the men with the guns called out the name of a village, the prisoners' faces would turn to the person from that place. "Come," a commander would say. The prisoner would rise, then walk to the front of the room. Here underlings would blindfold him, handcuff him, then lead him away.

Moments later, we would hear him screaming in another room. What had he done? Why had he been selected? He would be returned to us after twenty minutes. We would stare at the redness in his face and at his flaring eyes. "What did they do?" one of his colleague officers would whisper.

"Nothing," the victim would reply. Or: "Some hitting. End of story." Or sometimes the officer would utter a single word, then look away: "Sticks" or "cable," he would say, or "electricity." Anyway, he attached no importance to the matter. Neither should we. He would refuse to meet our eyes. He would ignore other questions. Over the following hours, these victims wouldn't speak. They would stare daggers at the walls.

Eventually, the big-bearded men began eliminating prisoners from our cell. The calling out of a place-name would be the same, and the handcuffing and the blindfolding would occur as usual. From the hallway came the same screaming. But as we waited for these prisoners to be returned, it would dawn on us that they were not going to be returned. What had become of them? Why had they been selected? We never knew. To replace these men, Jebhat al-Nusra began bringing new prisoners in ones and twos. These men would stay with us for a night, and then, during the following days, they, too, were blindfolded, cuffed, and led away.

One of the commanders who used to carry out these subtraction exercises seemed to feel that my fellow prisoners ought to be giving me, the only non-Muslim in the cell, proper religious instruction. My fellow prisoners had all day every day to convert me, yet they hadn't accomplished a thing. Why not? One afternoon, this commander, a certain Abu Dujanna, issued an order to the entire cell: "Teach him!"

"We're trying to teach him," Abu Sofiane told him. "He's a Christian. What can we do?"

Abu Dujanna tilted his head at me, smiled for a moment, stepped toward me, then launched himself into an Islam-for-children homily. "You see," he said. "The Jewish people believe Moses to be the Prophet of God, and this is a species of *kufr*." (The word *kufr* means "infidelity" or "unbelief.") "The Christian people believe that Issa," he continued, using the Arabic word for "Jesus," "may his name please God, is the Prophet, and the Alawite people believe that Ali, may his name please God, is the Prophet. All of this is *kufr*. The Prophet of God is Mohammed, peace and blessings upon him. For many, many years, the Syrian people have been asleep to this fact. Now, however, the Syrian people are waking up." As the words "waking up" fell from his lips, he nodded at the cell windows. He spread an arm toward the pleasant springtime weather. Jebhat al-Nusra's habit of burying windows under plywood, brush, old tires, and plastic tarps prevented us from seeing it. We could scarcely smell it. We could feel the presence of the springtime, but only faintly.

An awakening? I thought. Perhaps it was true. It had been six months since I had been out of doors. In the hours after Abu Dujanna delivered his homily, I imagined citizens throwing the blankets from their beds, sunshine streaming through the Aleppo parks, and schoolteachers and bank clerks resolving, in 10 million tiny ways, to slough off their old habits, to live holier, healthier lives, to be less afraid, and to stand up for universal rights. Untoward behavior of any kind would have frightened the Syrian government. The generals in Damascus despised anything that didn't bow and scrape before it. Now an unruly, uncontrollable mass awakening was underway. Probably the Assad government was trying to suppress it with artillery barrages. Probably this encouraged the awakeners. It could all be true, I thought. Why not?

On another occasion, in response to an officer's question about the progress of his negotiations with the Syrian government, Abu Dujanna recalled a parable, to be found somewhere in the sayings of the Prophet, in which three men take refuge in a cave only to be trapped by a giant boulder when it tumbles into the cave's mouth. For several hours after this speech, I pestered Ali, the military academy cadet, to explain the details of Abu Dujanna's parable to me. God had eventually caused the boulder to move itself from the cave's mouth, though of course the trapped men had spent their time inside the cave in prayer. Did not this mean that Abu Dujanna was telling us, "If you pray enough, God will set you free"?

Ali disagreed with my interpretation. During their prayers, the men in the parable had reminded God of the deep, inner virtue according to which they had lived their lives. God had examined the record. When he saw that they had indeed been virtuous, he nudged the boulder out of the way.

"Abu Dujanna thinks we have been bad, not good," Ali explained.

I argued: "How does he know?" and: "If we were bad, can't we make up for it in prayer?"

Ali's face fell. "Maybe you can," he said. "We're Alawites."

That spring, I learned to think about God as the Jebhat al-Nusra leaders wanted me to think. When they stood on the threshold of our cell, glowering, exhibiting their weapons, and rolling their weight over their haunches—that's when I learned to read his signs.

I understood then, for instance, that wearing the suicide belt as one goes about one's daily tasks signifies the depth of one's love of God. It suggests detachment from the plane of life we happen to be drifting across at the moment and enthusiasm for departures toward higher planes. The suicide belt also shows, by the way, that the wearer can afford expensive explosives. It establishes that he's important enough for the enemy to have identified him as a target, that he might be forced to climb to a higher plane in the next few minutes, and that he's at peace with the situation. A person like this is aware that life passes by in the blink of an eye. He's losing interest in the world of this life as he looks at you.

In contrast, the regime supporters think they're here forever, so they build up their villas, lay out ornamental gardens, and dig their swimming pools into the ground. They lust after baubles. A man who wears the suicide belt has nothing and wants less. He will swim in a pool, fine. A few minutes later, he will allow the angels to carry him away to the highest plane of paradise—finer.

That spring, I learned that the Jebhat al-Nusra wanted to be thought of as lovers of Syria's natural world. They symbolized their connection to it adopting names that recalled important natural features of their hometowns. A commander from a city by the sea called himself Father of the Seas. A person from the hill country in the northwest was known by the name Father of the Mountain. One of the fighters called himself Hud-Hud, after a bird, prized as a scout and mentioned in the Koran. Many called themselves after the towns in which they had grown up. We had several al Saraqibis and many al Taftanazis.

Often, the younger men in Jebhat al-Nusra liked to go around in bare feet. Were they showing their affinity with the time before shoes? With the pebbles and dust on the local goat paths? That they disdained adornment? I took them to mean that they were children of the nature of this place. They wanted its dirt in their toes.

In their Islamic-state-to-be, the rebel commander symbolized his coming into his own during the course of the war by his girth. He is fat and surrounded by the fruit of his loins. During this period of my imprisonment, Jebhat al-Nusra was feeding us a round and a half of bread per day, handfuls of olives, scatterings of rice, and, if we were lucky, a ball of falafel. It was our time to squabble over crusts. It was their time in the full flush of life. They were living off the fat of the land. We were being expunged from it.

A crevice in the pile of debris that had been stacked in front of one of our cell's windows permitted a view of a miniature willow in the villa gardens. Behind it, a swatch of gravel pathway twisted away into underbrush. Several times that spring, evening rainstorms sent sheets of rain crashing into this garden. These were dramatic, even violent events that made the scraps of plywood in front of our windows rattle and thud under the pelting of giant raindrops. Once or twice, there was hail. The willow writhed and thrashed. Inevitably, the hullabaloo outside would cause little knots of prisoners to rise from the floor as if in a trance. The prisoners would assemble themselves in front of the patch of window not obscured by the plywood. For ten minutes, the prisoners would murmur into the air, reach their fingertips through the bars, and watch as the sky emptied itself onto the willow in our little villa garden.

"In the Land of Sham, we are everything that comes from the rain." So went one of the lines in a pop song I used to hear, before the war, in the taxis and cafés in Damascus. Another number, by the same group, Kelna Sawa, foresaw a great civilization-ending cataclysm. It would come in the form of a flood:

> *Everything will drown, everyone will flee.*
> *The people who lived there, lived with fear in their hearts.*

In the songwriters' pre-war understanding of things, the great inundation to come was going to bring renewal and truth. It would itself be a kind of a deliverance:

> *But when the typhoon comes—*
> *but when the truth comes—*
> *when all have gone away,*
> *life will go back to the way it was.*
> *And so Noah will announce it: He has an ark. . . .*

Every time a storm wracked the villa gardens, I would rise with the other prisoner-spectators, drift toward the window, crane my neck at the rain, and agree that the powers of the natural world in Syria didn't speak through any pop rock band in Damascus but rather through the men with big bellies out here on the Aleppo plains. The torturing of the prisoners, the Tasers, and the wild hair of the young fighters, these were echoes of the force that dwelled outside the cell windows, in the grasses, the sheets of rain, and in the flailing of the willow boughs.

The more I watched these storms, the more certain I became that the power couldn't be negotiated with any more than one can negotiate with the moonlight. It was indeed in the raindrops and the groves of olive trees in which I had fallen into the hands of Jebhat al-Nusra. It was in the names of the places—Taftanaz, Saraqib, Binnish, Anadan—from which the commanders came. Naturally, it was in the people from those places. The officers' mistake, I felt, was to have left the mountains along the coast where their powers dwelled, and the other prisoners' mistake was to have gone wandering in territory ruled over by forces we couldn't fathom, couldn't appease, and couldn't see.

At the time, I was having trouble sleeping on account of the lice in my clothes. They seemed to attack in squadrons, but not at any specific point on my body. Under attack, my skin, especially along the backs of my legs, would tingle. The tingling would escalate into a burning sensation. I would scratch at my legs. Surely, this made matters worse. Seeing me scratch, the other prisoners would scold me. But they themselves scratched at their lice as much as I did. We tried to massage the lice away. We walked our fingertips through the hair at the back of our necks. But the lice were much too small to be found by fingertips, and massages didn't help. So we slept in half-hour segments. We woke, hunted down the lice in the darkness for a while, gave up, then drifted off for another half hour.

Of course, we were hungry. The hunger made me afraid. I felt our captors were capable of starving us to death. Their depravity made me angry, but I didn't have anyone to be angry at. "We're following orders," the captors told us. Whoever was giving the orders was much too important to concern himself with our needs. "Make do," the guards would tell us, "then shut your mouths."

Over time, their recalcitrance, I found, sapped my will. I knew that pleading with them wouldn't help. Nothing could help. I have been caught in a storm at sea, I told myself. I ought to have known about such storms. I didn't see this one. Anyway, now the wind had me. Perhaps it will let me go, I thought. Perhaps not. But there was no point in wondering about its psychology, since it had no psychology. I had stumbled into a natural phenomenon with which science had yet to reckon. And this made sense because scientists, it seemed to me, were smart enough not to go wandering through the hallways of the al Qaeda prisons. Someday ages hence, I thought, after I'm gone, someone will make sense of the prisons in Syria as Primo Levi made sense of his concentration camp in Poland.

But this was an idle fantasy. I thought an understanding of their Islamic state possible in a theoretical sense, the way it's possible, in theory, for peace to descend over Syria in an instant, in response to no particular surrender or collapse. I definitely didn't believe that the arc of the universe would bend toward justice, didn't believe in a book about Aleppo that would make sense of my nightmare, and did not believe, when I was being honest with myself, that I would come out alive. Deliverance of the kind I was dreaming of—walking away, without a scratch—was a fairy-tale ending. I couldn't take it seriously. It would have required rescuers who didn't exist, mercy Jebhat al-Nusra didn't have, and safe passage to the Turkish border no one could or would arrange for me.

During the daytime, the prisoners passed their copies of the Koran around among themselves. Of course, they were careful never to allow a volume to touch the floor. Now and then, a sergeant or lieutenant tried to lead the convert, Matt/Nasser, through a verse or two. One afternoon during the period in which the rainstorms were sweeping through our portion of Syria, a pair of Jebhat al-Nusra commanders appeared in the doorway, demanded to know where the Korans were being kept, strode to the windowsill, tucked the books under their arms, then strode from the cell without a word.

The subtraction of these Korans provoked exactly zero commentary among the prisoners. We knew what Jebhat al-Nusra was trying to tell us: We were unbelievers. We weren't entitled to the consolations of faith. Nor, as unbelievers, could we expect protection from harm. We had turned our backs on God. We were not his people. Why would he bother to help us?

Jebhat al-Nusra also would have been worried about the physical objects. The paddling of our fingers through the pages of their sacred books might somehow have worked an infection into the verses themselves. We might have cast spells. We might have opened the books only to mutter curses at God. Jebhat al-Nusra didn't know what we might do. To keep on the safe side, it removed the books from our cell.

I'm sure everyone in our cell felt that in removing these books, Jebhat al-Nusra had done something no Islamic authority, no matter how extreme, could countenance. In taking these books away, it had become the frightened, intolerant police state. Now Jebhat al-Nusra was policing its citizens' connection to God. It was jealous. It was afraid. But these were the charges the Jebhat al-Nusra commanders made against the Assad government. Now they were guilty of Assad's offenses.

I'm pretty sure the subtraction of the books didn't sadden anyone in our cell. If anything, the confiscation did for our cell what the regime's attempts to police religious faith in the run-down, disregarded Aleppo districts had done for the faithful out there. It redoubled everyone's commitment. It was a positive inducement to Koran love.

Anyway, one of the officers kept a secret, thumbnail-sized copy of the book in the breast pocket of his flak jacket. It hardly ever emerged. There was no need, since most of the officers had memorized the most important passages.

In this cell, we had no electricity. At night, the little piles of debris Jebhat al-Nusra had propped in front of our windows made the cell so dark that you couldn't see your hand in front of your face. Yet when the moon poked its way through the junk pile, it fell like a pale blue laser beam. It had the diameter of a lightsaber. You could have read a novel by this glow, not that we had any novels.

After the disappearance of the Korans, things changed in our cell. In the late evenings, after most of the prisoners had drifted off to sleep, a circle of officers took to gathering in a corner of the cell, under this beam of light. They collected around Abu Ayoub, the radar technician, who could recite for twenty minutes at a stretch without requiring a prompt. In earlier days, in their time of freedom, all of the men in this circle would have enforced the Syrian Arab Army's ban on the collective prayer. Perhaps they had discriminated against the more obviously religious men under their command. In the Syrian Arab Army it is not unknown for the brass to humiliate religious-minded conscripts. If these officers had done this in the past, they were regretting it now.

Other things were changing. In the past, Abu Ayoub, who was half the age of the captains and colonels who gathered in his circle, would have bowed his head in their presence. He would hardly have spoken a word. Now Abu Ayoub was the leader. The brass hung on his words. As the moon passed over this little circle, Abu Ayoub would whisper to the others, "The Surah of Yasin?" or "The Surah An-Nissa?"

"Yes, okay, good," the colonels and captains would whisper in reply. When he was done with one chapter, he would name another. "All right, then. Perfect," would come the reply. Abu Ayoub had what the brass wanted then: the Koran in his heart and his head. "Go ahead," they whispered to him as he proposed new chapters. "We're waiting." Out of consideration for the rest of us, who were, in theory, trying to sleep, Abu Ayoub would recite in a barely audible voice, as if the words didn't need to be spoken but could be hinted at by touching the tip of the tongue to the lips and by breathing. Sometimes, when the other officers knew the words to the verses Abu Ayoub was reciting, they whispered in synch with his whisperings. Sometimes I would wake up, listen a bit, and imagine that I was listening to the rustling of the trees in the villa garden. Sometimes I would wake up, look around, and see that a pair of officers was sitting under the moonbeam, in perfect silence. Perhaps they had recited all the verses they felt like reciting. Perhaps they just wanted to keep quiet. In their silence, one of the officers would hold the column of light with a single eye for a few seconds and then he would pass it on to his colleague.

Whenever I saw such scenes, I felt that the officers were trying to maintain connection with their lost power. Okay, their communication channel was a slender, useless moonbeam. So what? That moonbeam had found us in spite of Jebhat al-Nusra's complicated scheme to seal us away from the world. Its softness, its reliability, and its steadiness made me think it a countervailing force, faraway but powerful in its own right. This pair of officers, I guessed, knew they could count on the moon. So they waited up for it, and when it appeared, they held on to it with their eyes for as long as they could.

At the time, I found this communication strategy of theirs reassuring. To me, it meant that the officers were cooking something up, that not all of nature was on Jebhat al-Nusra's side, and that if things here got truly out of hand we might well be beamed away, as people on *Star Trek* were beamed away. In those moments, I was willing to believe in possibilities other people in our part of the world hadn't thought of yet. Just because it hadn't happened before didn't mean it could not happen in the future. I wanted to explore the low-end possibilities. I wasn't inclined to rule anything out.

Some time in early May, they moved us again—this time to a storefront prison in a much bombed-over Aleppo district called Al-Haydariya. This prison had once been a neighborhood grocery store. On the other side of the roll-down steel gate that served as the front wall of our cell, donkey carts drifted by. Children kicked soccer balls in the dust. Chinks in this gate allowed us a view of an elementary school–like building across the way and, in front of it, a line of pickup trucks whose antennae bore the al Qaeda flag. A shade-spreading eucalyptus tree hung over the trucks, and above the neighborhood, on the school rooftop, snipers kept watch.

Within the first twenty-four hours of our arrival, the army officers identified the snipers' guns, which they admired for their newness and their accuracy, as American guns—or anyway, guns made after an *American* design. The officers called these rifles Americans, as opposed to the standard-issue personal weapons in the Syrian war, the Kalashnikovs, which they called Russians.

Under the protection of the Americans, a kind of peace reigned in this neighborhood. Now and then, missiles—or shells or rockets (anyway, projectiles)—flew overhead. We could hear them crash into faraway buildings. Gun battles broke out from time to time but didn't seem to be occurring nearby. There were helicopters, sometimes, but no barrel bombs.

In the early morning, when most in our cell were still asleep, we could hear the donkey cart man hawking his cucumbers. In the evenings, after the Maghreb prayer, the trucks filled with soldiers then went rolling away into the night. Shortly thereafter, a van or a pickup loaded up with platters of rice, bags of bread, and sometimes pots of okra and lentils would pull up to the curb in front of the grocery store. "The dinner comes," the prisoner who was watching the street would say then. We could hear the deliverymen entering the grocery store by the main entrance, then laying out the platters on the floor in front of our cell door. When the door opened, men with guns slung over their shoulders would march heaping platters of rice and armloads of bread into the center of the cell. Often, the bread was still warm from the neighborhood oven.

The militants who controlled this prison wanted us to know that they had no official connection to Jebhat al-Nusra. "You are here on trust," the prison manager told us during the welcome-to-my-prison lecture he made on our first evening with him. By "trust," we understood, he meant that his faction, which, according to the T-shirts his men wore, was called the Islamic Dawn, had agreed to look after us as banks look after deposits. A Jebhat al-Nusra official or a group of officials, none of whom he named, had lodged us away in the manager's vault. Whenever the depositors wished to make a withdrawal, that's when the withdrawal would happen. What would become of us then the manager was in no position to know.

In the meantime, Abu Hajr, as the manager wished to be called, had a solemn obligation to uphold—the maintenance of the trust. He could tell us nothing about the depositors' state of mind, identity, or intentions. He himself knew next to nothing. "For you, everything we do, we do in the face of God," he announced. We understood by this that he intended to provide for us as the Koran requires prisoners to be provided for (in the Surah al-Insan, it requires that prisoners be fed, by the way, but doesn't go into details). We were to know that his relationship with the depositors was legal and aboveboard, that he was a cog in a system, and that the system was licit in the eyes of God.

This prison belonged to the neighborhood as the other prisons we had been in to date did not. There were six resident prisoners in our grocery store jail. All of them had grown up in Al-Haydariya. All of them had been arrested on suspicion of collaborating with the government. From one of them, a bricklayer called Abed, I learned that the neighborhood pharmacy was around the corner, that earlier in the week his mom and dad had been allowed to bring him some medication from this pharmacy, and that though he had lived in Al-Haydariya his whole life, he meant to leave it as soon as he had the money. In his mind, Al-Haydariya was the most unlovely, unloved portion of Aleppo. "We are poor," he said, holding his palms to the sky and grinning in mock hopelessness. He mentioned the lack of groceries in the grocery store. The cucumber cart man, he said, was what Al-Haydariya had instead of a neighborhood grocery store. "Probably he is also broke," Abed guessed.

So Al-Haydariya was poor. It did, however, have a business district. On our first night here, the prison manager sent out for thirty-odd falafel sandwiches. The following day, an electrician came to install a ceiling fan. He was not at all surprised (or successfully concealed it) on discovering that the grocery store now contained some twenty-five prisoners, in addition to the six neighborhood regime collaborators. The electrician was polite but distant with us, as any electrician would have been under the circumstances.

The local merchants, it seemed, had cordial relations with the prison authorities. On one of our first mornings in this prison, the cistern out of which we drew our drinking water ran low. Abu Hajr summoned a water tank truck. In order to allow the hose to reach our water tank, the storefront gate had to be unlocked, then rolled up from the floor at a height of about a foot. Abed leapt into action. He seized one end of the hose, then climbed up to the shelf, above the grocery store toilet, on which the cistern sat. From up there, he exchanged pleasantries with the water tank man through the roll-up steel gate, as the water poured into the cistern. Toward the end of this operation, the bricklayer asked the water tank man if enough water remained in the truck to allow the prisoners an impromptu shower. Abu Hajr had no objections. "Have at it then," said the waterman. The twenty-five-odd prisoners plus the six resident jailbirds stripped to their underwear. We rolled back our blankets from the floor. During the following ten minutes, a bemused but well-meaning waterman ducked into the cell, then stood by as Abu Hajr aimed a fire-hose torrent at the cell wall. The prisoners danced underneath the splashes like little children.

We became a neighborhood attraction. Had he been in the mood, Abu Hajr could have made a tidy profit by charging our visitors an admission fee. One morning, about a week after our arrival, a crowd of elementary school–age children came to stare at us. At midday that day a delegation of clerics dropped by, and later in the afternoon a passerby happened in off the street, apparently in order to harangue us about the unspeakable agonies God was preparing for us in hell. In the midst of his speech, this visitor lost his temper. He began to kick the prisoners nearest him in the ribs. Abu Hajr had to escort him from the cell.

Not all the neighborhood denizens admired the men of the Islamic Dawn. One afternoon, a flock of about a dozen demonstrators, upset, apparently, by some policy or habit that had developed under the Islamic Dawn's administration, collected around the alley that led to the grocery store's principal entrance. For ten minutes or so, they chanted in favor of a rival faction. There was much whistling and banging of kitchen utensils. Eventually, they had to be shooed away.

I found the men of the Islamic Dawn to be courteous, almost to the point of chivalry. They were conscientious guarantors of the trust. Never once did the men from this faction hit us. They hardly insulted us. They advised—but did not order—us to pray. They advised us to keep the cell tidy. When voices rose in our cell such that they might have been heard in the street, the guards advised us to lower our voices. They flogged the six resident prisoners with abandon, for no apparent reason, at random times. They dealt with us as if we were a delicate kind of merchandise, prone to spoilage and bruising.

One afternoon, a wall of sacks containing powdered cement had to be moved from within the cell to an alcove in the corridor outside the cell. Under the supervision of a line of Islamic Dawn guards, a handful of prisoners began picking up sacks. I picked up a sack. Abu Hajr hurried forward. He held up his hand. He made a gracious smile. "Afterward, when you go home," he explained, "you'll say that we employed you as slave labor." He asked me to return to my spot on the floor.

So the men of the Islamic Dawn were polite. And they weren't officially part of Jebhat al-Nusra. But the clerics who visited us threatened us exactly as the Jebhat al-Nusra clerics threatened us. They spoke to us in the same tones of trembling outrage. They hinted darkly at what was to become of us, as the other clerics hinted. All of our visitors foresaw a looming combat in which the forces of belief on planet Earth would confront those who insult God or discount him or cannot find it within themselves to believe in him at all. This combat was going to cause civilization as we knew it to crumble to the earth. All the clerics understood that an apocalypse now meant that afterward, in the great global Islamic utopia to come, Muslims would rule over Jerusalem, Rome, and Andalusia.

One of our first visitors, a father-of-the-family type, in his early forties, wanted us to know that he held no brief for any armed group at all, nor was he a learned man. He was merely a laborer. He happened to own several buildings in the neighborhood. He had built them himself, he said, and had worked within them. His buildings had lately been barrel-bombed away.

He wanted us to know that he wasn't at all unhappy about the situation. He rather felt that the calamity in whose midst we were living had been sent by God. "It is an education for all of us," he said.

Syrians in general, in his opinion, were discovering that buildings—and possessions and baubles of all kinds—were temporary, whereas the words "there is no god but God" would last forever. He himself had discovered that he loved these words more than anything, more than life itself, more even than his wife and his children. "Over there," he said to the officers, nodding toward a frontier in his imagination, "you kill people for saying the words 'there is no god but God.'" Over here, on his side of the national divide, he wanted us to know, the citizens were happy to see every building and tree go up in smoke, and to go up in smoke themselves, provided they were allowed to cherish the words "there is no god but God."

Another lecturer who came to us early in our stay in this prison directed his remarks exclusively to Matt and me. The burden of his speech was that whenever Matt and I were sent home we were to tell the Jews in America that they needn't send their armies into Syria, for Syria had a population that was yet worse than the Jews. They were called Alawites. Had the Jews ever tried to erase the Muslims from the map of Syria? No, but Bashar al-Assad had set his armies to accomplish this very task. Keeping his eyes on me but nodding at the corner of the room in which his enemies, some of whom were still wearing the flak jackets in which they had been captured, were sitting, he sank his fingers into his beard. "We are staying," he said. "We are ridding ourselves of them."

In our earlier prisons, it had been possible to imagine that an underground cult had taken over a building, converted it for use as a prison, then set about arresting unlucky passersby. In this prison, the visitors were too numerous and their dreams harmonized too much with the prophecies that had been communicated to us during the previous six months to imagine that a cult leader had brainwashed a band of malcontents and misfits. New understandings, our visitors told us, were settling over the society around us. At last, the time had come to do away with the Alawites, once and for all. The coming of this resolve, they said, had been in the works for ages. For generations, indeed, for centuries, the Syrian people had been too naïve and too frightened to face up to the evil that had crept across the nation. Now this period of slumber was over. The Syrian people, said one divine after the next in Al-Haydariya, were waking up.

In this prison, the visitors so often asked the Alawite prisoners to raise their hands, and so often stared in astonishment when they did, that I often thought the visitors had come to our cell to witness the fact of Alawites being rounded up with their own eyes. It was a dream. But no. It was a plain fact, witnessable all day long, every day, in the local grocery store.

Many of the preachers who spoke to us during this period didn't seem especially angry at the enemy army officers. They knew that a time of rounding up such people would come eventually. Now it had come. They weren't much surprised. They weren't even especially happy. Because other undesirables were being hunted down they felt a time of cleansing had come to Aleppo. It wasn't bad and it wasn't good, one visitor told us, of our imprisonment. He was equally sanguine about what was in store for us. "It's coming," he said, without saying what "it" referred to. "You can't stop it and neither can I."

Most of our visitors in those days made a point of reminding us that the combat in Aleppo was really just a prelude to a wider war, which would soon spread across the earth. Soon, the visitors felt, all the enemies of God would be routed and an era of Islamic hegemony would dawn. For the time being, many millions on both sides were going to be killed. The Muslim dead would ascend to paradise. Everyone else would live in agony in hell.

One afternoon about two weeks after our arrival in this prison, I met my old friend the Sheikh of Economic Science, in the hallway outside the grocery store toilet. He smiled as I was hurrying from the bathroom. He cocked his head at me. "Tell me about the girlfriend you have for me," he said, under his breath. I didn't reply. He smiled again. "Take me with you to America," he whispered.

I would have liked to have engaged this person somehow. He was the misfit of Jebhat al-Nusra, the terrorist who didn't want to terrorize—at least he was so in my imagination. Anyway, he seemed in the mood for an adventure. I judged that he wouldn't have objected to the kind that occurred in thirty seconds and came together with a wink and a flurry of believable-enough, true-seeming promises.

In the hallway outside the toilet, I didn't have the presence of mind to sketch out the fantasy he seemed to want, but during the following minutes, as I sat chatting with my neighbor prisoners on the floor of our cell, I whisked myself away.

I felt like having a look around the town in which I grew up, so called up the field in front of my mother's house in my imagination, then watched a troop of crows alighting from the crown of a venerable old maple. High off to the left, over the crest of a ridgeline, a bank of clouds was drifting in from the west. The temperature was dropping. Soon there would be snow.

I wished for a way to explain to my mother what had happened in Aleppo. I felt she trusted me to tell her the truth and knew that she would not have minded if, during the course of my telling, I paused to describe the weather, to relate a colorful snippet of dialog, and to opine a bit about the food.

The thing I most wished to discuss with Mom was the sleight of hand by which the Jebhat al-Nusra sheikhs had persuaded some significant portion of Aleppo that an era of killing had dawned, that this killing might somehow be good, and that in any case, it was an unstoppable thing, not so different from the rising of the sun. It felt to me as though now, in our neighborhood, the murders of a few dozen prisoners, even if carried out in front of the local elementary school—perhaps especially then—would be understood as a sad event, perhaps, but in harmony with the spirit of the times.

How had we come to this point? Since God was in charge of everything and since God was good, the audience attending our murders, I felt, would hail the killers. It would make videos. Helpful municipal workers would cart our bodies away, probably to the dump.

As I had observed the Jebhat al-Nusra sheikhs at their work over the previous six months and allowed their psychology to overwhelm mine, at least on occasion, it seemed to me that I had a basic grasp of what they had done to bring Al-Haydariya—and the many other neighborhoods and towns they controlled—to this place. I knew the affection they dangled in front of their acolytes. I knew the phrases they used to keep their underlings in check. I knew how they longed for their less religious neighbors to flee and what they did to those who wouldn't flee and wouldn't fall in line. Also, I knew about the lovely yesteryear in their imaginations. Not so long ago, they declared, in their speeches and anthems, there were no Alawites in Syria at all. Back then, according to their myth, the citizens of Aleppo lived in harmony with the earth and with one another like a sprawling family of farmers.

A proper letter home from an Islamic state, I thought, would jolt an audience into new awarenesses, as I had been jolted. During my first months in Jebhat al-Nusra's custody, it had seemed to me that powers that lived in the light and the shadows in this part of the world— forces beyond the reckoning of all journalists, all historians, and all scientists—coursed through the veins of the men with the guns. I had felt myself in the hands of something that operated through humans but wasn't quite human. Any true letter from an Islamic state, in my opinion, would have to make this sensation real to a reader. A good letter writer would want to invite his audience into the twilight zone where fact and fantasy mingled.

One doesn't normally try to frighten one's mother in letters home. Still less does one try to mess with her sense of what is real. What I ought to do, I told myself, is turn the empty hours here in jail to account. The right thing, it occurred to me, was to write out the script of a Hollywood blockbuster. When I got out of prison, I would hand the scribbles to an agent. Shortly thereafter, I would be rich.

Since I had scarcely been able to persuade the editors of the *New Republic* website to take an interest in goings-on in Syria, I judged that I couldn't set my blockbuster in Aleppo. But I had had quite enough of Syria by this point. Anyway, the phenomenon I wished to bring to life—the slide of a society into a little lake of blood—could happen anywhere. I decided to make my disaster take place at home, since I knew I could give an accurate accounting of how people talked at home and how certain kinds of weather wore on people's brains.

One of the less religious officers had hoped to take advantage of the empty hours in prison to learn English. He wanted to begin with the dirty words. In private colloquies, in a corner of the cell, with a pencil he kept hidden in the breast pocket of his flak jacket, I had written down the dirtiest ones I could think of. As the last moments of daylight drifted out of our cell, I asked this officer to lend me his pencil and his piece of paper.

Stretching the paper out on my knee, I thought for a moment about what it would take for the social contract in the disregarded mill town in which I grew up to disintegrate. What if someone, or some group of people, wanted to see it die, had allies and weapons, and so campaigned, under the cover of darkness, to make it come apart?

Wishing to be elsewhere, I stood for a moment on a bluff overlooking the disused woolen mill in this town. I was looking down through the early morning darkness. At that hour, I knew, most of the citizens in our town were either asleep or lost to a sleep-like state, thanks to alcohol or prescription drugs or a cocktail of the two. It seemed to me that anyone wishing to deal a blow to community cohesion in our low-self-esteem mill town would first of all do away with the Congregational church, since it was the tallest building, stood at the center of things, and really had, once, long ago, hosted meetings and dances and feasts.

So as the neighbors dozed, I imagined a fictional person into existence, imagined her dousing the wooden joists under the wooden nave with gasoline, and then watched as the flames crept through the pews.

I would have kept on scribbling in this manner—which is to say, whimsically, for the fun of being somewhere else—but the piece of paper my officer friend had given me was no bigger than a playing card. It took me about a minute to fill up the available space. Anyway, after a minute, the officer wanted his pencil back. I stuffed the chit in the pocket of my hospital pants. I'll finish this tomorrow, I told myself.

On the following evening, just before dark, Abu Hajr came to the cell to announce that Matt Schrier, Abu Sofiane, and I were to be transferred. To a new prison? To the Turkish border? To the custody of some other branch of the rebellion? Abu Hajr didn't say. He asked us to gather our spare T-shirts, to blindfold ourselves, and to stand in a line behind the cell door. Within seconds, we were being handcuffed. And then we were walking across a paved surface as a cluster of men pushed rifles into our ribs. These men brought us to the back seat of a waiting car.

CHAPTER 7

MATT'S ESCAPE

In our next prison, a warehouse basement ten minutes by car from the grocery store, Matt, Abu Sofiane, and I were the only prisoners. Abu Sofiane and Matt introduced themselves to the new prison manager as Muslims. I admitted that I was a Christian. Feigning outrage, at what I did not know, the manager, who turned out to be a reasonable fellow, screamed some curses at me, cuffed me across the side of the head, then attacked me with a heavy stick. Holding my elbow against the blows of his stick, I scuttled across the floor. When he caught me, there were more blows, some pleading from me, and a moment during which he held the butt of his stick over my head with both hands as if it were a pike he meant to plunge through my skull. "We are Jebhat al-Nusra!" he called out. "Who are we?"

I replied as he wanted me to reply. Some curses followed and then some questions: Why wasn't I a Muslim? What had I meant by coming to his country? How many Muslims had I killed?

In Syrian prisons, such beatings are known as "welcoming parties." The victims scream, the assailants scream, but these are strangers meeting for the first time. There isn't much feeling in the beatings, and when the new prisoner has exhibited his terror before the new jailers the assailants usually leave off. By this point, I knew how the routine worked. I was frightened but not so frightened that I couldn't be impatient at the same time. "Are you done yet?" I wanted to ask.

In this instance, the manager had brought along two partygoers. One of them carried a polished gnarled branch that looked to me as though it might have been somebody's walking stick once. A second assistant held his Kalashnikov on all three prisoners from a few paces away. After the first round of questioning, the manager had me crawl into a corner in which a used tire and a length of rebar waited. My hands were cuffed behind my back. My lower body was locked into the tire. I writhed on the floor like an overturned crab as assailants I could not see clubbed the soles of my feet. The Muslim prisoners, Matt Schrier and Abu Sofiane, watched from a pair of foam-rubber mattresses nearby. After about a minute, the manager ordered the beating to stop. I was released from the handcuffs. I unfolded myself from the tire. The manager issued some dark warnings against prisoner misbehavior, and then he and his assistants slipped through a steel door beyond which a staircase led upward to the warehouse's ground floor.

The following morning, the manager returned with a single armed guard by his side. Both of them were in a somber mood. The manager crouched by the side of the mattress on which I had slept. "I have done wrong by you," he said with deep feeling, as if my forgiveness might have meant something to him, which it couldn't have. Still, he was upset.

He explained that he had been under the impression that orders had been issued to beat me. In fact, there had been no such orders. On the contrary, the orders were that the three of us were to be treated with respect. The orders had been given by a sheikh so powerful that only God could say no to him. The manager asked me to forgive him.

So there had been a misunderstanding. Such things happen. Now all was well. "Of course!" I told the manager. I had forgotten the beating already, I said.

"Very well," the manager continued, "and soon perhaps they will let you go, all three of you." He didn't know when the release would happen or why. Probably, he said, we would be taken to Jarabulus, on the Turkish border, a city from which we could walk, if we liked, into Turkey. From the Turkish border, he said, we could walk straight into the office of the nearest American consulate. We pressed the manager for details. Abu Sofiane pointed out that he was not an American citizen. The manager shrugged. He knew nothing beyond what he had already told us. His advice for us was to comport ourselves, while in his custody, with dignity. "Respect yourselves," he told us, by which he meant "if there's any funny business from you, you'll regret it." We promised to respect ourselves. If all went well and if God was willing, the manager had every confidence that we would soon be sent back to our families.

I doubt any of us much believed him. He didn't seem in synch enough with the Jebhat al-Nusra command to know what it had in mind. I judged that an al Qaeda overlord somewhere was busy with more pressing matters. He would attend to the matter of his two American prisoners and their jihadi comrade whenever he felt like it.

During the following days, as Matt, Abu Sofiane, and I waited for news, we quarreled. Matt and Abu Sofiane had long since fallen out over Matt's devotion to Islam. At first, in the eye hospital, Matt managed to accommodate himself to his new life as a Muslim. He didn't mind being called Nasser. At prayer times, Abu Sofiane would arrange himself on his blanket such that his upper body faced in the direction we presumed Mecca to be. Matt would stand at his side. Abu Sofiane would recite for a few moments. Matt would bow his head. There would be bowings from the waist, then a series of prostrations, and then silence. That was all. At first, Abu Sofiane didn't insist on praying the dawn prayer at dawn. That prayer, in his opinion, could be prayed whenever he happened to wake. At the time, Abu Sofiane was pleased to have an acolyte. When the Jebhat al-Nusra fighters came to our cell, Abu Sofiane would trumpet the news of Matt's conversion as if a miracle had occurred inside our cheerless little cell. Matt would be asked to recite the testament of faith. He would mumble an approximation of the Arabic words. The Jebhat al-Nusra fighters would gape. "Is he really a Muslim?" they would wonder—at first only to one another, but then, seconds later, they would put this question to Abu Sofiane in Arabic and to Matt in English. Pointing to Matt, sometimes with their guns, they would ask: "You . . . Islam?"

"*Allah akbar!*" Matt would call out, mispronouncing this common affirmation of God's greatness.

Shortly after Matt's conversion, one of the fighters brought a gift to the cell: an English-Arabic edition of the Koran. Now Matt was meant to carry out his own study of the religion. In fact, he did read from the book now and then. During the prayers, as Abu Sofiane recited in Arabic, Matt would follow along in his English edition.

In the eye hospital, before relations between Matt and Abu Sofiane turned bitter, the arrangement suited everyone. By April, however, it was obvious to Matt that Jebhat al-Nusra was not going to free him because he had converted to Islam. Apart from flickers of interest at the news of his conversion, they didn't seem to take any notice of his religious feelings at all. By mid-April, Matt had begun to feel he had fallen into a trap. He resented having to perform ablutions, over and over. He hadn't dirtied himself. What was the point? He found the bowing and prostrating excessive.

After six weeks as a Muslim, he was no longer trying to conceal his impatience. He groaned when he heard the call to prayer. He hurried through the prostrations. He declined to read from his edition of the Koran. As for the officers' religious feelings: They enraged him. He felt that the officers were throwing themselves at God's feet when they ought to have been throwing themselves at our captors' necks. But Matt was in no position to defy the orthodoxies that reigned in our cell. Allegedly, he had lately fallen in love with these orthodoxies. If he had renounced Islam, the officers, some of whom he admired, would have thought him a fraud. The captors would have thought him an apostate. The punishment for apostasy, so the captors appeared to believe, was death.

What could Matt do? The situation confounded him. He felt he had made his conversion in good faith, out of respect for Abu Sofiane and Jebhat al-Nusra. He had, however, expected something in return. Neither Jebhat al-Nusra, nor Abu Sofiane, had made even a tiny concession to Matt. The longer the situation lasted, the more it infuriated him. By June, he was still speaking to Abu Sofiane, but only through clenched teeth. He had resumed his habit of sprinkling his sentences with curses. This brought out the scold in Abu Sofiane. A Muslim's heart could not be clean, Abu Sofiane remonstrated, if there was filth on the tip of his tongue. If Matt continued to use foul language, Abu Sofiane warned, and continued to ignore his obligation to read the Koran, he would effectively cease being a Muslim. "Just because you pray, that doesn't make you a Muslim," he scolded. Islam was an affair of the heart, he said. There could be no concealing the contents of one's heart from God.

When Abu Sofiane wasn't acting the part of the preacher in front of Matt, he liked to invite Matt to join him in reflecting on the sweetness of a martyr's death in Islam. Such thoughts came naturally to Abu Sofiane. He knew the verses that justified suicide bombing. He knew the language by which charlatans persuade teenagers to volunteer for suicide missions. He knew that talk of a terrorist attack on New York would make Matt see red. "Ah, the greatest thing I could do with my life," Abu Sofiane liked to say when he wanted to strike up an argument, "would be to walk into a café in New York—any one busy with Israelis—in a suicide vest. How beautiful would that be?" Abu Sofiane would pose such rhetorical questions to the air, inspect Matt's narrowing eyes, then smile for the two of us. "Very beautiful, right? So effective, too, right?"

I think we both knew that Abu Sofiane was trying to get a rise out of us. He was angry. He was bored. He wanted a debate. Both of us knew that he understood the logic of the suicide bomber, that he was capable of committing such a crime, and that engaging him, as he fantasized, would only draw him out of himself. So we tried not to react.

Instead, we argued with each other. Was Jebhat al-Nusra planning to kill us? Would a conversion to Islam save my life? We argued over these questions and then, with even greater bitterness, we argued over which of us could be proud of how we had comported ourselves in prison. Matt thought that by preferring Abu Sofiane's company to his, I had disgraced myself. He felt I had capitulated to the terrorists in an inner way, while he had retained his dignity. I disagreed. We argued.

When we ran out of things to argue over, Matt introduced topics: If the prison manager told me that I could go free provided I killed Matt, Matt wanted to know, would I agree to kill him? Some months earlier, in the eye hospital, we had agreed that if presented with such a choice, each of us would refuse to kill the other, but one afternoon in the warehouse basement, wishing to shock him into silence, I told Matt that, on second thought, I probably would kill him. He showered me with curses. He appealed to Abu Sofiane. Yes, Abu Sofiane agreed, if I were a Muslim, I would care about my fellow humans. But I was a pagan and a CIA agent. "It's because he has cold blood," Abu Sofiane explained to Matt, "which was why the CIA wanted him in the first place."

Our basement warehouse was a cavernous prison, about the size of a small airplane hangar. During the midday hours, a freight elevator shaft in one of the basement corners admitted a beam of strong summer sunlight. The opening through which this light shone was about five meters off the ground. Lying on my back and studying the opening from below, I judged that it might just be possible to scramble up the iron frame along which the elevator ran, when in service, to squeeze my head through the opening between the shaft and the floor of the elevator, and thus to wiggle away into freedom.

The operation, I thought, would require a slender frame. Also, steady nerves. Abu Sofiane's bullet-ridden right leg would have prohibited him from climbing up the elevator frame. If I were to tell Matt about the escape route I was eyeing, he would have blabbed about it to Abu Sofiane. Abu Sofiane would surely have scuttled our plans.

My escape, I decided, would have to happen when my fellow prisoners were asleep. They would wake to find me gone. My escape was thus a bit of a dirty trick, but I had spied the escape route, not them. It belonged to me, I reasoned. The circumstances precluded me from inviting the others along. It was too bad, but it was what it was. Anyway, the basement was cavernous enough and the elevator shaft dark enough for them to be believed, during the outrage my escape would unleash, when they said, "We were asleep. We never saw a thing."

Thus, early one morning, as Matt and Abu Sofiane snored—when nothing seemed to be stirring in all of Aleppo—I scurried up the elevator shaft. For an instant or two, as I felt the heat of the day pouring into the shaft, I believed my escape would work. I saw myself fleeing over the rooftops like a cat burglar. I felt the brilliance of the sun in my eyes and the pain of running through the gravel on the soles of my feet. Pushing my body through the slot between the elevator and the shaft was going to require a creative kind of dexterity. But I had been a rock climber in a previous existence. I knew how not to fall in such moments, how to keep cool, carry on, and so get the job done.

Underneath the freight compartment, I pressed the top of my head into the elevator's floor panel, then pushed. Nothing moved. I tried to slither my head through the crack between the freight compartment and the elevator shaft. That crack was no wider than a mail slot. Bracing a shoulder against a bottom corner of the freight compartment, I tried to jostle the thing. Nothing doing. Discouraged and covered in elevator grease, I shimmied back to the basement floor.

During the previous months, Abu Sofiane had been eager to exhibit to anyone within earshot how wise he was to the machinations of the World Bank, the Freemasons, the Trilateral Commission, and American Jewry in general. When he was frightened or frustrated, as he often was, he eased his mind by steering the discussion in the cell toward the sinister designs of Jews in the Middle East. I was his example of the seemingly innocent American traveler who, under the cover of "journalism" or "diplomacy" or "business," was plotting, in coordination with the World Bank and the CIA, to turn Syria into a sprawling plantation under the administration of Israeli settler families. When he had gotten the attention of a cluster of officers, he would put suggestive questions to me, in a loud voice, in Arabic. For instance, "How often do you go to Tel Abib?" and "Are you possibly a Jew yourself?" and "The newspaper you write for is a Jew newspaper, isn't it?"

I tried to ignore him. This allowed the doubts about me in the room to fructify. I denied his insinuations angrily, in no uncertain terms. This caused Abu Sofiane to smile. "Not a Jew at all?" he would say. "Not one little bit?"

"No," I would say.

"But you often go to New York, yes?" he would reply, grinning like a Cheshire cat. "There are many Jews in New York? About how many Jews would you say there are?" And so on. I worried that it wouldn't take much for Abu Sofiane's aspersions to crystalize into certainties, for the certainties to crystalize into a verdict, and, in this way, for Jebhat al-Nusra to justify an auto-da-fé. In the grocery store, I found that the only thing I could do to keep him from stirring up rumors was to massage his thigh. By June, three months after Jebhat al-Nusra had put a bullet through his femur, his upper leg was still a mess. The swelling had come down, but it still caused him excruciating pain. It wasn't as if he were not in need of a massage.

In the warehouse basement, I continued to massage his thigh, but down there, there was no audience for Abu Sofiane's the-Jews-are-our-affliction conspiracy theories. He stopped flogging them. He often day-dreamed about a future for himself away from the jihad, indeed away from Islam altogether. He saw himself at his seaside Moroccan restau-rant. He spoke of the cash that would pour into his pockets in such a situation, the women he would meet, the alcohol he would drink, and the elegant clothing he would wear. Because I wanted good relations between us and because I couldn't bear to hear him fantasize about blowing up public places, I was keen to summon his better angels. He liked to be sung to. I sang. He liked to fantasize about life as a dandy on the Moroccan coast. I listened. He wanted me to rub his leg. I rubbed.

Matt found my solicitousness unbearable. He denounced me for sucking up to terrorists. Abu Sofiane denounced him for denouncing his masseur. This led to bitterer arguments. In the warehouse base-ment, there were times when the tension between Matt and Abu Sofi-ane caused the two of them to seize each other by the throat. They would waltz through the warehouse columns in this manner as if they were on an insane kind of date, each of them sputtering with rage, nei-ther one willing to be the first to let go.

After such confrontations, Abu Sofiane would settle himself on the foam-rubber mattress, next to me, on which I had been trying not to pay attention to my prison mates. "Mais, il est *ma*-lade, ce type!" ("But this guy is a nutter!"), Abu Sofiane would exclaim, as if he and our jailers were conventional, transparent jihadis whose psychology made sense, whereas Matt lived way out there in the blue, in a private world of madness. He seemed to feel that only the French (rather than the Arabic or English) means of expressing incredulity at someone else's insanity (*"Mais il est malade!"*) could convey the depth of his astonishment. So he repeated this formula over and over, under his breath, as he gazed at Matt from the corners of his eyes.

Looking back now, I suspect we were all drifting away from conventional sanity then. We so mistrusted one another, were so tired of jail life, and so much wanted to be free of the others that if freedom and vows of silence were on offer, any one of us, I suspect, could have been persuaded to do in the other two.

In the beginning of July, the guards again came for us with their handcuffs and blindfolds. Again we were warned against sudden movements. Again we were piled into the back seat of a car, then driven at a crawl down quiet streets. We were unloaded from the car and led into a building, then down a flight of stairs. We were told to sit. We sat. A door closed. We removed our blindfolds. We found ourselves sitting on the floor of an airy, carpeted room. A pleasant breeze blew through the cell. Though I didn't know this then, we were in the basement of the municipal motor vehicles department in an Aleppo neighborhood called as Shaer.

Our new cell was about the size of a modest studio apartment. A bathroom in a corner, a bank of shoebox-sized windows high on the rear wall of the cell, some pillows on the floor, a stack of folded blankets—this was by far our most well-appointed prison to date. So far, so good, I thought to myself as I ran my eyes over the walls. Right away, Matt and I saw that the iron filigree, which had been welded over the windows in place of bars, had rusted away, in places, to a kind of friable chicken wire. Even from a distance of several feet, it was obvious, at least to me, that this filigree could be twisted into bits. Abu Sofiane was too big around the chest to fit through the foot-long channel on the other side of the filigree, through which an escapee would have had to slither. Matt and I, however, probably could have made it. He and I exchanged glances. The filigree in the rightmost window had begun to peel away from the window frame of its own accord. "That one could work," Matt whispered as he nodded at the damaged window grate.

I'm sure we would have turned to peeling back the rest of the filigree right away if not for Abu Sofiane. We didn't know whose side he was on. Anyway, there was no way that Abu Sofiane could have fit his bulkier frame through the window and no way that he would have kept quiet as Matt and I worked on an escape plan that did not include him.

Thus, during our first days in this cell, we ignored the rusting wire grille in the window. We devoted much of our mental energy then to thoughts of our former cellmates. Though Abu Sofiane had come to Syria to kill the members of the Syrian Arab Army, eight weeks in a pair of cells with seventeen of its officers had drawn him into their lives. "By god, their hearts are white," he had declared before a delegation of Jebhat al-Nusra authorities in the Al-Haydariya prison. Speaking well of Alawites could only have encouraged the Jebhat al-Nusra authorities to suppose that something had gone wrong in his mind. If he were to be released, he might conceivably infiltrate a nearby mosque, introduce himself as a Moroccan jihadi, then betray every worshiper in the place to the regime. Abu Sofiane would have known that in saying a good word, in public, about Alawites he was risking his own skin. That he had done it anyway gave evidence of a courage none of us knew he had. In our new studio apartment prison, Abu Sofiane kept faith with our former prison mates by remembering each of them, by name, during the portion of the prayer in which prayer leader communicates the congregants' most cherished wishes to God—the *du'a*. He asked God to return them to their families, safe and sound, at ease and in health, as Abu Ayoub had done for us when they led the prayers in our earlier prisons. I'm sure Matt, Abu Sofiane, and I hoped that if the officers couldn't be sent home, they would be sent down the block to join us here, in this cool, carpeted sitting room.

I, for one, felt that the Alawites might already have been released. I rated their chances of survival much higher than I rated the chances that Matt and I would be let go. It was true that the much-dreamed-of prisoner swap in which Jebhat al-Nusra members currently locked in the Aleppo Central Prison would be freed in exchange for the officers' freedom seemed to have gone into eclipse. I could not, however, imagine that the terrorists would store the officers away for half a year, lecture them, chat with them now and then, and allow them to call their families only to murder them, in cold blood, when the Syrian government proved itself intransigent. Of course the government was intransigent. The government's helplessness—its stubbornness and casual cruelty, I felt—was too well understood to serve as a motive for murder. For the time being, I assumed, the officers were like the crew of a ship that had gone down in stormy seas. They were clinging to a lifeboat. Because a spacious government rescue boat was only a few kilometers away, because no complicated international diplomacy would have been required to summon it, and because no government anywhere would abandon officers who had disappeared in the line of duty, in the fullness of time the rescue ship, I trusted, would come to the aid of the castaways.

I suspect now that the America-style guns I saw on the roof of the school across the way from our grocery store prison really were the fruit of a US government–sponsored initiative to train and equip the Syrian rebels. At the time, my mother and the mothers of other Americans who had vanished in Syria had begun to knock on doors at the State Department in Washington. I know now that as the diplomats there were explaining to my mother that the situation in Syria was opaque, with developments occurring every day that confounded even the State Department experts, the US ambassador to Syria, Robert Ford, was posing for photographs in opposition-held territory with US-vetted rebel leaders. Those leaders were becoming famous within Jebhat al-Nusra not only for the esteem the Jebhat al-Nusra leadership had for their religious scruples but also for their ability to bring in high-tech weaponry. I assume that in his zeal to help the Syrian people, the ambassador did not want to know how, once they crossed the Syrian border, his weapons would be passed from cousin to neighbor to friend until they reached the fundamentalists. In their hands, the American guns would have been used to beat the American journalists in their custody and to kill more Syrians. I assume Ambassador Ford didn't want to know about such matters. Anyway, after his Syria trip, when he met with my mother and Diane Foley, whose son James had also disappeared in recent months somewhere near Aleppo, he didn't mention the US weapons pipeline to the Syrian rebels. He spoke of the opacity of the situation in Syria in general. He spoke of alliances that shifted like quicksand and of the general inadvisability of traveling to Aleppo.

It seems to me now that, as the billion dollars in covert aid the Obama administration approved for the Syrian resistance in the spring of 2013 began to flood into Syria, some of the rebel commanders, feeling themselves buoyed by newfound alliances, lost interest in making deals with the Syrian government. Perhaps the guns that began to tumble into the rebels' hands then had the effect of bringing out their will to kill. Perhaps they hadn't been much interested in making a deal in the first place. Now new, richer deals beckoned on the horizon.

Because I keep in touch with two of the officers with whom I was imprisoned that spring, I know this for sure: After negotiations with their families, Jebhat al-Nusra released two officers. Two others escaped. Now, six years after the families' last contact, which came in the form of hurried cell phone calls from a villa basement, the parents of the remaining thirteen continue to search for news of their vanished sons.

I suspect now that toward the middle of July, Jebhat al-Nusra's patience with Abu Sofiane finally ran out. He had been promising to give the commanders information on a Médecins Sans Frontières doctor they hoped to kidnap. But Abu Sofiane had no such information. He had been hinting to them that the US might pay a ransom for him. But he was no US citizen. He made the mistake of telling them this openly, over and over, as if he felt that his captors would reward him for not being an American. Probably he misread the clues.

Anyway, about two weeks after Abu Sofiane, Matt Schrier, and I arrived in the as Shaer prison, a group of five men in balaclavas came for Abu Sofiane.

When the visitors called his name, a shock of wonder and happiness came over him. He had been waiting for his deliverance for six months. He shot up from the mattress on which he had been sitting. "Me?" he exclaimed as one of the soldiers called out his name.

"Yes, you. Pack your bags," said a voice.

The eyes of the man who spoke, however, were dead. The soldiers stared at us, then stared at the line of T-shirts and underpants we had hung up to dry on pegs beneath a window. They murmured but did not speak. All of their eyes were dead.

As they were leading Abu Sofiane out of the cell, he reminded them that he was barefoot. Out of deference to his feelings, it seemed to me, but not because he would be needing shoes in the place they had in mind for him, one of the men in the balaclavas kicked a pair of sandals across the carpet. They washed up against Abu Sofiane's feet. "We want you to travel in comfort, Doctor," said the soldier.

Though Abu Sofiane had not gone into details with me and though Jebhat al-Nusra never told him why they had arrested him, remarks he let slip about a bride in the Jebhat al-Nusra–controlled Aleppo suburb of Anadan—a bride he had yet to marry in an official sense but to whom he was committed in the eyes of God—made me think his real crime had somehow involved sex. Or an attempt at sex.

The men in the balaclavas, I think now, were the last to see him alive. Neither his brother on Long Island nor his ex-wife in Virginia—people with whom I know he longed to be in touch—have received messages from him. The FBI, which became aware of his presence in Syria at about this time and which knew him to be a potential suicide bomber, say that he disappeared from their radar screens in July of 2013.

He never wrote to me, though I think I knew him well enough to know that if he could have, he would have. A prison fantasy he cherished possibly more than all the others had caused him to believe that once I was freed I would vouch for the soundness of his character before the US immigration authorities. When the authorities had relented, he was going to return to Virginia. He would reunite with his wife and children, then carry on with life in the suburbs as if there had been neither a deportation nor any jihad at all.

Now I think that one day in July, the Jebhat al-Nusra sheikhs decided that the time had come to bring Abu Sofiane to an open field, and, out there, to make him kneel in the dirt. They would have known that he had come into Syria on his own, with no one to vouch for him and no connections to any authorities in the jihad. He had spent his first weeks in the country lying about medical training in America, avoiding the war, and insinuating himself into an Anadan family. Perhaps the authorities suspected him of being more interested in sexual adventures in Syria than in killing. I certainly did. Since he bragged so often about his training in America, at least some of his acquaintances would have supposed that, during his time in Virginia, he had discovered the personal advantages that came from moonlighting for the CIA. In Syria, freelancers for the Assad security services proliferate like fruit flies. It would have been natural for his Syrian friends to suppose that he was playing a double game.

As he knelt in the field, the men in the balaclavas would have prompted him to recite the opening lines of the Koran: "'In the name of the compassionate and the merciful, the king of all the worlds,'" he would have said, "'lead us on the straight path.'" These words are thought to stand a Muslim on the cusp of a departure from the earthly realm in the best possible stead. It is thought that any human at all who leaves planet Earth with these words on his lips earns a kind of paradise eligibility for himself, regardless of the creed by which he lived out his days. So his killers would have given him ample time to recite. They would have listened carefully, and only when the recitation was well and truly over would they have shot him in the back of the head.

In the wake of Abu Sofiane's departure, Matt stopped his observance of Ramadan, which that year came in the second week of July. He ate in the open, as the sun shone, as I did. He did not, however, give up the performance of the five daily prayers. Though I had never asked him to share his religious ideas with me, I think we both understood that his conversion to Islam had been a lie, invented to ease his way out of jail. Yet it was a strange sort of lie. Something in the prayers, evidently, had grown on him. "I bet you're wondering why I'm still doing the prayers," he said one afternoon, as he was preparing to make his prostrations.

"Nope," I said. "Not my business."

Looking back on those moments now, it seems to me that he might have been living through a touch of Stockholm syndrome. He liked the moral authority that came with being a Muslim. He loved to legislate. For instance, it had been Abu Sofiane's rule that an unbeliever mustn't be allowed to touch the pages of the Koran, lest the corruption in his soul pass though his fingers, into the holy book. Now, in the wake of Abu Sofiane's removal from our cell, this law became Matt's law. He presided over the English-Arabic Koran the authorities in the eye hospital had given him like a dragon guarding a hoard. He refused to countenance the idea of my hands touching his book.

What if I washed my hands before I touched it? I asked.

"No," he said.

I promised to kiss the cover before opening it, as he kissed it.

"Nope," he said.

One afternoon, I insisted. I hadn't read a word of any kind since the previous October. I was seeing bookshelves in my dreams. "Give me the book," I said.

"No," he said.

"Give me the fucking book," I repeated.

"No," he said.

I tried to tear the book out of his hands. We fought. In my many altercations with the Jebhat al-Nusra warriors, I had been afraid but never angry. Now I was in a rage. I wanted to tear Matt to bits. In our basement cell, as firefights echoed in the distance, he and I locked our hands around each other's necks. We throttled each other for a moment, then fell, then wrestled on the floor, grunting and gasping and saying nothing. After several minutes of this, he had me in a full nelson. He was pushing my chin into my stomach. "Okay," I whispered. "Uncle." He let me go. With his defense of his Koran complete, he returned to his corner. I returned to mine, empty-handed.

In the third week of July, the authorities brought us a third cellmate, a veterinarian who lived in an Aleppo suburb, as-Safira, famous for its arms manufactories and for having been taken over lately by a group that wished to be called the Islamic State of Iraq and the Levant. The veterinarian spoke of this organization as "Daesh." When they came to question him, the Jebhat al-Nusra authorities, learning that he was from as-Safira, asked him a series of questions about Daesh. Did Daesh preach to him? About what? What was his opinion of Daesh? He refused to utter a negative word, though it was obvious that the interrogators held Daesh in contempt. Instead of giving them what they wanted, he quoted a line of scripture to the effect that the casting of aspersions on other Muslims displeased God.

The veterinarian, Mustafa, likewise refused to utter a negative word about Jebhat al-Nusra, though they had hauled him away to jail for no reason he could discern. He assumed that there had been a mix-up. He was desperate to explain himself, to whom he did not know. Trusting that the person who had ordered his arrest would turn up eventually, he spent his days fasting and praying.

At first, on learning that Matt had converted to Islam inside a Jebhat al-Nusra prison, Mustafa betrayed not a hint of skepticism. He accepted. He behaved toward Matt as he would have toward any other Muslim. He prayed next to Matt and shook his hand after the prayers. But several days into Mustafa's detention, as Matt and I were conversing, some remark or look in my eye or change in my tone of voice caused Matt to fly into a rage. Suddenly he was trembling with fury.

Mustafa looked up from the Koran he was reading, then lowered it to his knee slowly, as if watching an event in a dream. He could speak only a few words of English. Still, there was so many versions of the word "fuck" in Matt's exclamations that it would have been difficult for him not to catch the gist of what Matt was saying.

"Nasser, my friend," Mustafa said softly in Arabic. "What is wrong?" He turned his eyes to me, then back to Matt. He asked me to tell Matt that a Muslim who allows himself to be overcome with rage as Matt had done has invalidated his fast. God would refuse to accept it. Matt would have to make up for the failed fast by fasting an extra day, at the end of Ramadan.

I relayed the message. Matt thought for a moment. He clenched his teeth. He waited for Mustafa to return to his Koran, then crept across the cell to where I was sitting. He cupped a hand around my ear: "Fuck you," he murmured, "and fuck your mother."

Given the bitterness between us, the collaboration he and I fell into, at the end of July, in the hours after the prison authorities took Mustafa away, was itself a kind of Ramadan miracle. Matt hated me because I had refused to convert, because he felt I was more willing to find the good in an al Qaeda suicide bomber than I was to spend a moment in conversation with him, and because I knew the secret of his bad faith. I hated him because he refused to understand that it wasn't me but the lunatics into whose clutches we had fallen who were driving him crazy, because he sometimes hit me as he held me by the scruff of my T-shirt, more or less as the Jebhat al-Nusra fighters had done, and because he inflicted Abu Sofiane's Taliban-like notions of who was entitled to touch the Koran on me.

The prospect of a jailbreak must have helped us put our differences aside. In undertaking it, we knew we were risking death. We could hear the snipers firing from nearby rooftops. The Aleppo quarter in which we were being held then, as Shaer, was a frequent target of the barrel bombers. Both of us believed that had Jebhat al-Nusra caught us in the midst of an escape attempt or had they detected signs of our preparations, they would have shot us. In this jail, the jailers allowed us pens and paper. Before our first escape attempt, both of us wrote out notes to our mothers. We folded the notes into envelope-like rectangles, then labeled these with our names and contact information for our parents so that, if the snipers cut us down in the street, the neighbors would have a means of sending the notes off to our mothers.

Though in this jail the jailers gave us ample, often tasty food, both of us felt that, on balance, staying was more dangerous than leaving. The barrel bombs that were falling over as Shaer in those days might have killed us. We might have been given or sold away to a group that really did want to kill us, or the jailers might have decided, in a fit of pique, to execute us as the *Wall Street Journal* reporter Daniel Pearl, about whom we tried not to think, was executed. We dreaded an American attack on an al Qaeda outpost in Egypt or Yemen. We dreaded the coming of the September 11 anniversary. "When the holy months are over, surround the idolaters and slay them wherever ye find them, and seize them, and beleaguer them, and lie in wait for them." So says the so-called Verse of the Sword, to be found in the ninth chapter of the Koran, the Surah of

Repentance. I knew enough of this verse to recite it to Matt in English. I was aware of our captors' prejudice in favor of literal interpretations of holy writ. I discussed these circumstances with Matt.

Looking back now, I suspect that even if we hadn't felt that our survival depended on an escape we would have tried to break out anyway, because the collapsing iron filigree too much invited our attention and because the jailers, busy with Ramadan, had all but forgotten about us. An hour or so before dawn, they brought us a plate of sliced melon, *labneh*, and bread. Minutes before sunset, they returned to the cell to bring us tea, more bread, lentils, a salty white goat cheese called *shanklish*, and rice. During each visit, the jailers remained with us for a matter of seconds. After they had delivered us our meals, they locked the door, climbed a flight of stairs, and were gone. We had our iron filigree to ourselves for twenty-three hours and fifty-nine minutes a day.

After about two days of steady work, we had reduced the structural integrity of the iron grille in the window to that of a pile of twigs. We tried to conceal the damage we inflicted by propping bits of wire against the sturdiest parts of the grille. But we had turned the thing into a swatch of wiry lace. A sneeze would have caused it to collapse.

The morning of our first attempt, Matt stood on my back, pushed the rusting iron mesh to the side, and then, holding the window frame with both hands, hoisted his head into the tunnel. He squirmed for a moment, got stuck, grunted, wiggled forward a few centimeters, then called out, in a whisper, "I'm stuck!" We had planned for him to rest his feet on my shoulders. I was meant to stand, and he was meant to thrust himself upward and forward, like an acrobat leaping from my shoulders, through the tunnel. When he was actually in the midst of the escape, his feet couldn't find my shoulders. They waved and kicked at the air. I tried to guide his feet to my shoulders, but they were bicycling through the air so violently that as I approached, one of the feet struck me in the face. It sent me reeling backward into the cell. By this point, he was too exhausted to carry on. He scuttled backward, then dropped himself onto the mound of pillows we were using as a stepladder.

Our failure left me shaken. I judged Matt too prone to panic to be capable of pulling off a stunt such as the one we were planning. If somehow he did manage to wiggle his way out of the cell, I didn't trust that outside, in the free world, he would hang around long enough to help me wiggle my way through.

Thus, over the following two days, we argued. I refused to try again. He insisted. I insisted that I be the first person out. He refused. He proposed that I allow him to climb away on his own, with no assistance from me. But the window was too high off the ground and the tunnel too narrow for this to be a realistic possibility. Anyway, I had no intention of allowing him to destroy our illusion of a grille as he scurried away to a new life, so I refused to allow him to try on his own. "If you do," I said, "I'll call the guards." My threat sent him into a rage. I was a rat and a traitor and an al Qaeda accomplice.

When this argument subsided, we argued over whether he should help me once he had squeezed himself through the tunnel.

"Once I'm out, I'm gone," he said. "Why should I wait?"

"Courtesy," I replied.

"What's a matter with you? This isn't a fucking country club," he said.

In one of our arguments, he recalled for me a lesson he had learned during his days (in the recent past, I suspected) as a cat burglar on Long Island. He and a friend had managed to break into a restaurant after hours, he said. They had piled cases of liquor at the door. The alarm had gone off. They managed to destroy the alarm but had had to flee in a panic. Several days later, however, in a cooler state of mind, they broke in again. Now there was no alarm. They took their time. They made off with many cases of expensive alcohol. For Matt, the story showed that great determination married with nerves of steel would carry the day.

"You should apologize to the restaurant owners," I told him, "and give them back their liquor."

He gaped at me. "What the fuck's a matter with you?" he said.

Our second escape worked like a charm—for him. By the time he had wiggled his way through the tunnel, the dawn was coming up over a ruined factory I could see now, for the first time, looming in the wide-open window. Crouching outside this window, he whispered instructions at me. He waited as I scrambled over the pile of pillows, climbed up the ladder of T-shirts I had built, jammed my torso through the tunnel, then poked my head into the open air. I needed him then to pull me by the hands or the hair or by the scruff of the neck, but we were both panicking then and though he tugged on my right forearm for a moment, he tugged for only a moment. Then he let the arm drop. "You can't do it," he whispered.

Again, we argued.

"Pull!" I said.

"I'm pulling," he said.

"Just one big pull," I said, gasping. "Please!"

"Shut your mouth!" he said. Somewhere above him, in one of the guards' sleeping rooms, perhaps, a window stood open.

"Just a few more seconds," I said. "It's working."

"I'm pulling," he said. "It's not working."

Inside the cell, my feet were flopping in the air. I kicked at the emptiness. I reached my hands forward toward a sandbag whose contents had spilled across the pavement. I searched through the sand for a handhold. "You're making a fucking racket," Matt said. "Would you shut your fucking mouth?" I sank my fingers into handfuls of sand. "I'll go for help, okay?" he said. He turned on his heels. He sprinted across an expanse of pavement, then disappeared behind a half-destroyed cement wall. I never saw him again.

During the hours that followed Matt's escape, I sat slumped against a wall at the back of our cell. Aleppo, to judge by the soundlessness of the world outside my window, was fast asleep. In the early morning quiet, I made myself climb through the window frame a second time, but I struggled to hoist myself off the floor. By the time I managed to poke my head into the open air, I was exhausted. I didn't have the strength to wriggle forward. I couldn't balance myself inside the window frame. I grunted a bit, then slid backward onto the cell floor.

If only I had insisted that I be the first one out, I told myself, I could have saved myself. I felt I would have had the presence of mind to stave off the panic, to reach inside the cell, and to pull Matt to safety.

That he would panic in the crucial moment had been, for me, a given. So why had I let him have his way? I had hoped to avoid a fight. I had assumed that even if he were to leave me in the lurch, as he did, I was lithe enough to scuttle through to safety on my own. My miscalculation, I supposed, was going to result in torture or death under torture. So it is in wars, I told myself. People who think themselves clever, as I had done, are crushed. I slumped deeper into the base of the wall. The room spun.

For several hours that morning, as Aleppo slept, I reviewed the errors that had led me into this spot—far away from the world, it seemed to me, at the very edge of life. Of course, long before I had ever set my eyes on the grille in this basement window, there had been strings of miscalculations. Had I not sealed my fate months earlier? In my heart of hearts, I told myself, I had long since conceded my life to my captors. Now the final moments were at hand. I may be shocked, I told myself, but can I be surprised? I sank my fingers to the roots of my hair. I stared into my lap. I waited for the sun to pass through the sky. Soon, I told myself, I will be at peace.

As it turned out, that evening, when the jailer who normally brought the evening meal discovered that Matt had fled, he gaped for a moment, withdrew, kept away long enough to pray and to break his fast, then returned in the company of a dozen angry, heavily bearded men. One of them—a leader, apparently—locked my head into the crook of his elbow. With a spare hand, he punched my face several times. As he held my head, he screamed questions at me. Why had I not alerted the guards as Matt was escaping? Had I helped him? After a minute or so, he released me. I sputtered answers at him through the blood that was dribbling into my mouth. I had not helped Matt, I lied. I intended to be "released with honor," I said, using an Arabic phrase that often comes up among prisoners. I was innocent of all charges, I said, it was beneath me to sneak away like a rat, and I meant to vindicate myself before a judge. Yes, I had summoned the prison staff, I lied, as Matt was escaping. I had banged on the door like a lunatic in an asylum. I had been ignored.

To my surprise, the Jebhat al-Nusra commander who had put himself in charge of this investigation seemed to listen as I spoke. This wasn't at all the normal Jebhat al-Nusra way. I assume now that on this occasion, my visitors were genuinely curious. They had believed the cell to be an inescapable dungeon. One of the Americans, apparently, had waltzed away. The other one, for no obvious reason, had refrained from waltzing away. Why?

Accordingly, that night, I did my best to cast aspersions on Matt's character. He had made his preparations as I slept, I said, probably because he felt I would rat him out if he had shared his plans with me. I showed the commander the cut on my forehead I had sustained during my struggle with Matt over his Koran. "We disliked each other," I explained. "Often, we fought."

"In truth, he understood Arabic, didn't he?" the commander asked.

"Probably, he did," I said. The commander glowered. He wanted to know if Matt had been a CIA agent after all. I shrugged my shoulders. "Perhaps?"

"Was his conversion to Islam also a lie?" the commander asked.

Again, I shrugged my shoulders. "Who can say?" I pretended to ponder the matter. "When he was alone with me," I offered, "he did not pray. Neither did he fast. You can judge his sincerity before God for yourself."

That night, my answers seemed to satisfy this commander. When I had ruined his reputation to the best of my ability, the commander harrumphed. All Americans were liars, he said, and I was as much of a liar as any. I held my tongue.

Thus, before this commander left, he allowed his adjutants to kick me in the ribs, and to slap my head. He screamed a few parting words of abuse. But he did not threaten to wring further, truer confessions out of me. Instead, he turned on his heels. All of my visitors filed out of the room. The last to leave slammed the door, as usual.

In the silence after their departure, I marveled at my good fortune. I had been anticipating a firing squad. I'd assumed, at the very least, that there would be torture. In fact, there had been a bloody nose, followed by a round of egregious lying.

The matter couldn't possibly have ended there, I supposed. Still, things had gotten off to an auspicious beginning. Later that evening, a prison worker appeared at the window out of which Matt had escaped bearing a welding torch. As I crouched in a corner, he affixed a sturdier, immovable set of bars to the window. A few moments after this worker had completed this task, he appeared at the door of my cell. He deposited a plate of rice on the floor, then slipped away. I ate. I listened to the back-and-forth of the neighborhood firefights for a while, inspected the welder's new bars, then gathered the throw pillows on which I slept into a corner. Within seconds, I was asleep.

The following morning, the jail staff moved me into a fetid cell, next door to the one from which Matt escaped, in one corner of which there stood a little lake of sewage. I languished here for two days, and then, one evening, for no apparent reason, I was returned to my former cell. Now the cushions were gone. Whereas before, meals in this cell consisted of melon, plates of rice, bread, and tea, they consisted now of a single round of bread and a single egg.

There came an afternoon, shortly after my return to this cell, on which one of the commanders I remembered from the eye hospital stood by as a pair of assistants subjected me to sustained flogging. They used their galvanized steel cables. One of the men supplemented the cable lashes with the application of a car battery. In the evening after this beating, a spell of dizziness caused me to collapse as I stood over the toilet in my cell. I summoned a jailer. A polite, well-meaning teenager appeared at the door. "May I have a pain reliever?" I asked. He disappeared, then returned, oddly enough, with a tablet of Panadol. I swallowed it, then slept.

The next morning, running my hand over the bruises and lacerations I had sustained during the cable beating, it seemed to me that I hadn't been injured in any serious way, that I felt about as I would have had I been in a high-speed bike crash.

After a bike crash, one's body aches. One's head rings. Sometimes, there are superficial wounds. One isn't quite oneself for a few days. I will rest up, I told myself. I resolved to focus totally on a proper recovery, as injured athletes do. I had sustained a series of painful blows to the head. I decided to keep my head still, and to sleep as much as possible during the coming days.

During this recovery period, the prison staff fed me a round of flatbread and a handful of olives per day. Once a day, a Jebhat al-Nusra fighter came to my cell with a branch that appeared to have been lopped from a nearby tree. It was much too heavy and too busy with twigs to use as a proper flail. This fighter waved his branch at me. He slapped my head and shoulders. Of course, he screamed. But after a few days of this, he seemed to lose interest. Neither he nor any of the other domestic workers in this prison ever breathed a word to me about Matt. They hadn't wondered at his presence. They expressed no interest in his absence. Within a day or so of his escape, it felt to me as though he had never been there at all.

That year, Ramadan came to an end on August 7. On the morning of the seventh, upstairs, in the Jebhat al-Nusra inner sanctums, there were feasts. I could hear the pots clanking. I smelled the mutton stewing. For me, in the afternoon, there was a new cellmate—Hamoud.

I warmed instantly to Hamoud, a Palestinian-Syrian who had spent most of his adult life in prison. He was in his mid-thirties. Some twenty years earlier, his uncle, he told me, had killed his brother. He had therefore killed the uncle. The Syrian government had sentenced him to life in prison.

In the regime prisons, he said, he had been permitted visitors, a hot water heater for tea and coffee, and a television. There had been exercise yards. There were smuggled cell phones. At the prison commissary, there had been pots of hummus.

I asked him how many stars, on a scale of one to five, with five being the highest rating, he would give to the Aleppo Central Prison. It had been a five-star facility, in his opinion. What about the prison in Palmyra? He felt that that prison rated only three. There had been inadequate ventilation and crowding. That evening, we cursed our Jebhat al-Nusra jailers for the crumminess of their prisons. We sighed over the luxuries afforded to the normal run of prisoners in Syria.

During the conversation that flowed, with occasional silences, through most of that night, Hamoud told me the story of his arrest by Jebhat al-Nusra. Earlier that summer, he said, the Syrian government had mysteriously commuted his sentence. A free man, he returned to the village outside of Aleppo in which he grew up. Sadly, he said, the Free Syrian Army squadron that had taken over his village suspected him of being an agent in the service of the Syrian intelligence apparatus, sent out to spy on the Free Syrian Army. This squadron arrested him. It held him in its own jail for three weeks, during which time it tortured him nearly every day. At the end of the three weeks, the Free Syrian Army turned him over to Jebhat al-Nusra.

As Hamoud told me of his tribulations, I couldn't help but feel that his appearance in my cell had been miracle enough for me. In the wake of Matt's escape, alone in the cell, I had been certain that Jebhat al-Nusra was planning a wicked, unbearable torture for me. But what? I fretted. I dreaded. I stared at the locked door. What evil thing was coming my way?

And then Hamoud had slipped through the door. Hamoud, a lifelong prisoner, knew how to be alone with his thoughts, and when to allow me to be alone with mine. He knew the geography of Aleppo much better than I did. Where were we, exactly? By drawing lines across the carpet with his fingertip, he made mysterious, labyrinthine, beautiful maps for me.

When he and I had spent several days together, I felt comfortable enough in his presence to sing to myself. To my surprise, he liked this. I've never known a soul to like my singing. Hamoud found something in it to appreciate. One evening, when I had been depressed during the day and so hadn't sung at all, he spoke up, into the silence. "You didn't sing today," he said. "Why not?" That evening, I sang a song for him whose melody he could remember, whose title he could recall only faintly. "Susanna?" he asked. "Yes, Susanna?" I smiled at him. I sang:

> "Well, it rained all night the day I left,
> The weather, it was dry,
> The sun so hot, I froze to death,
> Susanna, don't you cry."

As I was warbling for Hamoud, he was teaching me. What words should be uttered to a Jebhat al-Nusra warrior when you have finished your dinner and are hoping for a spot of tea? When you've been caught peering at their movements through a keyhole? When you'd like news about the progress of the war? Hamoud understood the language of the jihad. It came to him automatically, as if from a bottomless well of idioms. For instance, he knew that Jebhat al-Nusra fighters like to feel that somewhere in their prisoners' sinning hearts, the prisoners admire the jailers. We, the prisoners, were meant to love the warriors for their preparedness to die, for their devotion to God, and for their frank, childlike affection for the Syrian people. The warriors want to feel that while they are risking life and limb wandering the Aleppo streets, their prisoners are downstairs in the basement cells, rooting them on. "May God bring you victories, O Lord," he would tell the jailers who brought us our evening meal. When they quizzed him about his own commitment to Islam, he threw himself at their feet. "Teach me, my sheikhs, for I want to learn!" he would say. No, he didn't know how many prostrations were to be offered at the dawn prayer. Was it two? Four? "I have no idea. For the love of God, teach me!" he would exclaim.

Hamoud's arrival in my cell happened to coincide with Jebhat al-Nusra's restoration of my normal food ration. Again, they brought melon in the evening. After dinner, when Hamoud asked for tea, tea was brought. Sometimes, in the midst of a lazy afternoon, an urge for a chat with a jailer struck him. He summoned a jailer. Chitchat occurred.

A week after his arrival, I made an audit of my losses and gains over the previous weeks. I had undergone a week of light to moderate Jebhat al-Nusra abuse. On the other side of the ledger, I had gained an admirable cellmate. I had lost a disagreeable one. By now, the disagreeable one, I imagined, would have informed the CIA special operations team in Langley of my exact location. He would have drawn out diagrams of the cell and informed the men in "The Company," as he liked to refer to the CIA, of the routines that prevailed among my jailers.

I did not suppose then—or at any other moment—that the CIA might be willing to send its own people after me. In the wake of Matt's escape, however, I did begin to daydream about a hands-off, low-risk means of bringing my ordeal to a peaceful close.

If the US government was sending arms to the Syrian rebels, as I supposed it was, was it not possible that one of the US-approved rebel groups would be willing to drag its largest guns to the prison's front door, to knock, to smile, to utter a soto voce threat or two, and to let it be known that it wished to retrieve the American prisoner in the basement? "In exchange for Theo, we propose a gift basket of iPhones," the leader of the America-friendly group might have said. "Deal?"

It seemed to me then that Jebhat al-Nusra didn't quite know what it meant to do with me. The commander in as Shaer, I hoped, could well have been interested in thrashing out a deal. Probably, he would have rejected whatever initial offer happened his way. But he might, out of politeness, have ordered tea to be served. A theatrical exchange, filled with declarations of solidarity and invocations of the Prophet's name, would have followed. Such is the script by which business in Aleppo has always advanced, I told myself.

Thus the results of my internal audit: I had seen Matt off. Good riddance to bad rubbish, I told myself. God had given me Hamoud. I now had a new deliverance fantasy to ponder as I napped on the basement carpet. I was certain that Matt would have told my mother that although my life was in jeopardy, I remained quite alive. This comforted me. All in all, I judged, the bungled escape had proved itself a boon. Had providence presented me with such a deal before the escape, I decided, I would have agreed to the terms with joy in my heart.

One afternoon in the middle of August, two weeks after Matt's escape, a half-dozen Jebhat al-Nusra fighters stepped into my basement cell. "Where's the American?" said one, grinning. Another took a step toward me. "Stand," he said. He asked if I had belongings. "Get them," he said. "Blindfold yourself."

I turned a hurried glance to Hamoud.

"You're going home?" he exclaimed, whispering. His eyes lit up. He kissed my check. Within seconds, the guards had handcuffed me, and blindfolded me. One of them took hold of a plastic bag in which I carried a spare T-shirt, a pair of underwear, and some chits of paper on which I had been scribbling. I was led up a flight of stairs, across a patio, then into the back seat of an SUV. A pair of guards sat on either side of me.

CHAPTER 8

A VOYAGE INTO DARKNESS

Many months later, the SUV driver, a former engineering student at the University of Damascus, it turned out, with whom I developed a kind of a friendship, told me that my whole body shook as I climbed into his truck. He said that I looked to him as though I had been shot through the heart, that my blood had left my face, and that my legs trembled so much he could feel them clattering against the back of his seat. Perhaps it was so.

Ten minutes after I climbed into his SUV, however, as the SUV rolled through a succession of cloverleaf highway ramps, the young man who'd been posted to my left withdrew a handful of corner-store candy from a plastic bag. Did I know I was going on a voyage? he asked. He passed his treats around among his friends. I listened to the friends smacking their lips. The guard on my right opened a bottle of spring water. "Thirsty?" he asked me. Since my hands were cuffed behind my back, he poured a splash of water down my throat.

Some minutes after this, the driver addressed me. When I needed to pee, I was to say so. When I was thirsty, I was to say so. "If you move at all," he said, "even by a hair, we will put a bullet through your head." By this point in my captivity, I knew the rest of the prisoner-transport script by heart. Bullets were cheap, the driver was to tell me. So he did. In killing me, Jebhat al-Nusra would lose the cost of a single bullet, he said. "Are you like the other Americans?" he asked.

"No."

"You think you're clever?"

"No," I said.

Was I a liar? A fool? Did I mean to have a go at an escape?

I wasn't an idiot, I assured the driver. "I know well enough where my interests lie," I said. It was a line I had learned from Hamoud.

"Good," said the driver. "Then you will shut your mouth?"

I listened to the wind for a little while. I slouched against the seat back. I nodded my head forward, as if I were falling asleep, then lolled it backward, so that my neck rested on the back of the seat. In this position, peering out at the roadway from underneath the blindfold's bottommost flap, I could see the highway nearly as well as the driver could. I watched the sun glinting off the roadside signs. An hour or so into our voyage, it was striking the oncoming drivers in the face. It cast a pretty, coppery radiance across the single-story houses, more like cement storage units than dwellings, that lined the roadway.

Evidently, we were driving away from the sunset, into the east. Shortly after sundown, when we had been underway for about two hours, we came to a sign indicating the city of Raqqa to be a few miles to the north. Straight ahead, said the sign, was Iraq. I prayed that the driver would turn left, toward Raqqa. Nobody, as far as I was aware, was dropping barrel bombs on this provincial outpost. The snippets of rumor I had heard to date told me that, having expelled all representatives of Syrian government authority, the citizenry of Raqqa was carrying on with everyday life. It was neither on the government side nor on the rebel side. It meant to survive the war, I understood, by watching it from the sidelines. If I was to be transferred to this tranquil city, I thought, I might live for a few months in a pacific city-state. In due time, the common sense that prevailed among the citizens here would see me released. I would skip across the Turkish border. I would fall to my feet. I would kiss the ground.

Our driver scarcely glanced at the turnoff for Raqqa. "DEIR EZZOR IRAQ," said an unmissable sign hanging over the highway. A set of directional arrows pointed forward, into the east. My heart sank.

I suspect now that the true cradle of the war in Syria wasn't Deraa, where the famous graffiti "The People Want the Fall of the Regime" first appeared on a schoolyard wall, but rather the Euphrates River

Valley, especially the eastern portions of it, downstream from Raqqa, where Syria's oil and gas fields lie. Here, the country is poor, though the oil derricks that lie scattered across the desert floor attest to abundant wealth beneath the surface of the earth. Somehow, ever since the construction of a pipeline in the mid-eighties, this wealth has piped itself into the pockets of a tiny circle of presidential intimates. Naturally, it has flowed into the coffers of Shell and Total, the European conglomerates most responsible for building up Syria's oil industry.

For what it's worth, during my ten months of residence in this eastern half of Syria, I made a point of inquiring into the origins of the war as often as possible. I spoke with anyone willing to speak to me. I suspect I quizzed dozens if not hundreds of Deiris, as people from this region are known (after the provincial capital, Deir Ezzor). I was curious. I had time on my hands. I was among interesting, sometimes knowledgeable people. Why not inquire? As it happened, I did not encounter a single person in the eastern half of Syria who believed that peaceful demonstrators in Deraa—or mosque goers in the restive suburb of Duma or citizens anywhere else in the west—were the true fomenters of a rebellion in Syria.

The true fomenters, in the opinion of my prison interviewees, were the men of the jihad. The ISIS commanders and foot soldiers with whom I was sometimes imprisoned believed that their leaders, directing matters from planning rooms in Anbar Province in Iraq, dispatched fighters into Syria in late 2010, long before any child in Deraa scrawled his graffiti on a schoolyard wall. Their objective was to kill the Alawite potentates who, in their opinion, had used their talents in sorcery to wrest the land—and its seas of oil—from its native sons. Now the Alawites, it was thought, operated Deir Ezzor as a sort of slave colony. The native Deiris were the slaves. The Alawites, especially those in the intelligence services, were the slave drivers. The men of the jihad meant to repossess the oil, to plunder the colonists' arsenals, and to put these into the hands of the region's hundreds of thousands of unemployed young men. It was these young men, imbued with the piety of the desert, who carried the banner of the jihad into the well-behaved, demonstrate-but-no-violence suburbs of western Syria. My Jebhat al-Nusra jailers were inclined to believe in a similar origin story for the Syrian war, though in their telling, the planning rooms were not in Iraq but in villages along the banks of the Euphrates, south of Deir Ezzor, next to Syria's biggest oil fields. Fifteen years earlier, these villagers, the Jebhat al-Nusra fighters maintained, had slipped across the Iraqi border to assist in the jihad against the Americans. Now, they said, they—and their teenage sons and younger brothers—were bringing the jihad home.

None of my informants believed the war to have been a means by which rebels sought to advance a political objective. Nor did anyone suppose that the revolutionaries, whom they called mujahideen, or men of the jihad, sought to defend human rights. Rather, in the early dawn of time, my informants believed, God had decreed that a generation of heroes should arise, just now, in the Syrian deserts. Summoned to their destiny by God, these men thought, would in turn summon the world's truest, most devout Muslims to battle. In this battle, faith would oppose the disloyal, the inconstant, and the traitorous. In the fullness of time, the soldiers of God would erect the banner of their faith—the one that bore the legend "There is no god but God"—over every corner of the Earth.

Such was the official doctrine in Syria's east when I lived there. All my questions about the origins of the war led me into lectures that related this history. Yet my informants were opinionated, demonstrative, effusive people. Discussions about the deep causes of the war also brought us into the matter of the poverty in Syria's East.

The Syrian people were rich in oil, the Deiris believed. For too long, colonial administrators from Damascus had siphoned away the natives' birthright, while treating the natives themselves likes slaves. At last, they felt, the slaves had risen up in revolt.

Looking back now, it seems to me that as I was watching the road signs on the highway out of Aleppo, my captors were indeed whisking me away into the deeper, unknown, truer causes of the war. Here, the former slaves were dragging the colonists from their beds. Some were being hauled off to jail. Others were being put on trial in ad hoc courts, and many were executed on the spot. Later, the most hated colonists were crucified in village squares. Others were burned alive. Many never emerged from the rebels' rapidly expanding prison system.

That night, it took us about seven hours of driving to reach the city of Asheyl, on the banks of the Euphrates. In eastern Syria, I learned later, it was thought that this city had sent more fighters into the war in Iraq than any other in Syria. Now, a wave of Iraqi jihadists, intent on coming to the aid of their former comrades in arms, had turned Asheyl into a sort of forward operating base for the campaign against Bashar al-Assad. Some of these jihadists were aligning themselves with the newly formed rebel army in Syria, the Islamic State of Iraq and the Levant. Others arranged to join Jebhat al-Nusra. I know now that during this time, for everyone in Asheyl, there was instruction in the philosophy of jihad in the mosques. There were training camps in the school playgrounds. At the time, a stream of pickup trucks, new soldiers, arms, and ready cash was flowing into Asheyl. Everyone who was anyone was keen to get in on the action.

Asheyl, a scattering of squat, single-story huts, sufficient to house a population of about ten thousand, was lit up by the moonlight when the driver of our SUV rolled his truck down the central boulevard. There wasn't an electric light within sight. We coasted past shuttered shops and a mosque, then rumbled outward, into the fields beyond the settlement. After about ten minutes of potholed driving, we came to a stop in front of a walled compound. The pair of guards with whom I had been sharing a seat disembarked. A third guard, the front seat passenger, joined them.

The three of them banged for a moment on an iron gate. They called out to friends inside. No one answered. After a minute or so, one of the guards scaled the wall. He opened the gate, admitted his comrades, then closed the gate.

Alone in the moonlight, with only a silent SUV driver for company, I contemplated an escape. I might have been able to run a bit, I thought. I imagined breaking for the fields. It had been nearly a year since I had last run anywhere. I wasn't sure I could do it. I watched the stars for a moment, gazed at the shimmering field to our right, marveled as the SUV driver lost himself in his cell phone, then lost my nerve.

Instead of throwing myself from the car, I listened to dogs barking in the distance. I shifted a bit in my seat. "Is this my prison?" I ventured. The driver ignored me. I waited another minute. "Sheikh, please," I said. "What happens now?"

The driver sighed. He rested his cell phone on his thigh. "Maybe they'll kill you," he said. He returned to his phone. A few seconds later, boring his eyes into his screen, he added a thought: "Maybe they won't. Dunno, really."

I abandoned my questions. I turned my eyes to the potholed stretch of dirt road in front of the SUV. I admired the shimmering fields. In places, it seemed to me, some of the grasses might have been twenty feet tall. What crops did the farmers grow in this region? I wondered. Sugar beets, I supposed, and acres of cattails.

After several additional minutes of silence had gone by, the driver spoke up. Muttering again, he wondered if I had a phone number. "It's in the US," I told him. "Is that okay?" I gave him my mother's number in Cambridge, Massachusetts. He asked for my name and the name of the city in which I lived in the US. He recorded my information in his phone. Was he noting down my contact info in preparation for my being killed later that night? I thought this remotely possible. If I am to be killed, I thought, and if the driver does mean to tell my mom about what has happened, I ought to thank him beforehand. "That's my mom's phone number," I told him.

He shrugged. He yawned. "So?"

"If something happens to me," I asked, "can you call her?"

"Sure," he said. I said that she spoke no Arabic. I mentioned that a phone call to the US would be expensive.

"No problem," he said.

I murmured my thanks. He shrugged. "I thank you from the bottom of my heart," I told him. "You can come visit me in the US anytime," I said. I told him that he could have my car if he liked. Or money. "I have bicycles," I said. "Do you like bicycles?" He turned to me. He smiled.

"Keep your bicycles," he said. "I'm staying here."

It took about a quarter of an hour for a pair of jailers, both of whom appeared to have been woken from heavy sleep, to emerge from the gate. One of the jailers brought me into a courtyard. My handcuffs were removed. I was admitted into a bathroom. I was allowed to pee and to wash. When I emerged, I was conducted across a children's playground, up a short flight of steps, down a corridor, then into a large, airy classroom. A voice told me to sit. The door closed behind me. When I removed my blindfold, I found myself on a carpet, under a wide blackboard, facing two prisoners, who were seated cross-legged, as I was. We gazed at one another. One of them handed me a round of succulent Iraqi-style flatbread—*tanoor*, which are baked in clay ovens. "Welcome," he said. I ate. The prisoner offered me a glass of water, then pointed me to a spot on the carpet, beneath the blackboard. "Sleep there," he said. I rested my head on my blindfold, then fell into a long, dreamless sleep.

In the morning, a jailer whose black head scarf had been wrapped around his face came to the cell with a kettle of tea. He greeted my cellmates in cordial tones. He left us three rounds of bread, and three hard-boiled eggs.

Looking back now, I suspect that my desperation to find promising auguries in that prison classroom warped my perception of reality. One of the cellmates, a sad-eyed child of fifteen, had been a prisoner in this classroom cell for three months. He had been accused of theft. His father had declined to pay the ransom to get him out of jail. The father had, however, been allowed to provision the child with coins. The child used the coins to buy cigarettes from the guards. What a warmhearted prison administration there is here, I thought to myself, when I saw my cellmate slinking away to a window to puff his smoke through the bars.

The other cellmate was in his twenties. He had also spent the summer in prison. An Asheyl neighbor, by his telling, had made a false accusation against him. In the days following his arrest, he said, the Jebhat al-Nusra jail staff had tortured him. "Was it bad?" I asked. He gave me a dark look, which I ignored. Now, several months after his arrest, he said, Jebhat al-Nusra had become convinced of his innocence. He expected to be released in the coming days. The news filled me with happiness. I relaxed into a pleasant, peripatetic discussion, focusing mostly on sexual behavior in America, with my two new friends.

At that hour of the morning, when the sun was still casting long shadows over the fields outside our window, the temperature in our classroom was close to one hundred degrees. It is dry, desert heat, I told myself—and anyway, a slowly turning ceiling fan, operated by a switch within the cell, moved the air about. The heat, my fellow prisoners assured me, would kill the lice I had brought with me from Aleppo. Our Jebhat al-Nusra jailers did torture, the cellmates said, but as I had been arrested ten months earlier and had already been tortured in Aleppo, my case, my cellmates seemed to feel, had moved past the normal period for inmate torture.

"Are you really a spy?" the fifteen-year-old asked me.

"Of course not," I replied.

Both of my fellow prisoners greeted this news with smiles of relief. They shrugged their shoulders. Their good humor infected me. I made the elder prisoner promise to visit me in our classroom jail if he happened to be released before me. I assured the younger one that Americans did not, in general, have sex with one another in the street, as dogs do, as he seemed to believe. When our conversation dwindled away, I found a patch of sunlight, removed my shirt, then turned to hunting down the lice I had brought with me from Aleppo. Through the months, lice hunting had become an important kind of leisure activity for me. It brought tiny rewards. I could keep at it for hours. It was like reading in that I quickly lost myself in concentration. I looked forward to the hours in which I would have light enough and time to busy myself with my lice. Now, as I searched through the seams of my T-shirt, a wave of relief washed over me. Nobody's killing anyone here, I thought to myself. Nor was anyone threatening me. The *tanoor* had been lovely.

Later that morning, by holding on to a pair of bars in a window, I climbed to a sill, then peeked out over a cinder-block wall, a few feet beyond the window, that ringed the school compound. About half a kilometer from the school, a field whose grass was greener than any green I had seen since I left Vermont seemed to sway in a bend by a river. Inside this horseshoe curve, a cluster of farmers in straw hats walked through shoulder-high sun-dappled grass. From a distance, the hats looked like toy boats bobbing along on the surface of an undulating green lake.

Around noon, a pair of jailers stepped into the cell. Without saying a word, they wrapped blindfolds around my fellow prisoners' eyes. The prisoners rose and were led away. Later that afternoon, a jailer arrived bearing a heavy steel trucker's chain. Without saying a word to me, he knelt, then wound it several times around my ankles. When my ankles were properly bound, he pulled at the ends of his chain, then locked them together with a padlock. He had me hold my wrists in the air, applied a pair of handcuffs, then ratcheted each of the collars down carefully. When he had finished binding me up, he took a step back. He stared at his handiwork for a moment, then turned to the windows. He shook their bars for a moment, found them to be immobile, then inspected the lock on the door and found nothing amiss. Having satisfied himself, he left the room in silence, his eyes avoiding mine.

That night, I slept in the leg chains and the handcuffs. In the morning, there was no breakfast. Around noon the next day, four men in smock-like black shirts, with wild, unkempt hair, appeared in the doorway of the cell. The man who had bound me up in his chain the day before stood at their backs, poking his head over their shoulders. One of these visitors, an albino, strode to the blackboard like an angry schoolteacher. He squinted. "What is your nationality?" he demanded. I didn't want to admit it. "American?" the albino wondered. I nodded.

The resident jailer approached, unwound his chain from my legs, then unlocked my handcuffs. One of the albino's assistants dropped an armload of nylon webbing at my feet of the sort that might be used to tow a boat or a broken-down truck. The assistant bound up my ankles in his webbing. He cuffed my hands behind my back. I was blindfolded, then hoisted to my feet. Several of these men—more than two, at any rate—carried me from the room. I was borne through the school corridors in silence. Emerging into the light of day, one of the men lost his footing on the school's front steps. I heard him stumble, then mutter a curse. "Everyone, can you wait just a moment, please?" I said. For an instant, I was a thoughtful collaborator. I was at work on a project with colleagues. I wanted them to know that I was concerned for their well-being, so I uttered my little word of caution.

I suspect now that I meant to show this new band of abductors, who might have been stealing me away to my grave, for all I knew, that I had become a docile, institutionalized prisoner. I knew the prison-transport drill well enough, I wanted them to understand, and so needn't be dropped into the trunk of a car.

They dropped me into the trunk of a car. A hand slammed the trunk lid shut. The darkness within the cargo area, the heat, which was powerful enough to impede my breathing, the smell of soil, which pervaded the trunk, and the way my forehead bumped into the trunk lid when I tried to move the handcuffs from underneath the small of my back—all of this made me feel as though I were being locked into a coffin. I wondered what might happen if I screamed. I worried the men would plunge knives into my stomach. I decided to hold my tongue. It took a moment for them to climb into the sedan's forward compartment. As they settled themselves into their car, I told myself to keep my breathing even. I tried to let go of the tension in my neck. It seemed to me that I was close to suffocation, that if I were to allow the panic that was building in my throat to take over my body, things would get much worse, quickly. And so for the sake of my survival, I did not move.

When my abductors had settled themselves in place, the sound of a steel gate swinging open—somewhere in the school courtyard?—drifted through the car. An engine turned over, and then we were rolling through the dust. The air in the trunk filled with unbreathable soot. In the front of the car, an abductor, speaking in a pensive tone of voice, shared a thought with a friend: "He's a polite one, isn't he?"

"Well trained, rather," a second person replied.

We drove for about an hour. When the car at last came to a stop, I was dizzy. I was desperate for water. Hands trundled me from the trunk.

My body fell onto a vinyl floor. Was I in a garage? A warehouse? The light coming through my blindfold told me that I was indoors. When the nylon tow strap had been unwound, hands at my elbows escorted me to the base of a wall, at which I was made to sit. I pleaded for water. "Bring him a tea glass," a voice said. A pair of hands undid my blindfold. A shot glass's worth of water was brought to my lips. "Please," I said. "I'm thirsty."

"Stay thirsty," said the albino.

The blindfold was returned to my eyes. Someone locked a pair of plastic zip ties around my ankles. A foot kicked me from my sitting position. I toppled to the floor. Anticipating further kicks, I curled myself into a ball. My abductors stepped away from me, and then I heard a door sweeping across the floor with a muffled snapping sound, almost as if it were a refrigerator door. I know now that this cell had once been a janitor's closet in an employee gym on the site of Syria's largest oil field. The gym was part of a residential compound which, in a former time, had housed the employees of a Syrian petroleum giant, the Omar Company. I know now that this compound sits in the desert, on the northern bank of the Euphrates, about ten kilometers outside the city of Meyadin. A year after my arrival, it became an ISIS headquarters. By 2017, it had become a US military base.

During my first moments in the janitor's closet, I found myself marveling at the modernity of its construction. The school in which I had spent the previous nights had been a slapdash pile of stone blocks. Its wavy floors and crack-filled ceilings made me wonder if I wasn't, by any chance, being detained inside a ship.

When my abductors shut the broom closet door, it felt to me as though they were sealing me away inside a morgue. Only after they had left me to my own devices—when I had scuffed my head against a wall enough to nudge the blindfold out of place—did I notice the heat. I assumed that they had chosen this cell because they knew its air supply could be cut off, understood that inside, I would have to gasp and struggle to breathe, and that they had brought me here because they wanted to watch as I floundered and flopped at their feet.

In fact, this was no airtight box. I could breathe well enough. There was, however, no circulation. There was overpowering heat, as in a sauna. I was too frightened of the men who had deposited me in this cell to call to them. I curled myself into a ball on the floor. I tried to sleep. When I couldn't sleep I made an inventory of all the people on Earth who might be capable of rescuing me. Who might come? I needed Rambo, perhaps, or the mutant Wolverine.

Several hours later, around dinnertime, my abductors returned. I had rubbed and chafed the back of my head against a wall enough to cause the blindfold to lie in a knot around my neck. "Why? Why did you uncover your eyes?" the albino shouted. He prodded at my head a bit with his boot.

"I don't know," I told him. There wasn't a thing to see in this closet. It was an empty cube, about the size of the interior of a cargo van. A sliding window, as in a tollbooth, would have given a view into the room next door had it not been covered over, on the outside, by draperies. Such light as there was came through the draperies and slits between the door and its frame. "I wanted to see," I told him.

"What did you want to see?" he asked.

"I don't know," I stammered.

The albino declined to remove my handcuffs. He lifted me from the floor by tugging on my shirt, then propped me against the base of a wall. He untied my blindfold, then held a bowl of lettuce to my lips. "Eat," he said. He pushed a scrap of bread into my mouth. He poured a teacup's worth of water down my throat. The feeding finished, he lifted me to my feet. The zip ties at my ankles were too tight for me to walk. A pair of men at my elbows inched me into the back of the cell. The albino ordered me to stand with my toes pressed against the rear wall of the cell. I was to remain in this position until further orders. "If you sit, there is a punishment," his voice said. If I were to sleep, the voice said, the punishment would be worse. I was not to speak. "We have pliers for your fingernails. We have electricity. Do you understand?" I did not reply. The door closed.

At first, as the light drained from my closet, I imagined that my captors were spying on me, perhaps through a keyhole. I was being tested, I thought. Passing their test would show my respect for their rules. As soon as they understood that I was capable of respect, they would ease up. I focused on the task at hand.

During my first half hour at the wall, I refused to allow the thought of sitting to enter my head. I can handle endurance tests, I thought. After a half hour, my thighs were getting sore. I pressed my forehead into the wall. After an hour, the wall was swaying in front of me. In order to ward off the swaying, I tried to step in place. I crouched, then stood. This caused the wall to turn in front of my eyes like a pinwheel.

I wish I could say that I stood at my wall for hours. In fact, I gave in after about ninety minutes. I sank to the floor. I stretched my legs. Because I couldn't reach the lice in my hair—and because they seemed to be feasting on my scalp—I tried to crush them by lolling my head on the vinyl floor. Eventually, after an hour or so of this, I curled my knees into my chest. I slept.

During the following three days, I scarcely moved from this position. In the mornings, at around eleven, a pair of guards who slept and ate on a carpet immediately in front of the door of my cell would let themselves in. One of them would place a round of bread, a small cucumber, and a half-liter bottle of water on the floor. He would remove the handcuffs, then stand back. His colleague, observing the proceedings from the doorway, would hold his finger on the trigger of his Kalashnikov. The two of them would watch me eat for a moment, then withdraw.

After I had finished eating, I was meant to knock on the door. When it opened, I'd blindfold myself. A guard would enter the cell, take hold of my elbow, then bring me to my feet. I would shuffle into the light. The zip ties required me to take baby steps. On the far side of a twenty-foot stretch of vinyl flooring, inside a bathroom, I was allowed to remove my blindfold. I would baby-step into a stall, squat, wash myself, then drink from the hose with which I had washed myself. When I had emerged from the stall, I would reapply my blindfold. I would again be handcuffed. I would shuffle back to the cell, then sink to the floor. I would curl myself into a ball. In the evening, a half round of bread and another cucumber were brought to me. A similar toilet exercise followed.

In Syrian Arabic, a person in a position of power expresses contempt for an underling by appending the suffix "oolak" to the last word of a sentence. One hears the tic in the mouths of army officers and prison guards in TV dramas. An English equivalent might be "You stupid fuck" or "Okay, shit-for-brains?"

After ten months in prison, I had come to understand that guards who addressed me in this manner couldn't be negotiated with. They shouted at me but never spoke. When they had something important to say, they began the discussion by slapping the side of my head or seizing a tuft of hair. "Shut up—ooLAK!" they would say. In the presence of such guards, I kept my eyes on the ground. I did not speak.

It took me just a few hours in this cell to deduce that a certain guard, Abdullah, was in charge of the others and that among these extremists in Islam, he was known as an extremist. The first words I remember him speaking to me were "Stand—ooLAK." He had come to bring me to the bathroom. The handcuffs and the zip ties prevented me from rising to my feet. I wobbled on the floor. "Stand, Animal—ooLAK!" he screamed. On that morning, I wobbled and rocked at his feet. He stared at me through the scarf he never failed to wrap around his face before opening the door of my cell. Eventually, a smile spread through his eyes. "You really cannot stand on your own?" he said at last.

"No," I explained. He helped me to my feet.

. When he and I had come to know each other a bit, after I had eaten several meals in his presence and he'd taken me back and forth to the bathroom several times, I asked him why my hands had to be cuffed at my back. "Inside the cell, Abdullah," I said. "Why?"

I happened to be sitting then against the base of a wall. He put his boot to my shoulder. His foot pushed me to the floor. Holding his boot over my forehead, he invited me to repeat my question: "Say it again—ooLAK?"

During my third day in this cell, I decided that its heat, the thirst it induced, and especially Abdullah's refusal to release my hands from behind my back, a constraint that allowed the lice in my hair to attack as they pleased, were too much for me. The lice gorged themselves. My ability to hunt the lice, it seemed to me, had been my only measure of control. Now it was gone. I needed help. To whom could I turn?

I supposed that after ten months in detention, my case had worked its way through the middle managers in Jebhat al-Nusra, and through the analogous layers in the American bureaucracy. Had the Jebhat al-Nusra leader, whose name I did not know, wished to help me, he would have done so by now, I assumed. My thoughts turned to the American leader.

Probably, Barack Obama, I imagined, would have intervened if he could have. I was much too surrounded by Kalashnikovs and grenades for a black helicopter rescue to be of any use, but my captors, I felt, would have been happy to work out a deal with Obama over the phone. They would have asked for a ransom, or a prisoner swap, or an arms shipment, or all of these things. Such concessions, I knew, wouldn't exactly have been in harmony with US government policy. Yet Jebhat al-Nusra's treatment of me, I felt, was a greater injustice than the breach of a policy. The unfairness of it all pained me nearly as much as the heat did. It seemed to me that when swashbuckling reporters and Blackwater mercenary contractors and the like were kidnapped, they were always ransomed away. People of that sort courted danger, I told myself, were well paid, and so couldn't be thought of as blameless—no matter how pitiful their hostage videos were. Whereas I meant to avoid danger. I hadn't made a dime. It seemed to me that if Barack Obama could be made to understand that in rescuing me he wouldn't be rescuing the normal run of Middle East hostage but rather an idealist with a penchant for exploring the world—a person a bit like himself, really—he would be willing to relax his scruples about the importance of living up to the letter of every law.

If a discussion were to occur, I thought, it would be important for him to understand just how much we had in common. I would want to address that matter up front. The best way to do it, I thought, would be to tell him straightaway that his story of an outsider who drifts about after college, is haunted by an inscrutable father, stays true to himself, reads a lot, and finally comes into his own was my story, too. His *Dreams from My Father*, I would tell him, had held the mirror up to my own nature. Once he understood how genuine my admiration for him was, I would let him know that while the two of us were fellow travelers in a spiritual sense, in the material world, I happened to be in a spot of trouble at the moment.

If the matter were put to the president in this way, I thought, he was bound to act. He would help me out of a love of doing good works, I thought, and because he was the sort of person who could not not help me.

At one point during the afternoon of this third day, inside my heat-addled brain, I really did try to put in a call to the White House. I did it via mental telepathy. For a moment, it seemed to me that I could see the president huddled over his desk. He was quite lost in his work. I was reluctant to interrupt. Perhaps, I told myself, the matter could be brought to his attention in the customary manner, through appropriate channels.

I know now that when matters of this sort were brought to Obama's attention through official channels, he did not do much. The case I think of most often is that of the American ISIS hostage Kayla Mueller. I know now that a little more than a year after I was transferred out of this compound for oil workers, ISIS, which, by then, controlled all the oil fields in eastern Syria, transferred Kayla into this compound. It's not clear how much President Obama understood then about the program of organized rape to which ISIS was subjecting Kayla at the time. Perhaps reports from a pair of Iraqi sex slaves who had once shared a cell with Kayla reached him. Probably, he knew of ISIS's habit of subjecting all women under their control to varieties of sexual slavery. Certainly, he understood what Kayla's parents, Marsha and Carl Mueller, understood when, in the fall of 2014, ISIS began sending emails to them. Those emails said that in exchange for a ransom of about $5 million, ISIS was willing to let Kayla go. It seems that the White House decided nothing could be done for Kayla. The sexual attacks would have continued. Kayla was killed under disputed circumstances—not necessarily in a bombing, as ISIS claimed—in February of 2015.

•   •   •

Hindsight has helped me make sense of the US government's hostage policy. I know now that it works this way: Under circumstances much more unbearable than mine, the US government will cling to its dogmas. It will refuse to take the terrorists' phone calls. It will, however, allow the victim's family to take them. During these calls, I know now, the terrorists will make demands of the US government. The families will turn to the State Department, the White House, the FBI, and whatever senators and congressmen will take their calls. "What now?" the families will say.

Some of the officials will speak in sorrowful tones. Others will be curt. All will say the same thing: "Dunno, really. Anyway, it's not our problem."

Sometime during the evening of my third day in this cell, after my Obama fantasies had come and gone, it occurred to me that a strain of recklessness in my character, a trait that had hobbled my progress in life long before I ever saw Syria, had led me into an unknown and wicked social phenomenon—their caliphate.

It seemed to me that the people around me had pledged their hearts to the caliphate, had every intention of dying whenever it was blown to bits, and that because of their enthusiasm for death, everyone in the region, including those who despised the very thought of Jebhat al-Nusra, would also be blown to bits. If, somehow, I was to survive the sauna-like cell, I thought, I would be consumed in the apocalypse Jebhat al-Nusra was planning for the entirety of eastern Syria. I reduced my predicament to a formula: A flaw in my nature, plus their fantasy of collective suicide, equaled my destiny.

Would not a change in my nature, I wondered, allow me to alter my destiny? It seemed to me that I was adaptable in this way, whereas the Jebhat al-Nusra warriors were not. They believed that the angels of God had written down exactly how they would die fifty thousand years ago, at the dawn of time. Their personal identities were likewise immutable. Their word for immutability was *maktoub*—written down. Perhaps their destinies really were *maktoub*, I told myself, but I was no Muslim, didn't believe in their angels, and did believe in the virtue of adapting myself to the haps and hazards of life. I will adapt, I told myself, and thus change what has been written down for me.

I felt I ought to begin by making a few concessions. Earlier in life, before my encounter with al Qaeda, I had assumed, without ever thinking deeply into the matter, that I would arrange my life such that, every now and then, I would be able to return to Vermont. Vermont seemed lush and revivifying to me in my cell. During the hours in Aleppo in which I had been most frightened, I had clung to thoughts of a certain Vermont brook that, in real life, is nothing more than a chain of rock-strewn puddles, but seemed, in my cell, like a fountain at the end of the world. If I could only get there, I thought, its waters would wash away everything bad that had happened to me. They would restore what I had lost. In Aleppo, thoughts of this stream had buoyed my spirit. They had given me a reason to live.

Now, as I lay on Abdullah's floor, I decided that if, somehow, a deliverance without a return to my stream at the end of the world could be arranged, I could get along quite well in the world without it. Perhaps, I told myself, the authorities in our Islamic state would decree that I must live in their river valley. I would be fine with that, I decided, because the thing I longed for was life. I wasn't going to get all particular about a crummy brook in Vermont.

Several hours later, when the glimmers of daylight that leaked into my cell had gone out altogether—when I had been fed and was still hungry and very thirsty—I decided a further concession was in order. It had been an ambition of mine, even during my preteen years, and long before any thoughts of living as a reporter entered my brain, to turn myself into a writer. As a teenager, I loved Tom Wolfe. Later, I admired the *New Yorker* writer Ian Frazier, and Bill McKibben, the environmentalist. When I was in college and wondering what I ought to do with my life, I sometimes told myself: I'll be like Ian and Bill. That night, it occurred to me that my ambition had been a bit overwrought to begin with, that certain things must remain out of reach, that a human being required food and water but certainly not writing, and that the wise thing to do, under the circumstances, was to jettison all nonessential items. If there was ever a nonessential item, I told myself, it was this idea of myself. I don't want it in the least, I thought.

Toward morning, when the several guards who slept before my cell's door were snoring away—when I was frightened and delirious with thirst—it occurred to me that my earlier concessions had gotten me nowhere. The guards would have laughed at them if they had known of them. In any case, in a physical sense, my condition was deteriorating.

I had a final thing to give away. It wasn't a thing, exactly, but a person. I didn't want to let her go. It seemed to me that she knew of my ordeal in Syria, had been with me through every moment of it, quite understood what I was going through and that when I was finally released, I wouldn't have to explain a thing to her because she would know. This person was my mother. It seemed to me that if I were to relinquish her, I would be allowing the thing that mattered most to me to slip away from the world. That night, as I lay with my hands at the small of my back, I curled my legs into my chest. I clutched my mother to myself. I refused to let her go.

I clutched for fifteen minutes or so. Eventually, of course, I let her go, too. I felt I had to do it. I felt that they had given me no choice, that they were insatiable, and that they had forced this concession from me out of sheer wickedness.

When I had given her up, I thought for a few moments about the future I would earn for myself by giving up my reunion with my mother. If I were free but without my mother, my ordeal in Syria would be a secret thing, I imagined, devastating for me but unknown—a darkness in my past. I would never speak of it—not even to myself.

I can live with that, I told myself. I felt I didn't require understanding. I wanted to come away alive.

Nowadays, I know that in those hours, as I was making my concessions to fate, back home in America, the *Atlantic* publisher, David Bradley, who had become aware of a spate of disappearances in Syria, was refusing to accept what, by then, had become the conventional wisdom concerning Americans in the custody of terrorist groups in the Middle East: Nothing could be done.

By mid-August of 2013, I know now, five American families were staring into the void. Austin Tice, a freelance reporter, had disappeared somewhere near Damascus a year earlier. James Foley had vanished in Binnish, in Idlib Province, in November of 2012. The freelancer Steven Sotloff had been taken at a checkpoint in early August of 2013, and the aid worker Kayla Mueller had vanished in the company of her Syrian boyfriend, outside a hospital in Aleppo, also in early August of 2013. Another aid worker, Peter Kassig, was to disappear at an ISIS checkpoint in Idlib Province in October of 2013.

I know now these kidnappings confounded the authorities at home more than normal kidnappings do. The captors made shifting, uninterpretable, or unrealistic demands or—as in my case—locked their prisoners away without saying a word. Discussing matters among themselves, the families quickly agreed that they did not want to risk a rescue by commando raid, not that anyone was offering to perform such an operation.

The families understood that the kidnappers would eventually want concessions, especially from the US government, in the form of money, guns, or, possibly, a prisoner swap. The families understood that US law prohibited making concessions to terrorists.

I know now that my mother's initial reaction to this blockage was to shop government offices in Washington, DC, for answers she could bear. The State Department officials, it turned out, were, according to her, the most intolerable since they had a tendency to lecture. The US could not permit itself to give things to terrorist groups, they explained, because gifts would encourage terrorism. The FBI, she discovered, was keen to advise her in the theory of how to engage a kidnapper in a discussion but couldn't help her in practice since the things the terrorist wanted—concessions from the US government—were the things the law prohibited the advisors from offering. Samantha Power, then the US ambassador to the UN, proved helpful in that she introduced my mother to her (Power's) Qatari counterpart, Ambassador Alya Al Thani, whose government might have had ties to Jebhat al-Nusra, but unhelpful in that Power's project of kitting out the Syrian rebels with weaponry was turning into a bonanza for Jebhat al-Nusra and

ISIS. Provisioned with our high-tech missiles, the terrorists stiffened their negotiation postures. They built more prisons. They sold some of their weaponry. Flush with cash, they made further, more unrealistic demands. Some of them broke off conversation altogether. Others made ghastlier, more unspeakable threats.

I know now that as some parts of the US government were coming to the aid of the opponents of the Assad regime in Syria and all parts of it were refusing to help the American hostage families, David Bradley was brainstorming with his hostage rescue team. It consisted of Atlantic Media's in-house lawyer, Aretae Wyler, who helped the families understand the legal jeopardy to which a ransom payment might subject them; Atlantic Media's publicist, Emily Lenzner, who helped the families field questions from the press; a subgroup of four full-time researchers, who chased down rumors of prisoner sightings; and twenty volunteers from Teach for America, a nonprofit organization for which James Foley had worked, who helped however they could.

I know now that three indefatigable cousins of mine, Amy Rosen, Betsy Sullivan, and Viva Hardigg had already devoted their lives to pursing leads. By August of 2013, they had begun to coordinate their efforts with Bradley's team's efforts.

Nowadays, when I think of this rescue project, it seems to me that the TFA volunteers, the cousins, and the Atlantic Media staffers were indeed a match for the terrorists. They badgered ambassadors. They recruited bighearted former FBI agents. They took long shots on characters in Antakya who promised to track down leads in the suqs. They sought out advice from an elder generation of Middle Eastern journalists.

Over time, David Bradley emerged as a sort of foreign minister for the hostage families. I know now that during his two years of looking for us, he traveled to Beirut, Amman, Rome, London, and Istanbul, and three times to Doha—all at his own expense. In Doha, he waited in hotel lobbies for Qatari security officials, who were, as a rule, available for meetings only in the early hours of the morning. I suspect that these officials, the Qatari foreign minister, Khalid Al Attiyah, and his intelligence chief, Ghanim Al Kubaisi, regarded Bradley's quest to rescue citizens to whom he was not related, who were neither employees, nor friends, nor notable personalities of any kind, as quaint. Somehow, the Qatari officials warmed to Bradley's quaintness. Somehow, he passed his determination along to them.

"I have a theory we've used in business called 'wending,'" he told me when I asked him about the philosophy that guided this rescue project. "So, when you are walking across a field headed to an impenetrable forest, you worry that you can't get through it. But when you are right up close to the forest, you say: 'Well, I don't know if I can get through the whole forest, but I can get around this first tree, and then the next one, and around the bush up ahead.'"

During my time in Abdullah's broom closet, I doubt I would have been able to believe in a tale about an American publisher who saw himself as a wender in a forest. I certainly wouldn't have believed that a major figure in the magazine publishing world wanted to rescue me. I had internalized my captors' contempt for me. I wasn't altogether sure I was worth rescuing. I had been surrounded by hatred for America for so long that I had forgotten about the sort of citizen who brings out their best in his fellow citizens. Probably, such people are to be found on every street corner in America. In my prison cell, their existence slipped my mind.

Now I think that as I was relinquishing my reasons to live, one such person was encouraging his team to drop everything, to track down every clue, and to seek out every conceivable ally in its effort to bring me back to life. The team refused to give in, though there was only bad news. It kept up its work for nearly two years. Its only real strategy was to cast pings into the emptiness. "Hello out there? Can you hear? Is there anybody there?"

Looking back now, these seem to me like heartbreaking, beautiful messages to send, especially to vanished people. I suspect that in their cells, James, Steven, and Kayla were grasping at straws, as I was. Peter Kassig, who was arrested later, would have learned the routine in due course. Why is this happening to me? they would have wondered, and is anyone except my mom and dad actually looking for me? Had they known about them, those messages would have given the prisoners something lovely to daydream about. The thought of a team of idealists working under an idealist publisher would have helped them to keep on keeping on. Sadly, the four ISIS prisoners didn't live long enough to hear messages from home. Only Austin Tice, from whom nothing has been heard since his disappearance in Daraya in August of 2012, might conceivably be in a position to hear such messages now. I hope he's listening.

On the morning of my fourth day in Abdullah's broom closet, after I had eaten a round of bread and a cucumber, he agreed to cuff my hands at my stomach rather than behind my back. He loosened the zip ties at my ankles. This allowed me to stand without difficulty. He brought me a liter bottle of water. Now, in the privacy of my cell, I could hunt down the lice in my hair and my clothing—an immense relief. I poured water down my throat. I massaged the spots where the lice had bitten me.

That evening I strolled around my cell. I peered through a crack at the side of the door. A pair of sliding windows that had been covered over, on the outside, by a dark velvet blanket, gave on to the guards' room. Late that night, it occurred to me that, by sliding one of the windows a few centimeters to the left, I could bring a faint but meaningful current of air into my cell.

The purpose of the velvet blanket was to prevent me from seeing into the guards' room, but when I had opened the window, it was obvious that the curtain also prevented the guards from noticing the openness of their window. That evening, I didn't dare open the window wider than my finger, but the following afternoon, when the guards who normally lolled around on a carpet beneath the window had wandered away, I stuck my entire hand into the finger-width crack, then gave the window a solid shove. I pressed my nose through the bars, into the air-conditioned cool of the guards' sitting room. I turned around, then pressed the back of my neck through the bars. Though I knew the guards would return to their carpet momentarily, I resolved not to close the window. Why should I have? They were scarcely human. They were depriving me of light and air, without a thought, apparently, for a human's need for light and air. Part of me wanted to push it all the way to the side, to reach my hands through the bars, to seize hold of their hideous black curtain, and to dash it to the floor. Why should you breathe and see while I suffocate in the darkness? In my indignation, I wasn't far from screaming such words at them.

In the evening, after the guards had returned to their carpet, when they were drinking tea and chatting in quiet voices, one of them, a construction worker I subsequently came to know as Abu Qais, slipped into my cell. Crouching against a wall next to the door, he asked me if I was interested in having a chat.

Was I aware, he wondered, that recently, after archeologists found a copy of the Koran in a cave in the Yemeni desert then sent it off to Germany for carbon dating, the technician who examined the manuscript in Berlin found himself so overwhelmed by the truthfulness of what he was reading that he converted to Islam on the spot, though he had never had so much as a minute of formal instruction in the religion?

"No, not aware," I said.

He had a second question for me, he said, if I didn't mind. How could it be that Christians said that there were really three gods? "There are not three," he said. "There is only one. Why do you say three when there is only one?"

We discussed the doctrine of the trinity for a moment. I'm sure I explained it poorly. He allowed me to speak for a moment or two, then interrupted: "But do you believe there are three gods?"

"Of course not," I said.

He breathed a sigh of relief. "Thank God for that," he said.

Our discussion turned to a scientific demonstration whose details he wanted to share with me. Was I aware that when a man reading the Koran inside a glass room is photographed with infrared, temperature-sensitive cameras, the cameras show that an energy passes from the holy book, through the reader's hands and into his body? "You can see the body changing colors," he said. "The glass allows you to see that there are no other heat sources in the room." The energy had to come from the Koran, did it not? How could I say that the Koran was an inert object, like any other book, when over and over scientific demonstrations had established that it conveyed a quantifiable energy?

Abu Qais's bewildered tone made me think that our discussion had laid the groundwork for something that might turn out to be, if not exactly a friendship, then an awareness of shared experience. We shared in the mystery of life. This was a kind of kinship, I thought.

The following morning, when I tried to get him to give me a whole rather than a half round of bread, he sighed. He pushed the half round of bread he was holding into my hands. "Take this," he said. "Make do." He didn't know why these were the orders. "Maybe they're trying to weaken you?" he guessed. He was as bound by the orders as I was. He shrugged his shoulders. He was sorry. That matter did not lie in his hands.

Over the following days, during the hottest hours of the afternoons, I stood by my partially opened window. I pushed the crown of my head into the bars so that the air-conditioned cool of the guards' room would splash through my hair. I tried to feel the air down my spine. Out of hatred, I reached my fingers through the bars, eased their velvet curtain to the left a fraction of a centimeter—enough, in any case, to give me a view of a door, which opened onto the desert—then watched the comings and goings in the guards' room. In this way, I learned that every afternoon around five, the albino motorcycled to the guard room door, dismounted, pushed his motorcycle into the guards' room, parked it on its kickstand, then joined the guards on their carpet for a round of tea. Often, at about this time, Abdullah would rise from the carpet, then climb a set of stairs I could not see. He would vanish for a minute or two, then reappear with orders for his lounging colleagues. "Get up," he would say. "Path. Open the path!"

The colleagues would rise in silent unison, then disappear. Thirty seconds of quiet would pass, and then a train of women in gauzy, diaphanous gowns with babes in their arms and toddlers clutching their hands would process through the guards' quarters. The train would roll outside, into the stillness of the desert evening. Through my fold in the curtain, I could see the warmth of the setting sun in their gowns and on their faces. I watched currents in the air lifting their headdresses. Behind them, a field of desert scree glowed under a darkening sky.

These women would squint for a moment, then disappear around a corner. The sun would sink and fifteen minutes or so later, the train would come floating past my window in the opposite direction. It never made a sound.

Of course, eventually, when about four days of life with a partially open cell window had come and gone, Abdullah discovered my climate control system. He happened across my alteration as he chatted with friends on his carpet. He was yawning. He reached his arm over his shoulder, then pushed his hand through the curtain. The hand felt for the windowpane. Finding nothing, it waved itself in the air, inside my cell. It withdrew.

A moment later, in a quiet voice, Abdullah asked a comrade if the comrade had opened the window.

"No," the comrade replied. Had the comrade given me permission to open the window? Again, no.

There was silence outside my cell and then came the sound of keys jangling in the lock of the cell's door. Abdullah and a friend stepped into the cell. Abdullah spoke quietly, as if wondering over a mystery. "Animal, why did you open the window—oolak?" He raised his cable over my head. The friend made a similar gesture.

Over the subsequent months, I came to know these two men well. I learned about the dream of one of them, Zakaria, to finish his math studies, to be married, and to run away to Turkey. I learned about Abdullah's dream: He hoped to perish in the jihad. He was teaching his wife to drive, he told me one afternoon, so that when the time came, she could drive a suicide truck into a line of enemy troops.

Over time, Abdullah and Zakaria became something like my friends. I had no one else to talk to. I needed news. I needed their food. I wanted conversation. Somehow, in that world, their approval improved my state of mind.

On this particular afternoon, the two young men were my assailants. Their job was to make me pay for my crime. They flogged. I scuttled away from them. They pushed me into a corner. There were excruciating blows, especially to my hands and to my head. "Please!"

I screamed, in English. I held up my handcuffs. There was much more violence.

When they were done, after about a half hour, the two of them withdrew from the closet. They relocked the door. I ran my fingertips over the crown of my head. Blood was streaming down my face. It was dropping in clots onto the floor. The wounds on my head were not severe, I thought, but the force of the blows had caused the handcuff collars to ratchet themselves down over my wrists. The metal dug into my flesh. The cuffs seemed to cut off all circulation. When I twisted my hands, jolts of pain shot through my arms. Examining my feet, I saw that the cable blows had caused the zip ties to break into pieces. What to do? I feared that if I called my assailants back, they would return with their cables. On the other hand, I couldn't bear the pain in my wrists. If I said nothing about the broken zip ties, several hours would pass, and then in the evening, perhaps, or on the following morning, Abdullah would beat me for having broken his zip ties. So I called him back. He did loosen the cuffs, but he was angry at me for having inconvenienced him. I was insisting on special treatment. I was spoiled. I imagined myself in an American prison, but this, he wanted to show me, was no American prison. In order to help me understand the treatment I deserved, he had me sit at his feet. This time, as he flogged, I held my wrists to the side. In order to keep the zip ties intact, I sat on my feet.

The following morning, Abdullah returned to tell me that he had discussed my crime with a council. The council had determined that I was guilty of insubordination. In order to save myself from a second punishment, which was bound to be bloodier than the first, I was, in the first place, to repent. Second, I was to be deprived of food and drink. The period of repentance was to be twenty-four hours. During that time, I was to lie on the floor in a blindfold. I was not to touch the blindfold. I was not to speak. I would be permitted my normal trips to the bathroom. Did I have any questions?

Somehow, I managed to sleep through the heat of the day. In the evening, in secret, inside my toilet stall, I drank from the hose with which I was meant to clean myself. During the night, when the guards were sleeping and the cell was cooler, I thought about waterfalls. I imagined myself swimming under a sheet of cascading water. As I swam, I drank from the pool in which I was swimming.

By the time guards performed their dawn prayer, at about five in the morning, I felt I had their punishment under control. It seemed to me that my twenty-four hours of inertness on the floor of my cell had been like a flight in a glider, that I had been let go in the thin air, had been aware of the possibility of falling, had kept things under control, and now, in the early morning cool, it seemed to me that I could glide my way to an easy landing. Safety, for me, was ten o'clock. At ten o'clock a new liter of water would appear in my cell, along with a round of bread and a cucumber.

At ten, an unfamiliar figure whose face was wrapped in a scarf deposited a jam-smeared round of bread on the floor. The figure watched me eat for a moment, stepped out of the cell, returned with water and a cucumber, retreated from the cell again, then locked the door. Settling himself on the floor, on the opposite side of my cell door, the person initiated a conversation. He greeted me with a salaam—not at all the normal way to greet a prisoner. He spoke in a warm, forgiving tone of voice, as if he understood that I was going through a rough patch, knew I needed a friend, and wanted to listen.

"You were punished?" the voice asked.

"Yes," I said.

"You know why?"

"Opened the window."

And why had I not asked to have the window opened? Did I not know that the mujahideen were generous in their hearts? I did know this, I said.

"So the punishment was just?" the voice asked.

"Yes, very just," I said.

In general, how were the mujahideen treating me?

"Respectfully," I said.

Was the treatment here better than the treatment of the Muslims in Guantánamo?

"Of course," I said. The cell door opened a crack.

A hand held out a half round of bread.

I was grateful to God for the bread, I said, and for my life and my health.

As I spoke these words, I knew I was reciting from Jebhat al-Nusra's script. In this sense, I was mouthing lies to an enemy. But I was grateful for the bread and for my life. I had never been so grateful in my life. I wanted the person to believe in my gratitude, so I spoke quietly, from the heart, without hesitation. In this sense, I was sharing an intimate truth. The person outside the door was a confidante. We were on the same side of things, spiritually speaking, and allies.

A few days after this incident, when I was back on normal rations—when I had been given a sofa cushion to use as a pillow, and an extra water bottle with which to douse my head in the heat of the day—the albino brought me a new cellmate. Ibrahim was eighteen. He and his parents, whose fates Jebhat al-Nusra was sorting out elsewhere, were accused of flashing signs to passing fighter jets.

Ibrahim had a speech impediment. Perhaps he had other conditions. Was he aphasic? Autistic? Perhaps he was just frightened. During his first hours in the cell with me, he lay on his side in a corner. Though we had been told not to make a sound, he emitted a continuous high-pitched kind of moaning. Now and then, there were words of prayer in his piping. I whispered to him. Did he need water? Was he hungry? He was meant to keep quiet, I said. If the guards heard his prayers, they were liable to punish him. "Shh," I whispered. He moaned.

Toward the end of this afternoon, he stood up, walked to a corner, then plunged both palms into his crotch. "If you need to pee," I whispered, "you must ask the guards to bring you to the bathroom. Do you need to pee?"

He didn't need to pee, he said. A half hour later, when I was lying on the floor in my corner and not looking at him, I heard the sound of pee tinkling into a corner of the cell. I scolded him. I splashed some water over his urine. I returned to my corner.

Later, when the heat of the afternoon had passed, we had a discussion. I asked him where he had been arrested.

"On the road," he said.

"At a checkpoint?"

He did not answer.

"What for?" I asked. Again, a silence. Did he know who had arrested him?

No, he said. They had guns. "Was it Jebhat al-Nusra?" I asked.

"Maybe," he replied.

"Was it Daesh?"

"Maybe," he replied.

"Is your health okay?" I asked at last.

"I praise God for my health," he murmured.

"Is your family okay?"

"I praise God for their health," he murmured.

I resolved to leave him to his thoughts. In the latter part of the evening, his moaning brought the albino into our cell. We had been told to keep our mouths shut, the albino said. If he heard a word from either of us, he promised, he would make sure that both of us paid a heavy price. Did we want to play games with him?

"No, sheikh," I said. The albino slammed the door.

Almost right away, Ibrahim returned to his moaning. It was a sad, helpless kind of trilling—the sound a schoolboy makes when he's been set upon by bullies. Either he couldn't control himself or didn't want to. After the albino gave us his warning, he disappeared. The guards in the adjoining room, however, were on the case. At first, it seemed to me that they were too lazy to force Ibrahim to shut up. Instead of beating him or me or both of us, they called to Ibrahim from their side of the cell door: "Shut up, Animal," they yelled, in bored voices, or, more often, simply, "Hey, Animal! Your mouth!"

I knew they would come with their cables eventually. It happened in the evening of Ibrahim's second day in the cell with me. The guards appeared before us in bare feet, their faces wrapped in black scarves. This combination is an ill omen, I know now. The masked faces represent the impersonality of the state. The bare feet express the humility of the state's officers. There were three guards that evening. One of them watched from the cell's doorway. The other two strode into the cell.

There was a moment of quiet as the guards stared at Ibrahim. He raised an elbow to them. One of them kicked him in the head. Blood splattered across the floor. Ibrahim toppled to the ground.

During the ensuing scuffle, the guards screamed in anger and in order to encourage themselves. Ibrahim whimpered but did not scream. Probably, the guards knew they were committing a crime. Probably, they weren't as happy about it as they made out to be.

Eventually, a battery cable was attached to Ibrahim's toe. The guards wanted Ibrahim to count down from five. At zero, they would attach the second cable to a toe on the other foot. A voice called out. "Ready, Ibrahim?" Ibrahim was unable to count. Instead, he screamed: "Allah! Allah!"

Eventually, the guards agreed to count for him.

When they had shocked him several times, Ibrahim's body was writhing and fluttering against the flooring. "Shut up, Pig," the guards said to him as they left the cell.

Later that afternoon, when the guards were again chitchatting on the carpet outside the door of our cell, a thin piping, more like the mewling of a puppy than like a human cry, rose from Ibrahim's corner of the cell. He seemed to battle against this voice inside himself, to choke and cough, and finally, after several minutes of struggle, to give in. A louder, more uncontrollable kind of sobbing filled our cell then. Somehow, the guards allowed him this indulgence. By evening, he had calmed himself down. Somehow, both of us slept. In the morning, I noticed that Ibrahim had slept in a pool of urine. The odor of feces drifted from a pile of rags in a corner. I tossed my spare T-shirt to him. If the guards found out about the shit, I told him, they would make him clean it with his tongue. He didn't seem to understand. He put the T-shirt aside. Slowly, like a cat drawing in on himself, he curled into a ball.

Later that morning, when Abdullah discovered the urine and the feces, there was indeed another beating. I was told to look away. I listened as a cluster of guards kicked Ibrahim in the head and shoulders. Again, Ibrahim's blood went spattering across the floor. Again, he called out to Allah. At the end of this beating, however, there was a visit to the bathroom for Ibrahim. He returned with a clean set of clothing.

In the evening, Ibrahim lay in perfect silence as Abdullah deposited a round of bread and a bowl of soup on the floor in front of Ibrahim. Ibrahim refrained from whimpering. He did not speak. He hardly moved.

In the middle of the night, when a night-light in the guards' room was sending the faintest glimmer into our cell, my eye happened to fall on Ibrahim's partially eaten crust of bread. He had scarcely touched the soup. I knew he needed to eat. For all I knew, he was dying. I knew what I ought to have done. *Eat, Ibrahim, my brother*, I should have said. *Drink*. But I was hungry. I was frightened. They'll probably kill him anyway, I told myself.

As Ibrahim napped in front of his bowl of soup, I prodded his shoulder with a knuckle. I nodded at his bowl. "May I?" I said.

"Be my guest," he murmured. I devoured the remains of his bread and his bowl of soup.

Toward the second week in September, the weather turned. There was heat in the afternoons, as always, but I didn't have to fight against it. The nights were a fraction of a degree cooler. The dawns were positively enjoyable. In the mornings, when daylight trickled into the cell, I hunted down the lice I had brought with me from Aleppo. In the afternoons, I tried to sleep.

The cooling off was visible in the attire in the women's procession. Now, in the afternoon, the women wore shawls over their shoulders. Earlier, they had walked in bare feet or in sandals. Now the younger women wore sneakers. When I washed my face in the bathroom sink, I felt the cooling off in the water that was piped in from a cistern on the roof. I saw it in the rainclouds that happened to drift past the toilet stall window as I peed.

So Earth was moving through its orbit. Now and then in the Deir Ezzor sky, there were fighter jets. They did not bomb—at least they didn't bomb nearby, as they had done in Aleppo. It seemed to me that my captors were not on the verge of killing me. It seemed to me that my being alive for the coming winter was a likely happening, and that if I saw the winter, I would be alive for the spring and the following summer, too. Maybe I will come through, I told myself.

Toward the end of September, a commander who liked to tease me about how typical an American I was brought a genuine hamburger and a cool can of soda pop to my cell. He delivered these gifts in a brown paper bag. Opening the bag, I beamed at him.

"Tasty?" he asked, in English.

I nodded.

Soon, he said, I would be moved to a new prison.

"Will I be with other prisoners?" I asked.

"Of course!" he exclaimed. His eyes twinkled.

"Will there be light in the cell?"

"So much light," he said.

"Will the cells be small?" I asked.

"Big, spacious, gorgeous cells," he replied.

In my mind's eye, I saw a captured Syrian government prison. Shafts of light poured through towering windows. Crowds of prisoners milled in a refectory. I knew I was getting ahead of myself. But my hamburger commander was inviting me to fantasize. I felt he understood that six weeks in handcuffs in Abdullah's broom closet had been extreme.

"I'll believe it when I see it," I told him.

"Big rays of light," he promised. "Windows, too."

That night, when Ibrahim and I were sleeping, this commander opened the door of our cell. He blindfolded us, handcuffed my right hand to Ibrahim's left, then led us in bare feet to the trunk of a waiting car. Ibrahim climbed in. I climbed in. The trunk slammed shut. We drove for a half hour or so. The car came to a stop on a street busy with voices. Pedestrians strolled. A driver emerged from our car, exchanged greetings, then ambled away. On the street, passersby chatted. Someone rested a haunch against the side of our car. I whispered to Ibrahim: "All okay?"

"Yes. You?"

Another fifteen minutes of driving brought us to a stop in front of a steel gate. It groaned as it opened. The car advanced a few feet, and then the door clanked as it swung shut. Hands pulled me and Ibrahim from the trunk. We were trundled through a doorway, escorted by flashlight down a short corridor, then deposited on the floor of a construction site. Cement blocks littered the ground. Four cinderblock stanchions, like the side panels in a line of toilet stalls, were rising from the back of what appeared to be a windowless room. A flashlight pointed me to a spot on the ground. "Sleep," said a voice. The flashlight brought Ibrahim to a nook under a heap of cinder blocks. He was told to sleep. The flashlight stepped out of the room. A door slammed shut.

When I woke the following morning, I was surprised to discover that a tennis ball–sized hole in the ceiling did indeed cast a beam of light into the midst of the construction zone. The shaft lit up the dust in the air. It caused a dull refulgence to hang over the trowels and the half-built walls of the solitary confinement cells. Later that morning, the hamburger commander came with a pile of dates, two rounds of bread, and tea. I breakfasted in silence with Ibrahim. When the commander came to take away his kettle, he asked me how I liked his prison. "Very nice," I told him.

He pointed to a spot high on the wall above one of the partially built cells. "You asked for a window?" he said, smiling. He promised to make me one. "Birds. Wind. The moon!"

I doubted him, but that afternoon the sound of a pickaxe pounding against the outside wall of our prison woke me from a nap. Soon, the tip of the pickaxe was kicking little volleys of gravel into our cell. It sent plumes of cement dust through the air.

I joined Ibrahim in his half-built cell. Together, sitting at the base of a wall, we watched the making of our window as if we were moviegoers in a cinema. At first there was pale, lugubrious light, and then pebbles flew through the air, and finally the point of the axe was crashing through the wall. The opening allowed a broad beam of daylight to settle on a sack of powdered cement.

Ibrahim smiled. "Soon, *insha'llah*," he whispered, "you will be sent to your family, safe and sound." I wished the same thing for him.

CHAPTER 9

THE FARMHOUSE PRISON

The next part of my story is the happier bit. It starts in the early spring of 2014, in a solitary confinement cell, in the back of a farmhouse somewhere near the Euphrates, in the oil-producing regions of eastern Syria. Ibrahim, the companion with whom I spent my first days in this farmhouse-cum-prison, had long since been taken away. Whether he was sent to another prison, to his family, or to the grave, I cannot say.

Abu Qais, Abdullah, Zakaria, the albino, the commander who had brought a hamburger to the broom closet—these men had become my companions. They brought food to my cell. They brought me out of the cell when I needed to use the bathroom. Sometimes, when they were not busy, they flipped open the food hatch door in my cell, propped an elbow on its lower edge, and smiled at me. "What is your news?" they would say. I had a vague sense of what their lives had been like before the war. The albino, who was in his forties, had lived for many years in a regime prison. The friendly hamburger commander had been a laborer in Beirut. All of my jailers had grown up in and around the city of Asheyl, which was famous (in the region) for having been the cradle of the Syrian revolution. The townsfolk were frequent visitors to this jail.

By the spring of 2014, I had myself become something of an Asheyli, as the citizens of this place referred to themselves. Even the school-age children who occasionally toured the facility with their fathers and elder brothers seemed to know me. Everyone understood that I had been arrested some time ago, in Idlib, and that my case was now in the hands of the competent local authorities. I was not hated.

Our farmhouse prison consisted of a guards' room, a kitchen, and four two-by-six-by-six single-occupancy cells. By the spring of 2014, I had become the elderly jailbird in this facility. My fellow inmates were birds of passage. They came, were tortured, confessed, and were sent away. In this part of Syria, the part of the judicial process that occurred within my hearing range lasted about two weeks. By the spring of 2014, I had eavesdropped on an uncountable quantity—dozens, possibly a hundred—of such processes.

Though I knew what went on during their torture and their interrogations, I was not allowed to speak to my fellow prisoners. We communicated, of course—through whispers and taps on the wall—but we did so at the risk of being flogged, then deprived of our clothing and the blankets on which we slept for a twenty-four-hour period. Thus, on most days, our cell block was silent enough to allow us to hear the mice scurrying through our bathroom. I listened to the other prisoners grinding their teeth. Before they slept, I heard them praying. During the night, as they muttered to themselves in their sleep, I worried that the guards would mistake their dream-talking for conversation. In this prison, whenever one of the prisoners was caught whispering to a neighbor, all four of us were punished.

By March of 2014, I was confident that my case had moved past the torture stage. It had drifted into an intermediate realm—beyond torture, short of release, within range of abuse. Some of the guards seemed to feel that I was serving out a sentence. In due time, they said, I would be released—perhaps into the street in front of the prison. "Where else would you go?" one guard wondered. Others felt that I would be released, possibly into the arms of a US official across the border, in Iraq, but only when the US government had released its Guantánamo prisoners. Still others hinted that negotiations for a ransom were underway, though who was negotiating with whom they did not say. With these guards, I had a conversation that varied only in tiny particulars as the weeks passed. I would ask for news of the negotiations. No news, the guard would say. I would ask the guard if he, personally, believed in the existence of the negotiations. Personally, he would say, he did not know. I would ask the guard to tell me if any news about the status of the negotiations—even the faintest hint of news—came to him. He would assure me that he was no negotiator, that other people elsewhere were in charge of such matters, and that if there was news, it would be brought to me in the fullness of time.

By this point, I had come to know most of my jailers well. Abu Qais, one of the jailers who had slept on a mattress outside my janitor's closet cell at the Omar Company, had taken to revealing confidences to me. There were no major disclosures. Yet during the previous eighteen months, I had seen almost nothing of the outside world. Everything he told me about this place and the people who lived there fascinated me. Before the war, he said, he had dreamed of emigrating to Montreal. Currently, his father, a civil servant, was drawing a salary from the Syrian government, though its police and military forces had not been seen in the region in years. Abu Qais's father did not know of his job as a fighter and part-time jailer for Jebhat al-Nusra. "Why don't you tell him?" I once asked Abu Qais.

"He knows but he doesn't like knowing," he explained. Thus, when he was at home, Abu Qais did not discuss his work.

Abdullah and I had come to an entente, if not exactly a friendship. He wanted me to obey the prison rules, the most important of which was the prohibition against speech among prisoners. I submitted to the rules—as much as I could manage. He refrained from punishing me—as much as he could manage.

Now and then Zakaria spoke of a wish to return to civilian life, perhaps in Turkey. He and his family had suffered enough in this war to date, he often told me, without going into details. Though he was still in his early twenties, and though the war was far from won, Zakaria cherished a dream of living as a retiree, possibly in a refugee camp in Turkey.

Every once in a while in this prison, the commander who had delivered me a hamburger when I was locked into the closet at the Omar Company brought pieces of sweet, sticky baklava to me. He passed them through the food hatch on slips of old newsprint. I smiled at him. As soon as he had closed the hatch, I would slink into a corner of my cell. I would consume the baklava in tiny bites, over the course of hours, as if there might never be another piece of baklava, at least not for me.

It had taken some weeks for me to arrive at an entente with this Jeb-hat al-Nusra cell. At first, in the depths of the winter, when I was learn-ing to accommodate myself to the rhythms of life in this prison, I vowed to myself that if I were to survive, I would make it my mission in life to bring the members of this cell to justice. I couldn't forgive them their torture of my neighbor prisoners. A deaf man whose hearing aid had run out of battery power and so couldn't hear the questions his interro-gators screamed at him, a father whose wallet contained a photograph of a son wearing the uniform of the enemy Syrian Arab Army, a head-master thought to have pressured the female teachers in his school for sex—these were the first prisoners whose torture I overheard.

Their torture occurred in the guards' TV room, about fifteen feet from my cell. The deaf man was tortured several times, over successive nights. After his final torture session, he was not returned to his cell. The schoolmaster was electrocuted, sometimes inside his cell, some-times in the corridor, outside the guards' room. The bitterest, most drawn-out episodes of torture seemed to involve a simulated drowning. This portion of the torture occurred in the vicinity of the guards' bath-room. Were they stuffing the victim's head into a toilet? I assumed so, at first, but later, when a guard allowed me to shower in that bathroom, I saw that there was no water in the hole in the ground the guards used as a toilet. So the drownings occur in a bucket, I told myself. Perhaps the prisoners weren't being drowned so much as revived after faint-ing spells. I never discussed the matter with my fellow prisoners, nor with the guards. Thus, though they occurred several times a week and always within a few feet of my cell, I could never understand the mean-ing of the drowning sounds. Were real drownings occurring? Humilia-tions? Reanimations? I never knew.

During this period, the torture of my neighbors eventually wore me down. I found that I could live peaceably enough, provided I wasn't tortured. If I survive, I told myself, I will mount a crusade against tor-ture. I thought, I would hold the memory of my neighbor prisoners' screams in my heart, like a hot sliver of hatred. If I should live, I told myself, for as long as I would live, I would make it my business to bring these sadists to justice.

One afternoon in January, the members of this Jebhat al-Nusra cell admitted a *mokhtar*, or mayor, to the cell next to mine. Through the three-inch gap between the floor and the bottom of my cell door, I watched as his velvety robe swept across the cement in the corridor in front of my cell. I took note of his expensive-looking leather sandals. He first spoke to me shortly before the evening prayer.

"Where are we?" the *mokhtar* wanted to know. I didn't know, I told him.

"Are we with Daesh or Jebhat al-Nusra?" he whispered.

"Jebhat al-Nusra," I whispered back. "What's the difference?"

"No difference," he replied. "Just curious." He thought matters over for a moment. He asked me if I had been allowed outside, into the prison courtyard. In fact, every fifteen days or so, Abdullah allowed me a fifteen-minute stroll, within a parking area, inside the farmhouse gates. My strolls occurred in handcuffs and a blindfold, under armed guard. Yes, in fact, I had seen the prison courtyard, in a manner of speaking, I said.

"The soil outside out there," the *mokhtar* whispered. "Is it fine like sugar or brittle like charcoal?" I hesitated. I thought the matter over. "Is it red, do you happen to know, like clay, or is it more gray like the clouds?"

"I don't know," I stammered. He was a cotton farmer, he explained. He had lived in the river valley his entire life. He was fifty-eight years old. He knew from soils. Had I been able to see any vegetation? he wondered.

"Sadly," I said, "no."

Over the ensuing hours, I learned that Sheikh Hussein, as he preferred to be called, was the mayor of the city of Marat (population ten thousand), across the river from Deir Ezzor, that he had been accused of helping the Syrian government in its effort to conscript the young men in his city, that he had eleven children, the eldest of whom was studying law in preparation for becoming a *mokhtar* himself, and that his father and his father's father had been *mokhtars*.

He mentioned the family occupation to me in the afternoon, on the second day of his imprisonment. Now the distinguished-looking robe and the expensive sandals made sense. I stared into the cement blocks separating his cell from mine. In Jebhat al-Nusra's jails, all the guards, regardless of age or accomplishment, were to be addressed as if they were men of great learning. "Yes, my sheikh," we were to say to them, and "If you please, my sheikh," and so on. "For me," I whispered to my cell neighbor, "you are the real sheikh and everyone else here is a fake."

He did not reply, but a few minutes later, out of the blue, apropos of nothing, he cleared his throat. Sadly, he said, he had not had the opportunity to learn English. His eldest son, the mayor-to-be, spoke excellent English. He, however, did not. Yet there was one phrase he knew well, he said. "Do you want to hear me speak English?" he asked in Arabic.

"Of course," I whispered.

He took a deep breath. "I love you," he said. He spoke in clear, carefully pronounced syllables. In the silence after his declaration, he giggled.

I congratulated him on his pronunciation. But we were getting carried away. The prison guards had a tendency to press their ears into the keyhole in the door between the block of cells and their living quarters. "Your English is excellent," I told him. "Now, shh."

We lapsed into silence. About twenty minutes of dead air floated by, and then, out of the blue, again, as if struck by a burst of confidence, the sheikh tapped on the wall of his cell.

"Neighbor," he whispered. "Hello?"

"Shh," I told him.

"Neighbor of mine," he said in Arabic, "I have something to tell you."

I knew what he was going to say. The joke had been funny the first time. "Shh," I told him.

"I love you, neighbor," he said again, trying to whisper. Yet his whisper came out at conversational volume, as if he thought the stricture against inmate speech in our jail was to be taken with a grain of salt, like the other rumors and tall tales that floated through our cell block.

Perhaps he felt whispering was beneath him. Perhaps he just wasn't good at it.

For several hours that night, as he sighed and adjusted the little mound of blankets with which each cell was equipped, he stage-whispered the thoughts that happened to be passing through his head into the air above his cell. His central theme was his innocence. "There isn't a thing upon me, thank God," he would say to no one in particular. He would sigh, nap for fifteen minutes, and then his voice would return. "Thank God, not a thing," or, "Perfectly innocent, praise be to God." Toward midnight, new thoughts occurred to him. He was neither on the regime's side, nor on the rebel's side, he declared. "Neutral," he said into the air. "As neutral as neutral can be." He lapsed into silence for a while, and then, about an hour later, speaking in a casual, friendly voice, as if idle curiosity had jolted his mind, he asked if there was torture in our jail.

I didn't see any point in telling him the truth. "I don't think so," I lied.

Really, it was his wife he worried for, he whispered to me. "She doesn't know where I am." During thirty years of married life, she had always known how to find him. Now she was on her own. "Naturally, she's frightened," he said. He, however, was not frightened, since he knew that there wasn't a thing upon him.

After Sheikh Hussein's torture, which occurred on his third night with us, his body was dragged back to his cell. It left a streak of blood on the cement in front of my cell. At first, in his first moments in the safety of his cell, he spoke, in a weakened voice, to God: "Please, God. Oh God. Please. Please!" He, being a diabetic, had been unable to eat the potatoes and apricot jam we had been served over the previous days.

The torture had soaked his clothing in blood and water. That night, January 13, 2014, the temperature in our cell block would have been well below zero. In order for him to survive, I felt, he would have had to eat. I knew he had no food in his cell. To stave off the hypothermia, he would have had to remove his wet clothing. He would have had to bury himself under a mountain of blankets, as the rest of us did. Perhaps he wasn't thinking straight. Perhaps he felt that now, only God could help. "Please, God!" he whispered. "Please!" Yet he did not remove his wet clothing. I would have heard him shifting his weight inside his cell. I would have heard him pulling his undershirt over his shoulders.

That night, his pleadings to God eventually roused the torturers from their TV room. They must have felt he was carrying on. They returned to his cell with their cables. When they had finished kicking him, they screamed at him. He was an animal. He was filth. He was an enemy of God. After this round of insults, they flogged him. This took several minutes. Only when the sheikh was totally quiet—when he pleaded neither with his attackers nor with God—did they slam the door of his cell.

One of these assailants must have been aware, at least on some level, that Sheikh Hussein's life was in danger. This guard made the effort of opening the food hatch in my cell's door, of taking a spare pair of sweatpants and a clean T-shirt from me, and of flinging these into Sheikh Hussein's cell. "Cover yourself—oolak," the torturer said, as the clothing fell to the floor.

None of the torturers stuck around long enough to see if Sheikh Hussein was capable of removing the wet clothing. They certainly gave him no food. As they strode out of the cell block, they banged their fists against the doors of all four cells. The prisoners were to shut their mouths, they shouted. We were animals. We were enemies of the Syrian people. "Sleep, animals," a voice called out.

That night, we, the animals, were much too afraid to move, let alone speak. For a few minutes, after the Jebhat al-Nusra men had retreated to their room, I listened for the sheikh's breathing. I heard him coughing, I thought. When ten minutes of silence had come and gone, he seemed to sigh. If I could have, I would have climbed into his cell. I would have stripped away his wet clothing. I would have wrapped my body around his. I wanted to whisper reassuring words to him. I'm sure the other two prisoners did, too.

Of course, by that point, the sheikh was beyond our reach. The next morning, when the guards came to check on him, they found that Sheikh Hussein, who missed his wife, held a library of the region's soil types in his head, knew himself to be innocent and so did not doubt that things would work out well in the end, was dead.

That morning, our jail lived through a brief kerfuffle. The guards radioed news of the sheikh's death to a commander. As they waited for the commander to turn up, there was much whispering among the guards. There were hurried remarks and angry, whispered rejoinders. A further kerfuffle ensued when a troupe of commanders dragged the corpse from the cell. Then the cell had to be scoured and squeegeed. The sheikh's bloody robe had to be deposited in a bucket in the prison toilet. The other prisoners had to be screamed at and made to press their faces into the wall at the back of their cells, lest they guess that the sheikh had been murdered by accident, out of brutishness and stupidity, then left to die in the cold, in a heap of bloody clothing.

For most of that day, I was livid. I spoke to the sheikh in my imagination. I spoke to his wife and to his children. I promised to see the culprits brought to justice. I knew the excuses they would invent for themselves and how transparent the lies they would tell really were. "I will see them punished," I told the sheikh. I will never forgive, I told myself. I will never forget.

But later that day, Abu Qais brought a package of dates—almost a kilo's worth—to my cell. In the late afternoon, the two prisoners who had heard what I had heard of Sheikh Hussein's killing were removed from their cells, then driven away in a car. In the evening, three new prisoners arrived. I hardly spoke to them. I reiterated the prison rules. I ignored their whispered questions.

Several days later, a person who might have been a military commander, a civil authority, or a mixture of the two invited me to step out of my cell and to sit with him, in my blindfold, on a retaining wall in front of the prison. This man's voice had a warm, just-between-us frankness to it. Was I well? he wanted to know. Were "the *shabab*"—the youthful guards—allowing me to walk in the prison courtyard now and then? They were, I said. Was I being given enough to eat? I was. Was there any special kind of food I wanted? Not really, I said. He wanted to know what I had seen or heard during the previous week.

"Nothing much," I said.

"Good," he said. He spoke for a moment about mistakes. There was a war on. Mistakes were inevitable. If I were to talk about the mistakes I had witnessed, the young men of Asheyl, those who had fed me and cared for me over the previous months, could well find themselves in trouble. Indeed, all the Asheylis I had come to know, and others, too, from surrounding villages, would be put in a difficult situation. These citizens had devoted their lives to the struggle against Bashar al-Assad. Did I wish to make trouble for them?

I did not. The commander gave me his name. I had never met him before. I don't think I met him again. The name has slipped my mind.

"I can trust you to come to me if you have any problems?" he asked.

"You can," I said.

As he was bringing me back to my cell, he thrust a handful of sugar cookies into my palm. "You are a respectable prisoner," he murmured.

"I respect you," I told him. He clanked the lock on my cell door shut.

In that moment, as these words were leaving my lips, I was thinking, I despise you. I will never forgive and never forget. His overseeing of a torture farmhouse, his drowning and electrocution of the deaf man, his torture of the father whose son was in the army—I wanted to see him and his friends hanged for these crimes. I meant to see even the peons punished. In the minutes after Sheikh Hussein's torture, the guard, Zakaria, had been dispatched to squeegee away the streaks of blood the sheikh's injured body had left in the cell block corridor. Zakaria took to his task without a thought in his head. He might have been wiping down a table after a meal. The following morning, when the sheikh's body was being dragged from his cell, Abdullah was in the guards' room, chuckling over a cartoon show on TV. I longed for the day when all of these brain-dead killers were made to reckon with their crimes.

Such were my feelings, after my meeting, as I was being locked into my cell. A few minutes later, however, I was alone with the sugar cookies. It seemed to me the organization wished to entrust me with a secret. It had spoken to me, for the first time in more than a year, as if it understood me to be an observer—and so a human being. Moreover, it was giving me cookies and dates. I decided that it would do to remember the date on which they'd killed Sheikh Hussein. No one else would have done the sheikh this courtesy, I knew. I tried to make a mental note of the things he had said to me. I meant to push these memories down, into a nook in my consciousness. Perhaps I would dig for them later. For the time being, Jebhat al-Nusra seemed to have made, if not an apology, then at least a kind of a self-justification. They wouldn't have done this, I thought, if they didn't value my opinion. I wanted to be valued. I wanted more of the Jebhat al-Nusra men to seek me out and to trust me. I was keen for their cookies. I was keen to be taken into the out-of-doors, to be planted on a retaining wall like a flowerpot, and to peer at shadows through my blindfold. Above all, I didn't want the men with the guns to suspect me of disloyalty. Perhaps Sheikh Hussein really had been a regime agent all along, I thought. In which case, he had reaped what he had sown. Anyway, his death wasn't my business. My business, I told myself, was to live in compliance with the prison rules, to greet the citizens of Asheyl with salaams when they opened the food hatch door of my cell, and to keep my nose from poking into places in which it did not belong. Deep down, I wondered, am I a bit of a collaborator? If so, I decided, I am fine with collaborating. I wanted the men with scarves around their faces to smile at me when they popped open the food hatch door in my cell. I wanted them to push triangles of baklava into my hands and to ask me, as they sometimes did, in their joking way, when they wanted to make light, "What is the news with you, American friend? When you are released, will you tell lies about us?"

When they put questions like this to me, I knew that all was well between me and Jebhat al-Nusra. I knew the answer they wanted to hear. "My sheikhs," I would tell them. "I will speak, of course. How could I not? But I will not lie."

CHAPTER 10

THE CALIPHATE LIVES

In those days, in that place, we lived at a distance from the world. My cell permitted me inklings of life out there, on planet Earth. For instance, the window that had been knocked into the wall above the bank of cells allowed me a view of passing clouds. Abdullah had welded a chain-link fence that sat like a ceiling over my cell's side walls. This prevented me from climbing up to touch the windowsill, which was about eight feet off the ground. Still, at night I could see the moon. In the daytimes, I sometimes caught glimpses of desert birds.

I had a few possessions. Abu Qais had given me an English-Arabic copy of the Koran, an English-Arabic dictionary he had found in his family's library, and a Berlitz phrase book written for the Arabic-speaking visitor to the UK. I owned a toothbrush, a pee bottle, and a tin dish.

From whisperings among the prisoners in our jail, I understood that Jebhat al-Nusra was the reigning power in the region, that there were traffic police in the streets, order in the suqs, and that Islamic law, administered by Jebhat al-Nusra judges, ruled over the entirety of Deir Ezzor Province.

What exactly Jebhat al-Nusra did to maintain its power I did not know. I didn't have more than a hazy understanding of what Deir Ezzor Province might look like on a map, nor did I have an inkling of how many soldiers fought in its army. Fifty thousand? A hundred thousand? Abdullah wanted me to believe that in the mighty Islamic state Jebhat al-Nusra had brought to life, a million-man army stood at the ready. More soldiers were coming in every day, in his telling. I doubted him but because I had yet to be taken outside without a blindfold, and

321

so hadn't glimpsed so much as a blade of grass, the scope of Jebhat al-Nusra's power had to remain, for me, a mystery. In any case, I knew that Jebhat al-Nusra was powerful enough. It had driven away the Syrian government. At the time, no one else was interested in attacking the region.

Thus, we were a kingdom unto ourselves. I understood that to the citizens in this kingdom, the world beyond was about as distant as Deir Ezzor Province was to me—and had been so for about two years. I understood that everything had to be smuggled in to us, even the tomatoes. According to the rumors I was hearing in those days, only a trickle of outsiders, most of whom were European mujahideen, had been permitted in to our kingdom. The roads out were thought to be too subject to aerial attacks to allow the citizens of this river valley, of whom there were thought to be about five million, to leave. Anyway, most did not want to leave. Those who did had nowhere to go.

Which was just fine with almost everyone I spoke to in those days, since it was clear to them that we were living on the cusp of an ancient, much-loved Islamic dream. The dream was of a society cleansed, perfect equality for everyone, invincibility before the enemies of Islam, and oneness with the Koran. Everyone acknowledged that certain lingering ideas from the former way of life were blocking a perfect realization of the dream, for all 5 million inhabitants of this river valley. Still, much had been accomplished to date.

The outside world, I knew, would have referred to our society's leaders as "terrorists" or "extremists" or "fanatics." In our society, they were called "emirs"—or, in English, "princes."

These princes controlled the region's oil wells, the banks, the museums, the mosques, and five hundred or so Toyota Hilux pickup trucks. The Euphrates River Valley is Syria's breadbasket. The princes controlled the farms, too.

There was beauty in this society. It was generally held that the dream would come more quickly and more totally if everyone read a melodic early medieval poem called *The Reading* or *The Recitation* as often as possible. Military power, family happiness, and advancements in science were thought to flow from this poem. It predicted the future.

It warded off danger and instructed the community, even in the minutest particulars of everyday life, in how to live as God wished people to live. As it happened, the poem wasn't so much read as it was sung. Thus, inside the dream, it was in the air, all day, in every room and conveyance.

The leaders of this society sang with great self-confidence and attentiveness to the meaning of the lines. In this respect, they were artists. In their conversation, they exhibited masterful control over the details of the poem, which was hundreds of pages in length and, because of its arcane idiom, no easy thing to master. In this respect, they were professors. In honor of their accomplishments, they were to be addressed by the title "Sheikh." In Arabic, "sheikh" implies a pastoral function. Also, lifelong scholarship. It might be translated as "man of learning."

Though the men of learning were busy, in the daytime, with soldiery, their chief occupation was to usher humankind outward along a spiritual progress. The straight path we were traveling then began in the City of Destruction that was Assad's Syria—which is to say, in a wasteland ruled by misdeeds and corruption. At first little bands, and then all 5 million inhabitants of this river valley, and then all of humanity, were meant to set out for a new way of life, to find themselves in a strange land, there to pass through tests, to triumph over inner division and finally over all enemies everywhere. In this way, in theory, eventually the men of learning would usher planet Earth—and not just the bits of it that happened to have been born into Islam—into harmony with God.

Such was the theory. In practice, of course, in the spring of 2014 every settlement in our river valley remained a city of destruction in the most literal sense. The enemies who kept us in this condition were too far away to vanquish. The citizens couldn't be led anywhere because the highways were much too overrun with bomb craters and haunted by bandits and drones.

Thus the real work of the men of learning was to select citizens from within our society who might plausibly be taken as representatives of the enemy, to bring them before something or someone that might plausibly be taken as an instrument of God, and then to stage an event that might be taken as an instance in which the people of God triumphed over wickedness.

The carrying out of these selections was a prodigious labor. Because the entirety of the society had lived so long under the psychology of the Assads, the moral condition of that family was thought to have sunk itself into the collective psyche. Even the men of learning had, in earlier times, succumbed to it. They admitted this openly. But they had kept the dream alive within themselves, too, had kept the evil at bay, and at the first sign of the dream's dawning over the landscape they knew right away what was happening. Some were away at work in the oil fields in the Gulf. Others had exiled themselves to Beirut and Jordan. They all hurried home.

Arriving in our river valley, they discovered that their work was to fan out across the society, to identify the agents of the Assads, along with all others who had allowed the psychology of the Assad regime to infect their thinking, to roust these enemies from their beds and to chase them across the rooftops, if need be, then bring them to jail. Because the Assad family had ruled since the early seventies, everyone had been infected somehow. The men of learning couldn't very well arrest the entire society. Their task was to target the unrepentant, the unreformed, and all those who pretended to have extinguished the old ways of thinking but secretly, in their hearts, kept a candle burning for the Assads. There was no way to know how many such covert agents the society contained. The number might have been in the millions. Thus the prodigiousness of the labor before the men of learning.

It was understood that in the chaos of an arrest, errors could occur. "If there is nothing upon you," the sheiks would tell the new prisoners, "we will let you go." The new prisoners longed to believe. When the sheikhs had left the cell block, the new prisoners would whisper their thoughts into the air. "Praise God," they would say, "that I am as innocent as a child."

In the evening, the sheikhs would return with their lead investigator. The word for investigator—*muhaqiq*—means "bringer out of the truth." The *muhaqiq*'s job was to torture the prisoners until they confessed to whatever the sheikhs wished to accuse them of.

In our prisons, a prisoner could be a foreign agent or he could be a street criminal. The agents had slipped into the river valley in order to transmit bombing coordinates back to enemy air force bases. Or they disseminated lies and dissension within the dream and so sabotaged it from within. Street criminals lusted after money or sex or practiced witchcraft. Sometimes they insulted God.

In theory, it was better to be an agent, since agents could be ransomed away, whereas the criminals, especially when they were thought to have persisted in their crimes despite warnings, were irredeemable. I had not, however, heard of anyone being ransomed away. I certainly didn't think anyone would pay for me.

The distinction between the agent and the street criminal was a subtle matter. In theory, it was possible to be both at once. Practically speaking, the distinction didn't matter much because it was thought that all prisoners amounted to a form of corruption. Thus, it would have been unthinkable for the prisoners to be left, in their idle hours, to chitchat among themselves. Many of the mid-level sheikhs had done time in regime prisons. Almost all of the higher sheikhs had been locked away for years. They knew what happens when prisoners whisper among themselves. The whisperings lead to plots. The badly infected among the prisoners spread their sicknesses to the not-so-badly infected.

Accordingly, all prisoners in our society, except those so far beyond the pale that no hope could remain for them—rapists, for instance, and Alawites—were given copies of *The Recitation*. They were told to pray and to repent.

When a hint of chitchat emerged from the cell block, the men of learning would come crashing through the steel door that separated the cell block from the guards' living quarters. "Who spoke?" they would shout. "Who?" Within a minute, the prisoners would be lying on their stomachs in the corridor outside our cells. Our hands would be zip-tied behind our backs. The sheikhs with whom I had been trying to establish a rapport would use their galvanized steel cables to beat the contamination out of their dream.

"You will know who we are!" the men of learning would shout. "Who are we?"

"You are those who bring victories to the Muslims," we would reply, or, simply, "You are men of the religion."

"And who are you?" they would ask.

"We are filth," we would reply, or, "I am an animal," or, "I am an ass."

Once you knew the rules, life in our society, even in its worst places, in which, I'm pretty sure, I lived, was bearable.

The Syrian Air Force bombed occasionally. Most of the time, at this point in the war, in this river valley, the airplanes left us alone. The nearest enemy troops were hundreds of kilometers away, confined to redoubts in the desert, and in any case, vastly outnumbered by the defenders of our Islamic state.

Thus, inside the state, our days unfolded as follows: In the early morning darkness, there was prayer. The young men fighters liked to watch cartoons when they woke up, around noon. There were more prayers, then lunch, then shooting of the Kalashnikovs into adobe walls and into the sky. In the evenings, for the new prisoners, there were "welcoming parties" or "investigations"—which is to say, there was torture. When there was no one to torture, the commanders sometimes led the younger men in the singing of war hymns, many of which were addressed to the martyrs as they looked down on us from heaven. Though it wasn't strictly allowed, some of the guards didn't mind when I sang, to myself, in my cell.

I found it odd, at first, that the people who inflicted such a regime of violence and whisper-punishment on their brother humans also loved to play at make-believe, but all the sheikhs in all the prisons in which I lived in the eastern part of Syria (there were six, all told) were much more devoted to their imaginary worlds than they were, for instance, to looking after their rifles or filling up the tanks of their pickups with gas.

I noticed this quality of theirs many times a day. It was in their habit of dressing sometimes as black-robed avenging angels of death, sometimes in tracksuits, sometimes as MTV rappers, and sometimes as everyday citizens, out for a stroll in the sunshine. Of course it was in the sound of their voices as they sang to their friends in paradise. I experienced it most vividly during the "you shall know who we are" call-and-response dramas they staged for the new prisoners.

Of course, in Islam, the collective prayer invites practioners into the magic of the theater five times a day.

It happened that our prisons often lay outside the broadcast range of the nearest minaret. And so what? In Islam, a swatch of carpet may be your mosque. When you are far from an actual muezzin, you, the believer, should imagine yourself on a balcony, high over a city. You are to raise the right index finger to the right earlobe and the left finger to the left. "Come to the prayer," you say to yourself, twice, and also twice "come to the flourishing." The believer might not have any water on hand. Fine. Sand is like water. But if there is no sand, air is like water. You may bathe your face and arms in handfuls of air.

In this way, you wash the sins from your soul. The important thing is to extract oneself from the hurly-burly of everyday life, to cleanse oneself in an inner sense, and to bring oneself into alignment: with oneself, with one's community, and with God.

In this frame of mind, you turn yourself to the holiest spot on Earth. You sing from the poem, in rows with the young and the old, the poor and the rich, the sinful and the righteous. Elsewhere in the city and across planet Earth, following the arc of the sun, other believers are singing these lines with you. It is a dream of harmony come to life.

The purpose of this simultaneity is to cause the community to drift, just for a moment, out of earthly time. I realize this is not the sort of excursion that can be seen. No instruments can measure one's progress. That doesn't mean the voyage isn't a fact. In our river valley, it was the clock by which the society lived. It was its theater. It was as factual as the flooding of the riverbanks in the spring and as marvelous.

At the time, the prayer was hardly the only instance in which things that couldn't be explained by science intervened in daily affairs. Now and then, the airplanes that came to bomb us dropped out of the sky. The pilots turned up in the hands of the sheikhs. How had this happened? By accident? By a mechanical failure? Not a soul among the 5 million inhabitants in our valley could have believed this. Meanwhile, kindred spirits, which is to say dreamers from across the world, were slipping through the grasp of one police force after another, then trickling into our river valley. Somehow, American laser-guided surface-to-surface missiles were also falling under the control of the men of learning. Though they didn't all of them own shoes and often ate only a round or two of bread per day, somehow these men were conquering enemy military airports. This was also a dream come to life. The victories brought further weapons and new prisoners.

When the new arrivals turned up in prison, the sheikhs warned them in the starkest terms not to chitchat. But they were frightened. They were all badly disoriented. So late at night, long after their plastic zip-tie handcuffs had been cut from their wrists and their ankles—when they had prayed, eaten, tried to sleep, when it would have seemed to them as though everyone in the prison was sound asleep—they would tap at the cinder-block wall that separated our cells. "Neighbor. Hey, neighbor," they would whisper. "My brother. Where are we?"

I didn't know. I was too afraid to talk. But I was not capable of not talking. Eventually, of course, that night, or some night soon thereafter, as we were whispering, the steel door that separated the cell block from the sheikhs' TV room would emit a click. In the two inches of space between the bottom of my cell door and the floor, a half-dozen pairs of sandaled feet would appear. The hems of their black robes would hover over the floor. You could hear the motionlessness of the other prisoners then. We scarcely breathed. "Who spoke?" a voice would wonder. "Who? For the sake of God, tell the truth."

After the beatings, the sheikhs would prohibit all the prisoners from food or water until the following morning. So I would sleep. The mornings would be calm, a week or so would pass, and eventually, late at night, a newly arrested person would be brought into the cell next to mine. I was lonely. I was frightened. I needed friends. "Tap tap tap," I would say to the wall next to me. "Neighbor," I would say. "Hey, neighbor. What is your name?"

One afternoon late that spring, long after I had stopped wondering at the way of life in our river valley—when I was bored as I always was and longing to talk, as always—a mid-level commander called Abu Marouf al-Homsi stopped by my cell to chat. He had himself spent many years in a regime prison. I'm not sure the sentences in his prison would have had expiration dates. We certainly had no such things in our prisons. So he would have known what the passage of time feels like to prisoners in Syria. It is more a circular thing there than a linear thing. "Would it be possible for you to bring me a pen and a paper?" I asked him. He thought about it for a moment. "I don't see why not," he said.

During my first nights with the pen and paper, I decided to write a diary. I recorded a few thoughts. They had to do with the frequency with which the poem encouraged its readers to disengage from the details of life here on this plane, in favor of thoughts about the life to come. In the poem, dying was good, since it marked the beginning of eternal life.

That spring, disagreements between al Qaeda and ISIS over how to split up the proceeds from the river valley's half-dozen oil fields broke out into open warfare. When the al Qaeda men of learning captured ISIS princes, they brought these enemies to our jail. The ISIS princes, it turned out, were almost always talktative, genial types who had done years in prison in Iraq, under the Americans, or in Syrian jails, under the authority of the Syrian government jailers. I found my ISIS neighbors to be far more pious than my earlier, civilian neighbors had been. Sometimes, when the ISIS neighbors were feeling comradely, they invited me to follow along with them as they sang from the poem. "Following," in this instance, meant reading the line the ISIS prince was reciting in my copy of the Koran, listening for the vowels he elongated and the consonants he struck, then having a go at reciting the lines myself. If my recitation satisfied the prince, he moved on to the next line. As I recited with these ISIS princes, the poem's infatuation with romantic death began to seem to me its salient characteristic. This quality seemed to leap from every page. In earlier readings, the theme had escaped me. Now, in the company of the ISIS princes, the poem's authors seemed like dreamy, Thanatos-driven cultists to me, and the poem's modern admirers seemed little different. I wished for books that embraced life. But our prison had no library. We made do with the materials on hand.

Probably, for the ISIS prisoners, some of whom had been told they would soon be executed, the poem's loving way of speaking of the afterlife brought consolation. It promised and soothed.

The poem did not, however, soothe me. It made me feel that the powerful men in this society were resigning themselves to a world in which everyone killed everyone else.

The poem's contempt for humans who would not or could not reconcile themselves to Islam also discomfited me. In the poem, such refuseniks were called *kuffar*. The more carefully I read it, the more obvious it was to me that the poem considered the *kuffar* to be ingrates who deserved whatever fate befell them. Often, in the Koran, the *kuffar* were slaughtered en masse. Such killings brought the believers closer to God.

So much power did the poem have in this society that, as May wore on, it began to seem to me that the most unlikely outcome, for me, would be to emerge from this quiet river valley with my head. The poem, I sometimes thought, was my enemy.

You're meant to record private thoughts, even if they're improper, in a diary. So I told myself when I began writing. I wrote in English. No one in our river valley, as far as I knew, would have been able to decipher my English-language scribblings. So my diary and I were safe. So I told myself, but after that first night with pen and paper—when I had slept, picked up my diary, and reread—I knew that if they knew that I was having bitter thoughts about the poem, then setting these thoughts down on their paper, in the midst of their dream, they would have burned the paper. Then they would have cut my throat. I tore my diary into shreds.

Okay, I thought. Fine. A novel. I wanted to be home anyway. I wanted to revisit the spring storms I had written about a year earlier, in the grocery store in Al-Haydariya. At first, in my opening chapters, I found myself thinking a lot about a particular young woman called Gypsy Phelan. She had blond hair, glasses. I saw her in the Vermont spring. She was about to graduate from high school. I could see every detail of the village in which she had grown up because it was the village in which I grew up.

Probably I was needing some positive energy in my cell. I made my hero, Gypsy, the star of a high school musical. In my imagination, I saw her singing: "I'm in love, I'm in love, I'm in love, I'm in love, I'm in love with a wonderful guy!" I hadn't spoken with a woman in eighteen months. During a transfer from one prison to the next in Aleppo, I had glimpsed two of them at a bus stop, in front of the eye hospital. So I didn't know much about womankind in our society, but I did know—because I knew their husbands and brothers—that no woman in our vicinity—not one wishing to keep her head—would have stood anywhere near a stage. She certainly would not have sung those lines. That a woman might do this somewhere—and happily and without a twinge of guilt—seemed wondrous to me. But also ordinary and plausible.

I found that the more I wrote about Gypsy, the more I cared about her. For a person who didn't exist at all, she had a remarkable talent for getting under my skin.

Because our prison seemed to exist at some distance from other houses, I supposed that fields and trees were nearby. But I couldn't see them. Often I felt that the springtime might as well have been happening on the moon. Gypsy, I started to feel, was my springtime.

The ambient temperature in the afternoons late in May in Deir Ezzor Province, when I began to write this Vermont story, was about 110 degrees. In the afternoons, in that heat, I had to concentrate to keep from panicking. Thus I made my character, Gypsy, go swimming. She swam, um . . . a lot. I wrote about the deep pools in the rivers, the flotillas of tiny icebergs that poured out of the mountains in the spring, waterfalls, and a certain flat, sun-splashed, totally undiscovered rock above a millpond, high up, in an unvisited part of the forest. When Gypsy jumped from this rock, the shock the water sent through her body was powerful enough that halfway around the world, inside a solitary confinement cell, in the heat along the Iraqi border, it went through my body, too.

At first, since I was trying to take myself on a vacation to Vermont, I thought the book would be about a perfect place, under ideal conditions, but later, as the plot gathered momentum, it occurred to me that the effect on the human soul of drones floating through the night, suicide bombers drifting in from around the world, preachers broadcasting prophecies from the minarets, entire cities in flight, and no safe way in or out—the effect of year after year of this—was not known. A transformation was underway. What were we becoming? How had this happened? I felt that nobody in our war-ravaged river valley was likely to have the time or the energy to daydream about the pressures our society was exerting on the soul—and that if a person did daydream and did set the dreams down in Arabic, on paper, the story could cost the writer his life. As for the blank space beyond our valley, what could citizens of that other world, so far away, know about the dream underway here? The photographs from here would show normal citizens going about their lives in a time of war. Our dream, I felt, wasn't the sort of thing one could capture on film.

Toward the end of spring, in Vermont, in my imaginary world, Gypsy graduated from high school. Her university was to begin in the fall. She didn't have much to do. She found herself drawn to a classmate named Taylor who had grown up in a sort of a hippie cult, way out in the hills, among the stone walls and the apple trees.

The pioneer, the recluse, the man of principle who lives from the land, makes his own law, but goes on his knees before God—along the dirt roads on which I grew up, admiration for such people was a feature of the land, like the apple trees. This feeling mistrusts outsiders. It values defiance. Sometimes it collects guns.

I imagined that the young people in my Vermont town would have been too busy being young people to notice the first few acts of violence, since they had occurred far away, under the cover of anonymity.

Inside a local cult, resentments were stirring. The cult had always been there but now, for no particular reason—or, rather—for a dozen reasons, many of which were too convoluted for the cultists to express or understand, the cult leaders were on the march. They thought a shock to the system would do the system good. They wanted a fight. They dreamed of an apocalyptic battle. They made their first attacks by stealth, in the dead of night, against targets that had earlier held the community together. This, my ISIS comrades told me, was how they had got things underway in Syria.

In my story, as trouble brewed, Gypsy was absorbed in a teenage romance. It wasn't her first relationship, but she had never yet felt that she could love the person with whom she was getting involved.

The boy in question, Taylor, had a shy, almost courtly way of speaking. He never would have cursed, for instance. He did not drink. Though he had grown up in a religious family, he found most of the stuff in which he was meant to believe more humorous than true. "I don't understand God in the least," he told Gypsy when she asked about his feelings concerning the big man upstairs. She agreed that she didn't understand him, either. "Good," Taylor said. "Can we move on?" She was willing to move on.

So in the early summer, I had Taylor mention a clearing on a hillside called Delectable Mountain that he found very, sort of . . . um, impossible to describe? It was definitely a lot like a dream, sort of. Once she saw it, she would understand. Did she want to take a walk there sometime?

Delectable Mountain happens to be a real hill in my town in Vermont, though named after an imaginary range in the popular seventeeth-century allegory *The Pilgrim's Progress* by John Bunyan. In my cell, it didn't feel imaginary to me in the least. I had been free in that place once. Now that that world was lost to me, I saw all the splendors I had squandered. That I had enjoyed that many blessings, that I had tossed them all to the wind, and that my world now consisted of a succession of two-foot-by-six-foot cinder-block prison cells and, now and then, a go-round with the cable—try as I might, I could not make myself understand how this had happened.

I felt that my character, Gypsy, was the sort of person who liked to explore unusual places. She was curious about unfamiliar people, too. In my story, I had Taylor invite Gypsy to explore a patch of forest, beyond the apple trees and the stone walls, which the cult venerated as a kind of sacred space. To Gypsy, that part of the countryside was far from home. At first, she hesitated. Eventually, she gave in.

She found her first excursion into Taylor's forest positively entrancing. She didn't mind wearing the blindfold Taylor asked her to wear as he drove her along Delectable Mountain Road. She was about to be admitted into a sacred place. It was also a secret place. She meant to show respect. Deep in the forest, when she was allowed to remove her blindfold, the wind happened to wash a scroll of parchment-like birch bark up against her ankles. She plucked the bark from the grass and marveled for a moment at the fluttering of the forest canopy. She was standing on a bluff overlooking a meadow in which hundreds of white birch trees swayed in the wind. Taylor smiled at the scene. He took the parchment paper from Gypsy's hand. "We think these are letters from God," I had him saying, as a line in a poem I vaguely recalled said. "In every hour of the twenty-four," Taylor said, "in every forest in the world, he sends us these letters."

Gypsy gaped at the bark for an instant, turned her eyes to the swaying trees, then focused them on Taylor's eyes.

"My God," she whispered.

"Yeah," Taylor said. "We think it's a pretty cool spot, I guess."

"I guess so," Gypsy murmured.

At the time, I wasn't quite alone with my characters. Every few hours, one of the younger, twentysomething sheikhs, or several of them would pop open the food hatch in the door of my cell. "What are you writing?" they would ask.

"It's about some extremist Christians in America," I would say. "And about a girl I used to know in high school."

"Your girlfriend?" they would ask.

"Sort of," I would say.

"Is it true?" they wanted to know.

I told them it was very true. "Good," they said. They asked me to read it to them. If there was no girlfriend in the bits I read, they lost interest right away.

I wanted to keep them entertained. So as the summer got hotter in Vermont, as my cell heated up in Deir Ezzor Province, I made things between Gypsy and her boyfriend heat up, too. They went on dates— at first chaste ones in town but later to a lake, in the hills, at night. Up there, after they had taken off their clothes, then gone swimming, one thing led to another. I wrote about how Gypsy came to look forward to these excursions, how she loved taking off her clothes near Taylor, and how she felt when she was lying, without clothes, next to his body. She felt as she had felt in the birch grove: in the presence of something otherworldly—miraculous, even. She couldn't believe that what was happening was happening. She couldn't deny it, either. She found this confusion exhilarating.

Though the sheikhs could see me scribbling well enough, they had no way of knowing where my writing was taking me. I'm not sure I knew, either. Still, I had a rough plan. I meant to recall what love was like, to watch the heart in conflict with the structures of a society, and so, by going to Vermont, to get at the truth of things in our Islamic state. All day long, the men in the cells next to me were telling me true things about life in that state. So did their prayers, their singing, and their conversation with the Jebhat al-Nusra sheikhs. So every time I learned something true and factual, I put it in my story. The truer my story became for me, the more it drew me into my faraway world.

Looking back on that writing experience now, I recall how keen I was to drive my characters into a dark place. I found myself mesmerized by the instruments—the handcuffs, the galvanized steel cables, the blindfolds—with which the driving was accomplished. I wanted my narration to dwell on the barbs at the end of the cables, and to scrutinize the way these barbs sank through the skin after the shafts had wrapped themselves around the curve of a shoulder or a skull. The harder the tormentors thwacked, the more the cable ends tore at the flesh. I wanted to narrate the whole bloody mess, instant by instant. I didn't care if I repulsed my readers who were, in any case, a wholly notional construct.

In my story, things would have worked out well enough for Gypsy if it had not been for her love of exploration.

I knew she was going to die. I knew it was going to be an agonizing death involving heavy-gauge steel cables. I thought for a moment about how exactly they would draw her into their trap. Looking around my cell, my eye fell on my blindfold. I imagined that Taylor's father, a cult leader, had been spying on Gypsy and her boyfriend, as religious zealots sometimes spy on their teenage children. I imagined that Gypsy's nakedness had angered and excited him, which was how the sheikhs in my life, it seemed to me, felt about things they could never have.

In order to punish her, the father made the son arrange a date with Gypsy. The couple were to meet on the patio in front of the town library, their usual meeting spot, just before dark. In my cell, this patio appeared before me as if it had been projected across the rear wall of my cell. I could see the tiniest details of the scene. The maples that shade this patio rustled in my cell. From somewhere far away, outside the prison—in the desert, perhaps—came the smell of freshly cut grass. In my story, the patio was going to be the last spot on earth in which Gypsy was safe and in control. It was her jumping-off place. Looking back now, I'm sure the details of the scene came to me so vividly because even then, eighteen months after my own disappearance, I still longed to wind back the clock. I half-thought it was possible. Where on earth is a safe space for me? Such was the question my brain wanted to ask. An answer materialized: the library patio in a village at home.

In the event, I imagined that Taylor's father had arranged for Taylor to be away—far away, as it happened, in upstate New York, on a tour of a bible college—on the night he arranged to meet Gypsy on the patio. Trusting that he would turn up as he always did, Gypsy appeared on the patio at the appointed time.

In the event, a friend of Taylor's—amiable but simple-minded— turned up in Taylor's place. "He couldn't come down here tonight," the friend told Gypsy. "He's waiting for you in the birch grove. You wanna go?"

By the time I'd gotten to this point in my story, I knew roughly what the men in the birch grove were going to do to Gypsy. There were going to be head wounds, a period of drifting in and out of consciousness, and blood loss. I was going to kill my favorite character and before I did it, I felt a twinge of regret. Gypsy had woken me up from a period of slumber. It seemed to me that a person had drifted into my cell, that I had scarcely been involved in summoning her, and that now that she had come, I cherished her company. I didn't want her to leave.

But this character, I felt, had an important mission in life. She was setting out. In my imagination, her job in life was to discover what I had discovered about the cruelties men commit in the name of God. I wanted her to be led into these discoveries as I had been, that is, by a trusting nature and a will to discover what other humans get up to in the world. Accordingly, I gave the friend who came to pick up Gypsy on the library lawn a ramshackle car whose ignition was operated by a screwdriver plunged into the keyhole. The driver himself had a laid-back, almost sleepy way of talking. "Get in if you want, Gypsy," he told her. "Up to you, really."

As she contemplated these words, a wave of regret swept over Gypsy.

I saw her playing out dark scenarios to herself in her mind, which was what I had done in the moments before I got into a car I never should have gotten into. I saw her taking a hard look backward toward the safety of the library. How can I get out of this? she wondered. I made her get into the car because her curiosity about Taylor had been aroused, because she wished to discover more about his sacred space, and because everything she had learned about life to date told her that further, deeper mysteries would unravel themselves if she allowed herself to follow her heart.

In my story, I had the driver ask Gypsy to put on her blindfold once he turned onto Delectable Mountain Road. "Sorry, Gypsy," he said. "I guess it's a secret place and everything. Okay?"

She was okay with the blindfold. I arranged for Taylor's father—and a committee of cult leaders—to be waiting for Gypsy in the birch grove. The men stood in the darkness, in silence, their faces covered with balaclavas. Each of them held a three-quarter-inch galvanized steel cable in one hand. This was roughly the attitude in which my first group of torturers in the eye hospital basement had met me.

As the driver guided her over a stone wall, into the birch grove, Gypsy heard the rustling of the forest canopy, as she had heard it during her first visit to this space. Were there human voices in that rustling? She couldn't tell. "Taylor?" she whispered. She put her hands to her blindfold.

In that instant, it occurred to her that she had made a mistake. She had allowed herself to be led into the depths of a forest. By whom? She scarcely knew the driver. In the next instant, a cable crashed into the back of her skull. The force of the blow made her drop to her knees. "Oof," she said. A second blow caused her to topple forward. As she lay in the grass, a warm trickle of liquid oozed through her hair. What is this? she thought to herself. A boot kicked her head. "Oof," she said. And then her wrists were being locked into handcuffs. "You are our prisoner now," said a voice.

"Help me! Help me!" said other, younger voices—giggling apparently. A flurry of whispered remarks followed whose meaning she could not make out, there was more giggling, and then came another sharp blow to the back of her head. "Help me!" said a voice in the instant following this blow. "Oh please! Oh help! Stop!" Somewhere in the distance, there was giggling.

"Please!" Gypsy murmured.

"Oh please!" the voice replied.

In my story, I made this torture carry on for about twenty minutes. Afterward, a fake trial occurred as Gypsy lay bleeding on the ground. In Syria, such trials are always theatrical affairs. There are spectators arrayed in a ring around an empty spot of pavement or patch of field. In the center of the ring, there stands a man in a robe. At his feet, an accused person kneels.

In these dramas, the central conceit is that after many years of ignoring it, humankind has once again resolved to submit itself to the law of God. When there are trials, the spectators tell themselves that they have gathered to watch this terrifying but holy instrument at work. For their part, the men who spill the blood pretend to themselves that through their violence, they are ridding their sacred space of filth. In Syria, such trials are a ghastly kind of reality TV in that it is obvious to all that a drama is being acted out yet there are no actors, nor is there a script. These dramas are often filmed. Over the ensuing days, the dramas spread through the social networks.

In my fictional trial, Gypsy admitted right away that she had had sex with Taylor. Blood was streaming through her hair. She wasn't inclined to contradict her interrogator. She confessed to not being married to Taylor. She confessed to having had sex with other men. When these confessions were finished, there was a pause in the questioning.

"This makes you a whore?" a voice asked—softly, in a tone of fake wonder, as if a minor revelation was at hand.

"Yes," Gypsy confessed, "a whore." A man was holding his boot against the back of her head. Now he ground her face into the earth. The blindfold came loose. A man grasped a clump of her hair, then pulled her face toward his.

"What?" he said. "You are a whore?"

She did not reply. A rain of cable blows hit the back of her thighs.

"Yes, yes! Please!" Gypsy screamed. "A whore! Please! A whore!"

After her trial, when Gypsy could no longer move or see, she lay in her pool of blood. The cable barbs had sunk themselves into the flesh at the base of her skull. A boot had staved in a section of the frontal bone over an eyelid.

I made Gypsy fall sleep in her pool of blood since this is how victims of torture in Syria often pass the nights after their trials. Toward dawn, I made the dim-witted driver come to check on her. Wondering at her breathing, which was carrying on smoothly enough at that point, he asked her if she was asleep. She did not move. "Want some potato chips, Gypsy?" he asked. I knew this guard well enough. I had conversed with dozens of such people during my eighteen months with Jebhat al-Nusra. The foot soldiers are often zealous torturers but I'm not sure they mean anything bad by it. Afterward, when they see what they've done, they don't always know how to behave. Some regret. Some would like to make things right. But how? They don't know and so they chat with their victims as if the victims had been a little bit in on the game, as if a round of fun had been had by all.

I know now that at about the time in which I was writing out my scene killing Gypsy, my former captors in the eye hospital in Aleppo were putting an actual woman to death in an actual trial. Naturally, they filmed the proceedings, which eventually went out in video form over the social networks. Thus, I can see now, as I could not see when I was writing, exactly how the trials occur. I can hear every word of dialog. When I miss an unfamiliar phrase or quotation, I can play the voices back for myself, as I could not do when I was listening to the sheikhs in the villa basement, for instance, or in the eye hospital, as they brought out their truths. Here is a still from the videotape one of the onlookers made of that trial.

These men were frequent visitors to our cells in and around Aleppo.

Now I know that the scene in real life corresponded in all the important elements to the one I was seeing in my imagination, inside my cell. Naturally, the woman does not want to kneel. Her hands have been cuffed behind her back. The men who used to come to my cell in the eye hospital have surrounded her. They have accused her of seeking to spread filth, corruption, and enmity for Islam through their sacred space—roughly what these men accused me of doing. She is an enemy of God, they have told her, as they told me. In her case, the crime for which these sheikhs wish to hold her to account is prostitution. She doesn't appear to understand.

"Please," she says. "What?" Perhaps she's a bit disoriented. I know that when I was in such situations, I was badly disoriented.

"On your knees," replies one of the Jebhat al-Nusra authorities.

"I want to see my children," she says. "Please!"

"Sit," says a man.

"What?" she says. "Please, for the sake of the Prophet."

Having pleaded with these assassins myself, I know how little interest they take in listening. They know what is to happen next. You can talk all you like. Talking cannot help. It might make matters worse.

At the end of the video, one of my jailers shoots the woman in the back of the head. The onlookers raise their Kalashnikovs into the sky. *"Allahu Akbar!"* they cry. The woman's blood leaks across the pavement.

Nowadays it seems to me that my writing out my version of such a killing in my cell more than a year after I knelt at these men's feet was my way of coming to terms with what had happened to me. My brain was sifting through the facts. It was storing some of the details away. Other bits seemed useful to me at the time, and so they poured out of my memory. I hadn't been aware of their presence at all.

In the end, of course, in my case, there was no killing. Matters for me culminated in an imaginary trial, in a made-up birch grove, among fictional beings. To be sure, there was an imaginary killing. I made Gypsy cling to a thread of life, as the Arabic phrase has it, for a day and a half, as I suspected some of my fellow prisoners clung to life after their trials. She died in the early morning, on the forest floor, as her dim-witted driver fed himself from his bag of potato chips. Because this killing told the truth about my captors, I felt there was justice in it. In a way, I was proud of it because I felt that it showed the power that make-believe held over my world. In fact, it isn't so easy to believe that God's law has at last come to earth, that one's handgun is an instrument of God, and that in murdering a helpless woman in the street, one is bringing justice to Syria. Yet since the beginning of the war in Syria—and even now, under a different name, Hayat Tahrir as Sham-

Jebaht al-Nusra has been making such lies come true. When I was writing my drama, it seemed important to me to explain just how such wicked fantasies come to life. What words are spoken exactly? What is it like to witness such dramas and to play a role in them? I wanted to five the world my answers to these questions though of course I had no reason to suppose I would live long enough to have readers. I didn't care about this fact. I conjured imaginary readers into existence. In my mind, I spoke to them. I was keen for this public to see what I had seen of my Islamic state.

In those days, at the end of the day, when the light was dying in my cell, I would tuck my pen away, in a safe spot, underneath a blanket. The feelings that came to me after a day's writing weren't of satisfaction exactly, but I felt myself on a mission. I had a provisional sort of plot. I was sure that it was going to disclose important truths. Seeing the plot through gave purpose to my life, though of course I had no prospects, couldn't move much, wasn't allowed to talk to my neighbor prisoners, and could not press my face to any window. I didn't want to be killed, of course, but if destiny had written out a killing for me, I hoped it would be quick. And a long time from hence. In the meantime, I wasn't going to gnash my teeth over the matter. I felt I was living well enough, in a way, inside my cell. So during this period of my imprisonment, after my work was over, I sang to myself. I sang lots of songs. Sometimes, they were American folk songs. I liked to sing "Day by Day" from Godspell because it expressed sentiments of which I thought my captors would approve if they happened to hear me and because the words happened to have been stored, in a complete packet, in my memory. In those days, I especially liked to sing a song I listened to over and over the summer after my high school graduation. That song, "The Swimming Song" by Loudon Wainwright III, brought me back to time when everything in life stood before me. Death was a thousand years away. In my cell, the song made me smile. It buoyed my spirits and cooled me down. I had to trill and warble it to myself since, strictly

speaking, I wasn't allowed to sing. "This summer I went swimming,"
I warbled:

> This summer I might have drowned
> But I held my breath and I kicked my feet
> And I moved my arms around
> I moved my arms around.

CHAPTER 11

A VOYAGE WITH JEBHAT AL-NUSRA

One night in July of 2014, one of the two high commanders for al Qaeda in Syria, Abu Maria al-Qahtani, summoned me from my cell. He brought me to the Omar Company, in the desert outside of Meyadin, where he had established a training camp and an ersatz headquarters. "You will travel with us," he told me. He gestured at a crowd of fighters milling about in the darkness. They were to be my protection. We were soon to drive two hundred miles, at least, across the breadth of Syria, to the southern city of Deraa. After we arrived, he said, he would send me home.

During the subsequent voyage, which Abu Maria and I undertook in the company of some sixty pickups, two hundred fighters, and a dozen or so spiritual advisors, we drove overland, under the cover of darkness and without headlights. Allegedly, ISIS was pursuing us, though I suspect the commanders of the groups, who had been friends in childhood and maintained cell phone communication, had struck a deal.

During this voyage, our biggest danger was the Syrian Air Force. In the early mornings, after the prayer, when the planes began to appear in the sky our caravan blended into a village or a town. When there were no villages about we hid the trucks in caves or covered them in brush and parked them in drainage ditches or abandoned roadside shacks.

When we were moving, my attention fell on the countryside's new road signs. They appeared to have sprung up by chance: on the outskirts of the villages, on empty street corners, and sometimes all alone on a stretch of farming road. "All Muslims shall go to heaven. Happy is he who goes in the full flush of youth—Jebhat al-Nusra," read one. Other signs reminded people to turn off the lights on account of the Nusayri (Alawite) planes in the air and still others announced that a religious police enforced submission "to all things known"—which is to say, to the givens, the essential, universally agreed-upon framework of life under a Koranic dispensation.

In the mornings, at the end of our nightly voyage, as we arrived in a village, locals escorted the scholarly men in our caravan, the high military commanders, and me, their high-value prisoner, to a noble house. Here a man in a robe and slippers greeted the scholars with courtesies. Kisses were exchanged and then the host brought our group to the house's reception room. Usually, the curtains had been drawn. Usually, an immaculate, thick carpet such as one might find in a department store showroom stretched at our feet. There were stacks of pillows. Every divan we visited had a flat-screen television.

It was Ramadan then, but tradition allows for the traveler to eat during daylight hours, provided he makes up for his missed days later, so as the fighters laid their weapons across the carpet, bowls of a milky-lemony soup called *mlehi* appeared, and then came platters of chicken that had been decorated with sprinkled cashews and fresh coriander. Afterward, there were bowls of fruit, then tea, then sleep. We slept like hard-partying teenagers—everyone in his clothes, everyone sprawled on the floor, everyone out cold the second the hosts closed the sitting room door.

In the afternoons, there was more tea and the scholars received delegations of local sheikhs and the bodyguards of the sheikhs. The delegations appeared at the door of the sitting room in a single-file line. The travelers stood above their sitting cushions, at the periphery of the room. The delegation passed from traveler to traveler. The local sheikhs whispered pleasant words to the travelers. The bodyguards followed their bosses. God should give us health, they told us, and victory. He should guide us, and he should defeat the enemies of Islam, particularly the Jews and the Americans. After the greetings, the al Qaeda chief, Qahtani, made a speech. His speeches tended to say that ISIS exploited people's emotional connection to Islam, that ISIS was bound to come this way, and that when they did, they would lie about their intentions and lead the populace astray, as they had done in Deir Ezzor Province. The sheikhs must guard against the infiltration to come, he warned.

In one such house, after Qahtani had made his speech, a college-age fighter from Saudi Arabia came to pour my tea. Somehow, the jihad had brought him to this house in the desert. He poured the tea by tip-toeing to the sides of his guests, kneeling, holding out his platter with one hand, pouring from a teapot with the other, saying nothing, smil-ing not at all, then lowering his head. He held himself in this attitude until his guest decided to reach for his glass of tea.

I recognized this young man's head scarf as a Yemeni head scarf. Now we had the basis for a conversation. He spoke formal, well-educated classical Arabic and, by the way, excellent English. His two brothers, he said, had set out for the jihad in Syria some time ago. They had already been martyred. In his opinion, his parents in Saudi Arabia had been delighted by this news. The mujahideen were winning in Syria now, he said, and his generation of fighters was a charmed, destined generation.

I had been told to introduce myself to people we met along the way as an Irish fighter, Abu Mostafa al-Irlandi, who had come to Syria to seek martyrdom. Before our group left the house that evening, I sought out the Saudi fighter. I volunteered a bit of my Irish cover story. I doubt he believed me. My Arabic isn't drenched in religious locutions as is usually the case with the foreigners in the jihad. I would have stood out for my secular, informal way of speaking and for my questions about car racing in Saudi Arabia, the unchaste TV channels there, and the subjects he had studied at his secular English-language university.

Perhaps he had been an economics student? I can't remember. Anyway, he had hoped to pursue his studies in the West. Yet the jihad had intervened. Fighting now was an obligation. He thanked God for allowing him the steadiness of mind and body to carry on the jihad. It was a joyful time in his life, he said, and he had come to know the Syrian people as he never had before. Also, he had come to know brothers from all over the Earth, and this was a blessing. I was the first Irish brother he had encountered.

I half-hoped then to exchange email addresses or Facebook pages with this young man, but there was an unspoken rule against such exchanges, at least for me, and anyway, I had given him my cover story. It rhymed with the tenor of the time and place, even if the details would not have withstood much questioning. He had given me his. That was that. One doesn't probe for deeper truths in these sorts of situations, probably because the scholars know that the delusions the young men are asked to build for themselves in the jihad crumble like sand castles the moment two rational beings begin discussing them. So we shook hands. He wished for God's guidance for me and I wished it for him. In this way, nothing disturbed the fiction we had agreed on without speaking a word about it: that death was delightful, that we would both be martyred soon, that the sheikhs around us were wise, and that a benevolent God was guiding our jihad and so sowing victories across the land.

In the evening, an hour or so after we left the house in which this Saudi was employed, our caravan came to a crossroads in the desert. I happened to be riding at the head of the caravan, in the rear jump seat, in Qahtani's pickup cab. The last glow of daylight was leaving the sky. At the crossroads, Qahtani drew his pickup to a stop then asked me to get out of the car. For a moment, I stood in front of his pickup in my bare feet gazing into his face. What did he have in mind? His eyes smiled. Islam imposed upon him, the leader of this expedition, he explained, a solemn obligation: During the course of a voyage, it was his duty to ride at the front of his army. I nodded. The wind blew his curly black locks, which he wore at shoulder length, across his face. He pointed down the crossroad that led into the South. "Down there is Daesh," he said. He pointed into the North. "Up there is the regime"— the Syrian Arab Army. We were to follow the road leading into the West. In order to ensure that the sixty-odd vehicles behind us, some of which were trailing at a distance of several kilometers, followed the correct path, I was to plant myself here, at the crossroads. I was to indicate the proper path. "You can do this?" he asked.

"Happily," I replied.

The final pickup in the column of pickups was driven by Qahtani's nephew, an Iraqi from Samara, who went by the name Hud-Hud. In the Koran, Hud-Hud is a wise, all-seeing bird. I was to wait until I saw Hud-Hud's truck, then climb in with him. "You can do this?" Qahtani asked me.

"Happily," I said.

At first, when the first pickup trucks rolled by, I leveled blank-faced stares at the drivers. I pointed into the West. I had a job to do. I meant to do it well. Yet so many of the drivers seemed to know me, no doubt from visits to my cell block during the previous ten months, so many of them tooted their horns as they passed, and so many of the passengers waved merry greetings to me from their pickup beds that I found it hard, after a moment, to stand like a post beside the crossroads. The sheer zaniness of this Jebhat al-Nusra army made me smile. The first two dozen trucks in its column of fighting vehicles were regulation late-model white Toyota Hiluxes. After that the army became a circus caravan. There were doddering Syrian army troop carriers, a pair of Chevy pickups, possibly from the eighties (or seventies?), a little flock of Kia Rios (the Kia Rio was thought to be nimbler than other cars and so useful for urban combat), and toward the rear a fuel truck that tinkled the contents of its tank across the desert floor. When a merchant in an Arab souk wishes to welcome a group of customers into his shop, he will step aside, then sweep his hand over the path before him like a performer bowing on a stage. "Tafadaloo," he will say, meaning "Right this way, please." And also, "Welcome!"

"Tafadaloo!" I called out to the passing drivers. They wouldn't have been able to hear me. There was too much wind, too many tooting horns, and the truck engines were making a racket. They could, however, see me yelling. They flashed their headlights at me. They tooted their horns.

In some of the Damascus neighborhoods, the merchants call out to passersby in Farsi, since the Damascus tourist trade relies so heavily on revenue from Iranian pilgrims. *"Bi farma!"* I called out to the drivers, using the Farsi phrase the Damascus merchants used to welcome these passersby. So I was calling out in an enemy language. What did I care? I was feeling the wind in my hair. I was enjoying the wildness that is a Jebhat al-Nusra caravan. Probably, I thought, I could get used to this sort of life.

For reasons I did not understand or inquire into, our route took us through the eastern outskirts of Damascus. Out there, we passed through neighborhoods that looked like a film director's notion of the apocalypse. The director had clearly overdone it. Cement chunks hung from the upper stories of apartment buildings like slabs of frosting from a crumbling triple-decker cake. Lampposts flopped into the street. Balconies drooped; entire facades of buildings slid away from their foundations and sagged into the street. It wasn't one or two blocks that made you marvel at the destruction but the way it went on, mile after mile, each ruin leading into another, every street strewn with rubble, everything abandoned, and everything a live target. There were Jebhat al-Nusra rebels about. Why wouldn't they bomb more?

We drove through some streets that hadn't been inhabited in years. Greenish-yellow leafy stalks like Syrian goldenrod climbed the front stairs of the apartment blocks. Dead cars sat in front of chained-up gates. Everywhere, phone wires lay like loops of spaghetti salad over the property dividers.

In other neighborhoods, there were signs of life. Laundry fluttered. Children sold gasoline from oil drums. Now and then, beneath the bridge abutments or behind a crumpled roll-up storefront gate a circle of chairs had been arranged around a teakettle. Often, turning down a street, we came across little knots of resistance fighters. They lounged in the shade of a tank or milled about next to an artillery piece. We asked them about the state of the roads ahead. They consulted their radios, waited a few seconds for news, then waved us on.

When we arrived on the outskirts of the southern city of Deraa the roads were safe enough for us to drive in columns. Our columns sped through checkpoints, which had once been manned—but were manned no more—by the Western-friendly rebel army in Syria, the Free Syrian Army. Every once in a while, our convoy slowed to examine the roadside shacks from which the Free Syrian Army soldiers had once monitored their checkpoints. The shacks had been painted in the red, green, and white of the Free Syrian Army, as had the curbs nearby. The Free Syrian Army soldiers, however, had faded away. Now various black flags, all of which bore the words "there is no god but God," fluttered above the checkpoint shacks.

During this voyage, I was often seated over the Jebhat al-Nusra bank. It took the form of plastic shopping bags stuffed with cash. It was located on the floor behind the driver's seat in Abu Maria al-Qahtani's Toyota Hilux. It held US dollars and Syrian liras.

As we traveled, I watched the sub-commanders withdraw money from this bank. They would put the cash in the breast pockets of their robes, return to their trucks, then speed away in a cloud of sand. The more I watched these transactions, the easier it was for me to guess at how the Islamic armies had overcome the other rebel groups.

When the Jebhat al-Nusra brigades moved through Syria, many of the soldiers traveled in bare feet, as I was traveling then. The soldiers dressed in *shalwar kameez*, clothing for an Arab army of yesteryear. They used head scarves to control their hair rather than, say, a barber. This is how the Prophet of God is thought to have dealt with his hair. He ate with his hands, as we did, and brushed his teeth with a *siwak*, or minty stick. So did we. In our army, the soldiers didn't necessarily ask for food—or anyway, the fighters were happy to subsist on bread and NGO-donated tinned sardines. They slept in the sand when necessary. On those occasions, the soldiers made their ablutions with dust rather than water—a tradition of the pious and the poor.

They weren't doing this, as they often reminded me, to advance a military purpose; still less were they interested in politics or money. They fought to make the golden time of Islam come again. And now

Muslims from across the world had noted its coming. And so they, too, were pouring into the Land of Sham.

In other words, Jebhat al-Nusra had an excellent myth for Syria then. In the areas in which we traveled, that myth prevailed because an army of believing storytellers, excellent salesmen all, carried it from village to village. In each place, they recited the sacred texts, then lived out the myth. No doubt the villagers assumed, as I had assumed when I was a prisoner, that the army itself was propelled by inhuman powers, a force of nature. The villagers' role was to be bountiful hosts and to thank God for victories. This they did with appropriate, customary respect for ceremony—also with delicious tea.

Of course the scholars played a role in dressing up Jebhat al-Nusra's doings as natural phenomena. The scholars' function, as far as I could determine, was to tweet. As I discovered later, on coming home, they tweeted about ISIS's transgressions against the sharia, the foreignness of ISIS versus the Syrianness of Jebhat al-Nusra, and of their hero, the fourteenth-century philosopher Ibn Taymiyyah, who also had an apocalyptic turn of mind and also led a war, eight centuries ago, against the Alawites.

When they were not tweeting, the scholars sat on cushions next to Abu Maria al-Qahtani. They nodded as he spoke and embraced him when he finished speaking. (For instance, like this: On the next page is a photo of one of the big Jebhat al-Nusra scholars, Abu Hassan al-Kuwaiti, sucking up to his hero, the Iraqi Abu Maria.)

Qahtani needed these men's authority in small matters, for instance in deciding whether or not to permit the sale of cigarettes, and in more consequential ones, for instance in deciding when to deploy the explosive-laden suicide truck.

That summer in Jebhat al-Nusra, impassioned discussions concerning martyrdom operations swirled among the lower-ranking fighters. ISIS was thought to use the bombers much too frequently and at the behest of unlearned, uncaring commanders.

Jebhat al-Nusra was better because it sought religious counsel in

From Abu Hassan al-Kuwaiti's Twitter feed in
October of 2014: Abu Hassan, a Jebhat al-Nusra
religious authority, hugs Abu Maria al-Qahtani, a
military authority.

every case. Perhaps the counselors quibbled from time to time (I wasn't
present during these consultations), but because Qahtani controlled the
army's physical force and because the scholars seemed to leap whenever it was time to wrap their arms around the sheikh, I had the impression that Qahtani generally got what he wanted.

In their own way, the suicide bombers themselves conferred moral
authority on Qahtani. In this part of the world, when young men come
to you who do not cling to life but plunge themselves into death, when
they keep coming, year after year, the coming is understood as a natural phenomenon and a sign from God. "Our terror is a blessed thing,"
says a line from a Jebhat al-Nusra war hymn. "All the soldiers have

pledged themselves to the mullah, and our souls are now with God."
"To heaven we will go, martyred in the millions," goes another street
chant, and also: "We are all of us Jebhat al-Nusra." The children on the
street know the words to these chants. Often, as I discovered later, on
YouTube, the children lead the crowds.

So Qahtani's power over nature derived from the religious men
who accompanied us, the poverty of the soldiers, the soldiers' piety,
their willingness to be used as suicide bombers, and in a deeper sense
his power derived from the plastic shopping bags. What if he were no
longer able to buy gas for the trucks? Explosives for the suicide trucks?
What of the future of the jihad then? Everyone knows that there is no
future without the plastic shopping bags. Similarly, everyone knows
that the millions of dollars in cash a rebel army requires to pursue its
war comes from only two sources: the sale of Western hostages and
control over the oil fields.

The sixty-odd trucks following us through the desert were moving
west to open up new fronts: Some were to establish themselves in the
embattled Damascus suburbs, some were going to the Lebanese border at Qalamoun, and some would set up in the Syrian Golan. No one
would have traveled a centimeter farther if everyone were not confident that the black plastic bags were essentially bottomless, an ever-
flowing stream.

This is what I learned during my voyage: that the jihad is a conjur-
ing trick, that it shimmers like a mirage but is yet real because everyone
agreed that Abu Maria al-Qahtani and his former childhood friend, Abu
Bakr al-Baghdadi, would have cash until the end of time.

Most sheikhs in the jihad are wise. Many are wise and violent. Many
have wealthy friends in Qatar and Kuwait who throw them a suitcase
of cash now and then. But that kind of cash is pocket change compared
to what you get for a Western hostage. It's less than zero compared to
the amount you get from an oil well. In order to get the oil wells, you
need the suicide bombers who will drive the kamikaze trucks that open
up the roads. Once you control the roads, it's easy enough to control
the prisons that house the Western hostages.

Only a few sheikhs have the religious learning that attracts lieutenants, the wild violence that subdues the public, the will to get the Western hostages, the prisons to hold them, the wherewithal to negotiate with foreign governments, and the power to deploy the suicide bombers. Those sheikhs are at the top of the ISIS chain of command and at the top of the al Qaeda chain. There are other leaders out there in the field, of course. But no one brings in the cash, the suicide bombers, and the hostages like al Qaeda and ISIS. Since these were the essential elements for victory in the Syrian jihad, and since all the young men wanted to win, all the young men wanted to be with these two groups. The humbler, smaller, less ambitious military bands eventually picked up sticks, then faded into the undergrowth.

I found during this voyage, I could not take my eyes off the destroyed cityscapes but when you spend a few weeks traveling the countryside in Syria in the company of Jebhat al-Nusra, the changes that really take your breath away are the psychological ones. By the summer of 2014, the parts of Syria through which I was traveling had been under attack from the air for three and a half years.

You can observe the effects of the violence the world has been sending to Syria in the behavior of the children. When the planes left the sky, the eight-year-old kids would come running. They sprinted through the rubble, kicked their soccer balls into destroyed storefronts, and stared at the sky. They had been spared yet again. You could hear the joy in their voices. They had been terrorized. You could hear that in their voices, too. "God is greater than you, O Bashar!" they called out. They chanted, "O Allah, O Allah, we have only you, O Allah."

The state of mind that comes over you when you've lived in a bombing zone for years and have watched others die but remain alert and alive yourself isn't exactly PTSD. It isn't radical Islam, whatever that is.

It is certainly love of God. It is longing for revenge. It is a belief in the sufficiency of the Koran and the rituals, a fear of the consequences of not praying, and a hatred of anyone or anything that would get in the way of the prayer. It is not intense communion with jihadist philosophers of old. Perhaps a few of the scholars keep themselves busy in this way, but I'm not sure many people listen to these talkers. Anyway, the sustenance that people derive from reciting the Koran, a memorized form of music most Syrians learn in childhood, is a thousand times more powerful than anything a philosopher might say.

I know a bit about this state of mind because when I was held with other prisoners it took over our jail cells. The state of mind is a helplessness before the coming death. It is belief in a miraculous deliverance. It is poring through the Koran in search of a way to survive, then escape, then slip away to a better life. Yet the way out doesn't come. What then? There is more bombing and more praying. In the streets, deep into the night, by crowds of two hundred men, there is more chanting: "O Allah, O Allah, we have nothing left but you, O Allah."

One afternoon, during my voyage through the desert, a low-level fighter, one of the al Qaeda leader's bodyguards, told me of a prophecy to the effect that in a future time all the world was to abandon the Muslims and the great majority of the Muslims would themselves abandon Islam. In that hour, only a tiny kernel of believers would keep the faith. They would be under threat from enemies abroad and saboteurs within. In this hour of danger, they would memorize the sacred book. They would preserve the faith by laying down their lives at the slightest provocation and by transferring a love of memorizing and martyrdom to converts and to children. There would come a time, this fighter said, when every Koran in the world would be mutilated or burned and the only extant Korans would reside in the brains of the memorizers. God would never kill these memorizers, he told me, but would rather preserve them, even when the walls of their houses were crashing in on them.

The psychology in the bombed-over areas is a belief in this variety of prophecy. It is a belief that signs of the end of time are emerging in the land now. What is this destruction around us? What is this deepening of the faith? What is this ingathering of the world's truest Muslims if not a portent of the apocalypse?

The state of mind is the state of being under siege. Evil lurks in the darkness, just outside your door. Yet the whole world is against you. If somehow you were to kill the wolf at the door, what would this accomplish? Nothing. Beyond lie forests filled with wolves and the entirety of the globe, wherever Islam does not hold sway, is itself such a forest. Your protectors are the people who eat and pray with you. They are your truest, most loving family. The Koran is your moonbeam of hope. This is what will deliver you.

I was indignant at first when I saw how calm, even satisfied, the scholarly men were when the airplanes appeared in the sky. Every time the airplanes seemed to circle, they had their drivers race them away to hide in bunkers. What about us, the rank and file?

Later, however, after I got used to the Syrian Air Force, I saw the excitement that pulsed through the soldiers whenever the word *"Tayara!"* ("Airplane!") went up from the caravan. The soldiers tried to film the airplanes as they passed over us. They competed with one another in indifference to danger. Toward the end of our voyage, the reasons for the scholars' satisfaction at the appearance of the airplanes became clearer to me. They needed the planes and wanted them to come. Had they not prophesied of the tiny community of believers surrounded by enemies? So it had come to pass. Had they not foreseen how the enemy would destroy the mosques and the Korans? So it had come to pass. What about the empty cities through which we passed? The trains of refugees on their way, even then, to Europe? Had scholars not foreseen how the Muslims would turn their backs on their brothers, then flee into unbelief? So it had come to pass.

As for the airplanes, at this point, some of them were from Russia. Others might well have been from America. What did we know? What did it matter? Those airplanes showed how united the terrestrial powers were and how apocalyptic their destruction could be. Every bomb they dropped deepens the credibility of the men who channeled the prophecies. As the credibility of these men deepened, so did the power of the true authorities in the jihad: Abu Bakr al-Baghdadi, Abu Maria al-Qahtani, Abu Mohammed al-Jolani, and Abu Mohammed al-Adnani. When I was traveling with Jebhat al-Nusra, it occurred to me that one day, the war planners in Washington, London, and Paris would probably conclude that bombing Syria doesn't accomplish much. Yes, it kills civilians. Yes, it can drive an insurgency underground.

The state of mind mind in the rebel-controlled parts of Syria is also hatred of the enemy who lurks within. Many of the young men in these areas still listen, in secret, to Michael Jackson and to Britney Spears (pop music there can lag a few years behind the current hits in the West). So they have the Islam-destroying, treacherous thought patterns inside their heads. They are also sheltering the enemy. The state of mind in the rebel-held areas is a will to do violence to all people and things—foreigners, gays, sexy women, DVDs, and laptops—that recall for the fighters how intimate their relations with the forbidden things really are.

CHAPTER 12

MY WAY OUT

On the morning of August 20, 2014, when the James Foley video appeared on TV screens across the world, I happened to be sitting on the floor beside a plush divan in a villa outside the southern city of Deraa, with the remote control in my hand. At my back, a half-dozen mid-level al Qaeda commanders were playing video games on their mobile phones. I read on the crawl: "American journalist James Foley killed in Syria." I glanced at the commanders at my back. They didn't appear to have noticed what was occurring on TV. I changed the channel, but the man in the orange jumpsuit was on the Syrian state television, Al Jazeera, Al Arabiya, BBC, France 24.

I was living then under a kind of house arrest. During most of the day, I was confined to a bedroom in the back of the villa, but in the mornings, when the important commanders were still asleep, and in the late afternoons, when teatime came around, the villa majordomo, a gracious, timid man called Abu Kenan, would invite me to the divan. Here I watched television and shot the breeze with the al Qaeda middle management.

The middle management must have tuned in to the news during the course of that day. In the early evening, when the commanders had again assembled themselves in front of the villa television, I was again permitted to emerge from my bedroom. They winked at me as I arranged myself in my normal spot, on the carpet, at their feet. One of them flashed his cell phone at me. It bore an image of a man in an orange jumpsuit, a knife at his throat.

In fact, all the commanders had the same video on their phones.

That afternoon, they played the video for themselves over and over. As I watched them pore over their screens, I could see their admiration for ISIS in their eyes. In their murmurs, I could hear how pleased the sight of an American on his knees, in his last moments, denouncing the American government for its folly in Iraq made them. In the glumness of their remarks about their own video production department, I could hear their disappointment in Jebhat al-Nusra. The world, they felt, had passed them by. Now their former colleagues—their old friends from the eye hospital in Aleppo—had made a hit video. It had transfixed the world. The Jebhat al-Nusra commanders had been reduced to idling their days away in in front of the television.

When at last they tired of watching James Foley's decapitation, one of the commanders sighed. "You see what kind of a group these ISIS people are?" he said, nodding at his phone. This commander assumed an air of indignation, as if he meant to invite me into a discussion of ISIS's savagery, but the way he kept fiddling with his phone so that the clip would play smoothly, from beginning to end, told me that the video hadn't offended him. It had rather titillated him. It was having a similar effect on all the commanders in the room. It made them want to share it with another via Bluetooth, to leer at me, and to brag about how much more Islamic—and humane and decent—their group was than ISIS. Of course, ISIS, having won its war with Jebhat al-Nusra, now controlled the oil in Syria's east. It could draw on cash reserves from the oil in Iraq. It moved about in flashy, combat-appropriate trucks. It had bigger guns. It was the world's preeminent terrorist organization, and Jebhat al-Nusra was yesterday's news.

I knew these men well enough to know that if an invitation to join the ISIS middle management had somehow popped up on their screens in those moments these men would have leapt into their trucks, then sped away to Raqqa. These men were trend followers, not trendsetters. They wanted the fancy trucks. They wanted their own faces on the news.

In those moments, as I lounged with the commanders, I pretended, as everyone did, that Jebhat al-Nusra was much too kind to murder an American journalist prisoner, but later, in the evening, when I was by myself in the villa, my old terror before my captors took hold of me. It seemed to me that no time at all had passed, that I was back in my cell in the eye hospital basement, and that on the other side of the cell door, a little band of men, some in baseball caps, some in robes, was working out the most enjoyable way to kill me. I listened for their footsteps. When the wind caused a door in a distant room to slam, a jolt of terror went down my spine.

For ISIS, it seemed to me, the James Foley video had been a stroke of genius. It brought ISIS to the front page of every newspaper in the world. For a few moments, at least, it held humankind under a kind of a spell. As the world gasped, the ISIS assassin gave a lecture. "You, the Americans, are liars." "Today, we are slaughtering you." "This knife will become your nightmare." And so on. I had heard the Arabic version of that lecture a thousand times. Of course my captors will kill me, I thought, since they have always dreamed of entrancing the world. Now they knew just how to get the job done: by showing an American journalist on his knees in an orange suit, a knife at his throat. My captors had the motive. They had the weapons and the opportunity. When, I wondered, would they get to work?

In the villa bedroom, I fretted along these lines for several hours. Then I reflected: So my fate lay in the hands of a band of terrorists. The band might have been preparing to kill me. It might also have been planning to spare me. Perhaps my death had been decreed long ago. Perhaps not. I had been here before.

In the past, especially in my first weeks, in the eye hospital basement, my terror had incapacitated me. I had gaped at my captors like a victim in a slasher movie. My lot, I thought, was to be stupefied, to shriek, and then to die. Yet the longer I sat on the bedspread in the villa bedroom, the more that terror-struck person in the hospital basement seemed like a stranger to me. I understood his predicament well enough. I sympathized. But I was no longer he.

Now, twenty-two months on, it felt to me as though I could see through the Islamic statelet in which I had been living. All the middle managers fancied themselves mighty warlords. Each had a pickup truck, a Glock in a shoulder holster, and a line of talk about freeing the

Muslims of the world from injustice. I felt that while the outside world viewed these men as a threat to global stability, I knew them to be too dim to fix their own pickup trucks. Medicine was beyond them. So was organizing an elementary school.

I felt that I knew the details of their gimcrackery well enough to show how the operation worked. They fawned over their sacred spaces. They murdered the people who lived there. Their caliphate was an elaborate real estate scam. Their MO was to blow things up, to stride around in the guise of lawgivers for as long as the illusion held, to summon, via the world's social networks, all those dim or needy enough to submit to their law, and finally, when local conditions got too hot, to slip out of town in the night. Like all scam artists, their highest purpose was to keep their con rolling.

Though I was as terrified by my captors as I had ever been, I was less taken in. Their power was in their guns and their knives. They did not incarnate a principle in the nature of Syria, as I had supposed during moments of terror, or when I was stood in the desert, in awe, before their mighty columns of pickup trucks. I had bumbled into a colony of brutes. They were to be feared no more—and no less—than other brutes.

During the course of my voyage through the desert with Jebhat al-Nusra, the sheaf of papers on which I had scribbled out my Vermont story sat stuffed in the depths of my cargo pants pockets. I would not have dared to set pen to paper in front of the Jebhat al-Nusra army. Anyway, in the desert, I did not have a pen.

In the villa bedroom, however, I did. Now, as the image of the American journalist on his knees in the desert played before my eyes, my thoughts returned to my story. The men who killed Gypsy, it seemed to me, had done it because they were too lazy and too brutish to understand that their torture could crush the life out of a person. I had been thinking of my departed cell neighbor, the *mokhtar* of Marat, Sheikh Hussein, when I wrote about Gypsy's death. I had in mind beatings to which I submitted and Jebhat al-Nusra's general habit of pushing their torture victims outward, to the very edge of life. The Foley killing, in contrast, had been an expression of state policy. It had been designed to mesmerize the world. For his part, James Foley had been a mere prop. His killer had shaken Foley's head as if the killer felt that he was shaking a doll's head. It seemed to me that in drawing the portrait of my evil society, I had yet to reckon with this variety of cold-bloodedness. Yet was it not all around me? I had lived every moment of the previous twenty months within it, it seemed to me, and somehow, in my portrait of my society, I overlooked it. How inadequate to its purpose my tale is, I told myself, and how badly I have underestimated my captors.

I pulled out my pen and paper. I crossed out an earlier chapter. I set about correcting my oversight right away.

This turned out to be an auspicious time for writing. It was August in southern Syria. An unchanging, drowsy torpor had settled over the landscape. The sky was gray in the mornings, bluish gray in the afternoons, and turned through a range of pastel pinks in the evenings. All day long, a steady breeze rolled down from the Golan Heights. It lifted the lacy curtains in my bedroom window. It ruffled my T-shirt and, when I didn't think to weight them down, sent the pages of my Vermont story scattering across the floor.

At the time, the war, for Jebhat al-Nusra, was somebody else's business. It happened that a detachment of Free Syrian Army troops had arrayed its artillery in an olive grove a few kilometers to the east of the Deraa suburb, as Saida, in which Jebhat al-Nusra had settled itself. The Syrian Arab Army had arrayed itself along the Amman-Damascus highway, a few kilometers to our west. Now and then, the Syrian government would send artillery barrages over our heads, into the olive groves. The sound of the artillery whooshing over the roofs of the villas would rouse the commanders from their couches. They would wander to their villa rooftops, then stand around like spectators at an aeronautics show. As the sky filled with missiles, they would point their cell phone cameras at the sun. They would call out to the commanders on neighboring rooftops, wait for the sound of explosions to echo across the landscape, whistle at one another for a little while, and when the excitement had passed, after fifteen minutes or so, would wander downstairs, to the comfort of their sitting rooms.

At the time, the division of Jebhat al-Nusra of which I was a prisoner imagined itself to be a kind of high directorate of the international jihad. The division's leader, Abu Maria al-Qahtani, famous in Syria for having been an intimate of the al Qaeda in Iraq leader, Abu Musab al-Zarqawi, and a lieutenant of the ISIS leader, Abu Bakr al-Baghdadi, wished to build a new al Qaeda from the ground up. Naturally, he would be in charge. In order to accomplish his goals, he required more acolytes, more money, and more military equipment. That August, having too little of all of these things, he resolved to enlist the support of the important terrorist leaders in Jordan and southern Syria. Would they care to join him, he said in speeches he and an assistant recorded on video, in his villa in as Saida for a kind of rolling symposium on the purpose of terrorism in the twenty-first century? When these sheikhs turned up in our villa, vigorous discussion ensued. Was Bashar al-Assad to be ignored or dislodged? What use was the al Qaeda name? Should the men of ISIS be held to account for their crimes or should they be thought of as brother Muslims who'd gone astray? Qahtani was keen to punish the French government for its attempts to suppress the spread of al Qaeda in Mali. Accordingly, there was talk of opening a Jebhat al-Nusra chapter in Paris. But the idea presented difficulties. Qahtani didn't seem to know anyone in Paris. And should Jebhat al-Nusra allow worries over Mali to diffuse its fighting power? Such were the questions Qahtani addressed in his villa summits. As he spoke, the flat-screen TV at the head of the room played images from the war the Israeli air force had lately initiated over Gaza. After the speeches, there were ablutions, then a collective prayer.

Nobody was asking my opinion, of course, but al Qaeda's enterprises of great pitch and moment seemed to me to suffer under the endlessness of Abu Maria's speeches. Perhaps the torpor of the afternoons also worked to drain the energy from these meetings. Perhaps the rank and file were too aware that the nation of Qatar was about to drop a prodigious cash bomb on this part of Jebhat al-Nusra. Already some of the middle managers had discovered that a flashy white sneaker, evidently not available in the Deir Ezzor suqs, was to be found at an interesting price in the Deraa suqs. Among these men, there were new cases for their cell phones, new perfume, and talk of new pickup trucks. Kitted out in their "noolook," to borrow a phrase that has worked its way into Arabic, they drowsed during their afternoon meetings. From about three thirty in the afternoon to just before the evening prayers, Abu Maria pontificated about the future of the international jihad. Should the mujahideen move on to Jerusalem? Paris? In the future, when ISIS had been defeated, would it be possible to consider an ISIS fighter who had killed a Muslim a Muslim? Some of the voices in Abu Maria's divan said yes. Others said no.

Abu Maria wanted me to be present at some of these meetings. Before certain audiences, he wanted me to introduce myself, if the topic should come up, which it never did, as my alter ego, Abu Mustafa al-Irlandi, the martyr-to-be from Dublin. Other audiences seemed aware that I was a journalist, and that I was soon to be ransomed away. I suspect that for these colleague terrorists, who happened to be from Jordan and Iraq, my presence in Abu Maria's divan proved that he was about to be a very rich man.

When I wasn't trying to follow the gist of Abu Maria's speeches, I was in my villa bedroom, spreading fictional terror across a fictional countryside. In order to tell the truth about ISIS and Jebhat al-Nusra, I had to confront the inhabitants of my imaginary town in Vermont with a shock to the system. I wanted the feeling of something new, unknowable, and malevolent abroad in the land. The malevolence seeped into people's minds. It snatched bodies. It attacked places and people the town loved. Though this menace didn't want to build anything of its own—though it identified itself, in poems it posted in prominent public places, only as "we"—it could not accept the idea of the community's emotions attaching themselves to something other than itself. In order to bring the reality of everyday existence under such a psychology to life in my story, I did as my captors did: I caused random people to suffer ghastly deaths. When I was done, I allowed a few days to pass, enough time for the dread to work its way into people's dreams, then my story found something new to destroy. I destroyed that.

In the days following James Foley's murder, Abu Kenan, the man in charge of tea in my villa, brought ever more specific news about the nature of the deal under which I was to be freed to my bedroom. It was his job to serve tea to Abu Maria's inner circle. As important phone calls were made and received over tea, the tearoom, it seemed to me, was the place in which news broke. About two days after the Foley killing, Abu Kenan's news was that I was to be freed in the evening, in Jordan. But which evening? Where in Jordan? He didn't know. A few days later, the site of my freeing switched to a UN camp on the Israeli-Syria border. The ransom was to be $20 million. The following morning, as Abu Kenan poured tea in my bedroom, he whispered that the ransom had become €11 million. It had, he said, already been delivered.

A day later, Abu Maria appeared in the morning, in the TV divan in which he conducted his meetings. I was sipping tea on a couch. Abu Maria strode into the center of the room in his boots. He did not greet Abu Kenan. He did not greet me. He nodded in my direction. "Get your things," he announced. "Today, we are sending you to your mother."

Beyond the villa patio, at the edge of an olive grove, a line of three pickup trucks stood waiting. I climbed into the jump seat in the second truck. As we rolled down as Sadia's central boulevard, Abu Maria, who drove the pickup at the head of our column, barked orders over his two-way radio. He demanded that the convoy stop in front of a street-side shanty. On the sidewalk in front of the shanty, a rack of football jerseys fluttered in the breeze. A pair of teenagers who had been sitting in plastic chairs next to the football jerseys rose, took a step forward, then stopped themselves. They gaped at Jebhat al-Nusra's clean, white, late-model pickups. They eyed the guards in the pickup passenger seats. These men were dressed as if for a battle. They wore their bullet belts over their shoulders and strapped around their waists.

A lieutenant disembarked from our truck. He strolled to Abu Maria's window. The two of them began a discussion. A part of me thought it possible that Abu Maria was instructing the lieutenant in how exactly my execution was to be carried out. A plot twist of that nature would have been in line with what I knew of Abu Maria's character. He liked to keep people guessing. He loved surprises. It turned out that the purpose of our stop was to provision me with a new tracksuit. As the lieutenant handed me my new clothing, he smiled. He uttered a formal, polite phrase. They wouldn't be speaking to me this way if they meant to shoot me, I thought. They would only be giving me new clothes if they felt that I would soon be appearing, alive and well, on the news. Abu Maria had often hinted to me that, should I be released, he would appreciate it if I spoke well of Jebhat al-Nusra. Apparently, for my first appearance before the TV cameras, he also wanted me to look well.

As our line of pickup trucks rolled south, a guard with whom I had become friendly during the preceding weeks removed his cell phone from a pocket. Raising it to eye level and pointing the camera lens at me, he began an interview. "You are going home," he said, grinning. "What do you think?" I grinned back at him. He wanted me to say good-bye to the villagers of Asheyl. Over the preceding ten months, it seemed to me, I had come to know every last one of them. I salaamed a dozen *abus*. The guard, Muthana, prompted me to make comical remarks about a ten-year-old child, a certain Abu Jasem, the son of one of the commanders, who had often pointed his child-sized Kalashnikov at my head. When I used the villa bathroom, Abu Jasem liked to bang the butt of his Kalashnikov against the toilet door. "Hurry, you don-key!" he would call out. He had been a brat, it seemed to me, but he wasn't evil. I wanted him to laugh if he should watch Muthana's video. I wanted to leave all the Asheylis with good memories, and so as Abu Muthana fed me the names of the important villagers, I smiled into the camera. I made warm, funny remarks, as if they were my uncles, as if I were setting out for a distant land, as if my parting, for all of us, were a sweet sorrow.

Looking back now, I don't think my good-bye video was altogether a lie. I was aware that I was leaving their dream. During the previous weeks, it had not been an unpleasant place. The war had been close enough to supply occasional thrills but distant enough to be no business of ours. As the rockets sailed overhead, there had been ample food, sun-filled divans, and much talk about the brave, enchanting jihad to come. As the terrorists dreamed their dream, in my bedroom, eyeing my growing stack of manuscript pages, I dreamed mine.

It took us much of the morning and some of the afternoon to drive the thirty-odd kilometers from as Saida to the Israeli border. We followed a labyrinth of goat tracks. We crossed the blacktop roads now and then but never drove on them. During the late morning, a line of observation towers on the Jordanian side of the border appeared in the windows on the left-hand side of our truck. Shortly before the midafternoon prayer, the trucks rolled through a string of farming villages in the Syrian Golan. Walls made of disorderly piles of limestone blocks lined the roadways. Here and there, purple wildflowers poked from the clefts in the rocks, as in the Yorkshire highlands. In one of the villages, a cluster of shade-tree mechanics worried over a motorcycle that had expired by the side of the road. A few meters farther on, an elderly woman picked her way through the grass at the side of the road. The hem of her abaya trailed in the mud. She lowered her face as we passed.

Muthana was still playing with his mobile phone. He watched a moment of my video, then smiled at me. Whenever I liked, he said gently, I could come back. My return would be conditioned on a conversion to Islam. If I were to convert, Muthana said, I would be welcomed with open arms, as a brother. I could work for the jihad as a journalist.

I didn't like the idea of working for the jihad, but in those moments, a part of me regretted leaving my terrorist friends. I had learned so much about the jihad, Islam, life, and death in their company. Had I stayed, I might have learned so much more. I would certainly have gone deeper into my writing. Another part of me felt that during the previous two years, I had become a victim of the war in Syria, that my true kin were the shade-tree mechanics and the old woman hobbling by the roadway, and that if I were to rush away to America, I would be breaking faith with them. I didn't want to think about the suffering that lay in store for them. Would it not be right to stick it out with the victims of the war, come what may?

Toward sundown that evening, after Abu Maria had delivered me into the care of a garrison of UN troops at a camp on the Syria-Israel border, the UN troops brought me to a gate, on the western side of their camp, that opened into the Israeli Golan. On the other side of this gate, a pair of SUVs, dispatched from the US embassy in Tel Aviv, waited for me.

The sight of American officials in golf shirts brought me up short. Right away, it was obvious to me that they were Americans. But that they should be here, in leisure wear, in the midst of a war zone, when Jebhat al-Nusra was everywhere around us, didn't seem altogether plausible. Was I dreaming? I wanted to touch the officials. Only when I felt the solidity of their flesh in my hands, I thought, would I know that they would not dissolve, as mirages do, when I stepped toward them.

An FBI agent introduced herself to me. During the previous two years, she said, she and my mother had been collaborators in the effort to bring me home. I nodded. My mother? The FBI? I was willing to listen to this person on a provisional basis, to humor her, to see what might unfold, but I wasn't quite ready to believe in a tale about the FBI coming to the aid of my mother.

A few minutes later, when the SUV was coasting down an Israeli highway, the FBI agent pulled her cell phone from her pocket. "I have to call your mom," she said.

She herself could call my mother all she liked, I told her, but I knew that the sound of my mother's voice was going to cause a general system failure in my emotional circuitry. I worried that if I were to start crying, I wouldn't be able to stop. I declined the chat with my mom. I did, however, want to strike up a conversation with the FBI agent. I didn't care whether I came across as a chatterbox or not. I hadn't spoken more than a few words of English since the previous summer, when I argued with Matt Schrier over how we ought to execute our escape. So much had happened to me since then. I was anxious to share my news.

As things turned out, it took me several weeks to make my way to Vermont. A cousin was getting married in New Jersey. I felt like going to a wedding. There were other cousins to visit in Connecticut. My mother spends most of her time in Cambridge, Massachusetts. In late August, the Cambridge streets are busy with university students. The students schlep their belongings into dorm rooms. They flit along the Charles in sculls. Cambridge seemed like a land of dreams to me. I didn't want to leave it. As it happened, for weeks after my return, every remark, every falling leaf, every chance encounter, and every meal seemed like a miracle, designed by a loving providence just for me. When strangers in the street welcomed me home, as many did in those days, it was all I could do to keep myself from bursting into tears. Often I didn't bother.

It wasn't until October that my mother and I finally drove to the Vermont town I'd used as a model for the one in my novel. As we drove past the town green, my eye happened to fall on the village library patio. This patio—and especially the shade-giving maples that tower over it—had been much on my in my cell in Deir Ezzor. The place had seemed to me then the very picture of safety in small-town America. Yet in those days, I was anxious to tell a story about the smooth progress of evil in a place too serene to notice what was going on. Accordingly, in the story I wrote in my cell in Syria, the patio retained its aura of country calm but the place belonged to the evil forces in my book. They came and went as they pleased.

For an instant, as my mother and I drove past this library patio, it seemed to me that the fiction I had written about it in Syria was a matter of local fact. I was driving through a countryside beset by unseen killers, as I had lately been doing in Syria. The teenagers who lounged on on the library patio seemed to me, just for a moment, like lambs grazing before wolves. Because I had lately survived an encounter with such powers myself, it seemed to me that I knew how to cope with whatever was gathering in the shadows. And everyone else? The powers coming for the citizenry here, it seemed to me, couldn't be confronted because no one knew where they were and couldn't be reasoned with because they refused to communicate. They were, however, on the march. No one knew how to stop them.

A moment later, my mother and I drove past a high school soccer field. Already, I knew, a series of blood-curdling crimes had visited this community. In one episode, much reported in the local paper, a student—the star of the high school drama program—had been abducted, tortured, then left to die in a clearing in the forest.

I recalled some of the details of the crime. I knew, for instance, that during the torture, the victim had lost pints of blood. Afterward, some-how, she was able to sleep, but the next morning, when she woke, she felt she was dying of thirst. "Please!" she murmured to one of the tor-turers. He brought her a bottle of spring water. In order to make her more comfortable, he covered her body with his blue-jeaned jacket. Out of pity, he released her hands from her handcuffs. "You hungry, Gypsy?" he asked her. She could hear the young man speaking well enough, but because she was dying, she could not reply.

How terrifying the coming months would be, I thought.

For a few moments, as my mother and I drove, I was at a loss. The soccer jerseys flashed in the sunshine. I eyed a row of roadside houses. The evil that lingered in my imagination operated according to a logic no one could fathom. Perhaps it had no logic. When would it end? It goes on and on, I thought, because relentlessness is its nature.

My thoughts ran along these lines for a few moments, but even as I was thinking them, I was aware that I had come through my ordeal with my faculties intact. Was I so much bolder than anyone else? I was not and am not. If a destabilizing power were to establish itself here at home, I thought, my fellow citizens would live through a moment of shock, as I had done in Syria. But they were a robust lot. They were much stronger than they knew. In the fullness of time, they would gather themselves together. They would pitch themselves into the fray. Probably, they would come through it all with an enhanced apprecia-tion of life. Had not some such awakening of the spirit occurred to me after my ordeal in Syria?

After my ordeal, I had lived my first hours of freedom within a bub-ble of euphoria. It had seemed to me that I had died, been born again, and that a new life in America had been sent to me the way God some-times sends miracles to the bereft. I felt that the miracle could be taken from me at any moment. But the more I gazed at the field of soccer players, the more certain I was that the gifts I was looking on weren't only for me and that they had no expiry date. All of this is permanent, I wondered? Anyone can participate? Though I knew it would take a while for me to accommodate myself to such a world, I was pretty sure that, in the fullness of time, I would have at it.

ACKNOWLEDGMENTS

As of this writing, I know only a few details of the rescue operation that saved my life. Apparently, many millions of dollars were paid. By whom? To whom? How many millions, exactly? To what use is this money being put now? Certain high officials among the terrorists in Syria and the diplomats in Qatar, I assume, know the answers to these questions. I do not.

I do, however, know that three cousins of mine, Viva Hardigg, Betsy Sullivan, and Amy Rosen devoted two years of their lives to delivering me from Jebhat al-Nusra. I've tried to express a few of my feelings about these efforts in chapter 8 of this book. I'm aware that the little bit I've written there cannot do justice to all that these cousins did for me. Over the past six years, I've come to think that this family-based rescue project deserves a book of its own. Were such a book to be written, the imperturbability of my cousins Hill and Henry Carter, who devoted themselves to their mother, Viva, as she was devoting herself to my rescue would play a central role.

My mother, Nancy Curtis, was seventy-five when I disappeared. At the time, her job as the publications director for the Society for the Preservation of New England Antiquities in Boston entailed ninety minutes of commuting per day and a forty-hour workweek. When I was in prison in Syria, I knew, as children can know these sorts of things, that she was refusing to give up. I did not, however, suspect that she had established herself as the moral and spiritual leader of a kitchen-based command center for international hostage rescue. Of course, I ought to have guessed.

ACKNOWLEDGMENTS

In the hours following my release in August of 2014, I began to learn how many others came to our aid. My father, Michael Padnos, lobbied the world from his *péniche* in Joinville-le-Pont. When one is at death's door, as I was occasionally in Syria, love of this kind, which I knew he had for me, echoes in one's memory. I'm grateful to him for his passion on all important matters. I'm also grateful to the other members my *famille parisienne*, Sharron Welsh, Jacques Guyomarche, and Jöelle Chevalier. I realize that through the years, my father and I have been a handful. This Parisian family has responded to our many crises by offering us wine, food, and affection.

Since my return from Syria, five other families have looked after me. Though their graciousness has been obvious to all, they cannot know how much their kindness has meant to me. David and Katherine Bradley, John and Diane Foley, Ed and Paula Kassig, Art and Shirley Sotloff, Carl and Marsha Mueller—for the past six years, the bigheartedness of these people has accompanied me in everything I've done. Their selflessness humbles me.

When I was in Syria, the Atlantic Media staff members Shana Keefe, Aretae Wyler, and Emily Lenzner dedicated countless hours to my rescue. I am grateful to them beyond words. I'm also grateful to Enass Khan, Nasser Wedaddy, and to the many Teach for America volunteers who participated in David Bradley's search for American prisoners in Syria. The dedication the team at Atlantic Media exhibited for the rescue of their fellow citizens fills me with confidence in the future. I'm also grateful to the journalists Bobby Worth and David Rhode for providing wise counsel to my mother's team. James Harkin gave me wise counsel on my return. In Istanbul, Shane Harris and Sebnem Arsu aided my mother during a voyage to Turkey. My mother would not have been able to pursue her Istanbul meetings nor, for that matter, would she have been able to track down countless other leads if it had not been for the good will of the *New York Times* general counsel, David McCraw. I'm also grateful to Tik Root, a rising star in the journalism world, for the wise advice he offered my family during my absence.

For their kindness to me in and around Aleppo. I'm grateful to my fellow prisoners, Ali Ali and Cherif Makhlouf.

ACKNOWLEDGMENTS

I owe my deepest gratitude to the entire FBI office in Boston for its efforts to help my mother's rescue project. At the Washington FBI office, two agents I cannot name stood by my mother through the dark periods with the devotion of actual family members. They are breathtakingly competent professionals, as indeed are all the employees of the FBI with whom my family came in contact during the course of my ordeal. I'll never be able to express how grateful I am to these public servants. I'm also grateful to Ambassadors Frank Ricciardone and Rolf Holmboe for their efforts to guide my family's search. In Connecticut, Representative Jim Himes's counsel proved invaluable and constant. In New York, Ambassador Samantha Power removed many of the obstacles my rescuers confronted. Elliot Thomson, who understood more of Ambassador Power's effectiveness than my family did, encouraged my mother and cousins to keep after her.

For welcoming me home, I'm grateful to David Schisgall, Effie Peretz, and to Effie's wonderful dad, Marty Peretz. I feel that these New Yorkers adopted me, then awakened me to a dazzling new urban life.

For looking after my medical needs when I came home, I'm grateful to Dr. David Barrett at the Lahey Clinic in Boston. For help with my book, I'm grateful to Maria Carbone for her assistance with the photographs and to Loudon Wainwright for permission to quote from "The Swimming Song." I'm grateful especially to Jim Hornfischer whose early confidence in my idea gave me a feeling without which I wouldn't have been able to begin: confidence in myself. I'm grateful to my editors, Colin Harrison and Sarah Goldberg, for their inexplicable, inexhaustible patience. Also, for their writing wisdom. Last, I'm grateful to Karen Demas who has made my homecoming happier than I ever dreamed it could be.

ABOUT THE AUTHOR

Theo Padnos is the author of *Undercover Muslim*, which explored everyday life among Westerners as they studied in Yemen's religious academies. He was held prisoner by the Syrian al Qaeda affiliate, Jebhat al-Nusra, between 2012 and 2014. A documentary film called *Theo Who Lived*, about his experiences with Jebhat al-Nusra, was released in 2016.